Formula for Fortune

How Asa Candler Discovered Coca-Cola and Turned It into the Wealth His Children Enjoyed

Ann Uhry Abrams

iUniverse, Inc.
Bloomington

Formula for Fortune
How Asa Candler Discovered Coca-Cola and Turned
It into the Wealth His Children Enjoyed

iUniverse books may be ordered through booksellers or by contacting:

iUniverse
1663 Liberty Drive
Bloomington, IN 47403
www.iuniverse.com
1-800-Authors (1-800-288-4677)

ISBN: 978-1-4620-7168-5 (sc)
ISBN: 978-1-4620-7167-8 (hc)
ISBN: 978-1-4620-7184-5 (e)

Library of Congress Control Number: 2011961811

Printed in the United States of America

iUniverse rev. date: 3/5/2012

Formula for Fortune

How Asa Candler Discovered Coca-Cola and Turned It into the Wealth His Children Enjoyed

Other books by Ann Uhry Abrams

The Valiant Hero: Benjamin West and Grand-Style History Painting

The Pilgrims and Pocahontas: Rival Myths of American Origin

Explosion at Orly: The Disaster that Transformed Atlanta

Contents

PREFACE XI

Part One: Making Money

CHAPTER ONE
Farming and Praying. .1

CHAPTER TWO
Mixing Concoctions 21

CHAPTER THREE
Serendipity. 37

CHAPTER FOUR
Leaving Home 54

Part Two: Making More Money

CHAPTER FIVE

Changing World 81

CHAPTER SIX

Creating Families 99

CHAPTER SEVEN

Visions of Grandeur 118

Part Three: Spending Money

CHAPTER EIGHT

Prominence and Prosperity 139

CHAPTER NINE

In Control 159

CHAPTER TEN

Losing Control 183

Part Four: Enjoying Money

CHAPTER ELEVEN

Misbehavior 205

CHAPTER TWELVE
Trials and Tributes 226

CHAPTER THIRTEEN
Wild and Unfathomable Things 248

CHAPTER FOURTEEN
Murder in Druid Hills 270

CHAPTER FIFTEEN
And So It Goes 284

ACKNOWLEDGMENTS 299

SELECTED BIBLIOGRAPHY 301

ABBREVIATIONS IN NOTES 305

ENDNOTES 307

INDEX 333

FAMILY OF ASA CANDLER
(who appear in the narrative)

William Candler (awarded Callan Castle in Ireland)

Baronet Thomas Candler

Daniel Candler (came to America, (d. 1765)

William Candler (settled in Wrightsborough, GA, (1736-1784)

Daniel Candler (1779-1816)

Charles Samuel Candler (Sam) (1809-1873) m. Martha Beall (1819 – 1897)

Rep. Milton Candler (1837-1909)	Ezekiel (Zeke) (1838-1915)	Noble (1840-1887)	Florence m. James Harris (1842-1926)	Jesse m. Joe Willard (1845-1921)	William (Willie) m. Lizzie Slaughter (1847-1938)	Lizzie m. H.H. Dobbs (1849-1922)
Sam	Rep. Ezekiel, Jr. (Zeke)			Sam Willard	William, Jr. (Willie)	Sam Dobbs
				Jessie Willard		
				Joe Willard		

Asa Griggs Candler m. **Lucy Elizabeth Howard** (1877)
(1851- 1929)   (1859-1919)

	Samuel Charles, Jr.(Charlie) (1855-1911)	Warren m. Nettie Curtright (1857 -1941)	John S. m. Lula Garner (1861-1941)
			Asa Warren (1885-1929)
		m. Florida (Florrie) Anderson	

Charles Howard Candler (Howard)
(1878-1957)
m. Flora Glenn (1903)

- Charles Howard Candler, Jr.
- Catherine Candler Warren
- Mary Louisa Candler Eldredge

m. Mae Little (1923)

Asa Griggs Candler Jr. (Buddie)
(1880-1953)
m. Helen Magill (1901)

- Lucy Candler Thompson
- Asa Griggs Candler III
- John Howard Candler
- Laura Candler Chambers
- Helen Candler Hare Davidson (twin)
- Martha Candler York Callaway (twin)
- Samuel Candler

m. Florence Stevenson (1927)

Lucy Beall Candler
(1883-1962)
m. William Owens (1903)

- Elizabeth Owens Vann
- William Owens, Jr

m. Henry Heinz (1917)

- Henry Heinz, Jr.
- Emilie (Mimi) Heinz

m. Enrico Leide (1946)

Walter Turner Candler
(1885-1967)
m. Eugenia Bingham (1907)

- Walter Turner Candler, Jr.
- Asa Griggs Candler, IV
- Eugenia Candler Wilson
- Mary Candler Edmondson

m. Marion Penland (1919)

- Marion (Bootsie) Candler Ruffner

m. Rebekah Skeen (1939)

William Candler
(1890-1936)
m. Bennie Teabeaut (1913)

- Rena Candler Chambers
- William Candler, Jr.

Preface

Most of us growing up in Atlanta during the 1940s were familiar with the name Candler. It meant Coca-Cola, it meant wealth, and it meant all the mansions that dotted my Druid Hills neighborhood. In those days, Asa Candler, who founded the company that manufactured the famous beverage, was still considered an important figure from the city's recent past. When he died in 1929, the *Atlanta Constitution* called him "perhaps the most widely known citizen Atlanta ever had." Yet more than eighty years hence, his fame has been overshadowed by that of the product he produced and promoted. Few are aware that Candler was mayor of Atlanta during World War I, dominated the local real estate market, and provided the funds to transform a small college in Oxford, Georgia, into Emory University. Along the way, he developed a garden suburb, opened a major bank, and constructed Atlanta's then-tallest skyscraper, which he duplicated in New York while building major commercial structures and manufacturing plants throughout the United States. In short, he was the South's equivalent of Andrew Carnegie or John D. Rockefeller.

Asa Candler came from a farm in Villa Rica, Georgia, in many ways personifying Horatio Alger's fictional rise from rags to riches. Yet, notwithstanding his later stories about boyhood struggles, Asa was no child of poverty. In fact, his family lived quite comfortably during the antebellum years. His father, Sam Candler—a farmer and merchant—owned several slaves, but his wealth was seriously depleted as a result of the Civil War. Since Sam never lived to see Asa become one of the area's richest residents, he died thinking his eighth child was a failure, certainly in comparison to his prominent brothers. The oldest, Milton, was a Georgia lawyer, who served in the United States House of Representatives, and the second oldest, Zeke, was a lawyer and preacher in Mississippi. Sam Candler's tenth son, Warren, was a bishop of the Southern Methodist Church and president of Emory College during the 1890s, becoming the first chancellor when Emory University opened in 1917. John, the last of

Sam's children, was a distinguished judge of the Georgia Superior Court and a justice of the state Supreme Court.

In contrast, Asa refused to go to college and abandoned plans for a medical career to become a drugstore clerk. Within a few years after coming to Atlanta, he opened his own pharmacy, and then in 1888 he visited a local soda fountain in search of a headache remedy and swallowed a patent medicine that changed his life. Although that drink had been concocted by an eccentric druggist named John S. "Doc" Pemberton, Asa Candler manipulated the formula in order to buy it, tinkering with it awhile before producing the syrup that he marketed to soda jerks throughout the South. During the next decade, he turned the tonic into a nationwide marketing phenomenon. But that progression was not a smooth climb from soda fountain to international giant. A series of court cases instigated by the federal government questioned the inclusion of cocaine and caffeine in the syrup, and indeed a small amount of the narcotic remained in the formula until the company was forced to remove it. After battling his accusers and imitators for several decades, Candler grew weary of managing a large corporation and distributed his stock among his five children, leaving him free to devote the remainder of his life to charities and his city.

Much of this tale is in the public record, but the personal lives of Asa Candler and his children are not. His affectionate—if domineering—relationship with his wife, Lucy Elizabeth, produced four sons and one daughter, all of whom became prominent Atlantans in their own rights, spending their inherited fortunes to reflect their individual quirks. Asa himself was a generous but manipulative father, determined to mold the character of each child, while Lucy Elizabeth was typical of her era's hardworking mother, countering her husband's tough love with an overabundance of nurturing that provided a steadfast presence which kept her sons' disputes from splitting the family apart.

In many ways, the five Candler offspring exemplified the family dynamics that attract psychologists and sociologists. The oldest son, Howard, was the family good boy, responsible, obedient, serious, and thrifty. First working as his father's lackey at Coca-Cola, and then after he and his siblings sold the company, Howard freely—though cautiously—meted out his dollars to build a showplace home, served on corporate boards, and continued his father's support of Emory University. The second son, Asa Jr., was his older brother's polar opposite. He romped through a world that Jay Gatsby would have envied, living in extravagant luxury on his Druid Hills estate, owning several private planes and yachts, entertaining lavishly, and infuriating the neighbors by opening a zoo on his property. But despite his eccentricities, Asa Jr. negotiated some of the city's most lucrative real estate transactions, including development of the Atlanta airport (first known as Candler Field) and bringing the first Macy's department store south of the Mason-Dixon Line.

Next in line was the only girl, Lucy, the pretty, outgoing light of her father's life. From her spoiled and over-indulged childhood, she emerged as the cheerful arbitrator of her often fractious brothers. While reigning as a leading doyen of Atlanta society, Lucy enjoyed her own brand of '20s excesses, traveling extensively and supervising construction of her Italian-style mansion. Despite her sunny exterior, she suffered many personal tragedies: the loss of two children and two husbands, the second the victim of a brutal and controversial murder. Her next youngest brother, Walter, was almost as flamboyant as Asa Jr., but instead of a zoo, he had a large racetrack on the grounds of his estate and captured the headlines during a highly publicized adulterous affair. The last Candler child, William, was the only quiet and modest one of the five siblings. A well-respected businessman, he spent his share of the Coca-Cola fortune to construct Atlanta's Biltmore Hotel.

Asa Sr., a staunch proponent of propriety in his early life, succumbed to the wiles of younger women after Lucy Elizabeth's death. Partly caused by his declining mental abilities and partly by his naïveté and vulnerability, he became ready prey for fortune seekers. During that time, he shared an unwanted press spotlight with his son Walter when their two jazz-age romances led to simultaneous court cases. After the patriarch's death, the brothers let loose their youthful animosities, triggering inflammatory family gatherings and tumultuous meetings of their inherited real estate company. Yet, despite—or perhaps because of—their differences, their individual successes and failures, indiscretions and romances epitomize an era long forgotten.

Weaving through the narrative is the remarkable growth of Atlanta and the Candlers' contributions to it. Commercial properties—from the beautiful Candler Building to Hartsfield-Jackson International Airport—stand as testimonies to their dominance over the real estate market. And in Druid Hills, one of Atlanta's first suburbs, numerous well-known landmarks remain, including Howard's mansion, Callanwolde, and the campus of Emory University. Towering above all the family's accomplishments, the International Coca-Cola complex shines as a dynamic reminder of Asa Candler's once-dominant presence.

Formula for Fortune relays the history of shifting times as witnessed by members of a typical, yet suddenly wealthy family. From the slower-paced 1880s and 1890s through the dawn of a new century—with its concurrent technological advances and intellectual experimentation—they absorbed many of the shifting cultural mores, interpreted within the context of their deeply felt southern roots. Emerging from the desolation of the postbellum South, they contributed positively to bringing industrial and financial prosperity to their region and turning Atlanta into a commercial hub. If Asa Candler epitomized the optimism and drive of a quintessential entrepreneur riding the bandwagon of capitalism, he also projected an altruism and concern for his fellow man absorbed during his religious upbringing. Amidst the jingoism of World War I, Mayor Asa Candler waved the American flag more vigorously than most when he led parades down Peachtree Street. At the same time, his seemingly contradictory goals of entrepreneurship and generosity not only solved many civic challenges but unwittingly brought his city kicking and screaming into the modern world. Never fully comfortable with the acquisition of his mushrooming fortune, he fought hard to preserve the value system that he felt to be fast eroding.

As often seen in families of self-made men, Asa's five children had no such qualms about spending and enjoying the money their father made. Within the confines of their isolated southern world, they may only have peripherally heard of Sigmund Freud or Albert Einstein, Pablo Picasso or Gertrude Stein, but they could not escape the influx of new ideas forming far away that eventually led to the demise of old ideals and antiquated patterns of governing accompanied by new means of evaluating social behavior. After the sale of Coca-Cola in 1919 and the division of the proceeds, the five siblings embraced the Roaring Twenties, with all of its extravagances and misbehavior. Although the Depression of the 1930s barely caused a ripple in the Candlers' economic security, a series of tragic personal events paralleled the concomitant fracturing of Western civilization that preceded and followed World War II. In many ways, the trajectory of the Candler family replicated a nation and a world in flux, a microcosm of a society, emerging and prospering before fracturing and eventually changing to meet contemporary expectations.

When, several years ago, someone suggested that I write a book about the Candler family, I responded, "Oh that's been done many times." But when I checked it out, I discovered I was wrong. Except for pamphlets and articles produced by the Coca-Cola Company, there were only two biographies of Asa Candler: the first written by his son Howard and privately published in 1950, the other a thoroughly researched scholarly study by Katherine Kemp, published in 2002 by Mercer University Press. Asa Candler's great-granddaughter, Elizabeth Candler Graham, wrote a family history filled with anecdotes and personal reminiscences. But that's all there is. Although there are several good histories of Coca-Cola, Asa Candler and his family were given short shrift, a scant chapter or so in the books' opening chapters, overshadowed by the long reigns of Robert Woodruff and his successors. After much experimentation and rewriting, I decided to structure my book chronologically, realizing that an in-depth exploration of a family's history reads best if it progresses in the traditional evolutionary route from Asa Candler's ancestral background to the death of his last child. The story of Coca-Cola's founding fits well within this construction, since the business evolved along with the family. The impetus for the study happened when I discovered a huge collection of family letters in Emory University's Manuscripts, Archives, and Rare Books Library (MARBL) and in the Archives of the Coca-Cola Company. As I spent several years plunging into these treasures, I became familiar with the intricate personalities of the players, and I emerged feeling as if I knew them all—their shortcomings, their strengths, and their yearnings. Most of the letters came from the late nineteenth and early twentieth centuries, when the company was forming and expanding and the children were away at school or at work. By 1905, all of Asa's children had settled in Atlanta, so there were fewer communications. However, letters written during frequent vacations, or those connected with major events, provide many details about the separate households, their inhabitants, and their activities.

After the Candlers evolved into celebrities during the early years of the twentieth century, their names filled the Atlanta newspapers as well as those of other cities, thus augmenting and embellishing the letters in many surprising ways. To round out the picture, I interviewed several Candler descendants, each of whom contributed personal memories, never-before-published photographs, and even family secrets. Proud of their important heritage, Asa Candler's great-grandchildren provided insights into the lives of their ancestors that helped me construct a lively portrait of the past.

Ann Uhry Abrams
Atlanta, 2012

Part One:

Making Money

CHAPTER ONE
Farming and Praying

Asa Griggs Candler Sr., c. 1910, courtesy of Millennium Gate Museum, Atlanta, Georgia

S hortly after Asa Griggs Candler opened his gleaming skyscraper in downtown Atlanta in 1906, he orchestrated a ceremony to be held each year on December 6, the birthday of both his parents, an event that merited a brief write-up in the *Atlanta Constitution* in 1910. Although the article gave only facts and figures, a small stretch of the imagination—enhanced by information about the principal players—brings the ceremony to life. So let's begin this foray into the past by imagining that gathering.[1]

Staircase at the Candler Building, Atlanta, photograph by John Sumner

First we notice a milling crowd standing around the elegant marble lobby. The group watches hopefully as Asa Candler Sr.—a short, wiry man, with gray hair and rimless glasses, looking remarkably hardy for a successful businessman pushing sixty—smiles down on the group from his post on the first landing of the staircase. Except for the elegance of his attire and his commanding manner, unknowing observers would have never suspected he was one of the city's wealthiest citizens. Not only has he made a fortune from Coca-Cola, but he is also a prominent banker, realtor, philanthropist, and civil servant. Recently he so successfully completed a two-year term as chairman of the Atlanta Chamber of Commerce that people were suggesting he run for mayor. Despite all his accomplishments, Asa Candler managed to retain his distinctive southern drawl and the many colloquialisms that hinted of his humble origins. His own children, along with most of his grandchildren, nieces, and nephews, are present that morning, as are several of his siblings and his dignified wife, Lucy Elizabeth. Near her is their only daughter, Lucy, along with her husband, Bill Owens, an officer in his father-in-law's bank, and their young daughter Elizabeth. Asa's four sons dared not miss this command performance. Although each of the young men acts friendly and cordial to his brothers, the tension between them is palpable. That is especially true of the two oldest, Howard, vice president of the Coca-Cola Company, and the next in line, Asa Jr., called either "Bud" or "Buddie" by the family. He has recently become manager of his father's vast real *estate holdings and seems to be happy in his new role. Howard's wife, Flora, stands close by her husband's side, while their son and daughter are having an animated conversation with their Uncle Bud's children, who are there with their mother, Helen. Nearby Walter Candler, now a clerk at his father's bank, chats with one of his cousins, while his pretty but exhausted wife, Eugenia, who left a new daughter at home with a nurse, is watching her two little boys chase around her feet. William—the youngest of Asa Candler's children and the only one of the brothers still single in 1910—stands on the edge of the crowd, having just rushed in from the Coca-Cola plant, where he is treasurer.*

The crowd grows quiet when Methodist Bishop Warren Candler, a broad-shouldered bulldog of a man, steps forward to deliver the blessing. Heads bow and children are silenced as, in deep, sonorous tones, Asa's brother asks for the Lord's countenance to shine benevolently upon the descendants of Sam and Martha Candler, so many of whom are grouped about him that day. First he remarks how fortunate they are to have come from such an extraordinary heritage; then he entreats his Maker to bestow special blessings on the souls of his brothers Milton and Noble, who have passed on to dwell with their parents in heaven. Then Bishop Warren prays for the Lord to keep those esteemed parents in his company forever and grant his celestial benevolence on the remaining offspring of Martha and Sam, several being too old or too ill to be there that day. Restless now, the crowd shifts from one foot to the other. Throats clear, someone coughs, feet shuffle, and children giggle, only to be shushed by a firm parental hand. Finally, the bishop utters "amen" in Jesus's name as the assortment of Candlers raise their heads.

Then Asa Candler resumes his position on the staircase to explain that they are gathered for the annual celebration of his parents' birth, since Sam and Martha had both come into the world on the sixth day of December. Unlike his younger brother Warren, Asa's voice is high-pitched and reedy. His blue eyes grow misty as he recalls his childhood at the "old homestead" in Villa Rica in those far-off days before the War Between the States. Then he asks his brothers—John (a former judge and now chief lawyer for Coca-Cola), Bishop Warren, and Willie (a merchant)—along with his sisters Florence and Lizzie to talk about their favorite memories of that vanished childhood world. After they speak, a few of the oldest grandchildren add comments about Martha, the only one of the pair most of them had known. When the recollections end, Asa climbs a few steps higher to solemnly place wreaths on the marble busts of each parent, tucked into niches along the wall of the staircase, near similar statues of such favorite Georgians as General John B. Gordon,

Eli Whitney, Alexander Stephens, and Joel Chandler Harris. Then each of the children receive a white flower, and, one at a time, the little boys and girls step onto a temporary platform to insert their blossoms into wreaths draped around the necks of their stone ancestors.

Busts of Sam Candler and Martha Candler, Candler Building, Atlanta
photograph by John Sumner

Afterward, Warren delivers a final blessing before the ceremony ends with a flurry of applause. Now little faces wait impatiently, knowing that each year the man they either call "Pawpaw" or "Uncle Asa" distributes a wrapped gift to every child. Clutching their packages and bundled into their winter coats, hats, gloves, scarves, and muffs, three generations of Candlers bid each other good-bye, talking about their plans for the upcoming holiday. Slowly they push through the bronze-trimmed doors into the chilly December day, leaving behind the silent marble busts of the venerated ancestors amidst the hustle and bustle of office workers and bank customers, who brush past them every day. Sam and Martha are left in their staircase niches, staring in stony silence until next year's birthday celebration once more temporarily brings them to life.

This gathering of 1910 has its roots seventy-seven years earlier in another ceremony, that one taking place in the red-clay backwoods of Cherokee County, Georgia. At the time and in that remote place, Martha Beall, who had just celebrated her fourteenth birthday, married twenty-four-year-old Sam Candler. Sam, a recently appointed county sheriff, must have seemed extremely glamorous to a girl raised in the wilderness. Tall, dark, somber, and seemingly wise to the foibles of the world, he was taken with the bright, lively Martha, so tiny and doll-like that when he stood beside her, she barely reached his shoulder. The perky teenager—who readily took to the sheriff's advances—promised to develop into a warm and capable mate. As the oldest child of Noble and Justiana Beall, Martha had spent all of her young life helping around the house. Before she was thirteen, she had been responsible for tending the steady stream of new babies coming into the world almost every year. When she married Sam Candler, her next youngest sister, Eliza, was eleven, and six others were stair-steps down to the youngest baby, Charles, less than five months old. The older members of the Beall brood were the lucky ones, who had managed to survive the hardships of frontier living. Two of their siblings had succumbed during their first year, and little Charles wouldn't remain alive for much longer. Despite all the misfortunes, Justiana Beall would deliver five more babies after her daughter married, and all but one of them grew to be adults.[2]

Young Martha Candler, courtesy of Manuscript, Archives, and Rare Book Library, Emory University

Martha's father, Noble Beall, had moved to the northwestern Georgia frontier sometime in the late 1820s or early 1830s, when that territory was still under the jurisdiction of the Cherokee Nation. Through the years, the tribe had adapted to the white man's ways, eventually developing a prosperous farming community, replete with a school, printing press, and a newspaper in the Cherokee language. But after prospectors discovered gold there in the late 1820s, the tribe was doomed. In hopes of retaining its land, it sued the state in two separate cases that both ended up in the US Supreme Court. However, these attempts were futile, and Georgia won the right to take over the Cherokee's territory. In rushed the white man, and out went the original inhabitants.

The same gold rush that ousted the Native Americans brought Sam Candler into the former "Indian country," recently designated as Cherokee County by the state legislature. Before drifting northward, Sam had spent several months near the Alabama border in Carroll County, where prospectors had discovered gold on lands recently occupied by the Creeks. Family lore later claimed that he managed one of the mining companies, but chances are he was merely digging alongside the other fortune seekers, one of whom was his younger brother, Ezekiel, also a county sheriff. Having found little precious ore during his first mining experience, Sam convinced Cherokee County authorities that if they would appoint him sheriff, he would strive to remove the Cherokee from their ancestral homes. Conscientious in his new job, he worked diligently to round up the Native Americans and pack them off on the long trek to Oklahoma. But it was a tougher assignment than the young man had anticipated, as his targets often hid in the woods and refused to budge. At one point, Sam supposedly tied a Cherokee man to a bedpost so he wouldn't sneak away. This and other indications of his tough perseverance made such an impression on county authorities that they chose him as their representative in the Georgia legislature, then meeting at the state capital in Milledgeville.[3]

Like most rural southern families, the Candlers and the Bealls were Scotch-Irish farmers, and both families were fiercely proud of their ancestry. One of Martha's paternal forebears, Ninian Beall, had fought for Oliver Cromwell's Scottish brigade during England's seventeenth-century civil war, and when the Stuart monarchy resumed power, he was punished for that service by deportation. Thrown out of his homeland, Ninian crossed the ocean and settled in Calvert (later Prince George's) County, Maryland, where he began farming. Through hard work and fortunate connections, he was able to leave his offspring with valuable land holdings and a prosperous plantation. Many of his descendants dispersed to various parts of the South, and, somewhere down the line, one of them married a cousin of John Adams, thus allowing future generations of Bealls to claim a tenuous kinship to the second American president.

Sam's filial boasts were slightly different from his wife's, since one of his distant ancestors, William Candler, had ended up on the winning side of that same civil war. Awarded a castle in Callan, County Kilkenny, Ireland—for defending his village against Cromwell's invading army—William became a landholding aristocrat. Most of his children and grandchildren remained in the British Isles and mingled freely with Stuart royalty, but Sam's great-great-grandfather, Daniel, shocked his Anglican family by marrying an Irish Catholic, and as a result, he lost his inheritance. Disowned and penniless, he left for America, eventually ending up as a farmer in Wrightsborough, Georgia, about thirty-five miles north of Augusta. Daniel's son, William, bolstered the family's respectability by fighting as an officer in the Continental militia during the American Revolution and by serving as a member of Georgia's first legislature. But *his* son Daniel, Sam's father, did little to honor the Candler name, since he chose to operate a tavern and participate in frequent barroom brawls, some of them resulting in duels. In one such confrontation, Daniel unwittingly killed a friend, an unfortunate incident that sent him spiraling into a deep depression. Unable to recover and now under suspicion of breaking the law, he killed himself. This heritage of contradictory extremes—producing either alcoholism and self-destruction or temperance and notable achievement—passed intact from generation to generation of Candlers, as did the propensity for chronic depression.

When Daniel Candler took his life in 1816, he left his wife, Sarah, with seven children. Sam, who was only six at the time, was soon to discover that his father's profligate lifestyle had depleted the family funds. To help support her unruly brood, Sarah remarried, moved to Baldwin County near Milledgeville, and soon gave birth to four more daughters. With the constant arrival of new children, the house became so crowded that Sam and some of his siblings were farmed out to relatives. After an unhappy stay with an aunt and uncle, he landed in the home of his first cousin, Ignatius Few, a lawyer and Methodist minister, later to distinguish himself by founding Emory College in Oxford, Georgia. For the impressionable ten- or eleven-year-old boy, the Few household was the antithesis of his own. Few had attended Princeton University and studied afterward in New York City, thus providing his young cousin with a taste for books, tempered by an ardent dose of Methodism. However, this brief exposure to a learned and religious relative did not motivate Sam Candler to follow suit. Instead he went back to live with his mother for a while, until the packed house with all those younger half sisters got to be unbearable, and he left home for good, embarking on a trek that ended in the newly formed Cherokee County, where he began courting the young Martha Beall.

When Noble and Justiana Beall learned that their oldest daughter planned to marry a man ten years her senior, they were understandably opposed. How could they let their able helper marry a wandering gold-seeker, even if he did wear the sheriff's badge and represent the county in the state legislature? But after threatening to disown Martha and have any elopement annulled, Noble Beall—unable to dissuade his determined daughter—grudgingly agreed to host her wedding. As a dowry, he gave the couple a "claybank Indian pony" named Picayune and a slave girl named Mary, possibly a half-breed Cherokee. Sam and Martha wanted to wed on their shared birthday, but local superstition altered their plans, as December 6, 1833, fell on a Friday, and within the frontier culture, weddings on that day were deemed unlucky. Reluctantly, the couple agreed to placate her parents by delaying the ceremony for two days, and they married on December 8. Among the assortment of neighbors attending the wedding at the Beall home were reportedly two Cherokee chiefs in full regalia.

The newlyweds hung around the Beall farm while Sam continued rounding up Cherokee and attending legislative sessions in Milledgeville. But in a short time, Martha's parents decided to move, now that their peaceful rural life had been disrupted by the invading panhandlers. The Bealls relocated farther south in equally new and rugged Campbell (now part of Fulton) County, just west of what fifteen years later would become Atlanta. When her parents moved, Sam and Martha loaded a wagon with their belongings, including the young slave girl and pony, and headed back to Carroll County, where Sam's brother Ezekiel still lived. By the time the young couple arrived, the small vein of gold had been all but depleted, and most of the prospectors had moved on to a more lucrative lode in the foothills near Dahlonega. A few miners, however, did stick around the old pit in a tiny outpost they called Hixville, named after a local tavern owner. At the time, only about three thousand people lived in the entire county, and Hixville was little more than a scruffy collection of shacks. In hopes of transforming the mining enclave into a reputable agricultural community, Sam and Martha banded together with other residents and changed the name to Villa Rica, a Spanish phrase meaning "Town of Riches."

Sam lost no time in establishing himself as a community leader. To capitalize on the remaining prospectors, he contacted investors from Macon and arranged to lease rights to the mines, and by so doing, he received 10 percent of each gold lot sold. With the help of a mine owner named Ed Holland, Sam opened a general store on the muddy main street leading to the pits. Not only did he prosper from selling provisions to local residents for cash, but he began to accumulate gold dust in exchange for goods. Before long, he had amassed enough money to buy property two and a half miles northwest of what is now called "Old Villa Rica." There, on a knoll lined with oak trees, he built a small house and began farming the land. Gradually he purchased adjacent plots, so that eventually he owned three hundred acres of rolling hills, surrounded by hardwood forests and streams. Known in the community for his quiet disposition, wisdom, and ingenuity, Sam Candler became greatly respected for his honest, yet exacting, performance of business and community matters.[4]

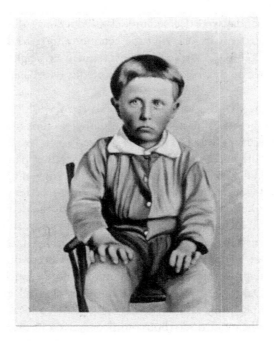

Asa G. Candler Sr., c. 1856, courtesy of Manuscript, Archives, and Rare Book Library, Emory University

Martha had her first child when she was barely seventeen. Frightened and lonely, she decided to give birth in her parents' Campbell County home, less than thirty miles away. They named the boy after a physician, Milton Anthony, one of Sam's relatives. Within a few years, their home was teaming with children. Martha was young, and apparently childbearing turned out to be easy, even with her small frame. Less than two years after Milton came Ezekiel (Zeke), then eleven months later, Noble, named after Martha's father. When this third son was small, he contracted an illness (probably meningitis) that left him mentally handicapped. Two years later, Florence was born, followed in three years by Sarah Justiana (Jessie), then William Beall (Willie) two years later, and Elizabeth Frances (Lizzie), two years after that. Asa Griggs Candler was their eighth child and fifth son, born on December 30, 1851. He was named for a young medical student—then tutoring Milton (almost fifteen) and Zeke (thirteen)—who had trained with Sam's kinsman, Dr. Anthony. Three more sons would follow in rapid succession: Samuel Charles Jr. (Charlie) in 1855, Warren Aiken in '57, and John Slaughter in '61, making eleven Candler siblings in all. Amazing for the time, all eleven survived childhood and most lived to old age, several of them becoming prominent Georgians during their lifetimes.[5]

As the family grew, so did the house. Land on either side of a wide hallway (or "dogtrot") soon gave way to additional wings that provided bedrooms for the boys. The smaller children played games in the central hall, heated by a fireplace in winter and cooled in summer by breezes blowing through the screen doors at either end. At mealtime, the ever-increasing brood gathered at a long table in the combined dining room and living room, placed at the rear of one wing. All of Sam and Martha's offspring fondly remembered sitting with their large family at that table, with Mama at one end and Papa at the other, bowing their heads in prayer before dining on sumptuous meals harvested from the farm and prepared by slaves in the detached kitchen out back. At one point, Sam Candler was said to have owned eighteen or nineteen slaves. A few worked in the house, but most tended the crops and cared for the animals. Mary, the girl who had accompanied them from Indian country, had been transformed into the children's "Mammy," teaching her young charges to ride on the pony, Picayune, and working around the house or yard, with the smallest baby in a papoose strapped on her back.

The presence of slaves, however, did not enable the Candler offspring to enjoy the languorous leisure characterized in so many antebellum myths. Quite the contrary, their disciplined upbringing left them with little time to waste. Since Sam and Martha had come up the hard way, they demanded that all of their children perform regular and often vigorous chores. Even though slaves carried out the most menial tasks, additional manpower was always needed, and for Sam Candler that meant recruiting his children, especially the boys. Each one spent part of every day, except Sunday, helping at the general store, working the fields, or tending the animals, while their three sisters assisted their mother around the house. Farming in rural north Georgia during the mid-nineteenth century was rigorous. Since the terrain was predominantly red clay hills unsuited for growing cotton, Sam and his neighbors planted corn and wheat, while simultaneously raising livestock. Wagons loaded with produce left the farm every week or so, headed for nearby towns, some great distances away. Traveling over rough, unpaved roads, Sam or one of his sons—accompanied by a slave or two—sold the goods at markets and then filled the empty wagons with goods to become merchandise at the general store.

Children performing obligatory farm chores occasionally had serious consequences, as Asa discovered when he was eleven. Riding across the fields atop a pile of corn, he tumbled to the ground when the cart hit a stone in the path. Although his brother driving the cart tried to stop, it was too late to prevent a wheel from running over Asa's head. The recovery was slow. Martha reported in a letter to her daughter Florence: "Though he can eat & set up, the nerves of his left eye ... were crushed so that he cant see or hear on that side but he can whistle yet." With her characteristic belief in providential happenings, she added: "His escape from death is a miracle and only by the thoughtful kindness of God was he saved."[6] The accident left Asa with severe migraine headaches, impaired vision, permanent deafness in one ear, and the deep-seated belief that he had been salvaged for greater things.

It was Martha who first drilled Christian piety into her children. When she and Sam settled in Carroll County, she attended Villa Rica's Old Pleasant Grove Missionary Baptist Church, the faith of her childhood, but her husband refused to belong to any church that required baptism by total immersion. Then shortly after the Civil War, when Sam heard a Confederate veteran and Methodist minister preach at a revival meeting, he decided to join Villa Rica's Methodist Episcopal Church, South. The itinerant preacher was so pleased with his newest convert that he came out to Sam's house to baptize him with a mere sprinkle of water. Thankful that her husband had finally embraced Christianity, Martha immediately transferred her allegiance and became one of the Methodists' most enthusiastic congregants. With zeal, she threw herself into church activities by becoming assistant superintendent of the Sunday school and donating a new bell to the congregation. Sam, too, taught each Sunday, bringing his four youngest sons—Asa, Warren, Charlie, and John—into his class. At home they held prayer services every morning, noon, and night, during which the family knelt together reciting passages from the *English Book of Prayer*. All of their children knew the scriptures by heart and quoted them often. After supper each evening, all gathered around to sing, while Florence, Jessie, or Lizzie plunked out hymns on the old Knabe upright.

Because Southern Methodism prohibited consumption of alcohol at any time, Martha and Sam were staunch teetotalers, insisting that all their children conform. But much of their county believed otherwise. In fact, near their home in the west Georgia mining town were a number of saloons, the best-known being the Buck Horn Tavern on the highway between Atlanta and Jackson, Alabama. Several times each day, coaches would pull up to let passengers refresh themselves inside, while their horses were watered and fed outside. During these stops, local residents and visitors clashed with advocates of temperance, leading to free-for-alls that spilled out into the road. Conduct of the bar's regulars was so abhorrent to the Candlers that when Milton was eighteen, he delivered a fiery condemnation of drinking at the Little Temperance Church in nearby Carrollton. That confrontation between the pulpit and the bottle revealed a curse that plagued generations of Candlers struggling to uphold unbending religious convictions to fight against the reappearance of destructive alcoholic demons.

Neither Martha nor Sam had much formal schooling. Her surviving letters are rife with spelling and grammatical errors and are peppered by descriptive southern colloquialisms. Sam, on the other hand, had developed a love of books during his brief stay with Ignatius Few, and, emulating that household, he filled his shelves with volumes of historical and theological studies. When time allowed, he pursued his quest for knowledge by reading, and he encouraged his children to do the same. Visiting tutors provided instruction for the oldest Candler children, several of whom attended college during the 1850s. Milton and Zeke graduated from the University of Georgia in Athens, and Florence completed the program at the Georgia Female College in Cassville. In the antebellum years, the younger Candlers attended a one-room, log-cabin church school, administered by migrant male teachers. Pupils learned the basics from "Blue Back Spellers," dictionaries, and readers, and when they were older they were allowed to "do sums." But all such education halted abruptly when the cataclysmic war closed all local schools and changed the lives of the Candlers forever.[7]

At some point during the 1850s, Sam Candler resumed his interest in state politics and served as county sheriff for one term, after his brother Ezekiel moved to Milledgeville to become state comptroller general. Subsequently, both Candler brothers were elected to represent their respective counties in the Georgia legislature. When Lincoln's inauguration (in March 1861) led southern Democrats to call a convention in Charleston to debate secession, Sam was chosen to be a delegate. Initially he was against breaking with the Union, hoping that the South and the North would settle their differences through peaceful means. But eventually he was persuaded to throw his support to the Confederacy. Milton and Zeke followed similar paths. Recently graduated from college, Milton was running a small newspaper and writing editorials opposing secession; Zeke—who had moved to Mississippi, where he was practicing law—spoke publicly against seceding from the Union. However, like their father, the two oldest Candler boys soon rallied to the Southern cause, and when war started, both joined the Confederate army.

At first, the war did little to alter the Candlers' daily routine, even though so many local boys were leaving for the front. But everything changed when the Yankee-imposed blockade eventually cut off merchandise for the general store, and Sam was forced to close it, although he continued to speculate in real estate by purchasing depleted land from neighboring farmers. But as the war dragged on, the formerly energetic and enterprising Sam Candler became a discouraged and helpless recluse, suffering from frequent bouts of "melancholy," a scourge inherited from his father. To add to his troubles, his mother Sarah—who had moved to live near him in Villa Rica—fell "out of her door and put her hip out of place," a mishap that incapacitated her so severely that Sam and Martha had to take her into their house for an extended stay. Now Martha was burdened with multiple responsibilities: a lame mother-in-law, a mentally handicapped grown son, a depressed husband, at least five of the younger children still at home, and a shortage of cash and provisions.

"Everything is in such distressed circumstances," she wrote her daughter Florence in December 1861, "that no one is able to hire negroes. Our hands are doing nothing except cut wood, cook & sleep & eat & grumble. We have done getting our crop in & have sown wheat rye & corn and have nothing to do now." Because of the war, Sam was forced to "gin his own cotton & keep it until times gets so he can sell it." As might be expected, Martha blamed these hardships on the enemy:

> How yet my heart burns against the hated hateful Yankees & when I see these that are living here going quietly about I feel as though I wanted to treat them to hanging … They are Yankees & nothing good clean or honest ever did or ever can come out of Yankeedom.

As the fighting continued, Martha witnessed the sad procession of casualties returning home, causing her to worry continually about her two oldest boys, fighting for "the Cause." A neighbor came back from Virginia with the bodies of his two sons, one dying of wounds at the battle of Richmond, the other succumbing to illness. Zeke wrote her every other week, and because he was far away defending his Mississippi town, Martha tried to answer his letters promptly. One of her younger sisters, Isabel (called Isie), was expecting a baby and begged Martha to be with her in her "confinement." One sister had already died "in childbed," and she was terrified that Isie would meet the same fate. But despite her concern, she was unable to help her sister at that time because she needed to spin and weave cloth and supervise harvesting the crops.

Although no actual battles took place in Carroll County, Sherman's assault on nearby Atlanta in 1864 brought scouting regiments into the area. Fearing possible capture, Sam fled into the swamps after being warned that the Yankees were planning to arrest him. But stalwart Martha, determined to defend her family from possible starvation, stashed away meat, grain, and cotton in the walls of the house and preserved the little money on hand by strapping it into a belt around her waist. Her most heroic moment came when one of Stoneham's raiders rode up to the farm and threatened to blow her "soul to hell" unless she gave him her silver. She sniffed and declared defiantly: "I do not think you will do anything of the sort, because I think hell is already full of Union soldiers sent there by Johnson's army between Chattanooga and Lookout Mountain." Her youngest son, John, was only three when the Union army came through Villa Rica. He remembered sitting on the front gate to watch out for approaching Yankees while his mother was in the kitchen feeding a battalion of Confederate soldiers.[8]

Asa G. Candler Sr. and sister Florence Candler Harris, c. 1865, courtesy of Manuscript, Archives, and Rare Book Library, Emory University

When the war ended, Asa Candler was fourteen, and his once well-to-do family was in dire straits. The farm had gone fallow without the help of former slaves, the store was boarded up, and all the schools were closed. Since Asa's education had been interrupted for four years, his parents decided to send him to Huntsville, Alabama, to live with Florence and her husband, former Confederate Colonel James Wyatt Harris. The youth remained there for a year, attending school and bonding closely with the sister nine years his senior. It was a good experience for the boy, who had never really been away from Carroll County, opening his eyes to the wider world and to the cultivation that Florence had acquired when she attended college before the war. Teaching and education had always been Florence's interest, and with no children of her own, she took it upon herself to educate her younger siblings. That appreciation for history and literature was especially valuable to her younger brothers and eventually to her nieces and nephews.

Asa G. Candler Sr., c. 1868, courtesy of Millennium Gate Museum, Atlanta, Georgia

After the year in Huntsville, Asa returned to the Carroll County farm. At age fifteen, he was short, for—like several of his brothers—he had inherited Martha's slight frame and small stature. Nevertheless, he was strong and clever enough to take over many of his father's farm duties, while Sam, with the help of Willie and Charlie, was preparing to reopen the general store. Recognizing that the real key to advancement was education, Sam enrolled Asa and his younger brothers in a school run by Dr. John H. Featherstone in the basement of the Methodist church. But this rudimentary education ended when the church burned down. Although Warren and John were able to take their lessons elsewhere, Asa chose to continue working on the farm and helping clerk at the store. Even in his youth, he showed an interest in making money, demonstrating an organizational and entrepreneurial bent that closely resembled his ambitious and clever father.

A good example of his penchant for commerce is a tale Asa loved to tell. One day when he was plowing the field, he "heard a commotion back at the house," and running as fast as he could, he discovered that his mother "thought snakes had disturbed a hen that made her nest beneath the kitchen floor." To pacify her, Asa crawled under the porch, only to be greeted by a big mink that scooted past him. The critter "ran down by the barn," he later recalled, "through a patch of woods and splashed into the creek." There in the shallow stream, Asa caught and killed the slithery animal after a fight that left teeth marks on his right forearm.

Thinking that mink skins might be marketable, he decided to send his prize to Atlanta. Since no trains yet linked Carroll County to the rest of the state, Asa persuaded a wagon driver to sell his treasure and bring back the cash. He hoped to earn a quarter for spending money, but, much to his delight, the pelt rendered a whole dollar. "And the man who bought the mink skin," Asa would laugh, "sent word that he wanted more and would buy them for that price." So he "started people in the neighborhood to catching minks, and the skins brought quite a sum." Then the farm boy seized the opportunity to turn the accidental encounter into a business by talking the wagon driver into returning with cards of pins that he could sell to neighbors. Just "plain everyday pins," he later explained, but they brought "a good profit in the country." Eventually Asa amassed "more than $100 saved up through the sale of mink skins and speculation in pins." It was enough for him to leave Villa Rica.[9] Apocryphal or actual, the anecdote characterized the grit of a young man determined to be noticed.

Shortly after Sam reopened his store in 1870, he told Asa that he had saved enough money to pay his tuition at either of two institutions: the University of Georgia in Athens or Emory College in Oxford, the Methodist school founded by his cousin Ignatius Few. But Asa refused his father's offer, believing he was not properly prepared for higher education. Instead, just after his eighteenth birthday, he announced that he once more wanted to live with his sister Florence, now settled in Cartersville, Georgia, where her husband was a district judge. Sam made it quite clear that he disapproved of Asa's move to Cartersville, since for years he had been telling his fifth son that he expected him to become a doctor. Not only had he named him after the young medical student, Asa Griggs—who by then had a successful medical practice in West Point, Georgia—but as the boy matured, he was showing an interest in science that seemed to justify his father's wish for one of his sons to study medicine. His eldest son, Milton, was also named after a physician, but he rejected that profession to become an attorney. Now the responsibility for fulfilling their father's dream rested on Asa. Maybe it was his name, or maybe it was the assumption from birth that he had a designated career, but Asa also believed he wanted to be a doctor. Later in life he told a reporter that being a physician shone as a more luminous boyhood goal for him than being "president or the world's greatest ball player."

Asa told his father that he planned to learn as much as he could about medicine in preparation for college, and to do so, he landed a job as an apothecary's apprentice at a Cartersville pharmacy owned by Dr. Fletcher Best. Next door to his drugstore, Dr. Best and another physician operated a clinic, which seemed like the perfect place for an aspiring doctor to attain medical experience. During the day, Asa mixed chemicals to gain a rudimentary knowledge of that science, and, when time allowed, he watched the two doctors as they treated patients. Every night, he poured over anatomy books and began learning Latin and Greek, then a prerequisite for medical school. Although he maintained this rigorous schedule for two years, he gradually began to study less and spend more time mixing medications.

By the time he reached the age of twenty-one, Asa had abandoned all notions of attending medical school, deciding instead to become a pharmacist. One of his first moves in that direction was to report his change of plans to Dr. Asa Griggs. In a long letter, he told the physician that he believed the country already had too many doctors, and besides "with a great deal less trouble of soul and body," he could make more money as a druggist. Fully aware that there was no room for advancement in Cartersville, he asked Dr. Griggs to help him find employment in a more promising location. "You are so widely known both professionally and socially," he wrote, "that I thought perhaps you would be the surest way through which I could get a situation." He further explained that he was "not particular about the place" and would move anywhere he would be able to succeed.[10]

Griggs may have helped his namesake obtain his first job in Atlanta, although Asa liked people to believe that he had pounded the pavement on a hot summer day in 1873 searching for work. He was hired, the story went, when he accidentally stumbled into George Howard's pharmacy late that night. This oft-repeated tale was inaccurate, for several documents indicate that he had already moved to Atlanta by January of that year and probably had procured the job before he arrived. According to his brother John, the Howards had a farm near Cartersville, and when George met the apothecary's apprentice in Dr. Best's drugstore, he was so impressed with Asa's spunk and drive that he agreed to take him on as a clerk.[11]

No matter what propelled Asa Candler to Atlanta, it was a fortuitous move that benefited both the young farm boy and the city where he spent the rest of his life.

Chapter Two
Mixing Concoctions

Asa G. Candler Sr., c. 1876, courtesy of Manuscript, Archives, and Rare Book Library, Emory University

When Asa Candler came to Atlanta in early 1873, the town was slowly recovering from the devastation of Sherman's advance, although reminders of the recent fighting were everywhere. "Red redoubts still marked the hilltops around the city," Asa recalled, while "breastworks, little changed by time, surrounded [the city] on every side and the trees of nearby forests still bore the scars of Minie balls and grape shot." There were no churches, no public schools, and only a few banks. "Telegraph facilities at high prices were none too abundant," he mused, "and the telephone had not been invented."

Although north Georgia still bore the scars of war in 1873, Atlanta was growing at a furious pace. Multiple tracks coursing through the downtown provided the most visible sign of the city's rapid recovery, enlarging the railroad hub that had spurred its founding three decades earlier. Unlike most of the postwar South—still mired in a rural economy with insufficient help to tend the land—Atlanta was a commercially aggressive urban center. Northern businessmen and an influx of enterprising Europeans were taking advantage of the available transportation and relatively mild climate to open factories and shops, while scions of depleted agricultural wealth were arriving to practice law or medicine, or to cash in on new business ventures. Five years before Asa came to town, the Reconstruction Georgia Legislature transferred the state capital from Milledgeville to Atlanta, further increasing the population so that it would soon outrank Savannah to become the state's largest city.

Asa made his way to George Howard's pharmacy amidst the confusion and cacophony of progress and recovery. Mule-drawn streetcars clanged down the major thoroughfares; wafts of sawdust permeated the air as carpenters were shoring up and repairing older buildings; bricklayers and stonecutters hollered back and forth while finishing the facades of new shops and offices. Maneuvering down the planked sidewalks that edged the unpaved streets, the young man from Villa Rica gaped at a variety of new hotels, dry goods stores, and drugstores alongside saloons and billiard parlors. He surely stopped to inspect the three-year-old Kimball House. The yellow wooden hotel was the pride of a city on the make, with its six stories above ground and another floor below that housed north Georgia's first steam-operated passenger elevators and central heating plant.

In subsequent years, Candler loved to describe the hardships of his first days in Atlanta, regaling listeners with tales of his bumpy journey from Cartersville in a wagon and the inconvenience of his first residence in "a tiny room on the ground floor at the rear of the three-story drugstore building" with a ceiling "so close to the floor" even his small frame was unable to straighten up. Relocation in a boardinghouse offered scarcely more comfort, since he was forced to share a bed with two other men and hang his meager wardrobe on one communal hook. Not handicapped by these disadvantages, Asa was so conscientious that George Howard soon appointed him chief clerk and began paying him the first real salary he ever earned. One thing was certain. This young man with an iron will and entrepreneurial resolve arrived in Atlanta determined to make a name for himself. Nowhere was that clearer than in a handwritten letter discovered by a Florida woman in an old medical textbook. On January 10, 1873, the twenty-two-year-old clerk used a sheet of George J. Howard's stationary to inform two men in Cartersville: "I have succeeded in getting into business in this city and as my success depends on the amount of good I can do my proprietor in the way of trade, I would very respectfully solicit any trade you are willing to give." He went on to assure the recipients that their orders would "be filled at as low rates as elsewhere outside the larger cities," and then he unabashedly confessed: "I am anxious to have Mr. Howard believe that I can do him good to such an extent that he will continue [to keep] me on his employ." Asa Candler was off to a very good start.[12]

But less than a year after he began working at George Howard's pharmacy, Asa had to put his career ambitions aside. When notified that his father was seriously ill, he rushed to Carroll County, reaching the farm just as the family patriarch—two weeks short of his sixty-fourth birthday—drew his last breath. Few clues explain the cause of Sam's death, although his obituary says that "he had been in feeble health for some time." On the other hand, Martha's letters indicate that he was performing farm chores up to the end. The burial, conducted with Masonic honors, took place in the new cemetery of Villa Rica's Methodist church, attended by a large crowd of mourners from all around the area. The local press memorialized Samuel Candler as a "quiet and unassuming" man with "sound judgment and a wise discriminating mind," with one eulogizer (possibly his son-in-law, Colonel James W. Harris) noting that he had been "rigidly correct in all his transactions and intercourse with men," thus rendering his very name "a proverb of honesty and virtue." In fact, his sterling character prompted the local saying "as honest as Sam Candler."[13]

Having a reputed paragon for a father presented a special challenge for Sam's many offspring, especially since they probably knew little about his early wandering days. By the time Asa came along as child number eight, rigid discipline was a family mandate, reflected in the achievements of the oldest children, then well-launched on careers. Milton was practicing law in Atlanta; Zeke also a lawyer, was a representative in the Mississippi state legislature and an itinerant Baptist minister; and Florence was beginning to tutor pupils in her home. All the rest were expected to follow suit after the family recovered from its wartime losses. Sam had chosen Willie and

Charlie, who seemed less inclined to scholarship, to take charge of the store, although for a while after the war, Willie taught at the local school. When Sam died, sixteen-year-old Warren was preparing for a ministerial career in his first term at Emory College, and twelve-year-old John was an astute, diligent student at the local school. But Asa, perhaps one of the brightest, was merely an assistant clerk in a pharmacy, having shattered his father's dreams by opting out of college and rejecting a career in medicine. But if there had ever been ill feelings between Sam and Asa, they diminished into reverential affection as time went by. On the day of his father's death twenty-four years later, Asa told his own son: "I love and miss him more today than I ever did."

Always close to his mother, Asa now dedicated his energies toward alleviating her distress by assuming many of his late father's tasks. Martha, who turned fifty-four a few weeks after her husband passed away, had spent all but fourteen years of her life with Sam, who—given her youth at the time of their marriage—had served as both father and husband. Her grieving was so intense that the local press observed: "Mrs. C. is very low and is not expected to live." But strong-minded Martha had no intention of dying, at least not in the foreseeable future. Times were tough, however, in late 1873. Sam's death coincided with a national economic downturn that severely curtailed her income from sales at the recently reopened Villa Rica store. The scarcity of hands around the farm was also a great burden for Martha, who complained frequently of aches and pains, colds and coughs. Making her even more miserable was the mentally impaired Noble "going around singing a mournful tune" and saying he hoped his "Pa would come back tonight." These worries were partially alleviated by frequent visits from her other children, grandchildren, and neighbors. Her daughter Lizzie Dobbs often dropped by with her young son, Sammy (named after his grandfather), and Willie came regularly with his wife (also called Lizzie) accompanied by their young children. Having this constant companionship during her early weeks of mourning meant Martha never had to leave the house, except for once riding with "Johnnie" to call on the "dear parson."

In January, after Warren returned to Emory, Martha admitted that it took all of her "strength of mind & body" to send him back to school. Milton came from his home in Decatur to help Warren pack, and Lizzie's husband drove the young man in a wagon to Atlanta to get a "neat suit of clothes" to go with the pair of "sown boots" that Martha had commissioned. When her daughter Jessie Willard, now living in Chattanooga, came for an extended stay, she confided in her mother that she had "missed her regular time" and suspected she was pregnant, although she had not yet experienced a "sick stomach." Later that year, Jessie gave birth to her oldest son, another Samuel. After Jessie returned home, Martha told Florence that she felt "very acutely" saddened watching each of her children ride away.

Their departures meant that Asa was stuck in Villa Rica. Although he had originally planned to stay only until his mother got back on her feet, he realized that he could not desert her now, especially since he was the only one among his brothers deemed to have no worthwhile career. His tasks were numerous, as the farm suffered from months of neglect. Fences had fallen down, animals had been ignored, and fields were unprepared for winter. In addition, the scant agricultural workforce was being stretched too thin, especially since most of the hands were required to double at the store. With the help of John, Charlie, and a few former slaves, Asa set about thrashing, mulching, plowing, tending the livestock, rebuilding the fences, bringing in broken rails for firewood, and generally getting the place back in order. His mother told Florence how much she depended on his organizational skills and ability to manage the seemingly disastrous situation. In fact, she wrote, he had been "as good as good can be."

Martha ended this and all other letters with prayers for the "good Lord's" blessing, assuring her oldest daughter that he would "save us all to gather in heaven with our darling dear one." These strong religious convictions helped her survive those difficult times through daily prayer services, church attendance, and frequent conversations with the minister. Faith for Martha was so fundamental that her beliefs in salvation through direct communication with God transported her from the dreariness of her everyday routine to her perception of a better life in heaven. Her intense piety had a profound effect on Asa, who accompanied her often to church and Sunday school. In the process, he became so devoted to Methodism that he pledged to become a steward of the Villa Rica church, thus embarking on a lifelong religious commitment. Martha must have been moved as well as gratified to have Asa join her church, for with the exception of Florence, Warren, and John, the rest of her children were not Methodists. Charlie never joined any church; Milton and Willie were Presbyterians; and the others followed their spouses to become Baptists.

Just as Asa was beginning to get the farm running smoothly, events at the family store grew desperate. During the spring of 1874, both Willie and Charlie came down with typhoid fever and were unable to work for months. Their illnesses meant that Asa had to run the store *and* tend the farm, with only thirteen-year-old John to help. After school, the youngest Candler helped gather crops and "haul cotton to the gin." However, with the recession worsening and no money for hiring additional workers, Asa and his siblings concluded, after much deliberation, that maintaining both farm and store was overstretching their sparse resources and manpower. Although it was difficult to abandon the home of their childhoods, by February 1875, they had found a buyer. With sale of the farm, Martha went to live with Florence in Cartersville, where her sister, Frances Beall Brame, ran a small school that John could attend. After his mother resettled and Willie and Charlie returned to the store, Asa was finally free to resume his job in Atlanta.[14]

Lucy Elizabeth Howard Candler, c. 1876, courtesy of Millennium Gate Museum, Atlanta, Georgia

Shortly after Asa went back to work at the pharmacy, George Howard's fifteen-year-old daughter, Lucy Elizabeth, began making regular visits to the store, ostensibly to get candy or supplies for her mother. Instead of leaving right away, however, she hung around to chat with the young clerk as he mixed vials of medicines and rolled out pills. Lucy Elizabeth, the fourth girl born to Maria Luisa and George Howard, grew up in a comfortable middle-class home on Houston Street, a few blocks from the pharmacy. Her family had moved from Augusta in the 1850s but fled back there when Sherman's army forged in from the north, returning to Atlanta when Lucy Elizabeth was six. Always challenged by his headstrong daughter—whose lively face and dark, knowing eyes revealed a playful spirit—George Howard tried desperately to shield her from the temptations of adolescence. When she was thirteen, he dispatched her with her two older sisters to Moravian College in what was then Salem, North Carolina. Two years later, with Asa Candler now on the scene, George became even more anxious to get his daughter out of town. This time he sent her to LaGrange Female College, a small Methodist school in western Georgia. A good student, Lucy Elizabeth took readily to the curriculum, especially development of her musical and artistic skills.

While she was in LaGrange, Asa made a definitive move. His relationship with Howard was becoming increasingly strained, partly because of his own ambitious agenda but mostly because of his growing attachment to Lucy Elizabeth. When the tension grew unbearable, George attempted to rid himself of the annoyance by offering Asa the chance to buy 47 Peachtree. This was just what the young pharmacist wanted: a drugstore of his own. But procuring it required a capital outlay he didn't possess, so to pay for the purchase, he formed a partnership with a pharmaceutical salesman named Marcellus B. Hallman. Then he borrowed the rest from his mother—now financially stable after selling the farm—and from Hallman's brother, as well as from his own brothers Willie and Charlie, who were now operating the Villa Rica store in the black. But the transition presented unforeseen obstacles. The first occurred when George Howard opened a competing drugstore a few blocks away, turning the feud between the two men into an advertising blitz. First Howard announced that he had attained the "skill and experience" of two well-known pharmacists, Charles H. Greene and John S. "Doc" Pemberton. Countering this, Candler placed a notice in the *Atlanta Constitution* to tell Howard's former customers that he and Hallman were now operating at "the old stand" equipped with "fresh and new" stock. Most importantly, the advertisement stated: "Asa Candler, known in Atlanta as THE prescription clerk with Mr. Howard," would be dispensing medications.

A month after this notice appeared in the Atlanta paper, Asa wrote Lucy Elizabeth at LaGrange College, the only remaining letter in what must have been a lengthy correspondence. Previously he had complained that she never answered his letters, a charge she countered by threatening to stop all correspondence if he failed to understand that studying took up most of her time. This explanation hardly sufficed. "Would I neglect you for two whole weeks," he queried, "just because I happened to have been extremely engaged night and day?" In fact, he made it quite clear that *he* always found time to write her "<u>some sort of letter</u>." (Asa liberally underlined phrases he considered important.) "But we will not quarrel about this," he conceded. "I shall as usual expect to receive your letters 'til you return home."

Lucy Elizabeth had invited him to attend the LaGrange commencement, where his brother Warren was speaking at the "Methodist Communicant." Asa, however, declined, explaining that Hallman was on the road and none of the clerks were experienced enough to take charge of the pharmacy. Pleading with her to drop out of school after that term, he insisted that she knew "enough in books for all practical purposes," especially since other things were just as important for her "future success as instruction usually imparted in college walls." That kind of education, he added, "is doubtless as much humbuggery as in any other of the world's money traps." Was this perhaps a defensive remark coming from a man who had elected not to attend college? Yet Asa allowed that, if after spending the summer in Atlanta, she still wanted to return to LaGrange in the fall, he would "quietly acquiesce." Satisfied that he had now placated her, he signed off: "Good night pretty pet. Your boy, Asa."

His tactics must have worked, for they saw each other constantly when Lucy Elizabeth spent the summer of 1877 in Atlanta, even though against his wishes she returned to LaGrange in the fall. No letters from that period can be found in the archives, probably destroyed deliberately to avoid having anyone read their romantic babbling. When she came home for Christmas vacation, they became engaged, and, not surprisingly, George Howard exploded. Not only did he deem his nineteen-year-old daughter too young for marriage, but he considered the farm boy from Villa Rica to be socially inferior. Therefore, without her father's permission, Lucy Elizabeth Howard and Asa Candler quietly married at Atlanta's First Baptist Church on January 15, 1878, in the presence of only a few members of the groom's family, since George Howard refused to attend the ceremony and demanded his wife and daughters do the same. For most of the following year, Lucy Elizabeth remained estranged from her family.[15]

A few months earlier, Martha Candler had moved from Cartersville to Atlanta and was renting a house at 61 North Pryor Street. To that small cottage, teeming with Candlers, Asa took his new bride. In addition to the newlyweds, Asa's brothers John and Noble also lived there, along with Warren—then serving as the pastor of Atlanta's Sixth Methodist Church—and his new wife Antoinette (called Nettie). Shortly after their marriage, Lucy Elizabeth and Asa accompanied Warren and Nettie to visit their family in Carroll County, traveling in a two-horse carriage on icy, rutted roads. The recklessness of hazarding such a journey in January gave Asa and Warren something to laugh about for years. By summer, Lucy Elizabeth and Nettie were both pregnant, meaning that space in the house on North Pryor would be stretched beyond its limit, as it was already bulging with seven residents. Crowding it even further, Jessie Willard came down from Chattanooga to be with her mother when she delivered her third child, bringing along her two older children, Sam and Jessie, to keep them safe from an epidemic of yellow fever then raging in Tennessee. It was just too many people for a tiny place to accommodate. So Martha began looking for a larger house to rent and settled on a duplex at 170 Ivy Street.[16]

Amidst all of the commotion, Lucy Elizabeth was miserable. Not only was she alienated from her parents and sisters, but the close-knit Candler tribe was overwhelming. Her great-granddaughter would later remark that "marrying into the Candler family was often like being absorbed. They were a dominating and clannish group." Florence Candler Harris was the exception. When she learned of her young sister-in-law's dilemma, Florence invited her to visit Cartersville. Suffering from the heat in her fifth month of pregnancy, Lucy Elizabeth was glad for a brief respite in a quiet location, where she hoped to find a sympathetic ear for the dual burdens of her own family's rejection and the close proximity of so many Candlers.

In a long letter after his wife's return to Atlanta, Asa told his sister: "Since I have learned what it is to love a wife and found you so willing to take her to your bosom" being "as kind to her as if she was [sic] always your sister, my heart can't contain the load of gratitude to you." He admitted that he had virtually stolen Lucy Elizabeth from her family, and with a hyperbolic flourish, he told Florence how grateful he was that his wife could unleash "her heart aches and bosom thoughts" to a caring soul who would listen to her "anticipated griefs and troubles." No proper gentleman of that Victorian era would have discussed pregnancy or the anxieties preceding childbirth. Asa merely told his childless sister of the "evil forebodings" that haunted Lucy Elizabeth after hearing "terrible" chatter from a bunch of "croaking crows." In October, Jessie Willard had her baby, Joe Jr., and she took her family back to Chattanooga. John went off to Emory College, leaving a little more space for the two expected babies. Much of Lucy

Elizabeth's anxiety dissipated when shortly before her due date, George Howard sent a note to his son-in-law: "I am disposed to 'bury the hatchet' and to be friendly in the future—if this should meet your approval you can let me know." Needless to say, his daughter was a much happier person as she entered her "confinement."

Nine days after receiving her father's letter, on December 28, 1878, she gave birth to her first child in the Candler's Ivy Street home. When the pains began, they called her uncle, Dr. William T. Goldsmith, a well-known Atlanta physician. It was a long labor, with Asa pacing up and down outside the closed bedroom, where only women were allowed. At last Dr. Goldsmith beckoned for him to come in, and it was then that he saw "a fine boy" lying "in the arms of his pretty mother, asleep." They named him Charles Howard Candler, after the baby's uncle and grandfather, but decided at once to call him "Howard," a conciliatory gesture that placed the final seal on the reconciliation with Lucy Elizabeth's family. Both grandmothers were in the room when Asa first saw his son. Martha Candler kissed the baby and said "'tis my boy," only to be reprimanded by the exhausted Lucy Elizabeth, who clearly had no intention of relinquishing her baby to a dominating mother-in-law. Calmly Maria Luisa Howard became the peacemaker by asserting: "He is ours." It was a gentle way of restating that the family feud had ended. Overcome by "the tremendous weight of parental responsibility," but joyful that a child would call him "Papa," Asa "grandly" walked the few blocks to his Peachtree shop. And so Howard Candler came into the world as the bond that mended the rift between his mother and her kinfolk.[17]

With his birth and Nettie's delivery of a daughter the following month, Warren moved with his wife and daughter upstate to Dahlonega, where he became presiding elder of the regional Methodist district. Yet the small Candler house was still so crowded that baby equipment had to be compact and practical. To help her daughter, Maria Luisa Howard produced a "swinging cradle equipped with two wheels at one end and a curved handle at the other for easy rolling from place to place." Though destined to become a family fixture passed on to future children, grandchildren, and great-grandchildren, the cradle proved costly to baby Howard. One day while Lucy Elizabeth's youngest sister was tending the baby, the buggy careened off the front porch and onto the ground. From that fall, Howard lost his front four baby teeth and damaged the buds of his permanent teeth. By the time that happened, the family was again ready to move, since Asa had saved enough money to make his first venture into real estate by paying $2,975 for a more spacious house at 99 Walton Street. Several months after they settled there, Lucy Elizabeth realized she was again pregnant, and on August 27, 1880, Dr. Goldsmith delivered Asa Griggs Candler Jr. whom the family nicknamed "Buddie."[18]

Now responsible for two children, Asa itched to make more money. Since in his current setup he had to share all profits with his partner, Marcellus Hallman, he decided to borrow again from his family and buy Hallman out. They arrived at an amicable settlement, and in no time 47 Peachtree sported a new sign that read: "Asa G. Candler & Company." However, no sooner was the sign in place than it had to come down, due to Asa's overestimation of his meager resources. Additional cash from his family was not enough to keep the business afloat, and he was forced to go hat in hand to George Howard. After complicated negotiations, his formerly estranged father-in-law agreed to buy half interest in the pharmacy, but only if Asa would agree to rename the enterprise Howard & Candler. Asa needed to have George Howard's input, because he realized Lucy Elizabeth deserved a home of her own. Not only had she been washing, scrubbing, and tending her two small boys, but she was helping her mother-in-law care for Noble and cooking for the entire household, which still included John, now beginning to practice law in Atlanta. Three generations living under one roof was definitely wearing thin, especially with a third baby on the way.

In June 1882, Asa paid $3,250 for a one-story clapboard farmhouse surrounded by a huge swath of land in the heart of a new suburb at the eastern end of the city called "Edgewood." His property sat on a hill overlooking the well-traveled—intermittently either muddy or dusty—highway that connected Atlanta and Decatur and ran adjacent to the railroad tracks. After they got settled, he established a small farm behind the house, replete with a horse and cow. The sloping front was a meadow, thick with field peas and bordered by a white wooden fence that Howard and Buddie crawled under to get front-row seats for watching the trains go by. Once the two brothers and a younger cousin were playing inside when they heard the engine's whistle. The three of them scampered out to the front porch and began tussling to see who could get the best spot for seeing the approaching locomotive. In the commotion, one of the younger boys shoved unfortunate Howard from the porch, and he landed on a jagged rock. To stop the bleeding Lucy Elizabeth covered the wound with chimney soot and hitched up the horse and buggy to rush the injured boy down to his father's pharmacy. Asa examined the cut and assured his wife that it would heal. A trip to the doctor for stitches might have been a better idea, since the fall left Howard with a permanent scar on his forehead. That scar, along with the damaged teeth, intensified the sensitive boy's impression that he was physically weak and unattractive.

Moving to Edgewood did not rid Lucy Elizabeth of her in-laws, however. Within weeks, Asa found a house down the road for his mother. Just before she moved, Martha explained to Florence why she had paid an exorbitant $800 for the four-room dwelling, "one half mile this side of Asa's." She rationalized the extravagance by telling her daughter that the house was "the best bargain & cheapest ever to its real value" she could find. Not only did the owner have to sell, but since it was "just out of the city limits," she would not be "city taxed." It reminded her of the country, with its level lot filled with "beautiful fruit trees & all kinds of grapes & a good well of water." Best of all, it was very near the Edgewood Methodist Church, where the whole family could worship together. Grateful that her son would be so near, Martha told Florence that Asa's assistance had relieved her of all the "work & worry" of moving. In fact, she prayed constantly that God would "bless and reward him by giving him just such sons" as he had been to her. Not everyone was thankful that Asa had assumed so much responsibility for his mother and siblings, however. Lucy Elizabeth—whose relationship with Martha had often been strained—once complained to her daughter: "Your papa has done so much for his folks and they don't try to do any thing in return."[19]

Several months after the Candlers settled into their new Edgewood home, Lucy Beall Candler was born. Given her mother's first name and her paternal grandmother's maiden name, the curly-haired blonde girl immediately became the darling of her family. Asa spoiled her with hugs and kisses that he rarely lavished on his sons, while Lucy Elizabeth—excited about having a daughter—was busy sewing little dresses. Her older brothers adored her from the start. Years later, when Howard congratulated his sister on her birthday, he wrote:

> I remember how proud I was that beautiful Spring day, when it was announced that I had a little sister. Bud couldn't understand it and when I would beg to nurse you, his infant jealousy would assert itself and he would say that I didn't love him any more, and that he was going to run away, and all such sweet baby talk and ideas ... I have watched you grow, dear, and develop into a sweet young lady from a

wee bit of a tot who would sit for hours between the banister rails on our high back porch and call the cow, "moo-cow" or "too-tow."[20]

But just as the Candlers were adjusting to their family's new addition, Asa faced a temporary setback.

Everyone knew that gas lights and flimsy buildings rendered downtown Atlanta a tinderbox. The perilous situation became even clearer when in the wee hours of August 12, 1883, the Kimball House Hotel—less than a dozen years old—burst into flames. The wooden structure was filled with guests and boarders as the fire leapt from the elevator shaft and tore through the building. It was a tribute to the efficiency of the hotel staff and Atlanta's newly salaried fire department that no one died as the building crumpled. Then it was Asa's turn. Two months after the Kimball House burned, a fire—attributed to paints and oils stored in the basement—broke out in his pharmacy, a stone's throw away from the destroyed hotel. Before the flames could be contained, they spread to several adjacent stores, including the King Hardware next door. Although swift action by the city's firemen prevented any buildings from collapsing, Asa's pharmacy was badly charred, and all his merchandise destroyed. An insurance settlement allowed him to repair the damage, replace some of the lost goods, and begin the long, tedious process of recovery. But it wasn't nearly enough. Then, just as he was trying to figure out how he would make ends meet, he received an unexpected boost. Shortly after the fire at 47 Peachtree, George Howard's former druggist, Doc Pemberton, decided to close his drugstore and put the entire stock up for sale, so he could devote all of his time to manufacturing patent medicines.

Always one to spot an opportunity when it arose, Candler scurried to acquire all of Pemberton's equipment and medications, transporting the lot to 47 Peachtree. Within weeks, the reconstruction was completed, the stock was replenished, and he was able to reopen the pharmacy. However, so many customers had drifted elsewhere that Asa had to find some way to lure them back, and it was for that reason that he decided to capitalize on the lucrative patent medicine market. It was a natural. He knew how to mix these elixirs and possessed the marketing skills that many others lacked, since the real secret of success in this potential moneymaker was owning the exclusive patents to products that could not be purchased elsewhere. Asa already had the rights to a cologne called Everlasting that was selling moderately well, and he soon purchased the formula for a dentifrice named De-Lac-Ta-Lave. With these new items, traffic in his store increased so noticeably that he decided to expand further by buying a blood purifying tonic called Botanic Blood Balm (or B.B.B), purported to cure everything from rheumatism to skin diseases. To capitalize on the popularity of this new patent, he hired salesmen to hawk his three exclusive products throughout Georgia and neighboring states. Increased sales from this expanded marketing provided him with enough income to buy out his father-in-law's share of the business, and once more the sign in front of 47 Peachtree read: "Asa G. Candler & Co." This time it would remain in place.

With the pharmacy and patent medicines producing sufficient revenue, Asa decided to construct a larger home on a section of his property across the railroad tracks from his present residence. The family's new one-story clapboard house sat on a twenty-five acre, heavily wooded lot fronting Seaboard Avenue, a new thoroughfare named after the Seaboard-Airline Railroad that coursed along its periphery. Even before he purchased the land, Asa and his boys often tramped over the grounds to collect scraps of ammunition, swords, and remnants of bayonets discarded after the Battle of Atlanta. Behind the new house, Asa had a larger farm, reminiscent of his childhood home, with a smokehouse and barn filled with pigs, chickens, cows, a bull, horses, a goat, and several ponies. Howard Candler had vivid memories of Lucy Elizabeth putting up the garden's produce in mason jars and of his father butchering, skinning, and dressing a hog, after which his mother ground the entrails for sausages. In the fall, Asa gathered apples from his orchard and made cider in an old wooden press, but given his frequent condemnation of alcoholic beverages, it is doubtful that he allowed the mixture to ferment.

In the late spring of 1885, two-years old Lucy came down with an intestinal illness. At first, Asa tried treating her with medications from his drugstore, but those elixirs did nothing to alleviate her discomfort, and the child seemed to be getting worse. Worried about the listlessness of his usually sunny, laughing, little daughter, he decided to send the toddler with her mother and the two boys to stay with his brother Zeke in Iuka, Mississippi, where she could bathe in springs known for their healing cures. For Lucy Elizabeth, who had protested vehemently against her husband's decision to dispatch her to the care of his family, the entire experience was a nightmare. Five months pregnant, with two active boys and a sick daughter, Asa's wife found the long journey in a hot railroad car to be only the beginning of a miserable visit. Although her husband was extremely fond of Zeke, she found little solace or assistance from him. He might have been one of Mississippi's most important citizens, but neither he nor his wife did much to help her or her brood, leaving the frazzled woman to tend the sick child, wash soiled clothing and diapers, prepare little Lucy's food, and find entertainment for the two boys. It was much worse than being at home.

At least on Seaboard Avenue she was in familiar surroundings, and Asa did assist with the chores, even though the burden of housework remained essentially in her domain. While she was in Mississippi, however, Asa had to manage all of her duties in addition to running his drugstore and doing much of the farm work. Making things worse, his mother was in Cartersville visiting Florence, so he had the added responsibility of providing meals for Noble and Zeke's son, Dan, both staying with him while the rest of the family was away. During his wife's absence that early summer, Asa spent his limited spare time sitting at his desk behind the pharmacy, scratching out letters to Lucy Elizabeth, dotted with paragraphs of baby talk for the children. He told how every morning he rose at five to "feed kittens, pigs, cows, horses," and cultivate the sprouting beds so that when she returned, she would "get a big mess of snaps, butter beans and Irish potatoes and peas, squash and cabbage and watermelon, roasting ears and cantaloupes and ---- kisses." After finishing his chores, Asa wrote, he went back inside to prepare "fried middling" eggs, biscuits, batter cakes, coffee, milk, and fresh butter" for Noble and Dan's breakfast, sitting down to eat with them before hitching up the buggy and riding five miles to his Peachtree store.

Bred in the rural South, Asa possessed a wry sense of humor, colored by colloquialisms. When his family first left home, he wrote jokingly that Lucy Elizabeth should arrange for his "blue eyed baby" to get "everything to eat," and then "slip off without paying" her board. However, if she did this, he quipped, his "ugly old" brother would be watching "mighty close" and might decide to steal little Lucy as ransom. Chances are, however, he would tire of her "about August" and claim one of the boys for pay. No doubt Lucy Elizabeth failed to appreciate her husband's wit as she scrubbed diapers and pulled the boys out of trees. Her letters (which he didn't save) must have griped that the whole hot journey had been a mistake. That made Asa's humor dissolve into concern about his daughter. "Is she worse than when she left here?" he worried. Had Lucy Elizabeth filled the prescription he sent and given it to the child immediately? She should tell Zeke to telegraph him right away with information about "Sister's" condition.

"I pray she is not going to be sick," he wrote gloomily. "Mr. Read's baby was taken sick Sunday and died today at noon — so bad." This ominous message surely added to Lucy Elizabeth's anxieties. Asa had bad news for the boys, too. Their four "little chickens were drowned" and the cat "we all loved so much" was found dead under the barn. "Now her poor little kittens have not any Mama except me." In order to keep them alive, each day Asa milked the cow and carried the warm milk up the ladder to the barn loft. "Now ain't that bad," he jibed, "poor old hen with no chickens and poor little kittens with no mama."[21] This news probably made things worse. Little Lucy survived her illness, and after several weeks the family returned home.

In October 1885, Lucy Elizabeth delivered another boy they named Walter Turner Candler. Now with four children to feed and clothe, Asa desperately needed to earn additional money in order to make his wife's life easier. Besides, he was itching to do something more significant than managing a drugstore. Not that pharmaceuticals wasn't an honorable profession. But frankly he was growing tired of dispensing pills and mixing concoctions, even though the patent medicines did provide some new avenues to explore. Still, there had to be something else, and he was determined to find it.

CHAPTER THREE
Serendipity

The answer to Asa Candler's prayers was waiting a few blocks away in a house on Marietta Street, where Doc Pemberton was experimenting with patent medicines. Doc had always been a peculiar fellow. Tall and gaunt, with deep-set brooding eyes and a long, dark, scraggly beard, he suffered from persistent illness, which probably contributed to his haggard look. A few years after the Civil War, he moved his family from Columbus, Georgia, to Atlanta and spent the next two decades working at a series of drugstores, barely earning enough to make ends meet. Asa had known Pemberton ever since he came to town, mostly because they were competing pharmacists. But where Asa was ambitious and determined to make money, Doc was more interested in his hobby, or more accurately, his obsession: tinkering with concoctions to heal everything from gout to high blood pressure. One of these was an elixir made from wine mixed with the recently discovered coca leaf. He bottled the mixture under the name "French Wine Coca" (or "Wine Cola"), a syrup to be mixed with water and taken to ease nerves and cure ailments. Finally Pemberton came up with a balance of water, sugar, extract of kola nut, caffeine, coca leaf, and a pinch of cocaine, producing a refreshing drink that doubled as a healing remedy.

After the syrup pleased him, Doc convinced a pair of local drugstores to give it a test run. The more popular of the two was Dr. Joseph Jacobs's pharmacy at the corner of Whitehall and Marietta Streets, where Willis Venerable operated the soda fountain. As local businessmen, young people, and nearby residents began demanding Wine Cola, Pemberton realized that he had a potential winner. Deciding that the best way to capitalize on his invention was to form a partnership, he teamed up with his son Charley and Ed Holland, scion of one of Villa Rica's leading families, who agreed to loan the start-up money. Soon after the trio formed the Pemberton Chemical Company, Doc hired two Maine natives, Frank Robinson and David Doe, both having recently settled in Atlanta after touring the country selling advertisements produced on their own portable printing press. Although Robinson and Doe had no formal contract with Pemberton, they poured all their savings—along with that of a few friends and relatives—into ads placed in local papers.

The first thing Frank Robinson did was coin the catchy name "Coca-Cola," combining two ingredients found in the mixture. Then employing the familiar rhetoric used by patent-medicine salesmen, he hawked the brew as an aphrodisiac, a panacea for exhaustion, a nerve stimulant, a cure for intemperance, and a substitute for alcoholic beverages. In an attempt to make the product more salable, he hired a local printer to design a unique trademark displaying the name "Coca-Cola" in a curved Spenserian script, similar to that then taught in penmanship classes. The initial advertising was so successful that he ordered five hundred streetcar cards, sixteen hundred posters, and forty-five tin signs. Meanwhile, according to Coca-Cola lore, one day at the Jacobs Pharmacy soda fountain Venable tapped the wrong spigot, thus mixing the syrup with carbonated water instead of the plain water prescribed by Pemberton. And, *voila*, a new phenomenon was born. Whether this actually happened or not is unimportant. It was the fortuitous addition of carbonation that gave the "medicine" its pizzazz.

At first Pemberton was able to keep up production of the syrup. But soon he began suffering from so many ailments that even his own potions couldn't cure him, and thus supplies to the soda fountains lagged behind. Discouraged by the uncertain future of their enterprise, David Doe renounced his shares and disappeared, leaving Robinson and Holland to flounder around hoping Pemberton would recover. Always curious about new (and competing) products, Asa Candler had no doubt been reading Robinson's ads in local papers and was well aware of the new "Delicious! Refreshing! Exhilarating! Invigorating!" cure-all that promised "the relief of headaches and nervous affections, neuralgia, hysteria, melancholia, etc." Since his pharmacy a few blocks away from Jacobs's had no soda fountain, he often wandered down to Five Points to chat with Joe Jacobs and sample Venable's latest concoctions. In a city as small and interconnected as Atlanta was then, Candler no doubt already knew that Doc was once more scrounging around for money. But nobody was aware—until after the fact—that Pemberton had signed a contract to sell the Coca-Cola formula to Willis Venable and his friend George Lowndes for $283.29. It was a deal comparable to Peter Stuyvesant's purchase of Manhattan!

Now assuming they were sole owners of the formula and everything necessary to produce the syrup, Lowndes and Venable hauled off the brass pot, chemical equipment, and all the advertising materials to the basement of Jacobs Pharmacy. Not only had wily old Pemberton failed to tell Holland and Robinson about the sale, but unbeknownst to anybody else, he had applied for the Coca-Cola patent in his own name, omitting all the others. That way, Pemberton figured he could collect an extra $1,201 by allowing Lowndes and Venable to buy two-thirds interest in the patent. This sleight of hand infuriated Frank Robinson. After all he had done to promote Coca-Cola, he was cut out with seemingly no recourse. A few days later, he and Holland were attending a property auction on the front steps of the Fulton County Courthouse. While mingling with the crowd, Holland spotted John Candler, his old friend from Carroll County, and they began to chat. Newly launched in an Atlanta law practice, Asa's youngest brother listened as the frustrated investors explained their dilemma. John—who remembered Doc Pemberton from the days when he came to Atlanta with his father to buy products for the general store—said he wouldn't mind calling on the chemist to see if he could persuade him to give the men their fair share of the business. But when John stood at Doc's bedside, Pemberton adamantly denied that he had cheated Holland and Robinson. No, indeed, he insisted. They could not have rights to either the formula or the promotional materials. Disappointed at this outcome, John trudged back to call on the two men, explaining that any kind of suit would be futile because Pemberton was sick, penniless, and stubborn.

But John Candler did feel sorry for Frank Robinson, "a little dried up sort of fellow," who had wasted the better part of two years promoting a product that was sold behind his back. There would be nothing to lose, John thought, by introducing Frank to his older brother on the odd chance that Asa might invest in Coca-Cola. Although at first Asa rejected the idea of taking on another patent medicine, he did offer Robinson the position of part-time bookkeeper, a largesse readily accepted. When he wasn't pouring over his double-entry ledger, Robinson began pushing his employer to buy the Coca-Cola formula, which he had secretly copied when he worked for Pemberton. But with no soda fountain in his shop, Asa decided against investing. Besides, he argued, the patent now belonged to Venable and Lowndes, meaning no one else could produce the beverage without their permission.[22]

At this point of his career, Asa Candler was far happier riding in a Governor's Horse Guard parade wearing full cavalry dress than he was in confronting the ornery Doc Pemberton. He had joined the volunteer cavalry troop just in time to lead President and Mrs. Grover Cleveland to the 1887 Piedmont Exposition, a trade show to promote southern products in Atlanta's newly created Piedmont Park. Slightly over a year earlier, the fifty-year-old president had married his ward, Frances Folsom, in the first wedding ever held in the White House. Curious Atlantans poured out in the rain to catch a glimpse of the young Mrs. Cleveland and the rotund president, when he spoke to a large crowd in front of the Markham House Hotel. That evening, when Cleveland was the honor guest at a private banquet at the newly rebuilt Kimball House, Governor's Horse Guard Lieutenant Asa Candler stood on guard outside the ballroom door.[23]

Asa's new bookkeeper, Frank Robinson, had no doubt been standing in front of the drugstore watching his boss parade down Peachtree to escort President and Mrs. Cleveland to their hotel. The two men had been working together amicably for several months, during which time the persistent Robinson kept trying to convince Asa to purchase Coca-Cola. Candler was listening but not admitting any interest, still cautiously waiting to see how things were shaping up. And what he observed was stagnation. Although Venable had leased storage space for the equipment from Dr. Jacobs, the soda jerk had been too busy to keep up any semblance of regular production and was beginning to regret that he had made such a foolish investment.

When he learned that Venable was agonizing over the unused equipment, Joe Jacobs offered to buy his employee's shares of the patent medicine, and—relieved to be shed of it—Venable readily agreed. Just about that time, Asa Candler came around for one of his frequent chats. In the course of their conversation, Jacobs told him he had helped out his soda jerk by buying some worthless stock, and, as a gesture of friendship, Asa agreed to take it off his hands. He would be happy to trade shares in a glass company he had recently bought, throwing in some "odds and ends" from the pharmacy in exchange for Jacobs's Coca-Cola stock. Seeing this as a good swap, the two men shook on the deal. Soon afterward, Jacobs regretted having been so gullible. As it turned out, the uninsured glass company burned, offering no recompense for the shareholders, while Candler walked away with a windfall.

But even though Asa now owned a portion of Coca-Cola, the situation was mired in complications. By late 1887, several people had bought shares from Pemberton, among them one of Doc's former salesmen named Woolfolk Walker. He and his sister, Margaret Dozier, had each paid $1,200 to purchase part of the business, and now they were demanding something in return. Then Pemberton's son Charley showed up in Atlanta asking for his cut of the proceeds. Clearly too many hands were reaching into the pot that was being hauled back and forth between the basement of the Jacobs Pharmacy and Pemberton's quarters, where it finally remained.

In the spring of 1888, Asa informed his brother Warren that he had discovered a miraculous cure for his headaches called "Coco-Cola." Up to that time, no one realized that Asa Candler had been quietly making deals with small investors in Pemberton's formula. As soon as he acquired a majority of those shares, he went down to the Fulton County Courthouse to file incorporation papers for a partnership between himself, Woolfolk Walker, Margaret Dozier, and Charley Pemberton. Then he contacted Doc Pemberton with a proposition. He would forgive an old debt of $550 in exchange for one-third of the original business. When Pemberton agreed, Asa paid Walker and his sister $750 for half of their shares, thus acquiring a controlling interest in Coca-Cola. In April, he moved the equipment from Pemberton's basement to the rear of his Peachtree store. Wasting not a moment, he and Robinson adjusted the formula to their liking and immediately began manufacturing a new syrup. Two months later, he told Warren: "We are doing moderately well with Coca-Cola," the "only obstacle" being Pemberton. Doc, Asa wrote, had been "continually offering a very poor article at a less price," thereby cheating "the public who pay for Coca-Cola" but are not informed "that it is a fraud." To Asa's dismay, the ailing chemist had dragged himself out of bed to once more produce Wine Cola, claiming his was the real product and Candler's was merely an imitation.

The competition came to an abrupt end, however, in August 1887 when Doc Pemberton died. Now Candler could afford to be magnanimous. On the day of the funeral, he asked all Atlanta pharmacists to close their shops and assemble at 47 Peachtree to pay tribute to their late colleague. Even though Pemberton had been erratic and fractious, he had been a leader of their profession and a pioneer in inventing patent medicines. The gathered pharmacists agreed that his nonconforming presence would be missed, and they issued a statement acknowledging as much. Asa then joined eleven other druggists in a slow procession of buggies, driving down to attend their old colleague's burial in his hometown of Columbus.[24]

At first, Asa's purchase of the Coca-Cola formula did nothing to change the daily routine of his family. Life on Seaboard Avenue still played out before a rich background of jostling youngsters. Although Lucy Elizabeth attempted to run an orderly household, the children often invaded her territory with their kittens, puppies, and rabbits. Chickens might escape from the henhouse and lay eggs under the porch; cats would scratch the upholstery; small, muddy footprints would soil the carpets. After eight years of marriage, lifetime patterns had set in. Lucy Elizabeth—her youthful mischievousness now tempered by maturity and responsibility—remained outwardly serene, with a soothing and forgiving demeanor that contrasted markedly with Asa's edgy restlessness and tendency to overreact. Although both worried constantly about their children, Asa administered discipline with a firm hand, expecting his offspring to be dutiful, God-fearing, and obedient. His wife, on the other hand, conducted her daily routine with tranquil resignation, gently requiring her progeny to learn manners and adopt social graces.

As soon as they were old enough, the children were assigned chores. Howard milked the cows before breakfast each morning, and together he and Buddie took care of their pet goat, also helping their father plant, hoe, and weed the vegetable garden. For Lucy there were different expectations, so that even when small, she was trained to do housework. In the warmth of the kitchen, Lucy Elizabeth taught her daughter how to bake cakes and cookies or put up preserves. Sometime, the little girl would sit beside her mother, watching her turn out pretty dresses or shirts for the boys, her feet bobbing back and forth on the pedal of the sewing machine. Martha Candler lived right down the road, and the children often walked there to play with the constant parade of visiting cousins. Noble—whose impairment led to declining health—had died during 1887, but Martha was seldom alone, since John and his wife Lula moved in with her while he was establishing his law practice. The couple's first child, Asa Warren, (named after his two uncles) grew up as a veritable member of Asa and Lucy Elizabeth's family. By the time Howard was seven, he was allowed to take this cousin, along with his younger brothers and sister, on excursions around the neighborhood. He remembered pushing Walter in a baby carriage and holding Lucy by the hand as they walked "along a rough path, most of it through woods and along the edges of fields" to a "nearby Negro settlement, known as Reynoldstown, where the house servants" lived. While visiting, they would play with the children of the "help," since the rules of segregation didn't apply to servants in the privacy of their homes or yards.

With no public school near their Edgewood residence during the 1880s, the Candler children were taught the fundamentals of reading and arithmetic at home until they were deemed old enough to enter a private institution. When Howard was almost eight, Asa walked with him across the tracks and down a red clay road to the Moreland Park Military Academy, where he paid the first trimonthly tuition of two dollars. Always sensitive, Howard recalled being teased by the children because Asa insisted that his son bring the same lunch that he and his brothers had taken to school in Villa Rica. So in a small tin bucket, his mother placed "left-over-from-breakfast-biscuits" with syrup poured over them. It was a mess to eat, and Howard suffered the humiliation of sticky fingers and constant taunting. Although considered a "modern" building, the school did not have indoor plumbing, meaning that the boys had to go outdoors to the privy in all weather. Their home on Seaboard Avenue not only had indoor facilities, but the heat and gas lights were powered by a kerosene contraption. Not true at the Moreland Academy, where classrooms were warmed inadequately by potbellied stoves. This was fine, Asa decided. The boy needed toughening up, and the school noted for its strict discipline was the perfect place for him. Each day the students had to participate in military drills, and the older ones were made to attend rifle practice. If they misbehaved, they had to carry a heavy Springfield rifle on their shoulders and march in circles around the parade ground.

Howard adapted to the regimentation of the military academy, but Buddie could not. An inquisitive and rambunctious boy, he had trouble sitting still in school, while at home he frequently disrupted the routine with his unconventional pranks. Family members claim that he once dangled his little brother in a bucket down the well and cut up his father's expensive new harness to use for driving the pet goat. Such escapades led to frequent paddling by his father, during which the headstrong youngster refused to cry. When Asa's punishments failed to work, Lucy Elizabeth found her second son too hard to handle, especially after she discovered in mid-1889 that she was once more "with child." She protested, however, when her husband decided to send his namesake to the small school that his sister Florence had opened in Cartersville. In his youth Asa had been dispatched to her care, and therefore he deemed it logical that his unruly son (who seemed to have inherited his father's quick mind and boisterous disposition) should do the same. Both Florence and Colonel Harris would keep him in line in an authoritarian regimen that would be good for the recalcitrant youngster. Before Buddie arrived, Florence had been teaching only girls, so the new pupil's antics presented a challenge to his aunt and great amusement to her giggling students. But neither his Uncle Joe nor his Aunt Florence were tyrants, and under their critical but loving attention, Buddie did manage to do his work and stay out of serious mischief. [25]

After Buddie left, the family on Seaboard Avenue drifted back into its familiar patterns. Howard returned to the Moreland Academy, Lucy, now six, followed her mother around the house helping in the kitchen and watching after four-year-old Walter. Asa was more absorbed than ever in his business, yet he still rose early each morning, going out to milk the cows, gather the eggs, and perform garden tasks that Lucy Elizabeth couldn't manage. Then after prayers and breakfast, he would hitch a horse to the dray or buggy and drive five miles to work.

His pharmacy served as both factory and shop. In the basement, the new owner of Coca-Cola mixed his patented products in a makeshift laboratory; at street level, he operated the pharmacy with the help of three new assistants; and in the rear, Asa and Frank Robinson—now his second in command—maintained their offices. Several of his nephews were brought in to help. Lizzie's son, "Sammy" Dobbs, managed the top-floor shipping department, and, when they were old enough, Jessie's sons Sam and Joe Willard joined Zeke's son Dan in production and sales. By employing so many close family members, Asa not only displayed allegiance to his kin but emphasized that he only trusted close relatives to promote and guard his patent medicines, especially Coca-Cola. Extremely cautious not to reveal the secret ingredients that they labeled "Merchandise Number 5," Candler and Robinson memorized the recipe so they didn't have to write it down. In the early days, Candler only manufactured Coca-Cola syrup on Saturdays, producing twelve barrels per week in the summer and far fewer in the winter when most soda fountains were closed. One hot summer Saturday, a nearby druggist ordered a gallon of the mixture, but because they were in the midst of production, no single gallon was available. To fill the order, Asa siphoned some melted sugar-water from the cooling batch and approximated the other ingredients to fit the container's size. At this early stage, the consummate entrepreneur allowed no request to go unfilled, even if it meant a lack of uniformity.

Although most other businessmen in Atlanta closed shop at noon and went home for the day's big meal, Asa never allowed himself that luxury.

Instead, Lucy Elizabeth would pack his midday dinner and have it delivered to the pharmacy, usually by the driver and all-round handyman, Bill Curtwright. When Howard was not in school, he sometimes transported his father's basket, walking a mile down to catch the mule-drawn streetcar. One day he boarded an empty car, while the driver was having a beer at a nearby saloon. The honest boy dropped his nickel into the slot and sat down awaiting the driver's return, but when the motorman mounted his high seat, he turned to ask Howard for his fare. With no more money in his pocket, the nine-year-old could only tearfully protest, as the driver forced him to get off and trudge four uphill miles lugging the heavy basket. After he arrived at the Peachtree store, he watched his father sit down at his desk, tuck a napkin into his collar, and line up the bowls of vegetables, meat, cornbread, and dessert, all stone cold by the time it reached him. Howard's reward for delivering Asa's meal was permission to hang around the shop and watch assistants place medications and elixirs into bottles and label them. Then the biggest thrill of the day came with the journey down Edgewood Avenue, perched next to his father atop the buggy pulled homeward by their horse named "Ol' Bird."

On many occasions, Asa would arrive at the house on Seaboard Avenue so exhausted that he had to lean over a basin, while Lucy Elizabeth poured a pitcher of cold water over his aching head to relieve the migraines that had plagued him since his youthful farm accident. Asa also struggled with periodic depression, an affliction that he had inherited from his Candler forebears. His children were always mindful of their father's heavy workload, for their mother constantly reminded them that his delicate constitution was being stretched to the limits by his efforts to provide them with a good home.[26]

47 Peachtree, Asa Candler Sr.'s pharmacy, courtesy of Manuscript, Archives, and Rare Book Library, Emory University

Finally the hard work began paying off. A year after Asa bought controlling interest in Coca-Cola, the *Atlanta Journal* ran a feature article calling his enterprise "possibly the largest drug business" in the city, "known especially for its three patents: Botanic Blood Balm (B.B.B), De-Lac-Ta-Lave, and Coca-Cola." A sketch of Candler depicted a serious, dark-haired, clean-shaven man wearing a high collar and wide-lapelled jacket. In the same paper, an ad for Asa G. Candler & Co., "sole proprietors of Coca-Cola," pictured 47 Peachtree with five figures lined up in front. Asa stands at one end and a boy of about eleven at the other. He might have been a delivery boy working for the drugstore or perhaps Howard, who had just transported his father's lunch and was hanging around the shop on a summer day. The drugstore was an exciting place for a young boy to be. Each week, the sales force loaded bottles or kegs of Botanic Blood Balm and Coca-Cola syrup into their buggies and set off to traverse Georgia and surrounding states peddling their wares.

Although his new product was gaining recognition, Asa Candler still watched his pennies. On New Year's Day 1890, he pulled out a scrap of paper and scrawled across the top: "WE Stood January 1, 1890." Beneath that, he gave an accounting of his assets and liabilities, valuing his home at $6,000, the Coca-Cola patent at $2,000, and his personal net worth at $55,226. At last he was on comfortable financial footing, even though he still had to pay off a few commercial notes and owed small amounts to the Merchant's Bank and to his brother Willie. Shortly after Asa wrote this memo, his fifth child, William—named after his brother and the venerated ancestor of Callan Castle—was born. Howard had turned eleven a month earlier; Lucy was not quite seven, and Walter was four and a half. Even with nine-and-a-half-year-old Buddie at school in Cartersville, Lucy Elizabeth had her hands full. Gradually, Asa was able to lighten her burden by bringing home enough money to enable hiring extra servants. By the spring of 1890, the business was grossing slightly more than $100,000, a tidy sum for those days. In a letter to a druggist in Cartersville, Asa boasted: "The sales of one fountain in Atlanta during the month of January 1890 amounted to $320 for Coca-Cola alone—equal to 6,400 drinks." His situation was definitely improving.

In April 1891, Asa decided to stop dispensing medicines and devote full time to manufacturing and selling Coca-Cola, although for a while he also continued to make and market B.B.B. After closing the pharmacy, Candler rented a twenty-five-by-one-hundred-foot space at 42½ Decatur Street, above a pawn shop, second-hand clothing store, and saloon, giving him enough space to increase production. Often Lucy Elizabeth brought the younger children to town so they could watch transfixed as their Papa stood on a wooden platform holding a large wooden paddle and leaning over a forty-gallon copper kettle. The pot was suspended over a fire coming from a square brick furnace with its stack jutting through the roof. Sometime Sam or Joe Willard, with help from Bill Curtwright or his brother George, would help stir the mixture of sugar and hot water until it boiled down to become syrup. Occasionally the gooey combination would trickle over the sides, seeping through the floor into the businesses below. Men hunched over the bar in the saloon or customers in the shops complained loudly as they wiped the glop off their heads. More seriously, the shop owners ranted furiously when the syrup ruined their merchandise.

But the diligent crew upstairs continued manufacturing Coca-Cola. After the concoction mixed sufficiently, they would dip it into fifty-gallon barrels and let it cool. Then Candler and sometimes Frank Robinson—the only two who knew the formula— would climb back onto the platform to add the ounce of Merchandise Number 5. After shaking the barrels, the crew would then transfer the syrup to containers that ranged from one-gallon earthenware jugs to ten-gallon kegs. It was such a hot operation that windows and doors had to remain open, allowing swarms of bees to congregate on the sweet, sticky surfaces. After they finished mixing each batch of syrup, Candler and Robinson tasted a spoonful to make certain it was satisfactory. The children were not allowed to take even a tiny taste of the concentrated Coca-Cola syrup. But when Papa brought jars of the mixture home on hot afternoons and combined it with soda water, the family on Seaboard Avenue would sit around on the porch to cool off with sips of the "refreshing" beverage.

Not every customer was satisfied, however. An Atlanta physician, Dr. J. M. Alexander, questioned the ingredients and expressed concern about the presence of cocaine in the syrup. Candler was quick to respond, explaining that he would abandon his business if "a single case of the cocaine habit" was "contracted from using coca-cola." He assured the public that each batch contained less than a half-ounce of coca leaves. After considering Candler's remarks, Dr. Alexander retracted his criticism and said that "as prepared and sold here," the concoction was "perfectly harmless." He even admitted: "I use it regularly, and find it has a delightful effect when I'm tired."[27]

Now that Candler had dispelled local skepticism, he decided to go public. In December 1891, he petitioned the state of Georgia for incorporation, and by the end of January the following year he chartered the company with an authorized capital of $100,000, divided into one thousand portions to be sold at $100 each. Asa retained five-hundred shares, allocated ten to Robinson, and one apiece to his brothers John and Warren. Then he sold another segment to distributors in Iowa, Boston, and Baltimore, with the understanding that they would have exclusive rights to sell Coca-Cola syrup in their territories. The remaining shares went on the open market. Although a few local people did buy stock, the offering was not the nationwide success Asa had envisioned. One reason for the disappointing response was the Panic of 1893. As the gold supply dwindled, banks called in their creditors and refused new loans, resulting in widespread unemployment and business failures, which made potential purchasers apprehensive about investing in such a new company. Compounding these unfavorable economic conditions was the localized nature of a business that only sold its product in a small segment of the Southeast.

That limited recognition, coupled with the poor results of his stock offering, led Asa to make another important decision. He needed to develop a nationwide clientele. Frank Robinson agreed to rethink their methods of advertising, and within the next year, magazines began carrying colorful lithographs of stylish young women holding glasses of the fizzy beverage. Friends speculated that the first model might have been Lucy Elizabeth, although neither Asa nor Robinson acknowledged the rumor. Throughout the early '90s, the Coca-Cola ladies resembling Gibson Girls adorned outdoor posters, trade cards, fans, car cards, and calendars, thus spreading the penmanship logo to faraway locations. Robinson also rewarded cooperative soda fountain owners with porcelain urns, wall clocks, and showcases, all carrying the increasingly familiar Coca-Cola script. Probably the most successful advertising ploy of all was the distribution of free sampling tickets, which salesmen handed out personally or sent through the mail as enticements for recipients to taste the new drink at local soda fountains.[28]

Although Asa remained preoccupied with managing his growing business, he never neglected his religious obligations. Every Sunday, he took Lucy Elizabeth and the children—along with his mother and visiting relatives from Villa Rica—to Sunday school and services at the Edgewood Methodist Church. When he was in town, Warren Candler preached the sermon. As he stepped up to the podium, the broad-shouldered, barrel-chested minister would wave his "massive head," a lock of hair falling over his forehead, before launching into a long, erudite sermon in a pontifical voice, that Howard later described as seeming to emanate "from the bottom of a well." Warren had been rising rapidly in Methodist ranks. After holding several ministerial positions around Georgia, he moved his growing family to Nashville, where he became assistant editor of the *Christian Advocate*, the official mouthpiece of the Methodist Episcopal Church, South.

Then in 1888, Warren's career took a dramatic turn. After learning that his *alma mater*, Emory College, was planning to offer him the presidency, he consulted Asa for advice. In response, his brother felt the move would be a comedown for the brilliant young man, providing a smaller salary and diminishing his prestige. Those disadvantages, Asa argued, meant he should definitely "declaim the Oxford place" and remain in Nashville, where he would surely be better rewarded. No question about it, Asa insisted, when the offer comes, "decline it." But Warren didn't listen. Against his brother's better judgment, he accepted the offer, moved to Oxford, and became president of Emory College.

Asa might have been considering Warren's career from a businessman's perspective, but when it came to their shared faith, he had no doubts. Tutored by their pious mother, Asa was a dedicated churchgoer. In addition to teaching Sunday school, he regularly attended weekly prayer meetings and participated frequently in conventions of the Methodist Episcopal Church, South. Often he acted as a watchdog to ensure that members of the congregation met the high standards their religion demanded. When one man was found to be drinking heavily, Asa made certain the transgressor was swiftly dismissed from the congregation. Similarly he laid down firm rules for his own brood. All meals were preceded by grace, and Asa had the family kneel each morning before breakfast, while he led them in prayer. Then the children had to listen attentively as their father read passages from the Bible. When one of the boys snitched that his brother had opened his eyes during prayers, Asa frowned and asked: "How do *you* know?" Once when Christmas fell on a Sunday, Howard and Buddie were not allowed to open their gift—a varnished oak box filled with assorted tools—and were forbidden to play with its contents until the following day. But most of the Candler children's memories of their religious upbringing dwelt on happier times, such as evenings when Asa asked Lucy Elizabeth (and later young Lucy) to accompany him, while he stood next to the piano, opened a large family songbook, and sang hymns in his high-pitched tenor voice.[29]

Sometimes, Asa took his Sunday school pupils on picnics, often including his own children in the mix. One summer day, he chaperoned the class to Houston's Mill, about three miles east of Atlanta. The boys wanted to splash around a shallow pond on the property, and after inspecting it, Asa granted them permission. Although Howard was twelve at the time, he had never learned to swim, a failing he dared not admit to the other youngsters as they scuffled in the waist-high water. But before long, Howard lost his footing, stumbled, and went under, not once but twice. It was a terrifying experience. One of his classmates, "an expert swimmer," tried to pull him out, but unable to move him, he yelled for Asa to come quickly, and together they tugged Howard onto dry land. The rescue left the embarrassed and humiliated boy with an indelible memory.

Another memory was Asa's running battle with a "coal-black" pony named Frank. Gentle and obedient when Lucy Elizabeth or one of the children hitched him to the buggy, Frank would "spread his feet apart, squat and tremble" when Asa picked up the reins. The Coca-Cola president would jump angrily down from the buggy, yell at the recalcitrant pony, and lash his flank with a willow. Nevertheless, Frank held his ground and refused to budge. Humiliated, Asa was forced to watch his wife or child soothe the animal by patting his head and whispering into his ear. Thus placated, Frank would slowly proceed on the journey. On one of his rare days off, Asa took Howard to visit Buddie and Aunt Florence in Cartersville. Because Frank was pulling the buggy, Howard believed he was asked to go along so he could coax the pony to move. Around noon on that warm, autumn day, they stopped for a picnic lunch near Kennesaw Mountain, about halfway to their destination. After they watered the pony and progressed up the road, they noticed that Frank was unusually sluggish. By the time they reached Cartersville after dark, he appeared to be ill. Asa attributed his listlessness to colic caused by the icy well water at Kennesaw and predicted he would soon recover. But sadly, that was not the case. Although they tended Frank all night, the pony could not be roused, and by the next morning he was dead. It was such a heavy blow to the children, who had known the animal all of their lives, that Lucy Elizabeth gilded Frank's horseshoes and had them framed.

Howard also remembered his father's playful moments, demonstrating a sly lightheartedness that caused his eyes to twinkle. In the evenings, for example, when he finished reading a Bible verse, he would pick another book, sometimes a classic. More often, however, he chose the recently published *Uncle Remus* tales by Atlantan Joel Chandler Harris or the popular folk tales from *Sut Lovinggood's Yarns*. The latter book caused quite a stir in the household, because Lucy Elizabeth deemed it unsuitable for children. So when she wasn't around, Asa would gather the offspring and secretly read aloud the earthy stories that sent them into gales of laughter.[30]

In the early 1890s, Asa once more realized his current business facilities were inadequate. Not only did the additional production of Coca-Cola require more space, but shopkeepers beneath the Decatur Street workshop were complaining more than ever when the pot boiled over and oozing Coca-Cola syrup trickled through the wooden floorboards to annoy their customers and damage their stock. So with the help of his nephews and the Curtwright brothers, Asa moved all the equipment to a three-story house on the corner of Ivy Street and Auburn Avenue that provided enough room to expand the staff. When settled in the new building, he engaged a stenographer and promoted Sam and Joe Willard to supervise the more spacious shipping department. In the larger quarters, the furnace was in the basement, heating a much larger copper kettle on the floor above.

After getting the Atlanta company settled into efficient and more sanitary facilities, Asa decided to issue the first stock dividend of twenty dollars per share. In addition, he decided to expand his operation by opening a Coca-Cola plant in Dallas, Texas, and he assigned his nephew Dan Candler to manage the facility. He was definitely on a roll. A year later, he opened similar factories in Chicago and Los Angeles, the latter under the supervision of his brother Milton's son, Sam. The expansion meant that soda jerks—from Georgia to California, Pennsylvania to Illinois—were dispensing the "refreshing and delicious" beverage, no longer touting it as a medicine but as a special treat, a feature soon reflected in Coca-Cola ads. Expanded distribution led shop owners to begin talking about selling the popular beverage in bottles. One of the first to actually do that was Joseph Biedenharn of Vicksburg, Mississippi, who experimented by mixing Coca-Cola syrup with soda and putting it into Hutchinson bottles. This container had a rubber stopper that made a popping noise when it opened, thus giving rise to the name "soda pop." Biedenharn was so thrilled with his ability to capture Coca-Cola in a bottle that, in 1894, he sent a crate to Asa Candler in Atlanta. The owner of the formula had no objection to this novel utilization of his product as long as Biedenharn bought the syrup from the Coca-Cola plant. And thus the Mississippian acquired offhanded permission to open the first bottling operation, beginning a process that would take off five years later.

Biedenharn's discovery was just one of many indications that Coca-Cola was becoming a national phenomenon. Now, for the first time, Asa's business was beginning to change his family's daily lives. With an increased income, Lucy Elizabeth could have a cook, a part-time dressmaker, and servants to help with the cleaning and gardening. They now had electricity in parts of the house and were enjoying the luxury of a telephone, which had first arrived in Atlanta during the late 1880s. An electric streetcar had been recently installed near their home, connecting downtown to the new subdivision of Inman Park, developed by the Candler's friend Joel Hurt. Asa bought several parcels of land in the city's first garden suburb abutting his Seaboard Avenue property. It was only one of several such real estate investments he was making, now that he was feeling more financially secure.

Increased income also meant that Asa was able to think about expanding his house. The older children were growing up and starting to discover the greater world around them. At fifteen, Howard was finishing up at what was now being called the Georgia Military Academy and preparing to enter college.[31] Buddie was completing courses at his Aunt Florence's school and happily anticipating living at home in Atlanta for a while. Lucy, now eleven, was still helping her mother in the kitchen and supplementing her chores with daily studies in reading, arithmetic, and music. Walter, soon to be nine, was attending the nearby Donald Fraser School for Boys, and little William, aged four, still clung to his mother's skirts and played beside her while she worked. This typical Victorian family had no idea that they were on the cusp of a modern world that would soon transform their lives.

Chapter Four
Leaving Home

As Howard Candler approached the small town of Oxford, Georgia, in the fall of 1894, he was elated about being an Emory student but apprehensive about the unknown pitfalls that awaited him in the new, alien environment. Tall, awkward, and not yet sixteen, he was a bundle of nerves when he approached the campus but must have breathed a sigh of relief when he walked onto the welcoming tree-lined quad. It was a beautiful place, full of charming old buildings and interesting new ones, like the library then under construction, being part of his Uncle Warren's attempt to raise the school's academic standing. A good bit of Howard's anxiety was related directly to his uncle. It was bad enough that his father's exacting brother presided over the college, but it was even more distressing that Asa had arranged for him to board in his uncle's home. In the six years that Warren Candler had been at Emory, he had made significant strides toward transforming the former agricultural school into a serious institution of higher education. Much to the consternation of many alumni and students, however, that meant de-emphasizing athletics and terminating the school's intercollegiate football program. Discontent among the students about abolition of the football team made Howard's adjustment even more difficult.

Part of Warren's new emphasis on scholarship was a mandatory entrance exam that Howard had to pass before being admitted to the freshman class, and, to his horror, he failed. Not surprisingly, his father was appalled, writing in shocked disbelief:

> How on earth is this my boy? You have so often assured me of your thorough knowledge of the studies for entry that I am just simply stymied. I know there is something radically wrong ... you ought

not willfully to have deceived me. Had I known or even suspected that there was a doubt of your success, I would have seen to it that you were taught during the Summer vacation ... Do for my sake get <u>down </u>to your books. Don't join yourself to any society, any club or any boy or boys 'til you have made honorable entry into your class ... I am not satisfied for you to fail <u>right</u> on the threshold of your life ... I slept none last night thinking of you. You have never given me trouble. This has been my first anxious night about you.[32]

No matter how frightened he was, Howard was well aware that giving up was no option. In order to redeem his self-esteem, he would have to repeat the test. On the second try he passed, and, to everyone's relief, he became a freshman.

Assured now that his son would not return home, Asa began issuing a barrage of letters, designed to orchestrate Howard's every move and, in the process, further increase his son's insecurity. "I expect you to be first in your class," Asa wrote, shortly after school began. "Do right my dear boy. Don't let any <u>body</u> <u>swerve</u> you from that <u>line</u>." Howard diligently attempted to follow his father's instructions, going against them only to pledge Kappa Alpha shortly after he arrived, hoping that the fraternity would provide a chance for him to meet other boys and feel part of campus life. Uncle Warren probably approved since he, too, had been a KA. Even as a fraternity member, Howard remained lonely and uneasy. He begged his father to let Buddie come visit now that he had finished at Florence's Cartersville school and was back in Atlanta. But Asa objected, telling his oldest son that if he studied harder, he wouldn't have time to be so homesick.

First and foremost, Asa was concerned about Howard's spiritual well-being at the Methodist college. In an early set of admonitions he wrote: "Don't be religious in word only but in your life. Be thoroughly consistent. Live so as that it will not be needful for you to tell people you are religious — but [in] your life constantly <u>exhibit</u> <u>Christ</u>." Another time, he instructed him to attend church every Sunday and deposit at least a nickel in the plate. Asa worried about his son's physical health as well, often sending medications such as Quinine tablets and prescribing a tablespoon of salt per day to keep his "bowels open." When the November winds blew, he warned that in order to avoid a cold he should keep his chest protected when he went outside.

After piety and health came frugality. Even though the family's fortunes had risen considerably, Asa was perturbed that Howard spent almost fifteen dollars during his second month at Emory and had to borrow five dollars from his Uncle Warren to make ends meet. If requested, Asa would occasionally send small sums of two dollars or five dollars but not without demanding a detailed monthly accounting for every penny spent. Although he did give his son permission to buy a lamp, he insisted that it be neither expensive nor fancy, and when Howard considered buying a bicycle, he reprimanded him for even considering such an unnecessary extravagance. "It takes all the money I can get to pay needful expenses," Asa fussed. "Quit thinking about things to buy. Use such as you have and try to learn something." Secondhand items, he insisted, were just as good as new ones. So in the packages of the sweets, sausages, and preserves coming every few days from Seaboard Avenue, Lucy Elizabeth tucked in "Sister's umbrella," old textbooks, a Bible, and other items from home.

In addition to attending church, taking medicine, pinching pennies, and excelling in his studies, Howard was expected to trudge from soda fountain to soda fountain in Oxford and vicinity, selling Coca-Cola syrup and collecting money owed the company. Although Asa frequently warned his son not to neglect his "College duties for Coca-Cola affairs," he kept sending him shipments of syrup, calendars, urns, trays and other paraphernalia to distribute in Oxford. The conflicting responsibility of studying hard and working conscientiously only exacerbated Howard's anxiety. In January 1895, Asa told him that a Mr. Johnson had telephoned for a barrel of Coca-Cola syrup, threatening that if the company failed to send it, he would serve Wine Cola instead. As a result of that phone call, he instructed his son to tell Johnson that he could do whatever he pleased, but if he did sell Wine Cola to students and tell them it was Coca-Cola, Howard must set the boys straight. But when he talked to his classmates, he must never brag about his family's business. His duty was to snoop around at various soda fountains and gather as much information as possible to report back to Atlanta.

The following fall, Buddie joined his brother at Emory, his presence on campus being both a comfort and a burden for Howard. The two boys' adjustment to college—and indeed to life—was diametrically opposed. While conscientious Howard seemed unsure about his every move, Buddie, an old pro at being away at school, eagerly embraced campus activities with jaunty self-assurance. This only made Howard more uneasy, reviving their many boyhood confrontations, especially since he felt that his younger brother was invading territory that he had established for himself with great difficulty. Buddie accused Howard of criticizing him among his fraternity brothers, and in retaliation, the younger Candler openly ridiculed members of KA. When each complained about the other's behavior, Asa made it clear that he would not tolerate such rivalry, demanding that they stop their wrangling at once and start "living in love with each other." They should try to get along not only for the sake of their parents but to avoid damaging their future relationship. He reprimanded Buddie for worrying and teasing Howard about his fraternity and suggested that he "make so splendid a record in college, both as a gentleman and scholar," that he would be "desired by all good clubs."

While Howard and Buddie were battling it out in Oxford during the fall of 1895, their parents, sister, and two youngest brothers attended Atlanta's greatest World's Fair: the International Cotton States Exposition. As they strolled around Piedmont Park, the family viewed the agricultural, manufacturing, and fine arts displays in large structures positioned around the sloping grounds. They looked curiously at the Women's Building and especially the Negro Building, one of the nation's first such exhibitions to applaud the accomplishments of former slaves. But what the youngsters enjoyed most was the midway, with its panoply of exotic foreign villages, a mining camp, and a beauty show. One of the greatest thrills was being swept up in the air on the Ferris wheel, a brand new ride that made its debut only two years earlier at the World's Columbian Exposition in Chicago.

At the opening ceremonies on September 18, Booker T. Washington, the prominent African American president of the Tuskegee Institute, told the audience: "The wisest among my race understand that the agitation of questions of social equality is the extremist folly." Advancement, he continued, must come from "severe and constant struggle rather than of artificial forcing." Southern white spectators applauded this Negro gentleman in his suit and tie who knew his place and promised not to encourage racial mixing. When the sun set that night, the crowd was treated to one of the largest displays of electrical illumination it had ever seen, centered on a bouncing fountain with colored lights in the middle of Lake Clara Meer. The entire spectacle was illuminated, so they said, when President Grover Cleveland pushed a button in the White House. Although clearly a publicity stunt, the crowd loved it and applauded enthusiastically. A month later, the president—now reinstated in office after four years of

Republican rule—returned to Atlanta to again parade through town. And again a uniformed Asa Candler pranced down Peachtree leading his Governor's Horse Guard unit.

Martha Candler and her sons, Villa Rica, 1891, (front row, left to right) Warren, Milton, Martha, Zeke; (back row left to right) John, Charles, Asa, William, courtesy of Jim Candler

On December 6, 1895, as the Cotton States Exposition was winding down, the Candlers gathered to celebrate the seventy-sixth birthday of the family matriarch. Martha had been failing noticeably for the past two years. Although she had worked hard all of her life and was forceful and often tough, she suffered from frequent bouts of illness, especially in her later years. As her condition worsened, her daughters took turns coming for lengthy stays, preparing her meals, instructing the servants, and doing much of the hands-on care. Asa walked down the block to check on his mother in the morning before work and at night when he came home, and his brothers visited as often as they could. But as Martha's health further declined, she needed more than makeshift care. Because of family obligations, Florence, Jessie, and Lizzie—who all lived out of town—were unable to stay for long periods, so Asa decided to move Martha into his own home and hire a practical nurse to care for her, with Lucy Elizabeth and her daughter on hand to help out. They had enough room for extra people now, since during the previous year, a contractor had added a second story to the Seaboard Avenue house. The addition gave the family seven bedrooms, three below and four above, with a bathroom on each floor, a decided luxury in the mid-1890s. Connecting the two levels was a stairway with a hand-carved balustrade crafted by an artisan neighbor, and for the landing, Asa commissioned a local artist to create a stained-glass portrait of Lucy Elizabeth seated in a garden.

With larger quarters for entertainment, Asa was able to host the party for Martha. For the past several years, most of her children, grandchildren, and remaining siblings had visited on her birthday, showering her with gifts. One year, Asa, Charlie, and John, along with their wives, a number of her grandchildren, and two of her sisters, sat down to what she described as a "bountiful dinner" that included a "fat turkey" and a "beautiful cake." However, now with her weakened condition, the celebration at the end of 1895 took on poignant overtones. Several people delivered personal tributes, and Florence Candler Harris read a poem she had written for the occasion:

> *In fancy let us gather, at the old home on the hill*
> *Where the sound of happy voices, in our memories haunt us still.*
>
> *Let us dream, we are your babies as we were so long ago,*
> *Before your steps were feeble and your hair so flecked with snow.*
>
> *Let us come to you, sweet mother and lean upon your breast;*
> *Put your loving arms around us and bid us 'Be at rest.' …*
>
> *We will look unto the Father, for He grace and strength will give,*
> *We will look up into Heaven, we can 'Look to Him and live.'*
>
> *May the great the blessed Savior shield us here from every harm*
> *May the Holy Spirit's guidance keep us safe from every storm.*
>
> *And may you, dear, sweet mother, when the toils of life are past,*
> *Go in joy to meet your loved ones, to the Heaven of heavens, at last.*
>
> *We promise there to meet you—a reunited band,*
> *Where, with father, brother, sister and the angels we shall stand.*[33]

Nothing better exemplifies the basic orientation of the siblings from Villa Rica. First and foremost came an unquestioning faith in the basic tenants of her Methodism: a personal relationship with God and Jesus that promised good deeds on earth would be rewarded by a heavenly reunion with loved ones. Next it revealed the strong bond that united Martha Candler's offspring. Their "old home on the hill" had become a retrospective catchphrase for those halcyon days, during which the children learned immutable values of good and evil and experienced the ties of blood kinship that were life's most important allegiance. In a letter to his brother a few years earlier, Asa had expressed these same sentiments. "We are scattered here on earth never more to live together as our band again," he wrote Warren. "Never more to look to a common father and mother for protection, care and guidance … but blessed be our God, after it is all over we are to come together again now, never to part."

As Martha Candler's condition gradually worsened during 1896, Florence—who had recently lost her husband—moved her mother to Cartersville and assumed responsibility for her care. For the next six months, all of Martha's children and grandchildren took turns visiting her bedside. Asa drove there frequently, often with Lucy Elizabeth and some of the children along. Much of the family was there on July 3, 1897, when Martha died. All were, no doubt, sadly aware that her passing would transform their Independence Day celebration into rituals of mourning. After a funeral service at the Edgewood Methodist Church, the Candlers traveled to Villa Rica to bury Martha next to her husband. Each year for the rest of their lives, Asa and his siblings drove over to their hometown on the Fourth of July to say a prayer at their parents' graves. An obituary in the Cartersville newspaper paid tribute to the seventy-seven-year-old "mother of distinguished people," reputed to be "among the brainiest in Georgia." In listing her sons' accomplishments, the article praised Rev. Warren Candler, a doctor of divinity and president of Emory College, as well as Judge John Candler, presiding officer of the Stone Mountain Circuit Court and colonel in the Georgia state troops. But Martha's eighth child, Asa Griggs, was mentioned merely as a "well known druggist and capitalist.[34]

Maybe Asa was not yet well known in Georgia, but by 1897 his product was beginning to warrant the attention of Washington. For the past year, federal authorities, whom Candler angrily called "food people," had been investigating the contents of Coca-Cola. Because consumers of the carbonated beverage frequently mentioned its restorative powers, health officials were beginning to suspect that the formula— guarded like a top-ranked state secret by Candler and Robinson—contained a larger percentage of cocaine than its manufacturers claimed. Encouraged by aggressive advertising that still emphasized the health benefits in a glass of Coca-Cola, young people were visiting their favorite soda fountains to request "a glass of dope." These persistent associations with narcotics convinced Candler to ask the Georgia Pharmaceutical Association to test the syrup, certain that the results would prove it safe for consumers. The board concluded that although the sample did indeed contain a small amount of cocaine, it was not enough to be harmful when mixed with soda. Nevertheless, Candler and Robinson again reduced the coca derivative in Merchandise Number 5, so that each barrel had less than one-thirtieth of a grain. Yet even that miniscule amount could be detected by sophisticated tests, thus giving federal investigators additional proof that they must continue to monitor the contents of Coca-Cola.

One telling note about the composition of the original Coca-Cola was Asa's misgivings about the effect on his own family. At the same time "food people" were investigating the company, its president was worried that his fourteen-year-old daughter was drinking too much of his product. Her mother warned her: "Papa says it [Coca-Cola] is not good for you," and he "won't let me drink it often" either. When Lucy received that advice in the fall of 1897, she was enrolled in her Aunt Florence's Cartersville school, now called the West End Institute. During the previous summer, she had left home on her own for the first time by visiting her relatives in Villa Rica. Her absence was a traumatic wrench for her parents. Asa's "jewel" was barely out of the door before he wrote: "How Papa misses you! Seems like you have been gone a week. Your bed looked so cheerless this morning when I went to get my bite." At the bottom of his wife's letter, he drew a red dot which he identified as a kiss, and added a funny stick figure labeled hugs. When she went to Cartersville the following fall, they missed her even more. Shortly after her departure, Lucy Elizabeth burst into tears when the cook mentioned her daughter's name, and Asa felt like crying when he saw she wasn't at the piano in the parlor playing "Somebody's Child," "My Mother's Bible," and his other favorites.

Lucy missed her parents, too, her homesickness exacerbated by constant reminders from home about the things she was missing. The household now revolved around Walter, almost twelve, and William, seven. Each morning they drove a pony cart to the Donald Fraser School not far from their house, and although both boys were doing fairly well with their studies, Walter kept getting into trouble with his teachers, which was a disturbing reminder of Buddie's behavior. But within a few weeks, he began to improve, at least for the time being. Whether completely true or not, Walter told his sister that he was "the best boy in his room." William was no problem at school, Asa told Lucy, especially since he was studying "like he thought the country would be lost" if he failed to work so hard.

A near catastrophe occurred during the fall of '97, reported in detail to the older children by both parents. One Sunday afternoon, the family had joined some friends for an excursion in "the trap," accompanied by three ponies "under saddle." On the way home, William was riding a pony named Robin Jr., when all of a sudden he shocked his parents by dashing away. Asa described the scene in a letter to his oldest son: "Robin supposed a race was wanted and away he went," he wrote. "The little darling could not hold him and as he went out of my sight I felt that my baby was lost to me for this life." In a panic, Asa "whipped the horses" to go faster, but they couldn't catch the bolting pony. "As he started up the hill" he continued, "the baby fell off and Robin, Jr. stopped." Although William was stunned by the fall, he miraculously escaped without injury. "To see my poor baby flying through the air," Asa remarked several days later, "going further and further every minute and no hope of helping him simply broke me up. I could see his white jacket like a spec. Thank God he was not hurt."

Lucy Elizabeth usually imparted more ordinary family events in correspondences with her children, revealing glimpses into the daily routine of a housewife in the late-Victorian American South. Many letters were filled with details about food: harvesting it, preparing it, preserving it, and most of all eating it. On one special occasion, they had baked pork and jelly with whipped cream, on another they ate turnips, baked beans, baked Irish potatoes, sweet potatoes, turkey, celery, cranberries, rice, and mustard pickles, followed by syllabub and cake. She regularly sent food packages to Lucy and her older brothers, either by mail or by asking family members and friends to drop them off when their train passed through either Oxford or Cartersville. These parcels would be left with the station master for her children to pick up later. One day Lucy Elizabeth apologized to her daughter because the cow had been "sick all week," so there was no butter to bake anything other than sponge cake. Another time, she sent her leftover buttered rolls from breakfast, along with candy "pulled" with some difficulty. One package was invaded by ants, because the cake's icing was still soft when she packed it.

Food preparation was only part of Lucy Elizabeth's daily routine. "I am still busy sewing," she told her daughter, with more to do than she could possibly "finish off in a month." Sometimes a seamstress would come in to help, but Lucy Elizabeth did most of the work herself, staying up late at night to complete it. One week, her output included five shirts for Walter, a waist for herself, and three nightshirts for Asa, as well as petticoats, dresses, and a purse for Lucy. The hard work took its toll on her health. She often complained of neuralgia, heart problems, headaches, a fever blister, and grip. Once she wrote Lucy: "I had one of my front teeth to fall out today. I will have to go and have it put in just as soon as I can in the morning, for I look like an ugly old woman." Much to her dismay, the dentist took longer than she had anticipated, and she was left "snaggled tooth" for almost a week. Her favorite pastime was attending the theater. About once a week in good weather, she went alone or with her sister Pauline (Paul) to shows at either DeGive's Opera House, the Grand, or the Lyceum.

Her daughter would respond to these newsy letters by describing her own loneliness and various minor illnesses. But despite the complaints, she remained a conscientious and achieving student, getting along easily with the other girls and enjoying outings in the small town of Cartersville. Florence's school apparently had a fairly rigid curriculum of basic skills, as well as an active program of china painting. So when Lucy wasn't attending class or studying, she spent hours practicing the piano and decorating plates, pickle dishes, and candlesticks to distribute among her family and girlfriends as Christmas gifts. Bubbly, vivacious, petite Lucy was beginning to attract young men. A boy named George Reed—a friend of her older brothers who worked for Asa at the plant—sent her a box of candy and a container of Coca-Cola syrup. Her Aunt Florence thought it unseemly for girls of fourteen to receive presents from young men, so she reported the gift to her sister-in-law. Upset by this news, Lucy Elizabeth commanded Lucy not to *ever* accept presents from "any one but Mama and Papa." At the same time, she warned her not to mention this in letters home, because her brothers and father seemed "down on Mr. Reed." Prompted by her mother, Lucy returned some of the items. But this wasn't enough. Lucy Elizabeth took it upon herself to reprimand Reed for his inappropriate behavior, making him promise never to mail any more gifts. Knowing nothing of these confidences between mother and daughter, Asa continued to heap praise on Lucy. From time to time, he would send her money or medication, filling the letters with loving hints that he wished she had stayed home.[35]

Back at Emory for another semester, Howard and Buddie were still quarreling and still infuriating their father. Not only was Buddie constantly cutting up, but both boys were letting their work slip. "Your marks are just as low as they can be to admit of your rising," their father growled. "Can't you do better? Ain't there some way for you to learn your lessons." Angry that Buddie had eight absences and Howard ten, Asa lambasted them both for not attending class. At one point Howard told his parents that Buddie expected deferential treatment because his uncle was the college president. Upon hearing this, an irate Asa chastised his namesake for being so brash and lit into Howard for creating an atmosphere that forced Buddie to make such boasts: "He is your younger brother," his father complained. "You have never treated him as it is your duty to," and seem to "prefer other boys to him, speak disparagingly of him to others, and allow others to speak to you evilly of him." Furthermore, he railed: "I sent him down there under your protection, and if you do not love him you ought for your parents sake to treat him right." Then he added: "You must know I live and labor for you boys ... It is bad enough for classmates to treat each other wrongfully—infinitely worse for brothers."

While such guilt-producing admonishments devastated Howard, they seemed to roll off Buddie's back, and he continued to flaunt college rules. Once he was accused of filling the chapel with hay and another time of taking a goat up to the chapel's belfry. Then his uncle caught him smoking in his house, a taboo that only Buddie dared break. Infuriated by his disregard for rules, Warren reported these incidents to Asa, saying that if Buddie didn't shape up, he would have to leave Emory. Asa responded by issuing a warning to both boys. "For my own son, who bears my name and for whom I labor and work and pray, to deliberately disgrace me is more than I can bear," he wrote Buddie. To Howard he complained: "I cannot think that Buddie has deliberately made up his mind to kill me with remorse. He knows how to behave and ought not to treat me so."

Finally Warren Candler had enough. In the middle of October, he threw both boys out of his house, alleging that Buddie was smoking and being excessively rowdy and that Howard often went along with his brother. This was the last straw. Such behavior, Asa wrote, took him to "an extremity to which I never dreamed that I would be driven." He advised them to leave their uncle's home at once and find another place to live. Although he would forward the rent money for their new quarters, they would have to pay back every cent. Elaborating on his feelings in a letter to Howard, Asa delivered another burdensome diatribe:

> Upon your good conduct depends not only my peace of mind and your best interests, but the future welfare of your younger brothers ...

I hope Buddie will remember his promises as to the use of Tobacco.
He knows that I will not stand that. I believe his uncle is mistaken.
I can't think he would violate my laws.

Lucy Elizabeth, on the other hand, blamed her brother-in-law for not
understanding young people. Convinced that he ousted Howard and
Buddie simply because their noise made him nervous, she was certain
that other boys had caused the mischief. This was confirmed when Willie
Candler Jr. came to visit his aunt and uncle in Atlanta and reported that
his cousins were innocent. Lucy Elizabeth was so pleased to receive this
information that she baked her boys a special cake and sent it back to
Oxford with Willie.[36]

By the end of 1897, the crisis of a few months earlier was long forgotten;
the two brothers had settled into a comfortable cottage, and the Candlers
were all anxiously awaiting the Christmas holidays. Weeks beforehand,
Lucy Elizabeth began making fruitcakes and fixing up the house. "I
can't realize that it is nearly Christmas again," she told her daughter. "I
am going to try and get everything ready so I won't have anything to do
but have a good time when you all come." Twelve-year-old Walter was
also excited that his brothers and sister were returning home. "Oh! What
a fine time we will have," he told Lucy. "I hope you have not forgotten
how to shute [sic] fire-crackers, if you have I will learn you over again."
The only thing marring preparation for the upcoming holiday was an
outbreak of smallpox. Everybody in the Candler family and their servants
were vaccinated, and even though she had not bought all of her Christmas
presents, Lucy Elizabeth was afraid to go downtown during the epidemic.
Then a swollen face and "siege" of illness—coupled with a weeklong visit
by the presiding elder of the church, his wife, and five children—had her
pleading with Asa to let their daughter leave school early so she could help
around the house.

Lucy, who had been begging to come home, was more than ready to
comply with her mother's wishes. But Asa would not allow her to return
before the term ended. He rarely denied her anything, he admitted, but
this time she must remain in Cartersville. "You are Aunt Florence's niece,"
he wrote, "and if you come away others would think they ought to also
and it would do harm." With only one week until vacation, he begged
his "precious" to wait it out with patience. As compensation, he enclosed
a new two-dollar bill to pay her railroad fare, with a little pocket change

remaining. On the following Tuesday, her parents met her train, and the next day their sons arrived from Oxford. The holiday was made even merrier when Lucy's report card came from the West End Institute. Her deportment and attendance received perfect grades, and she made As in reading, arithmetic, geography, composition, Latin, and elocution. Only in algebra did her marks drop. But that didn't hurt much, and she ended the term with a general average of 97+.[37]

After Christmas, Lucy got her wish and was allowed to stay home. In mid-January 1898, her father became ill, apparently suffering from depression, coupled with a severe case of flu. His daughter was, therefore, able to persuade her parents that she should quit her aunt's school and remain in Atlanta to help her mother. Shortly after Lucy left Cartersville, Florence Harris closed the school and moved to 20 Hurt Street, near her brothers John and Asa. Lucy probably walked over to her aunt's house for informal instruction to prepare her to enter college the following fall. The first month of 1898 had been cold and dreary, but by February the temperatures rose, the smallpox scare passed, and Asa recovered from his unspecified ailment. He could not afford to be laid up with so many things pressing. Most important among them was dedication of the new Inman Park Methodist Church, constructed on property that he had donated. That spring, the small, yet elegant, granite building on Edgewood Avenue was almost ready for occupancy, and Asa wanted to supervise installation of the large stained-glass window that he and his brothers had contributed in memory of their late mother.

Everyone was looking forward to the upcoming ceremony in the long-anticipated church, but their enthusiasm was marred by a family tragedy. Lucy Elizabeth's parents, now living in Augusta, were in town to attend the dedication. But two days beforehand, George Howard stopped by Asa's office in the morning and then went to call on another son-in-law, W. B. Ansley, in the afternoon. Suddenly while sitting in Ansley's office, he felt weak and keeled over. Now unconscious, George was rushed to Grady Hospital, where he was diagnosed with having suffered a severe stroke. The doctors could do nothing to save him, and he died within a few hours. Lucy Elizabeth and other members of the Candler family must have missed the dedication to attend the funeral and burial in Augusta. Despite their absence, an overflow crowd filled the wood-paneled church interior on the afternoon of April 17, 1898, to hear duets and solo performances, accompanied by the choir, and listen to a sermon by a distinguished visiting dignitary.[38]

Within weeks after the Inman Park Methodist Church dedication, America was at war with Spain, a controversial, one-sided conflict that divided the nation between those endorsing Congress' declaration of war and those disapproving it. Mixed feelings about the confrontation did not discourage Atlantans from coming out in droves to cheer as trainloads of soldiers passed through Terminal Station, among them Lieutenant Colonel Theodore Roosevelt taking his cavalry unit known as the "Rough Riders" to Tampa, where they would embark for an invasion of Cuba. By the middle of June, about seventeen thousand soldiers had landed in Santiago, and, amidst desultory attempts by the Spanish to defend their colony, the Americans fought their way up San Juan Hill to "liberate" the country. A month before that assault, Asa's brother John—a colonel in the Third Georgia Volunteer Infantry—was mustered into the army, first serving in Georgia and then going with his unit to Cuba.

The brief war, which ended less than four months after it began, offered a golden opportunity to Warren Candler, who had recently become a bishop of the Methodist Episcopal Church, South. When his replacement as Emory president arrived, he moved back to Atlanta to live in Inman Park near his two brothers and older sister and began concentrating on church affairs. From the lofty perch of his influential new position, Warren lost no time in organizing a mission to predominantly Catholic Cuba, convinced that the defeat of Spain created a welcoming atmosphere for Protestant proselytizing. With Asa's financial assistance, he established the groundwork for a Methodist school in Havana, which opened several years later as Candler College. The American victory also sent Asa on a Latin American "mission," and within the next year, he opened Coca-Cola offices and plants in both Cuba and Puerto Rico, the company's first expansion outside of the continental United States.

In light of these new endeavors and Coca-Cola's growing nationwide prominence, the makeshift quarters on Auburn Avenue seemed so inadequate that Asa decided to build what he hoped would be a permanent factory and headquarters. The contractor George E. Murphy promised that the building would be ready for occupancy in six months, but when that date arrived, the job was far from completion, and Murphy announced that he was too ill to continue working. His illness was no doubt caused by spiraling expenses that sent him into bankruptcy. When Asa discovered the real cause of the delay, he agreed to pay Murphy double the originally estimated cost and placed him on the Coca-Cola Company payroll. It turned out to be a fortuitous marriage for both men.

The following December—less than a decade after Candler purchased Pemberton's formula—the Coca-Cola Company moved (for the fourth time) into a state-of-the-art facility on a triangular lot fronting Edgewood Avenue, a few miles from Asa's home. At the gala opening reception, Asa, his nephews, and other members of the staff distributed free samples of the soft drink to the crowd that came to ogle at the modern equipment. All afternoon visitors tromped around admiring the huge boiler, giant-size mixing and cooling tanks, "steam-jacketed" kettle mills, and large percolators that the *Atlanta Constitution* reporter mistook for smokestacks. No longer did employees have to raise and lower their goods on a platform hoisted by a rope; now a hydraulic, steam-powered elevator did the job more efficiently. On the first floor was a small fireproof laboratory, fortified by an iron door with a combination lock that only Asa Candler and Frank Robinson could open. The secured safe had been built for one purpose and one purpose alone: concealing the Coca-Cola formula. Since both men knew the secret ingredients by heart, they removed all bottle labels, intercepted all letters and invoices, and omitted names of the formula's oils in their annual inventories.[39]

Asa and Lucy Elizabeth Candler and their children, 1898, (front row, left to right) William, Asa Sr., Walter, Lucy, Lucy Elizabeth; (back row left to right) Howard, Asa Jr., courtesy of Millennium Gate Museum, Atlanta, Georgia

The same time that the new factory opened, the Candlers posed for a photographer. The resulting picture offers an interesting insight into the dynamics of this unique—and yet quite typical—family, on the cusp of enjoying the fruits of Coca-Cola's success. Asa, sitting at one end with young William leaning against him, appeared to be the typical affluent paterfamilias, stern yet proud of his five offspring. At the other end is Lucy Elizabeth, with her daughter snuggled up next to her, smiling knowingly, her dark eyes sparkling. Standing behind are their two eldest sons, who looked very much alike. Buddie was about the same height and build as Howard; both wear their straight, dark hair parted in the middle in the popular style of the day, and both have their mother's sharper features and deep-set dark eyes. But their facial expressions reveal their opposite personalities. A mischievous twinkle lurks in Buddie's eyes, and a smile twitches his lips, while Howard looks cautiously at the camera, as if expecting something or someone to pounce. Fifteen-year-old Lucy is a contrast to her older brothers, with her fair coloring and round face that exhibits Asa's blue eyes, yet she also has Lucy Elizabeth's more angular nose and jaw. The two younger boys also resemble their father; both have his coloring and stocky frame, although eight-year-old William's face is still soft and angelic, while thirteen-year-old Walter was developing the more pronounced features of early adolescence.

Each of the five Candler siblings had personalities as individual as their appearances, fine-tuned by reactions to their powerful father. Howard spent his life striving to please his demanding parent. Not only was he diligent and obedient, internalizing most hurts and criticisms, but his compliance created an outward equanimity that covered internal insecurity and self-effacement. Buddie, on the other hand, was assertive, cheerful, and not afraid to confront Asa; yet more than any of the others, he could be effusive in his expressions of love. Like a friendly puppy, Buddie was naïvely sweet one minute and naughty the next. Lucy—squarely in the middle balancing the two sets of boys—was her father's darling and mother's constant companion, occupying a secure niche that made her spoiled, outgoing, optimistic, and confident. In many ways Walter's behavior resembled Buddie's, although he was never as mercurial. Often infuriating his father with unpredictable antics, he knew how to toe the line when required. In his youth, William was the sickliest of the five, leading both parents to overprotect and often pamper him. As the youngest, his personality seemed to be a composite of all the older children: adept in his studies, independent in his thinking, reckless at times, and always able to avoid his father's harsh criticism.

Despite his expanding bank account, Asa Sr. was determined to teach his sons frugality, hard work, piety, and moral fortitude, correcting them constantly for the very things he ignored in his daughter. All four boys accepted the double standard because they, too, overindulged Lucy. In public, however, Asa always defended his sons, even when he was criticizing and chastising them at home. On the other hand, when they obeyed or excelled in some pursuit, his enthusiastic praise could be equally as intense. Guilt was his favorite disciplinary weapon, making "disappointing Papa" something all four boys (and later men) strove assiduously to avoid.

C. Howard Candler, 1898, courtesy of Manuscript, Archives, and Rare Book Library, Emory University

During his senior year at Emory, Howard Candler informed his sister that he had acquired "a 'kit' of instruments, a magnifier, and some pickled subjects," the first step, he said, for becoming a physician. No doubt that decision originated from a desire to purse the career that his father had abandoned, although at the time he told Lucy that he was anxiously anticipating medical school, where he hoped to become a tremendous success. In preparation for that profession, he entered the Atlanta College of Physicians and Surgeons shortly after his Emory graduation. The last year of the nineteenth century brought an unusually cold winter to Georgia. Snow and ice blanketed the city when Howard rode the streetcar downtown to study anatomy and chemistry. That same winter and spring, Buddie was finishing his senior year at Emory, while Lucy was attending classes at Agnes Scott College in nearby Decatur and still living at home. At sixteen, Lucy Candler definitely attracted boys, as the unsolicited gift from George Reed the previous year revealed, and her outgoing friendliness made her a favorite among her college classmates, who continually filled the house on Seaboard Avenue. During one such gathering, her father read passages from *Sut Lovingood* "to those dignified girls," and, as Lucy gleefully told Howard, the book made all of them blush like "you never saw."[40]

Howard's tenure at the Atlanta medical school that year was limited to only one term, for in the spring of '99, Asa recruited him to hawk Coca-Cola in the Midwest, at a salary of $12.50 per week. He left home in March, working his way through Alabama, Tennessee, and Mississippi before finally ending up in Kansas City. During his first two months on the road, he was so successful in boosting sales that his father began writing him the same contradictory letters that had haunted his college career. For example, after one of his son's productive sales trips, Asa wrote:

> I don't know whether I can let you be a doctor or not. If I felt sure that this business would hold over perpetually I believe I would resign and give you the place. But my boy I can't take such a risk on your future ... I have no right to limit your usefulness to the narrow company of a 5 cents Soda Fountain business. You are capable of grander achievements than such a field promises.

Under the cloud of these confusing messages, Howard trudged through Kansas and Missouri, selling Coca-Coca and distributing advertising materials. He kept a pocket-sized order book—a souvenir of the J. J. Douglas distillery of Louisville, Kentucky—with a liquor bottle on its cover, an incongruous illustration in light of Asa's avid opposition to alcohol. On the note pages, Howard meticulously recorded sales and receipts from each little town he visited, sending frequent reports and requests to the Atlanta office. Following his father's instructions, he kept a separate record of his daily personal expenses, listing everything he bought, even ten cents spent for two glasses of Coca-Cola. No ownership privileges here! Meticulously, the young man listed every disbursement: hotels averaged two dollars per night, his three meals were usually about the same, and train fares ranged from two dollars to six dollars. Each week he would submit these accounts for his father to tally, appraise, and criticize.

At every stop, Howard received specific directives from Asa and Frank Robinson, both treating the twenty-year-old man as if he were a puppet on their strings. His father's correspondence was filled with the names of relatives, fellow Methodists, or business associates who might provide contacts for possible sales, intermingled with a string of medical instructions, orders for choosing hotels, banks, churches, and even where to eat breakfast. Howard, no doubt, obeyed such suggestions to the letter, and his compliance seemed to pay off. By the spring of 1899, sales were skyrocketing. "Demand for goods has been in excess of our ability to supply since about 20th of April," Asa wrote his son. A month later, Robinson told him: "Our business is much larger than it has ever been before … the sales for the first six days of May were over 12,000 gallons."

But the frantic attempt to meet the demand was taking its toll on the company president. When a Methodist convention came to Atlanta that summer, Asa nearly reached the breaking point, as he tried to juggle his service to the church with the increased workload. "Papa is completely exhausted," Lucy wrote her brother. "He is so nervous that he can't sleep, eat, nor rest. He has been going to town at five o'clock every morning and returning at eleven that night." Candler's fatigue was so obvious to the Coca-Cola board that its members suggested he "take an extended vacation." Asa did what they asked but only to the extent of briefly accompanying Lucy Elizabeth to her favorite summer resort near Toccoa in the north Georgia foothills.

He might have asked Howard to cut back on sales in light of the overstretched workforce, but instead he encouraged his son to persevere. Determined to fulfill his father's expectations, Howard pushed harder than ever, his diligence paying off with so many orders that both Asa and Frank Robinson praised his efforts. By May, however, Howard was moving so fast that his father advised him to slow down, fearful that the Kansas City heat would be harmful. Robinson cared little about Howard's health, sending such coded commendations as: "We feel quite sure," that "future sales will be much larger than they have been in the past on account of your personal efforts and the advertising you are doing." This encouraged the young man to slog on with a renewed resolve. And his father, too, could not conceal his glee as he exclaimed: "It is the unanimous opinion that you are making a first class commercial man and that The Coca-Cola Company interests in your hands are well cared for." Poor Howard. His life was getting to be more and more perplexing. On the one hand his father wanted him to pursue the study of medicine, but on the other, he desperately needed him in the business.[41]

The most important occurrence during the summer of 1899 went largely unnoticed by most of the Candlers. In July, two men paid Asa a routine visit in his new Edgewood Avenue office. One of them, a Chattanooga lawyer named Benjamin Franklin Thomas, had recently returned from serving in the quartermasters corps in Havana, where he noticed residents walking around with bottles of a carbonated pineapple drink. If that beverage could be bottled and retain its flavor, why wouldn't it work for Coca-Cola? After Thomas returned to Chattanooga, he contacted a fellow lawyer, Joseph Brown Whitehead, and a distant Candler cousin named Sam Erwin. The three men made an appointment to visit Asa in hopes of interesting him in becoming a partner in a bottling operation.

Four years earlier, Joseph Biedenharn had received Candler's permission to bottle the drink, and a Valdosta, Georgia, merchant was selling a similar product with the company president's blessing. Howard, while still a student at Emory, had even arranged an experiment in bottling by selling gallon kegs of the syrup to a general store owner, who mixed it with soda water and sold it in Hutchinson bottles. These localized operations brought profits to Coca-Cola, without the company having to worry about maintaining the drink's quality after it was bottled. The latest proposition, however, turned out to be very different.

At first, when the men from Chattanooga approached him, Asa scoffed at their offer. His cousin, Sam Erwin, had made a last-minute decision to remain in the waiting room, and Candler mistrusted Thomas and Whitehead because they had little capital to invest in the project. Besides, Asa had become wealthy through clever advertising and merchandising to soda fountains, and he was afraid to jeopardize his success by venturing into an unexplored enterprise. Yet, it would be bad business to turn the men down flat, so he suggested a compromise. Since he had no interest in a partnership, why not a perpetual contract that allowed them to purchase the syrup at one-dollar per gallon? Under this deal, they could merchandise bottled Coca-Cola in all states except those restricted by prior arrangements. At the time, it seemed like an easy way to make a profit. Nobody—except perhaps Thomas and Whitehead—realized the magnitude of that casual deal. [42]

Asa G. Candler Jr., 1899, courtesy of Manuscript, Archives, and Rare Book Library, Emory University

Around the time his father was negotiating with the men from Chattanooga, and Howard was making record sales in the Midwest, Buddie graduated from Emory accompanied by a week of parties. After several attempts at persuasion, he convinced his father to let him drive the "trap" from Atlanta to Oxford, while Lucy and a group of her girlfriends came over the next day by train. Wearing a new wardrobe of summer dresses her mother had recently completed, Lucy found Emory to be very exciting, with all the festivities and all the boys. She went to one party at the KA house and another in "the club room" with a young man named Douglas Feagin, who gave her his fraternity "badge." Howard's presence hung over the graduation despite his absence, especially when Buddie failed to earn the "first honor" that his older brother had achieved the previous year. Although Asa was disappointed with his namesake's record, he pleaded with Howard to tell his brother that "he has taken a good education" and thus possessed the "equipment necessary to be successful." Years later, in preparation for writing his father's biography, Howard penciled in the margin of that letter: "Could not do this with a clear conscience." Nevertheless, he did write his brother a letter of congratulations, and Buddie responded with enthusiasm, describing the commencement as the most fun he'd ever had.[43]

Buddie's seeming inability to shoulder responsibilities left his father in a quandary about finding a place for him in the company. At first, he considered sending him to Kansas City to follow Howard around and learn to be a salesman. Not only did Howard object to the idea, but Buddie was downright negative, begging his father to send him to the new Los Angeles Coca-Cola office. Father and son clearly had two different ideas about what that would entail. Asa Sr. wanted his namesake to acquire discipline and begin to understand the intricacies of the business; Buddie, in contrast, envisioned a California assignment as a pathway to adventure. But worn down by his son's persistent pleading, Asa finally gave in and assigned him to assist Milton's son Sam, then manager of West Coast manufacturing, shipping, and sales.

Slowly Buddie made his way westward, stopping for a brief visit with Howard in Kansas City, then getting stalled on the train for thirty-six hours in the Nevada desert before he reached Los Angeles. Upon his arrival, he received a letter from his parents telling him how much they missed him, and he answered with his usual candor:

> I don't see why you are so lonesome without me for I have never been with you much in my life. I am not at all lonesome because I found such a hearty welcome for me from Sam. To tell the truth about it . . . I believe him to be the best cousin I have. I never was more charmed with anyone than I am with him.[44]

In time, Buddie became disillusioned with Sam, who often disappeared for days at a time, leaving his cousin to manage the office. Sam's failure to communicate so frustrated Buddie that he complained to Howard: "Now do not that beat all, a traveling man out on the road and his nearest office does not know where he is?" Wondering why the company would keep someone so incompetent, Buddie insisted that *he* was working extra hours to keep the West Coast venture afloat. Within weeks, however, that resolve began to falter.

Buddie's first misstep was his penchant for adventure. Having often expressed his yearning to see the "Wild West," he spent much of a supposed business trip climbing Pikes Peak on a burro and swimming in the Great Salt Lake. Clearly these detours were not on the agenda for selling Coca-Cola syrup. To make matters worse, when Sam returned to Los Angeles, he proved to be the worst possible influence on his mischievous and impressionable cousin. Under Sam's influence, Buddie seemed to be learning more about the lowlife of Los Angeles than about managing a Coca-Cola office. Together they frequented saloons and pool halls in the company of prostitutes and shady characters. These excursions caused Buddie once again to change his mind about Sam, telling Howard that their cousin was really "a good fellow." At that time, Asa Sr. knew little about his son's transgressions, because Buddie continued to dispatch rosy reports of his progress and admiration for his older cousin. Based on these letters, his father allowed him to remain in Los Angeles, hoping sales on the West Coast would improve.

In stark contrast to his younger brother, Howard was slogging doggedly through Kansas, diligently pushing to set sales records. After finally finishing his grueling tour in early September of 1899, he set out for home. Scheduled to contact soda fountains as he traveled through Texas and Louisiana, his plans were curtailed by an outbreak of yellow fever. Nervous as usual about his son's health, Asa maneuvered him around quarantines and possible danger spots while still allowing him to "earn expenses." As Howard moved eastward, his father supplied him with shipments of quinine, so that he reached Birmingham without becoming ill. The journey ended on a high note, when he surprised his parents by appearing unannounced at Atlanta's Grand Opera House, just in time to hear his Uncle Warren deliver a sermon at a Methodist prayer meeting.

Shortly after his return home, Howard reenrolled in classes at the Atlanta College of Physicians and Surgeons and spent another winter studying medicine. But when the term ended in the spring of 1900, he once again hit the road; this time his assignment was to check up on Buddie in Los Angeles and see why the California office was doing so poorly.[45] Because of that deficiency, Asa had decided to replace his nephew with a new manager named George Patterson. Yet, even with a different man in charge, profits from the West Coast still lagged, and Asa became more convinced than ever that he had made a mistake to stretch his operation that far. All hopes of turning things around now seemed to be pinned on Howard, who was not only instructed to help his brother get the office in shape but given specific directions for how to improve sales. Therefore, as soon as he reached Los Angeles, Howard boarded another train headed to northern California. Once again Asa burdened his "noble boy" with avoiding "the exposure of evil," that seemed to hover over the wicked West. He had faith, he said, in Howard's "ability and disposition" to "withstand any temptation." It was another tough task, especially when Asa kept repeating how confident he was that his two sons would reverse business prospects in California.

Once again, Howard's efforts were so successful that a month after he got to the coast, sales began to increase. But back in Los Angeles, things were falling apart. Because Patterson was also on the road, Buddie was left in charge of both manufacturing syrup and managing the office. That meant Howard had to depend on his brother to ship orders to every client he solicited. Given their different ideas and orientations, it didn't take long for that situation to explode. Howard accused Buddie of messing up the shipments, and Buddie complained that Howard kept changing his requests without understanding the difficulties involved in having to manufacture as well as package orders. Frustrated and feeling helpless, Buddie told his brother: "I am trying to do everything I can for you, and do it in a way that will please you," including getting the orders out as soon as they arrive.

But despite his protestations, Buddie could not quite admit how deeply their temperaments clashed or how impossible it was for them to work together. He continued to remain cheerful and boastful, while Howard's outlook was dour and pessimistic. From the letters they shot back and forth to each other, it seems pretty obvious that Howard was depressed, while ebullient Buddie responded to his brother's cries for help with naïve attempts to cheer him up. "You must not get discouraged," he wrote, "for you knew before you left here that you were going to strike a very hard job. Keep your spirits up and remember that I am back here ready ... to help you along. You can do anything and I will back you." Beneath such simple expressions of concern for his brother lurked Buddie's growing awareness that he was out of his element. Not only was he unable to understand Howard's mood swings, but he knew deep down that he had made a mess of running the office.

Soon none of it would matter, for within weeks, the lives of both young men would be changing dramatically.

Part Two:

Making More Money

CHAPTER FIVE
Changing World

Buddie's life was the first to change. By the early summer of 1900, Asa realized that his namesake was having serious problems handling the complex duties of managing, manufacturing, and marketing. No doubt, Howard's appraisal of the situation added to their father's apprehensions, since he probably reported that Buddie lacked the capacity and experience to handle the job. And even more disturbing to their father, Howard surely mentioned his brother's unsavory lifestyle. Upon hearing these negative assessments, Asa sprang into action. First he assigned family friend George Reed to be West Coast office manager, and then he brought his son home. Not long after he returned, Buddie admitted to his sister that he had gotten into trouble in Los Angeles, because he socialized with the wrong crowd. Asa—who realized now more than ever that he had to keep his second son away from all such temptations—began seeking a solution.

It came to him aboard a Seaboard-Airline train, en route to a Methodist conference in New Jersey. During the two-day journey, Candler spent a great deal of time in the club car, sipping Coca-Cola with his old acquaintance Billy Witham, a Georgia banker, mill owner, and real estate investor. In the course of their conversation, Witham told his friend that he owned a failing cotton mill in the small northeast Georgia town of Hartwell and asked the Coca-Cola president if he had any ideas about how he might pull the deteriorating business out of its slump. Asa then told Witham about his bright and capable son, who had been working in California. Aware that semi-rural Hartwell would keep Buddie far away from the evil influences of a larger city, yet near enough to Atlanta to be within the purview of his watchful eye, Asa agreed to invest in the faltering enterprise, on the condition that Witham employ his son. Within weeks, Asa Candler owned a controlling interest in the Witham Cotton Mill, assumed the role of company president, and Buddie had a job as the business's assistant secretary. Shortly thereafter, Asa wrote Howard: "If he takes hold well and is pleased with the business, he will be president in my place ... and will eventually own the stock."[46]

In his new job, Buddie asked to be known as Asa Jr. a name that he hoped would establish him as a grownup, although his parents and siblings rarely called him anything other than "Buddie" or "Bud." The young man did seem happy with his new position at the Witham Mill, and with his usual naïveté and general optimistic outlook, he expressed appreciation for being charged with such weighty responsibilities. "We have such sweet dear parents," he told Lucy, "we should always do and be what they would like," and the best way to demonstrate that gratitude was "to obey them and love one another. No one loves their parents more than I do," he protested, "and I love them more and more every day I live." Part of Asa Jr.'s problem was a tendency—perhaps deliberate or perhaps unconscious—to wander away from the straight path he was supposed to follow. This pattern of rebelliousness, balanced by expressions of frustrated admiration for a demanding father, is a bifurcated inclination often found in second children from families where the older sibling behaves according to expectations.

When Asa Sr. conversed with Witham aboard the train headed to the Methodist conference in June 1900, he had another mission to perform. After the conference ended, he and his wife accompanied Howard to a Philadelphia dock, where he joined a group of recent Emory graduates for a tour of Europe. As their eldest son waved good-bye from the ship's deck, his parents struggled to hold back tears. Like most provincial southerners at the opening of the twentieth century, they felt as if they were dispatching their boy to the far reaches of the moon. "Oh my child," Asa wrote, "when that old red boat carried you out of my sight ... I trembled for your health and safety." Although Lucy Elizabeth was attempting to be cheerful as she waved, she too had pangs of regret as the ship grew smaller and smaller. Later she confessed that she "could hardly sleep or eat" until she knew he was safe, and both of them breathed a sigh of relief when a phone call from an Emory official informed them that Howard had arrived in England, and the tour was going well.

Even before the ship landed at Southampton, Asa was busy issuing ways Howard could combine his vacation with work. "You must carefully note business conditions in the countries and governments visited," he wrote, and investigate "whether or not we can do anything in Europe." If Coca-Cola were to be sold abroad, he advised, it must be somewhere with plenty of "ice, hot weather, long summers, etc." Just in case an opportunity arose, Asa equipped his son with a one-gallon bottle of Coca-Cola syrup, a fortuitous move as it turned out. While the group was in London, Howard wandered into an American-style soda fountain at a department store near St. Paul's Cathedral, pulled a container of the syrup out of his pocket, and showed the fountain attendant how to mix a Coca-Cola. Pleased with the result, the soda jerk served it to his bosses, who were so taken with the beverage that they not only ordered five gallons of syrup but soon opened a regular account with the Coca-Cola Company. Thus Howard's trip abroad produced a small opening wedge in what would eventually expand into a phenomenal international trade. Ironically, London met none of Asa's requirements as a place to introduce Coca-Cola: it rarely had hot weather, the summers were short, and few people used ice in their drinks.

While still touring Europe, Howard received a letter that significantly altered his future plans. "Our New York manager is not at all equal to the requirements of that position," his father wrote. "I think you had better go there and look after our interests. New York is the American metropolis and requires first class direction." Aware that his son harbored different career aspirations, Asa noted that attending medical school in Manhattan would surely enhance his chances of success in his chosen profession. But to the president of Coca-Cola, business definitely came first. Thus a representative of the company—armed with calendars, posters, an order book, and a sales-trip itinerary—greeted Howard on the pier. Lugging all this paraphernalia, the young man made his way through Pennsylvania and New Jersey. Then, ever dutiful, he returned home for a brief visit with his parents before taking the train back to New York to enroll in the Bellevue Hospital Medical College.

For the next few months, Howard divided his time between studies at Bellevue and dealing with the tangled business of Coca-Cola's Washington Square office, a double duty that left him nervous, frustrated, and plagued by frequent illnesses ranging from sore throats to aching eyes. Although his first set of exams was "long and difficult," he passed them successfully and was admitted to Bellevue's junior class. Yet he still felt lonely and isolated in the big northern city among unfriendly strangers, especially those in his boarding house. In describing his unsatisfactory lodging, he wrote: "Last night, I sat down to the table, knowing no one, no one spoke to me, nor had I a word to say. I ate pretty much as a farmer would feed a gin—just as if I was a machine." After dinner, he returned to his room and attempted to read, but when that proved fruitless, he dragged himself down to the hustle and bustle of Broadway, where he happened into an Otis Skinner play called *Prince Otto*, and that dispelled his gloom. Later in the fall, the Coca-Cola office manager, H. T. Applewhite, introduced him to two young southern women. Before he took one of them out, he purchased "a swell suit, hot tie, and some broadcloth gaiters," in hopes the outfit would "cut quite a shine." He must have impressed the unnamed lady, because she invited him to tea at her house and to a church bazaar. "I find that I enjoy this diversion very much," Howard told Lucy, and the new contacts worked temporarily to quell his depression.[47]

Shortly after Easter in 1901, Asa Sr. rushed off to Philadelphia to try and solve a crisis in the family of his sister, Jessie Willard. He wrote Howard to solicit his advice, saying merely that his niece, also named Jessie, had a "serious and curious condition." Written above this in Howard's handwriting is: "she was pregnant." In the early twentieth century, premarital sex was neither tolerated nor mentioned in open conversation. In his correspondence, Asa never referred to young Jessie's condition openly. Instead, he told his son that he "carried her and her mother (my poor widowed heartsick sister)" to a private home, where he would "attend to having her treated." The matter, he insisted, was not to be discussed with anyone. In the next letter, he spilled out more of the story, still using euphemisms that Howard obviously understood. Feigning "bad health," young Jessie Willard had traveled to Atlanta and was examined by Dr. Hurt, the family physician. He "found her in such condition that he recommended that she be without a moment's delay carried to New York or Philadelphia for treatment such as he had no facilities for giving her." Apparently they were seeking an abortion.

Asa, therefore, returned with the young woman and her mother to their home in Philadelphia. Because no one seemed able to help them there, Asa asked his eldest son if he was "on such intimate terms with any of the faculty" to find out the name of a Philadelphia doctor, not one "so eminent as to make a big bill" but somebody "able to treat her" or one "to direct me to a place in Philadelphia to which she can be carried for treatment if necessary." The girl, he said, had "lost her mind" and was "not disposed to talk." Her mother is "almost heartbroken." Again he warned Howard not to say anything about this in his letters home.[48] The correspondence stops here, leaving the results of this incident a mystery. In the Candler family genealogy, young Jessie Willard is listed as "unmarried" with no descendants. So we must assume that the "treatment" succeeded.

When Asa Sr. returned from his secret mission to aid his niece, his attention shifted. Concerned about how his second son was handling his job at the mill, he made frequent visits to Hartwell to check on his new investment. During one such visit, Asa Jr. told his father that he planned "to marry a country girl," although he didn't "intend to do so for some time yet." Lucy already knew that her brother was engaged to Helen Magill, a petite, blue-eyed redhead, whose father published the local newspaper. Wanting her fun-loving and attentive brother to remain in the bosom of the family a little longer, Lucy advised him to wait awhile and not rush into marriage, especially since he and his bride-to-be were both only twenty. But Asa Jr. ignored her pleas, responding that he would never leave Hartwell and intended to make "a little home" for himself in northeast Georgia. Besides, he had been promoted to secretary and treasurer of the mill, which was "a very responsible place" to be. They had already set the wedding date for June 12, he confided, begging his sister not to say anything to the family until he told his parents at the end of May.

Since that conversation was not recorded, we can only imagine the reaction of Asa and Lucy Elizabeth, which must not have been entirely positive. When they told Helen's father, he was furious, probably worried that his young daughter was marrying a reprobate, whose reputation for recklessness no doubt followed him to Hartwell. But the couple was determined to marry and acquiesced only to Asa Sr.'s request that they postpone the wedding for another month. On July 16, 1901, a small, simple ceremony took place in Hartwell at the home of Helen's uncle, with Bishop Warren Candler officiating. Although most of the Candler family was present at the service, Helen's father refused to attend, repeating the same inflexibility that overshadowed the wedding of Asa Sr. and Lucy Elizabeth twenty-three years earlier. Two days after they married in Hartwell, the newlyweds traveled down to Atlanta for a reception hosted by the groom's parents on the grounds of their Seaboard Avenue home. Five hundred people wandered around the palms, daisies, and pink carnations in the house and garden, enjoying the music of a small orchestra seated under a festoon of Japanese lanterns. Exhausted after a round of additional parties, the young couple returned to begin their life together in Hartwell.[49]

Two months after Asa Jr. wed, the nation was stunned to learn that President William McKinley had been shot while shaking hands with well-wishers at the Pan-American Exposition in Buffalo, New York, and when he died a week later, the far more progressive Vice President Theodore Roosevelt moved into the White House. But Howard Candler scarcely noticed the changes in Washington, since he had too many personal matters on his mind. Possibly spurred on by the marriage of his younger brother, he had begun seriously courting Flora Glenn. They had grown up within minutes of each other, sharing many childhood memories and mutual friends, especially those they met at the Inman Park Methodist Church, where both families worshipped. Flora—with her dark hair and plain features—was no beauty, yet there was something compelling about her sparkling friendliness and quick wit that captivated a wide circle of friends and admirers. Lively and outgoing, she posed a contrast to Howard's reserve and introspection. The couple began to correspond regularly after Howard returned to his job and school in New York during the fall of '01. Fortunately, she saved his letters, which not only describe their growing romantic involvement, but also document the many emotional problems tearing Howard apart.[50]

After she graduated with honors from La Grange Female College (Lucy Elizabeth's alma mater), Flora promised Howard that she would visit New York in mid-October. Since both of them loved music, theater, and literature, he began making plans to take her to concerts, plays, and his favorite restaurants, where they would discuss the books he had been reading. But to his bitter disappointment, she had to cancel her planned trip. Instantly, he leapt to the conclusion that she wanted to stay in Atlanta to be with another suitor. But it wasn't only Flora's mention of other male friends that made Howard so despondent. From the day he arrived in New York, he had been unable to concentrate on his studies and complained constantly of being sick with an undiagnosed illness. To find out the cause, he consulted three different doctors, each of whom advised him to suspend his medical studies for a few months. The physicians had no idea what was wrong, Howard wrote, and he was certain that they used the term "nervous condition" merely to cover up for their inability to make a more accurate and serious diagnosis. Long before the term "clinical depression" entered the vocabulary as a form of physical illness, doctors attributed his kind of complaints to an excessive amount of strain. Exacerbating his gloominess was an overwhelming sense of failure. He explained to Flora that he felt extremely discouraged, after having already devoted seven years of his life to medical school. "So much time spent for nothing," he lamented. All that work had accomplished little other than destroying his nervous system.

As part of his recovery, Howard asked his father if he could be assigned to the Los Angeles Coca-Cola office, now under the supervision of his old friend George Reed.

Asa dismissed Howard's plan to return to California as well as his intentions to suspend his studies at Bellevue, advising him to move slowly and consult with another physician before making the final decision. But if he must quit, his father insisted that he would recover more rapidly at home. Then he added his assessment of the situation:

> It has not been because I could not give you work to do that I have kept you in college but looking to your future usefulness and personal interests I have thought it will not [do] to involve your life in a <u>mere money</u> getting machine. That is the plan with many I know. Enough money to buy fashionable clothes, show tickets, etc, etc, etc. Enjoy ourselves is the style, but I have not arrived to be stylish but [to be] useful in myself if possible and also in my children. [51]

Underlying Asa's comments is the lurking suspicion that he contributed to the breakdown by insisting Howard combine work with medical school. Yet he seems to be communicating a deeper apprehension. Struggling with his inherited frugality and religious conscience, Asa was being forced to face the reality of his own phenomenal success. Although the Candlers still lived simply compared to others of their economic strata, the rewards of a "mere money getting machine" were significantly changing his life and presenting unwanted temptations to his offspring.

At that critical moment in the fall of 1901, Howard's awareness of potential luxuries seemed irrelevant. His immediate need was to pull himself out of the troubling "nervous condition." So, in hopes of alleviating his depression, he accompanied a friend to a Hungarian café, but even though he felt better listening to the music there, his gloom returned when he got home. He admitted to Flora that he "had to get into a hot-pack and take opium to relieve the pain." Still trying to overcome his suffering, he attended a few comedies and musicals with friends in the ensuing weeks. But his depression remained acute, and he could not shake his "abominable humor." Eventually, Howard decided to follow his father's advice, and he returned home at the end of September.

After less than a month of nurturing by Lucy Elizabeth and long rides around town with Flora, he was ready once more to hit the road for Coca-Cola. Going by rail through Georgia, he stopped almost daily at a string of small towns: Lawrenceville, Athens, Lexington, Crawfordsville, Greensboro, Madison, Social Circle, Covington, Milledgeville, and Macon. Slightly later, he followed a westward route that took him to Americus, Moultrie, Valdosta, Troy, and over to Dothan, Alabama. At each stop, he wrote long letters to "Miss Flora" complaining of his physical ailments and telling her of his business disappointments and accomplishments, the latter appearing only rarely among gripes about his frenetic schedule and terrible accommodations. Adding to his loneliness were apprehensions about the men escorting Flora to parties, plays, and operas, and he constantly told her about those worries, which he feared were preventing her from not corresponding with him regularly.[52]

Despite his protestations, Howard's travels did include some bright moments. He kept running across friends from the military academy, Emory, and the Atlanta Medical College, and he even seemed to enjoy a stay with his mother's family in Augusta. These diversions bolstered his mood and helped him gradually emerge from the doldrums. "Under the balmy influence of a traveling man's life," he began to improve. In Ozark, Alabama, he attended a street fair, where he lingered until his train left at 12:30 a.m. "I decided to come down off my dignity and try to have some fun," he conceded. "You see I haven't had any real fun since leaving home, and very little I had while there." That outing meant donning his "best costume" and treating a group of strangers to Coca-Colas and bags of confetti. They showed their gratitude by "showering the abominable small bits of sand and paper" over his head, and that "almost succeeded in blinding and choking" him. Characteristically, he concluded: "To tell the truth, I was right glad to take the train away from the scene." Finally, after many weeks on the road, he wended his way to Atlanta, arriving just before Christmas. During the holidays, he and Flora spent a great deal of time together, and although the word "engagement" was never mentioned in their correspondence, they clearly had an understanding and possibly were making secret plans to be wed.

But before that could happen, Howard was again obliged to ride the rails. As he journeyed through Alabama and into Florida, he resumed the familiar routine of late-night train trips, little sleep, and treks from pharmacy to pharmacy. Occasionally he would reluctantly admire certain aspects of the scenery, and his observations could be quite poetic. Look, for example, at this description of the ride between Pensacola and Tallahassee:

This morning [the bay] was as calm as a lake. For twenty miles we traveled along the shore and watched the sun rise, showing blood-red through the haze ... We crossed a neck in the bay upon a trestle which was so long that we, when at its middle, could see neither end of it. Immediately we plunge into a dense luxurious green jungle which arched by the long clinging moss completely hides the sun and almost obscures its light.

But such positive comments were exceptional, and he continued to grumble until he reached Atlanta in the middle of February. After only a few days to relax and see Flora, he was dispatched to resume his job in New York.

Howard's continual grousing provoked his father into embarking on a familiar theme: "Only a few years at best and I will have to sit down and wait for the <u>Reaper</u> to carry me off like the street cleaner [carries] the trash." When this occurred, Asa repeated, his oldest son would direct the company. This onerous reminder, little altered since he began working for his father, was the only consistency amidst the rapid changes that Coca-Cola's mushrooming popularity demanded. For one thing, Asa promoted his nephew, Sam Dobbs, to supervise the sales department, giving Frank Robinson additional time to update their advertising. As a result, the old-fashioned fans, dispensers, glasses, and other paraphernalia—which Howard had so dutifully dragged around the country—slowly gave way to twentieth-century fashions and synchronized nationwide promotion. Attractive drawings of sports stars and stylishly dressed young people gradually began replacing the corseted, Victorian actresses, and the very first ad in a nationally circulated publication appeared in *Munsey's Magazine* during 1902.

The improved publicity brought such unprecedented success that the company could not keep up with syrup production. Daily they were shipping two thousand gallons from Atlanta, five hundred from Dallas, one hundred from Los Angeles, and two hundred from both Chicago and Philadelphia, totaling three thousand gallons per day and over one hundred thousand per month. From these sales in the spring of 1902, the company gained 25 percent over the previous fiscal year. Despite this phenomenal success, Asa was not about to spend their profits needlessly. If delivery wagons and horse-drawn carriages had taken them this far, why splurge on anything else? He was thus outraged to learn that Howard wanted the New York office to purchase a steam-powered Locomobile. "Certainly you must not invest in one," he scolded. "I very much fear that the use of a machine like that on the streets of New York City will ultimately get us into trouble [and] probably hurt one of you." Emphasizing that he had no confidence whatsoever in the automobile, he was convinced it was merely a momentary fad, just as the bicycle had been a decade earlier. Eventually, however, he authorized spending $500 for the Locomobile, as long as Howard and the New York manager deemed it to be "in the interest of the Coca-Cola Co." and not merely "a toy." Under this stricture, the business bought its first motorized vehicle in the summer of 1902.[53]

While Howard was chugging around Central Park in the new "machine," his father was demonstrating his frugality in an Atlanta courtroom. The case—*The Coca-Cola Company v. Henry A. Rucker*—stemmed from an 1898 Congressional decision to levy a federal tax on medications to help finance the Spanish-American War. Since early ads claimed that Coca-Cola possessed curative powers, the government collected $1.75 per gallon, which totaled almost $29,502 over a three-year period. However, when Congress repealed the measure in 1901, Asa rushed to sue the federal tax commissioner, claiming that his product was not medicinal. During the trial that dragged on for several years, the government called Assistant District Attorney George L. Bell to present a chemist's report analyzing the ingredients of Coca-Cola, and, in so doing, he revealed that a small amount of cocaine could be found in the analysis. With this disclosure, the emphasis of the trial changed dramatically. In cross-examination, Dr. George Payne, the company's own witness, agreed that a minimal amount of the narcotic was in the formula, although it amounted to less than four hundred thousandth of a grain per ounce. Asa Candler, when questioned, conceded that the report was correct. It was a shattering public disclosure. Now Washington had evidence—confirmed by the company's president—to prove that Coca-Cola contained cocaine! And to make matters worse, a federal witness, Dr. J. P. Baird, testified that the drink could be habit-forming, and even though he followed that claim by saying he doubted that such a miniscule amount of the narcotic could make it addictive, the damage was done.

Still fixated on redeeming what he considered an illegal tax, Asa persevered through more months in the courtroom. Actually, Coca-Cola had little need of the refund because the company was now raking in more money than ever. But Candler didn't see it that way. Since he had initiated the legal process, he was determined to win. At first he was very pessimistic about his chances of success as the trial dragged on. "It will probably be a lost case for us," he complained to Howard. "The government resorts to every means to defeat us." But after a few days, he decided that the verdict would either end in a mistrial or swing in his favor. His instincts were correct. A jury of Atlantans ruled that the company should be reimbursed for the amount paid in taxes, and subsequently it received a refund. But it was a hollow victory that opened a Pandora's box of future legal entanglements for the Coca-Cola Company.

Asa had other distractions during the spring of 1902. Asa Jr. and his wife Helen were expecting his first grandchild in June. They had decided the baby should be born in Atlanta, where family members and qualified doctors were on hand to help. But an unanticipated occurrence caused them to leave Hartwell sooner than planned. During one cold day, Helen had helped a barn cat deliver her litter in the warmth of their house. This kindness was rewarded by a bite on the hand from one of the newborn kittens, and within a few days the hand became infected. When by mid-March the wound still festered, the couple decided to consult an Atlanta doctor, and they traveled down to stay with at the Candlers' Seaboard Avenue home. But their consultation turned into an emergency when, only hours after the couple arrived, Helen began having labor pains. Luckily, Asa was able to reach his friend and neighbor, Dr. John W. Hurt, and tell him to come at once.

After a brief examination, Dr. Hurt told the family that her weakened condition and the rampant infection had precipitated premature labor. Since the baby was breach, the only way he could save both mother and child was to try and reverse the infant's position. Several nervous hours ensued, but thanks to the doctor's skillful manipulation, Helen delivered a healthy 5½-pound girl. They named her Lucy Magill Candler, jokingly called "Lucy 3" by her proud father. But Helen's condition was no laughing matter, for they soon discovered that the birth left her not only fatigued but seriously ill from the ongoing infection. Since she was far too sick to care for the baby, the new grandmother would have to take over. Family lore contends that when Lucy Elizabeth determined that premature infants required an incubator, she retrieved an egg hatchery from the barn, placed her tiny namesake in it, and tended her day and night with constant changes of boiling water and hot towels. Helen was also too ill to nurse, so baby Lucy was reportedly kept alive for the first few days with Coca-Cola fed through an eyedropper. This sufficed until Asa bought a goat, thus replacing the narcotic-bearing soft drink with more nutritious goat milk.[54]

With Helen and the baby in the protective care of his mother, Asa Jr. returned to the Witham Mill, assuming that his wife and child would be joining him shortly. But the weeks dragged into months, and Helen continued to run a fever. Her temperature would shoot up precariously high, stay for a few days, and then drop, leaving her weak and listless. Two generations later, Helen probably would have been diagnosed with a severe case of "cat-scratch fever," an illness transmitted by felines, especially kittens. But in 1902, neither the family nor the doctors knew of this illness, which remained unidentified until the mid-twentieth century. Not understanding what was wrong with his daughter-in-law, Asa remained fully convinced that she was malingering to avoid taking responsibility for her infant. "The baby grows some," he told Howard, "but the feverish condition of the mother makes it fretful." Then he added, unsympathetically: "Helen appears to be utterly short on judgment [and] maternal wisdom," and his wife was "all out of sorts with everybody and everything." There was clearly turmoil on Seaboard Avenue.

To escape the disruption of his household during the spring of 1902, Asa Sr. poured himself into a more rewarding project. He had recently decided to capitalize on the phenomenal success of Coca-Cola by building a new home for his family on property he owned at the corner of Elizabeth Street and Euclid Avenue, a few blocks from his present residence. Although the pie-shaped lot (128 feet frontage and 215 feet in the rear) in the heart of Inman Park was considerably smaller than his ten-acre farm, the house itself was notably larger. George Murphy, who had built the company's headquarters on Edgewood Avenue, was the contractor. True to the reputation for procrastination, evident while constructing the Coca-Cola offices, Murphy was behind schedule, and once again Asa complained that the job was moving at a "snail's gait." But by the end of May, the basic structure had risen, and it was time to begin applying the brick facade. In typical Candler fashion, the bricklaying gave cause for a family ceremony. With help from her grandparents, two-month-old Lucy laid the first brick; twelve-year-old William laid the second, sixteen-year-old Walter the third, and Lucy Elizabeth the fourth. Then came the extended family. Asa's sister Florence, his nephew Charlie from Villa Rica, and Warren's wife Nettie each placed a brick on the stack, but Helen was still too weak to accompany them.[55]

Throughout the long hot summer of 1902, Helen and little Lucy continued to stay with the Candlers in Atlanta. In the middle of August, Helen was well enough to attend the baby's baptism at the Inman Park Methodist Church, with her great-uncle Warren performing the ceremony. Asa asked Howard to buy a silver bowl and have it engraved: "Lucy Magill Candler, August 17, 1902 Saved by Jesus." The inscription should cost no more than five dollars to ten dollars, he instructed his son, and it should be charged as a refund item on the Coca-Cola account. "She is a lovely baby," glowed the proud grandfather, and "is fat and getting fatter every day." With so many relatives in town for the ceremony, he wrote, his wife was "running a nursery with herself chief nurse." After the baptism, Helen and the baby were finally able to join Asa Jr. in Hartwell.

The baby's Aunt Lucy took great pride in her new niece, although her time to play with the baby was limited. Two years earlier, she had entered the freshman class at Wesleyan College in Macon, Georgia. Still dependent on her parents, she had difficulty adjusting to college life and required frequent visits from her mother to quell her homesickness. Before long, however, she began to enjoy school, especially as her social life improved. Young men frequently invited her to attend fraternity parties at Emory and the University of Georgia. Even though these dates occupied much of her time, Lucy still managed to make good grades. Howard, in his role as wise elder, encouraged her to keep up her music. "It will give you a certain refinement," he wrote, "an <u>entrée</u> where most young ladies are not permitted." When she sent home a prize-winning essay, her father teased that he would show it to her when she got "married to the Prince of Denmark or some other fine fellow, about 50 years from now." Lucy, however, had no intention of waiting another half-century to be married. She had informed her friends, but perhaps not her parents, about a new suitor named Bill Owens.[56]

Lucy boasted of him to her Willard cousins—Jessie (the young woman that had the secret medical emergency a year earlier), Florence, and Mary—when she visited them in suburban Philadelphia during the early summer of 1902. Bill, she explained, was a twenty-six-year-old banker, a Florida native, who had surprised her with an engagement ring a few days before she left to go north. At nineteen, Lucy was an animated beauty, with blonde curls and a warm, engaging smile, while he was a contrast, with dark hair and serious dark eyes. Several of her letters written to Bill during her visit to the Willards survive. Paragraphs of cooing are interspersed with insightful glimpses into the customs of the era and telling bits about her teasing control of their relationship. Since we only have her half of the correspondence, we can only surmise from her responses that Bill's family knew nothing about their engagement, and he was annoyed because she was displaying the ring to her cousins. Admitting that she had already dropped hints to her mother, Lucy said she had decided not to say anything to her father until Bill had a chance to formally ask for her hand, a visit she hoped would take place while she was away. "You will find it very easy," she assured him, and "you won't need me there."

Bill was apparently concerned that he wasn't earning enough money to properly support a wife, especially one who was enjoying the benefits of her father's fortune. Lucy not only dismissed that worry but admonished her fiancé "never to mention it again." In one letter, she begged Bill not to enlist in the Georgia Horse Guard, her father's old cavalry regiment. Why "join in such a disgusting, outrageous" company, she fussed, adding: "You care very little for your future, if you are willing to go and put yourself up as a target for such as a negro to shoot at," adding that the "last one of the negroes should be shot anyway, although they are not worth shooting." Lucy was possibly referring to a recent incident in Atlanta in which a white boy shot and killed a black youth, and a race riot ensued. [57] Yet her comment is a sad testimony to the then-common attitude toward African Americans in Georgia, where they were being outwardly abused (as the shooting indicates) and frequently lynched for not obeying the expected code of behavior. Not that Lucy or her family formally endorsed racial violence, but her seemingly lighthearted acceptance of prevailing fears indicates just how ingrained racial prejudice was in the early-twentieth-century South.

After her sojourn in Philadelphia, Lucy traveled to New York to see Howard. Afraid for her to be in the huge metropolis alone, her father insisted that she take one of her Willard cousins, dictating where they should stay and eat, what sights they should see and not see, and the route she should take home. He issued the same instructions to sixteen-year-old Walter when he visited Howard during that summer of 1902. Like his older brother, Asa Jr., Walter believed that travel meant having fun, despite his father's more restrictive plans. The New York stay, Asa Sr. insisted, was intended to be "an educational move," primarily for keeping his rambunctious son's nose to the grindstone. The young man was expected to work at the Coca-Cola office every day, and if he failed to comply, he would have to come back to Atlanta at once. So when Walter seemed to be enjoying the sights and jaunts in the Locomobile more than performing dull business tasks, his father summoned him home to work under his watchful eye in the Coca-Cola shipping department.

Howard, on the other hand, worked hard that summer of 1902. Except for a few excursions in the Locomobile, he diligently monitored the intricacies of the Coca-Cola office. That responsibility grew more demanding when one of their salesmen, W. A. Slaton, was accused of excessive drinking. Because of his adamant opposition to all forms of alcohol, Asa wrote that if Howard and office manager H. T. Applewhite had "indubitable evidence" to prove Slaton was not "a moral upright gentleman," he must be dismissed. "I have never allowed any person of bad morals to remain in the employ of this company in any capacity after discovering his unworthiness." Within days, Slaton was gone.

For Howard—far away from his family and yearning to be with Flora—this matter seemed insignificant. In letters to his parents, he complained that life in New York was injurious to his health, a condition confirmed by his great-uncle, Fred Beall, who was spending weeks in Asbury Park, New Jersey, representing Coca-Cola in a copyright-infraction case. All of Howard's pleadings were in vain, however, because his father needed him to continue supervising the troublesome New York office. Possibly depressed during that hot August, Howard revived the idea of returning to medical school. And once again, Asa sent mixed messages:

> If I thought you could get your degree by taking another course which would end as I understand it next Spring, I am satisfied you should do this. There may be two dangers. 1st: Having been out of school for a year and during that time intensely busy mentally and otherwise in commerce, you might not be able to pass. 2nd: Your health might give way and each time this happens it is more difficult to recover. Consider earnestly the above two contingencies. After you get your degree it may not be decided best for you to practice medicine but for you to take a responsible place in connection with this business.[58]

Those comments no doubt convinced Howard to forget medical school once and for all, because a few days later, his father wrote: "I take it that you have decided to abandon the profession of medicine and cast your lot in Commercial Lines." Although he claimed he had reservations about his son's decision, he agreed to accept it as final. With this issue settled,

Asa decided to reconfigure the staff by transferring H. T. Applewhite to Georgia and making Howard manager of the New York office, a promotion that provided his first important role in his father's company.

Lucy Elizabeth Candler and friends in the New York Coca-Cola office, 1903, (she is third from the left in black hat and white lace collar), courtesy of the Coca-Cola Company Archives

Shortly after Howard became office manager, Lucy Elizabeth visited him in New York, ostensibly to buy furniture for the new house, but more likely she wanted to check up on her son's health and lodging. Even though her duties at home had lessened now that Walter had entered Emory's freshman class, the generally pessimistic Howard still worried that his mother would change her mind. However, as planned, Lucy Elizabeth arrived in early October with a group of her friends and remained for a week.[59] During her stay, Howard invited his mother and her traveling companions for dinner at the Coca-Cola office, then on South Washington Square. A photograph survives of the six women, dressed in silks and large feathered hats, gathered around a potbellied stove, in front of a wall adorned with Coca-Cola calendars and posters. Howard prepared their meal in his small apartment behind the office. "The ladies professed to enjoy" the food, he later wrote, but he suspected they were most taken with "the novelty of such an occasion." His mother, however, was irate about his living conditions, claiming that the cramped apartment was making him ill. Thus, as soon as she returned to Atlanta, she told her husband that an office was no place for her son to live, and, within months, both Howard and the New York Coca-Cola office changed addresses. He moved back into a boarding house, and the office was relocated in the Mallincrodt Building on William Street.

As Howard became more comfortable in his managerial role, he relieved the daily tedium of sales and manufacturing with occasional trips to the theater and gatherings of his fraternity brothers. But his usual taciturnity—tempered by the insecurity that had always haunted him—kept him from feeling fully content. Above all, he feared that he would not be able to meet the exacting standards his father demanded. In one telling letter, he wrote: "I will continue to do the very best I can. I hope you will never be ashamed of me," for "my whole object is to please you and never give you any trouble." In fact, he stressed, his goal was simply to relieve his father wherever possible. Under the weighty burden of this obligation, Howard plunged headlong into his work during the cold opening months of 1903.

In February, Asa Jr. arrived in New York to investigate an attempted purchase of the Witham Mills by a group of New York financiers. Both Asa Sr. and Jr. were skeptical about the proposed deal, which never actually materialized. Nine months earlier, when Billy Witham lost almost $5,000 at the New York Cotton Exchange, Asa Jr. informed his father that if his boss continued to gamble away all the profits, he would have trouble staying in his job. Although shortly before that Witham had won $8,000 at the exchange, Asa Sr. condemned all such speculative involvement as being "wrong regardless of profits or losses." To help his son manage the books, he sent a nephew to Hartwell, but such stopgap measures only emphasized his nagging realization that the "mill investment" was proving to be more of "a nuisance" than a benefit.[60]

For public consumption, Asa blamed the mill's failure on his friend Billy Witham's wasteful practices—not on his namesake's negligence—writing Howard that he was convinced his "brave good boy" had been "standing square and fair and will do his duty." Asa Jr. was no doubt buoyed by his father's outward expressions of trust, yet he must have suspected that such limited praise contained a large dose of condescension, since no one could prove that he did not somehow contribute to the business's downward slide. For the time being, however, Asa Jr. attempted to retain his father's confidence by returning to Hartwell and watching the mill limp along, as the only loser in the ever-expanding Candler financial empire. But all of this would soon be inconsequential when Asa Jr.'s life once again took a different course.

CHAPTER SIX
Creating Families

L ucy Candler and Bill Owens formally announced their engagement in January 1903 and planned to be married in the Candler's new Inman Park home the following spring. Work had been progressing during the fall of '02, and the family hoped to move in February. But as they were packing up, a fire in the furnace of the new house caused extensive smoke damage to walls, woodwork, and some of the furniture already in place. When the fire set the moving date back several months, Lucy decided to postpone her wedding, so she could be married in the mansion. As repairs crept along, Asa complained that "scarcely an hour passes" without having to solve some kind of problem. He even brought Howard into the project, by asking him to visit a New York showroom to investigate a cast-iron fountain for the garden. After visiting the place, Howard reported that the fountain his father had found in a catalogue was "a beautiful thing but rather expensive." Nevertheless, Asa decided to buy it, but not without telling Howard to see if the vendor would lower the price.

Callan Castle, Asa Candler Sr.'s home in Inman Park, photograph by John Sumner

By April 1903, the Candlers were finally able to move into their new fourteen-thousand-foot classical red-brick home, and two months later they displayed all of its finery to five-hundred members of the community attending the marriage of their daughter. The estate—named "Callan Castle" after the Candler family's legendary ancestral home in County Kilkenny, Ireland—announced Asa's entry into the city's upper crust. This message was reinforced when guests entered through a portico supported by six Ionic columns and viewed stained-glass windows on either side of the front doorway bearing the Candler coat of arms: a tricolored shield with an angel perched over six horses and the Latin inscription "Ad Mortem Fidelis." Above their heads in the grand entrance hall hung a huge light fixture, illuminated by sixty-four bulbs. Since only 10 percent of Atlanta's homes had electricity in 1903, Asa's lavish display proclaimed itself as a modern marvel. All of the wood-paneled doors on the ground floor were flung open, so guests could wander into the parlor, music room, library, and dining room, admiring the specially ordered stained-glass windows and see the stairway with the stained-glass portrait of Lucy Elizabeth in her garden, transferred from Seaboard Avenue. As they strolled through the house, visitors noticed the ceilings plastered by hand with rosettes surrounding specially designed electric chandeliers, shaded for the occasion in green and white silk and festooned with white roses, sweet peas, and carnations.

Some of the wedding guests wandered out to the large veranda circling two sides of the house and several strolled through the gardens, where the cast-iron fountain Howard purchased in New York created a stunning focal point. A few people even went behind the house to see the smaller version of Asa's "miniature farm," replete with a vegetable patch, chickens, and a cow. Others might have been allowed down in the complete basement with its bowling alley and steam room for drying clothes indoors, copied from a similar one in George Vanderbilt's Biltmore estate in Asheville. None, however, could get into the large basement vault, where it was rumored Asa kept the secret Coca-Cola formula.

Promptly at nine, Bishop Warren Candler entered the front parlor and stood under a canopy of roses and smilax, awaiting the slowly approaching groomsmen in tuxedos and bridesmaids in white dresses with wide green sashes. Howard was Bill's best man, and Laura Witham, the daughter of Asa Jr.'s boss, was maid of honor. Then on her father's arm came Lucy, looking radiant in a white satin gown trimmed in lace and embroidered in pearls. A reporter for the *Atlanta Constitution* described her as "one of the most beautiful young women in the city," who "has by her gracious and attractive manner endeared herself to a large circle of friends." Her groom, the writer continued, "is one of the most popular young businessmen in Atlanta."

The next day Asa wrote Florence, who was spending time with her sister in Philadelphia: "The wedding is over. My girl is gone and I am feeling blue." Not only was he depressed over his daughter's departure, but he was upset because he had no idea where Lucy and Bill were going for their honeymoon. They had no doubt kept their destination a secret, fearing that her father might well decide to join them. Without knowing their whereabouts, Asa told his sister, he would just have to pray for their rapid return. When the couple did come back to Atlanta, after touring the northeastern United States for two weeks, they moved into the family's new Elizabeth Street home, a decision probably mandated by Asa Candler. Although it's less common today for newlyweds to live with their parents—especially if there was no financial need to do so—it was a common practice in the Southeast at that time and definitely a tradition among the Candlers, since Asa, Warren, and John had each taken their brides to their mother's home after they married.[61]

The wedding of his younger sister prompted Howard into action. A short time afterward, he announced his engagement to Flora Glenn. For several months, he had been growing increasingly anxious to return to Atlanta. Not only was Flora constantly on his mind, but he missed being part of family activities. During March, he once again complained about the deleterious effects of New York weather on his health, and, as usual, his father responded by telling him to buck up. During a recent visit to New York, Asa Jr. reported that his brother was not only in good health but was looking better than he had in years. This tidbit of sibling rivalry did little to ameliorate Howard's stress.

He had already pleaded with his father to send a replacement to manage the office, or at least hire an office boy to perform some of his many chores. Then he added an admission that provides an insightful glimpse into the workings of his mind. "I really enjoy the office part of the work," he wrote, "but I don't like to have to be sociable with the trade such as is demanded to a certain extent here. I mean that the salesman for an article has to go in frequently and talk to a proprietor" or the "Soda-men and clerks. I don't like that." Most tellingly, he told his father: "I am more anxious to please you and that is now my whole object ... I would never be baby enough to just lay down and let you do the work, my big regret is that I can't do all of it."

That plea seems to have worked. Asa Sr. soon decided that since there was no one to run the shipping department in Atlanta, he thought his eldest son might like the job. Without hesitation Howard accepted, confessing once again: "I will never be satisfied in New York" and "I feel that I can be of more aid to you at home than here." He remained in Manhattan only long enough to familiarize his replacement with the routine, and in the middle of April, he boarded the Seaboard-Airline train to return home for good.[62]

Following several weeks of entertainment by friends and family, Howard married Flora on the evening of December 4, 1903, at the Glenn's Edgewood Avenue home. In many ways, the wedding duplicated Lucy's nuptials six months earlier, except that the guest list was smaller. The color scheme was the same green and white, the bridesmaids wore white with green sashes, and once more Bishop Warren Candler presided. Two days later, while the newlyweds were honeymooning in New York, Asa wrote a letter to his son and new daughter-in-law. "Dear Children," he began:

> The new daughter takes in her keeping the <u>well being</u> and to a very large degree the well-doing of my first child. My <u>Man</u>, oh how vividly my mind recalls the moment of his arrival <u>here</u> a dear little body which I quickly discovered was faultless … I thank God that he has been allowed to grow into physical manhood and now taken unto himself a Christian girl to share his successes, to lean on in sorrow or apparent failing … He has ever been dutiful and devoted to [his parents] … and they have delighted in doing by God's grace all for him that in this finite nature they have been capable … We wish for you on this first "trial trip" together—a pleasant recreation and safe return. We want you to come to this home that was our boys' home and shall be yours as much and as often as you will.[63]

As is obvious in this letter, Asa was pleased with his son's choice of wives. Not only was she the daughter of a well-known Methodist minister, but her parents were close friends and neighbors. What more could he want for his "faultless" boy? In the warmth of Howard's pleasing marriage, he once again showed his approval of his dutiful eldest son. But satisfaction with his new daughter-in-law did not dispel Asa's parsimony. When Howard found himself short of money during their New York honeymoon, he withdrew a fifty-dollar draft from the Coca-Cola Company account at the Western National Bank. After his return to Atlanta, Howard discovered that he would be paying it back by having ten dollars docked from his salary for the next five weeks. Another deviation from paternal expectations was his living arrangements, for as acquiescent as Howard was to most of his father's requests, he did not obey Asa's pleas that he and his bride reside in the family homestead. Instead, the couple moved into the Glenn's home, a few blocks away from Callan Castle.

Candler family, 1903 (front row) Asa Jr., Helen, Asa Sr., Lucy Elizabeth holding baby Lucy Magill Candler, William; (second and third rows, left to right) Walter, Bill Owens, Lucy Candler Owens, unnamed friend, Flora, Howard, courtesy of Millennium Gate Museum, Atlanta, Georgia

One warm afternoon in June 1904, Asa dashed out of the Coca-Cola Building on Edgewood Avenue to catch the Inman Park trolley. In his haste, he jumped across a ditch where workmen had been laying pipe and found himself in the path of an oncoming streetcar. The motorman tried to apply the brakes, but they didn't hold. Fortunately Asa jumped back just in the nick of time and was spared being crushed beneath the trolley's metal wheels. He may have been rushing home to check on his daughter, who was expecting a baby momentarily. Four days after that near accident, Lucy produced a healthy girl named Elizabeth Candler Owens, giving her the first name of her grandmother, which also happened to be the name of street where the family lived. Only two days after the birth of Lucy's daughter, Helen and Asa Jr. had a son, and much to the delight of his grandfather, they named the baby Asa Griggs Candler III. Then three months later, Howard's wife Flora delivered their first child, Charles Howard Candler Jr. Suddenly, Callan Castle was brimming with life. The upstairs had ample space for Lucy, Bill, and baby Elizabeth; fourteen-year-old William (still attending the nearby Donald Fraser School); and nineteen-year-old Walter, who spent part of the year in Oxford, attending Emory College. But the joys of the growing family were soon to be marred by tragedy. [64]

In early January 1905, an ice storm paralyzed Atlanta and all of north Georgia. With frozen trees crashing onto phone and power lines, Asa Jr., Helen, and their two children—Lucy, almost three, and little Asa, seven months old—were totally isolated in their cold, dark Hartwell home. As the storm grew worse, and their house grew increasingly frigid, the baby developed a high fever and cough. With the roads like skating rinks and all phone lines down, Asa Jr. and Helen had no way to obtain medical help when the usual remedies of alcohol rubs and ice failed to bring down the baby's temperature. Although the frantic couple did everything they could, his condition steadily worsened, and within hours the boy was dead.

Having no telephone, telegraph, or even postal service, they could not inform the other Candlers about the tragedy. All they could do was take the train to Atlanta and board the trolley to Inman Park from Terminal Station. Asa got word (probably from a station master) that his son and family were traveling to his house on the streetcar, so in happy anticipation, he drove his horse and buggy up the few blocks to the car shed to await their arrival. To his horror, he saw Helen and her daughter descending the steps, followed by Asa Jr. carrying a tiny homemade coffin. Losing his namesake—who had only weeks earlier been a strong, healthy baby—was such a tremendous blow to Asa that every family photograph made during the next decade included someone holding a portrait of the deceased baby.

Devastated by the loss of their infant son, the young couple wasted no time in having another. In December 1905, nine months after the death of Asa III, Helen delivered a healthy boy named John Howard Candler. Around the same time, Asa Jr.'s predictions were confirmed, when Billy Witham finally gambled away all the mill's profits on the Cotton Exchange, allowing the company to sink into excessive debt and ultimate bankruptcy. Since there was no future for him in Hartwell, Asa Jr. brought his family back to Atlanta, and by early 1906 they were settled into a temporary residence on North Jackson Street.[65]

By the time Asa Jr. returned to town, his father had already found the right niche for him. Never one to sit by and watch others make more money than he did, Asa Sr. decided in early 1904 that he wanted to capitalize on Atlanta's booming commercial real estate market, since he already owned a fair amount of residential property. For that purpose, he formed the Candler Investment Company and made Asa Jr. supervisor of real estate purchases. In the days before the federal government regulated businesses, the Candlers were allowed to borrow funds from Coca-Cola to buy stock in the new real estate corporation. Asa distributed the shares to himself, his two oldest sons, three nephews, and a few employees.

As soon as he organized the new company, Asa Sr. moved on an idea that he had been hatching for several months. A man of his wealth and stature, he decided, should erect the city's tallest skyscraper. With that in mind, he bought an elevated site at the intersection of Peachtree, Pryor, and Houston Streets, then occupied by the First Methodist Church. Deciding to hire numerous people to carry out specific duties during construction, he appointed his official builder, George Murphy, to be both architect and contractor, and Howard to act as project coordinator. But they would have little real authority, since Asa made it clear that he planned to approve every design and choose all materials. While workmen were boring holes into the granite-laden ground for the first steel beams, he proved his determination to control the project by traveling to the quarries in Cherokee County and personally selecting the marble to adorn part of the façade and interior.

Upon learning that the Fourth National Bank rising nearby would also be sixteen stories tall, Asa sent Murphy back to the drawing board even though the blueprints were completed. Obviously, he decided, they would have to add another floor to make his skyscraper the city's highest. Although this change of plans slowed down the job somewhat, the building was ready for occupancy two years later. During construction, Candler informed the local newspapers that he would open his own bank, the Central Bank and Trust, on the building's ground floor. When he released that information, he said emphatically that he would not preside over the new institution. However, before long he changed his mind and announced that he intended to be its president, appointing his son-in-law Bill Owens to be assistant cashier, and he promised Walter the same position after he graduated from Emory.

Candler Building, Atlanta, entrance, photograph by John Sumner

The local papers carried full sections describing details of the gleaming white Candler Building, which opened formally on February 5, 1906, with alarms in the bank vaults clanging in celebration. Crowds surged through the brass, plate-glass, and bronze doors, only to see they were standing in an unfinished lobby cluttered with debris and building material. However, they bypassed this mess to enter the shining and clean Central Bank and Trust, with large floral arrangements in the tellers' cages circling the marble interior. Even the "armor plate steel" vaults were thrown open for viewing. So sensitive were the alarms leading to the safes that ladies had to remove their hats, lest a hatpin set them off. In the bank's rotunda, Asa Candler, outfitted in his customary cutaway jacket and vest, welcomed city officials and Atlanta socialites, dressed in their finery, inviting them to enjoy refreshments before touring the still-unfinished building.

If the visitors chose not to ride the six electrically operated elevators, they could walk up the grand marble staircase. On their way, they were invited to admire the busts of Sam and Martha Candler, placed not far from the panoply of Confederate heroes and famous Georgians. Outside, they could stare up at the themed friezes that surround the façade, carved by Florentine, French, and British sculptors. These individual reliefs depict everything from natural history, invention, and agriculture to the arts, literature, and the Wild West, each centered with busts of men who had distinguished themselves in those fields. Among these historical notables—which still grace the building's façade today—are artists Michelangelo and Raphael, authors William Shakespeare and Sir Walter Scott, musicians Richard Wagner and Ludwig von Beethoven, and founding father Benjamin Franklin. Other panels feature American celebrities from Candler's own time: Admiral George Dewey, showman Buffalo Bill, industrial giant Cyrus McCormick, astronomer Sir John Herschel, architect Henry C. Hunt, painter Edwin Austin Abbey, and sculptor J. Q. A. Ward.

The eclectic character of these sculptural tributes—personally planned and authorized by Asa Candler—turned his building's staircase and lower exterior into a confection of early twentieth-century trends and tastes, as he interpreted them. His decision to place this assortment of recent newsmakers alongside iconic historical figures tells a great deal about his preferences and tastes and also serves as a demonstration of his acquired knowledge, erudition, and high principles. The grand staircase displays his adherence to the Ten Commandments (honoring his parents) and loyalty to the state, region, and the South's "Lost Cause." The outdoor friezes represent the veneer of learning that Asa had acquired through years of reading historical tomes, along with his reverence for industrial pioneers and notorious adventurers. Atlanta's then-tallest skyscraper thus rose as a self-devised tribute to the city's most successful entrepreneur. The short country boy, with only a rudimentary education, now soared over the city, tall, elegant, and grandiose.[66]

As Asa Sr.'s real estate empire began its lucrative climb, he and his namesake moved forward to purchase and develop a variety of downtown properties. It was a perfect combination of entrepreneurial talents, for with Asa Sr.'s business acumen and Asa Jr.'s willingness to take risks, the Candler Investment Company thrived. Now comfortable in his new role, the younger Asa Candler made up his mind—as his father had done two decades earlier—to attract the public's attention. However, his first attempt to make the headlines fizzled. In June 1906, he announced his candidacy to be Fourth Ward representative on the Atlanta Board of Aldermen. But a few weeks later, after a long list of well-known Atlantans also entered the race, he withdrew.[67] This does not mean that he was shrinking into the background; rather, Asa Candler Jr. was merely stepping back and searching for other ways to gain recognition.

While his son was searching to make a name for himself, Asa Sr. was beginning to disengage from management of Coca-Cola, even though he retained the title of president and continued to offer opinions on every major transaction. His position as bank president had so delighted him that Asa moved his main office to the Candler Building and set about reorganizing the Coca-Cola hierarchy. In 1906, Howard took over as vice president in charge of manufacturing, a step long anticipated. Coincidental with this promotion, Howard also improved his domestic standing, when he and Flora moved out of the Glenn's home and into one of their own, about a block away from his parents on Elizabeth Street. Like his father, he personally chose the best materials for his house, specially selected Georgia marble for the foundation, tongue-and-groove heart pine for the exterior siding, and an elaborate stained-glass panel for the stairway. Shortly after they moved into the new home, Flora gave birth to their second child, a daughter named Catherine Harper Candler.

In his new position as Coca-Cola vice president, Howard began his own reordering of the company, establishing a Traffic Department to organize shipments, monitor transit, and generally coordinate the transportation of syrup from plant to soda fountain. Because Robinson, now well into middle age, was ready to relinquish some of his responsibilities, Asa released him from running the sales department and turned that job over to his nephew, Sam Dobbs. This switch—coupled with Howard's dislike for meeting the public—created the perfect opportunity for the outgoing Sam to act as company spokesman, often upstaging his uncle. From his lofty perch, the aggressive younger man began edging himself into Robinson's former territory by engaging his friend Bill D'Arcy of St. Louis to manage the lucrative Coca-Cola advertising account. After D'Arcy took over, the ads changed again. Now appealing, yet glamorous, beauties and well-known celebrities participated in folksy vignettes centered on enjoyment of the refreshing beverage.

Asa Sr. was actually glad to remove himself from the daily operations of Coca-Cola, because the company was undergoing increased inspections by federal authorities, egged on by muckraking journalists and authors pressing for reform, the best known being Upton Sinclair. When politicians jumped on the bandwagon, Congress voted in June 1906 to pass the Pure Food and Drug Act. A principal catalyst for this legislation was Dr. Harvey W. Wiley, longtime head chemist for the United States Department of Agriculture. In his zealous pursuit of tainted products, Wiley dispatched what soon came to be known as a "poison squad." Well aware that these inspectors had targeted Coca-Cola for scrutiny, the company completely removed saccharin and cocaine from the formula. It also changed its advertising to emphasize such words as "pure" and "healthy." Nevertheless Wiley—who rivaled Asa Candler's in missionary ardor—further intensified his moral crusade against the Atlanta beverage maker.[68]

Now that Asa Sr. had emerged as one of Atlanta's most prominent citizens, he found himself playing a key role when the city erupted into chaos. Tensions between whites and blacks had been simmering for decades, exacerbated by implementation of strict Jim Crow laws that paralleled the rise of a substantial black middle class centered on Auburn Avenue and in the neighborhoods surrounding Atlanta University. Further inflaming the situation was the heated rhetoric accompanying the gubernatorial campaign between two Atlanta newspapermen: right-leaning Hoke Smith (publisher of the *Atlanta Journal*) and slightly more liberal Clark Howell (editor of the *Constitution*). With the support of renegade politician Tom Watson, Smith won by a landslide, giving license to an upsurge of racial discontent.

On the night of Saturday, September 22, 1906, everything exploded. Mobs of white men stormed into shops and saloons, slaughtering two barbers in an African American barbershop, before forging on to the Union Depot shouting their intention to "kill every damned nigger in the town." Echoing Lucy Candler's similar but private comment several years earlier, this endemic animosity was the prevailing sentiment among whites. At the station, the gang dragged a black Pullman porter from the train, beat him mercilessly, and left him on the ground for dead. In an attempt to quell tempers—ostensibly aimed at protecting "negro" victims—a white military regiment took over the city's center during the night. Meanwhile, African American leaders were reacting to the carnage by organizing a meeting in suburban Brownsville to express their fears and declare their rights. An assembly of angry "negroes" was sure to get a rapid response from the community, and to no one's surprise, a posse of policemen from the all-white force charged into the outdoor gathering and arrested numerous participants. On their way back into town, one of the white officers was shot and killed, only inciting the mobs to further violence. Rampaging through downtown, an enraged white hoard dragged innocent blacks from streetcars and away from their jobs in hotels and restaurants. Upon hearing that an African American man standing on Marietta Street had accosted a white woman, the mob threw him to the ground and shot him, while police nearby ignored the turmoil. In response to this and other unwarranted attacks, blacks began throwing stones and randomly shooting into crowds, further terrifying whites and creating additional mayhem. When the city finally calmed down after three days of violence, the official tally (probably far too low) estimated the death of ten blacks and two whites, with sixty blacks and ten whites wounded.

On Tuesday morning following the weekend debacle, about two hundred civic and religious leaders—including a group of black ministers and newspapermen—gathered at the Chamber of Commerce room in City Hall to assess the damages. Just as the meeting opened, a cacophony of voices began demanding that all saloons serving Negroes have their licenses revoked. Asa Candler was one of the first to chime in. "We are talking too much," he yelled over the din. "Every rumor we hear we repeat on the street." Then he told a story about seeing a young white boy "with a big pistol buckled around him," the sight of which made him decide that "these things do not tend to preserve peace, and we should not blame the poor, weak, and ignorant portion of our population with all of this trouble." Although today that statement seems fraught with racial stereotyping, Candler's comments were a remarkable call for moderation, given the atmosphere of racial hatred that shrouded the city.

That same afternoon, Asa joined a committee of businessmen, clergy, and manufacturers to petition the Georgia Superior Court to request closure of all "dives, restaurants, saloons, pool and club rooms frequented by negroes." After hearing a chorus of complaints about "the dens of vice and idleness," the court passed the measure unanimously. With that accomplished, Candler jumped to his feet and waved his hand in the air, insisting that the proposition was too narrow. Instead of just shutting down saloons frequented by negroes, the city should eliminate every bar in town. "We are trustees of this great nation," he shouted. "There is never a time in our life when we should not try to govern ourselves with Christian righteousness." Repeating his call to quell the rumors, he welcomed the support of several black clergymen, who shared his plea for stopping all liquor service in public places. It was a rare moment of racial accord.[69]

Such harmony, however, was short-lived, and the ministers were rewarded for their cooperation with a gradual tightening of racial divisions, followed by legislation to make the city's whites feel more secure. The Candlers were no exception. The *Atlanta Constitution* reported two months after the riots: "For the past few days it has been noticed that instead of negro men cleaning and scrubbing up the stone floors of the magnificent [Candler] building, there are white women and men." Asa Jr.—speaking as manager of the real estate company—refused to comment, although he did admit that they were trying out some new white laborers.[70] Despite Asa Sr.'s willingness to join forces with members of the black community in time of crisis, this small retreat indicates that, like the rest of Atlanta's business establishment, he was cautious about personal contact with African Americans in the workplace.

However Asa's crusade to shut down alcoholic sales did prevail. Shortly over a year after the riot, *all* Atlanta saloons and *all* liquor dealerships were permanently closed. But that wasn't all. Blaming the riot on excessive consumption of alcohol, the Georgia Legislature voted for statewide prohibition. Then, much to Candler's distress, his crusade backfired when the state senate placed Coca-Cola on the list of outlawed beverages. Convinced that crooked "liquor men in the Legislature" were to blame for that decision, he told his brother that ultimately the company has nothing to fear, even though "these villains are able to suborn witnesses, doctors and others who will charge evil against Coca-Cola."[71] He needn't have worried. When prohibition became a state law—one that remained in place for the next six decades—Coca-Cola was not listed among the forbidden beverages. In fact, with liquor, wine, and beer no longer sold in Georgia, consumption of Coca-Cola increased dramatically, thus adding to the Candlers' already bulging coffers and giving rise to the suspicion that Asa's initial call for total prohibition was not founded entirely on his religious convictions.

This resolution by the state legislature and the rhetoric accompanying it did have negative repercussions for the Coca-Cola Company, when the federal government intensified its probe into the beverage's damaging effects. Based on Asa Sr.'s statement during the IRS trial of 1901, the US Army banned the soft drink on hearing that the syrup still contained a small amount of cocaine, a misconception that triggered a five-month loss of military sales and precipitated a plunge in the company's profits. Reacting to the army's detrimental decision, John Candler—who had resigned from the Georgia Supreme Court after ten years on the bench to become Coca-Cola's chief legal advisor—sent federal authorities a chemical analysis conducted by an independent researcher that proved all traces of the narcotic had been removed. Based on this report, the army lifted its ban, and within a few months the company recouped its losses.

In her luxurious Inman Park home, Lucy Elizabeth Candler was starting to enjoy the benefits of her husband's phenomenal success. Although she never lost her quiet, modest demeanor or dislike of excessive ostentation, her children and close friends were pulling her into the social scene. That meant attending and hosting teas and receptions or doing volunteer work for the Inman Park Methodist Church and the YWCA. During the summers, she began to travel on extended vacations with her daughter and little Elizabeth, leaving their husbands behind to work in the heat. In 1905, they went to the Hotel Continental in Atlantic Beach, Florida. When not relaxing by the sea, they visited with friends, who were staying at the same hotel or living in the vicinity. Two years later, they vacationed at the De Soto Hotel in Savannah. Even though the Georgia coastal city was warmer than she would have liked, Lucy preferred it to Florida, she wrote Bill, especially when they wandered around to shops and occasionally purchased a "good Coca-Cola and chewing gum." From Savannah, they went by sea to New York to spend several additional weeks. Even though Lucy was now a wife and mother, she was as vivacious and talkative as she had been as a young girl, meeting people easily and finding ways to enjoy herself wherever she ended up.

Shortly before that journey, she and her mother had hosted an afternoon reception to honor one of Lucy's in-laws and their visitors. Once more Callan Castle was bedecked with palms, ferns, and a profusion of flowers, while a small orchestra played in the dining room. Serving punch on that April afternoon was a young lady named Eugenia Bingham, Walter Candler's girlfriend. Daughter of a Methodist minister, "Genie" was a graceful beauty, with an interest in music that she shared with several members of the Candler family.[72]

Two months after his mother's tea, Walter received a bachelor's degree from Emory College, but like Asa Jr., he had failed to receive top honors, although he did well enough during his four years in Oxford to make the D.V.S. Honor society and gain the "Speaker's Place" in 1904 and 1905. Most of all he had plunged himself wholeheartedly into various campus activities, including the MIE Social Club and the Kappa Alpha fraternity, as well as the intramural football and track teams. He left college with such a love of Emory that he later helped found the school's first alumni association and remained an active participant for the remainder of his life. The December after his graduation, Walter and Eugenia married. It was a repetition of his siblings' weddings, except that the ceremony took place at the Trinity Methodist Church, and instead of the traditional long white gown, the bride wore a pale blue "cloth tailored" gown trimmed with white and gold braid. Following the ceremony, Walter took his new wife on a short wedding trip before they set up housekeeping on North

Jackson Street. Five months later, the couple's first child, Walter Turner Candler Jr. was born.[73]

Shortly before the birth of that baby, Asa Candler Jr. and Helen had another daughter named Laura, born on Christmas Eve 1907. Now a respectable businessman and the father of three children, he moved his family into a large house on Euclid Avenue in Inman Park, described by an Atlanta reporter as "one of the most beautiful of the palatial homes in the city." All the while, Asa Jr. was attempting to get his name in the papers, once more announcing a second run for the Board of Aldermen. But again his hopes were dashed, this time by losing in the Democratic primary. Not deterred by the setback and still determined to be noticed, he joined the Atlanta Automobile and Good Roads Association. During its first meeting during the summer of '07, he was elected the organization's treasurer.[74] His fascination with cars would soon win the young man the recognition he sought.

Walter T. Candler, 1907, courtesy of Manuscript, Archives, and Rare Book Library, Emory University

As Asa Jr. was looking for his own niche in Atlanta, his father was establishing his credentials as one of the city's leading philanthropists. Although Asa Sr. could be extremely parsimonious when it came to doling out money to his children, he was the opposite where charities were concerned. As soon as he began reaping the profits from Coca-Cola, he gave liberally to various Methodist projects, beginning with a large contribution for the First Methodist Church to relocate after the Candler Building dislodged it from its downtown home. At the same time, he became one of the principal benefactors of the Wesley Memorial Hospital, sponsored by the Methodist Episcopal Church, South. Then, in 1906, Emory's Board of Trustees chose him to be chairman, since he had already demonstrated his charitable generosity and shrewd investment management as head of its finance committee. Chairmanship of Emory's trustees began a longtime close association of Asa Candler—a man who never attended college—with the school's financial well-being.

Sometime his altruism meant rescuing troubled businesses. That notion first came to him during October 1907, when a shortage of cash in New York banks precipitated an economic panic. Worried that the crisis would distress the Atlanta real estate market, Asa announced that he would purchase any house threatened with foreclosure for its value *before* the recession began. In addition, he allowed the owners to remain in their residences, as long as they paid him rent. When the panic subsided, Candler found himself landlord of at least 250 small dwellings, which he subsequently sold back to the original residents, or to prospective buyers, for a cash deposit of 10 percent, the rest to be paid in one hundred monthly installments. It was a brilliant combination of business acumen and humanitarianism, since in the long run Asa profited from his investment, and for the short run he helped thousands of people.

Then two days before Christmas, the Neal Bank—a respected local institution—informed customers that it had turned all of its assets over to the state bank examiner. Atlantans soon learned that the bank had overstretched its capital by borrowing money to purchase properties in Alabama and Cuba, which left it with no resources for repaying its creditors. This collapsing house of cards (that would be repeated with slight variations in the century to come) was troublesome for investors, especially as crowds of dismayed customers, swarming around the locked doors of the Neal's office, incited alarm that the city was on the verge of a catastrophic run on banks. It was at this point that Asa G. Candler came to the rescue.

On Christmas Day, he dramatically announced that he would take over the failed bank as "a kind of Santa Claus gift" to the nine thousand frightened investors, advising depositors "to be patient," because they would soon "reap the reward of their self denial." Most of all, he promised that within thirty days customers would not only recover all of their money, but they stood to gain a possible increase of 10 percent. Asa Sr. spent a good part of the Christmas holidays working with bank officials to put matters in order, and during the next year, state regulators cleared the way for the Central Bank and Trust to acquire all of the Neal's holdings. Although it took several months to settle matters, Candler was able to begin paying the depositors in stages, and ultimately he reimbursed them all, with some actually receiving a bonus. Again this heroic rescue was not entirely unselfish. By taking over the assets of the Neal Bank, the Candlers received a chunk of valuable property in Atlanta, Alabama, and Cuba.[75]

Early one autumn day in 1908, Asa and his nephew Sam Dobbs embarked on a business trip to New Jersey that included a motorized jaunt with a local advertising man to Atlantic City, where all would attend a meeting with Coca-Cola salesmen and wholesale druggists. They were riding happily along until they hit a problem caused by a high coastal tide that had flooded the roads. With the nervous company president urging him to keep going, the reluctant driver ploughed through a deep puddle, warily watching the water creep closer to the car's hood. It didn't take long for the rising current to kill the carburetor, meaning the car was literally stuck in the mud. For an hour and a half, they were stranded on the country road, waiting for the tide to ebb enough for the carburetor to dry out. When they finally succeeded in pulling the car out of the muck, the "Coca-Cola King" and his companions chugged onward toward Atlantic City, arriving when the scheduled meeting was almost over. Undaunted, Asa strutted into the hall and was greeted by loud welcoming cheers from the assembled body, which rose to hail their company's "Big Chief."

Nothing could stop the indefatigable Candler in any difficult situation, and he relished in that reputation. In fact, he and his namesake had little regard for the quagmires that might hinder their progress as they moved aggressively to purchase large swaths of downtown Atlanta for the Candler Investment Company. During February and March of 1908, for example, they bought a theater, seven stores, and an office building. Under Asa Jr.'s daring oversight—tempered by his father's scrupulous supervision—the Candlers were becoming synonymous with high-profile real estate trading, especially after they sold the theater for a profit and used the proceeds to reimburse former Neal Bank customers. The Atlanta Chamber of Commerce rewarded Asa Sr. for his growing prominence as the city's foremost businessman and leading philanthropist by electing him its president. That job, which he assumed in early 1908, provided the perfect platform for him to demonstrate his dedication to his hometown. Within weeks of taking office, Candler became the organization's most active and vocal advocate for completing the city auditorium—then being slowly, and not so efficiently, constructed. As a result of his diligence in directing this and other civic projects, the Chamber of Commerce selected him to preside for another year.

His second term as Chamber president began with a flurry of activity surrounding the visit of William Howard Taft in early 1909. To arrange details of this Chamber-sponsored event, Asa and a few other city officials visited the president-elect at his vacation retreat near Augusta, Georgia. They "were charmed with Mr. Taft's democratic manner, his unaffected personality, his cordiality, his sunny smile, and his tactful way of making them feel perfectly at ease," the men told the *Atlanta Constitution*. During their one-hour conversation, Taft asked to meet personally with a group of Atlantans, including "members of the leading negro organizations," who had requested a short session with the incoming president. When Taft arrived at the Union Depot a few weeks later, Asa led the delegation to meet his party. For the first time in Atlanta history, a covey of automobiles—not carriages—escorted a visiting dignitary around the city. A photograph appearing in *Leslie's Weekly* pictured Candler in the flag-draped car, his small frame dwarfed by the enormous president-elect.

The highlight of Taft's visit was a banquet at the almost-completed Atlanta Auditorium Armory. Waiters bearing large platters of roasted Georgia possum walked up a center aisle and placed the treat before the affable, portly guest of honor. As toastmaster, Asa Candler introduced the Reverend J. W. Lee, pastor of the Trinity AME Church, who sang a song about the possum in vernacular typical of the period. In response, Taft told the sold-out audience that he immensely enjoyed his first taste of the southern delicacy. Then as Candler launched into a lengthy address, he suddenly paused, seeming momentarily disoriented. People in the audience wriggled in their seats, wondering if the Chamber president was ill. But it was nothing like that, Asa later explained. As he was facing the huge crowd, he experienced a poignant moment of *déjà vu*, during which he saw himself as a young officer in the Governor's Horse Guard, standing

116

sentinel outside the hall where President Grover Cleveland was speaking at a similar banquet. Now, two decades later, he was an important city leader addressing a prestigious assembly in the civic auditorium he had spurred along to completion.[76] One thing was certain: the boy from Villa Rica had come a long way.

CHAPTER SEVEN
Visions of Grandeur

Asa Candler's newest endeavor as city benefactor started during the late spring of 1908 in the guise of helping his old friend Joel Hurt, the developer of Inman Park. Eighteen years earlier, Hurt had established the Kirkwood Land Company and through it purchased a huge tract of rolling terrain east of the city limits that he called Druid Hills. To design the suburban area, Hurt engaged the renowned landscape architect Frederick Law Olmsted, and although Olmsted's health was declining, he agreed to make preliminary drawings. Following his plan, which called for a wide boulevard divided by a chain of parks, the developer began installing essential utility lines and clearing the land for the major artery, Ponce de Leon Avenue, named after a popular spring, farther east on the same road. At that time, the landscape architect was spending a great deal of time in Asheville, where he was designing the grounds of George Vanderbilt's Biltmore Estate. Olmsted and Hurt selected rare specimens of shrubbery and trees from the flora ordered for Biltmore to plant throughout Druid Hills. But even before Olmsted died in 1903, Hurt realized that his new venture was costing more than he had anticipated, a worry exacerbated by investors pushing him to speed up sales to offset the expenses of developing the infrastructure.[77]

Sinking deeper and deeper into debt, Hurt finally decided that the only way out was to sell Kirkwood and all of its holdings. When Asa Candler got word that Hurt was offering the property for sale, he agreed to pay an unprecedented $500,000 for it, and the deal was finalized. It was the largest real estate transaction ever to have taken place in Atlanta. Candler's contract not only allowed Hurt to keep two mules and a wagon, but it granted him limited permission to dig up a prescribed number of the landscape specimens from unsold lots, as long as the removal did not "mar the beauty or value of any of the plantations."[78] As chairman of the new syndicate, Candler immediately accelerated installation of sewers, water pipes, and utility lines. In the early twentieth century, most Atlanta streets were still composed of compacted dirt, and the few that were paved were topped with expensive and impractical cobblestones. So when Candler announced that Ponce de Leon Avenue would be covered with macadam, then a mixture of stones and cement, the novel paving innovation distinguished Druid Hills from Atlanta's dustier suburbs, which were less accommodating to newfangled motorcars.

In another departure from custom, the Druid Hills board of directors, which Asa largely controlled, decided at its inception not to exclude religious minorities, as so many other neighborhoods were doing. Therefore, many Jewish families built homes in Druid Hills and lived there comfortably during the first half of the twentieth century. This decision to avoid overt anti-Semitism during an era when it was so prevalent sheds an interesting light on Asa Candler's determination to differ from other prominent Atlantans, despite (or perhaps because of) his devout Christianity.[79] However, his open-mindedness did not apply to African Americans, who—in conformity with prevailing southern customs—could only live in a Druid Hills home if they were servants.

Asa's brother John built the first house in the new suburb, on a four-acre lot at the corner of Ponce de Leon Avenue and Williams Mill Road (now Briarcliff). His first wife, Lula, had died several years earlier, and when he remarried Florrie Anderson, the couple wanted to start their new lives in a house of their own. By the summer of 1908, John's one-story red brick bungalow was under construction. Unfortunately, the project was delayed when a raging fire swept through the neighborhood, threatening devastation. Asa and his brother Warren, who owned land across the road from John, rushed to the scene and grabbed branches to beat back the flames. Finally, firemen were able to quell the blaze, saving John's house and barn just in the nick of time. Within hours, mounted policemen picked up two eight-year-old boys, who admitted starting the blaze.

Warren hoped to begin building his own home right away but was worried about the cost. So to help him out, Asa devised a plan. He would buy his brother's present home in Inman Park "at a minimum price," allowing Warren to build the new residence for less than $6,000. After the old house sold, he said, Warren would probably emerge with a profit, which he could use to repay the loan. Asa's assistance to Florence ran along similar lines: he helped his sister manage her expenses but rarely gave her money outright. Instead, he charged rent for her Inman Park house (which he had purchased) and lent her money from time to time, making certain she repaid every penny.[80] In short, when Asa—by far the wealthiest of the siblings—aided his brothers and sisters, he followed the same plan that he had devised to assist his city. At first glance, the idea of bestowing loans instead of gifts seems to demonstrate the Coca-Cola president's parsimonious nature, but perhaps by avoiding outright charity, he was allowing his siblings to maintain their dignity.

A decisive incident in Asa Candler's life happened during the early months of 1909, when he was traveling on an extensive vacation with Lucy Elizabeth and their son William. Perhaps the brightest of Asa's children, the youngest had been sick much of his life, although his ailments were never specified. His parents blamed poor health for causing William's less-than-stellar performance in the classroom, especially after he reached the upper grades and transferred from one school to another, finally completing his secondary education at the Culver Academy in Indiana. Like his older brothers, William entered Emory College at Oxford, but unlike them, he dropped out before graduation, ostensibly due to illness.[81]

To improve William's health, his parents decided to take him on a Western tour, but as their departure date neared, Asa began having misgivings. Although he almost never traveled for pleasure, Lucy Elizabeth often went away with her daughter, staying months at a time while Asa remained at home to work. Now for the first time *ever*, he would be leaving the office for an extended period, and the very idea terrified him. "I hate to leave Atlanta now, "he wrote Warren. "There are so many matters that no one but myself will or can attend to, and if not done now will never be done." Still, he agreed, "it is best for me to make this little stop now." At the beginning of the trip, Asa had a purpose. In New Orleans, he had been invited to deliver a speech at the city's banquet for William Howard Taft. Not to be outdone by Atlanta's possum feast, the Louisianans served the president-elect their local delicacy, alligator, which Asa ate and seemingly enjoyed. Moving westward, they stopped in San Antonio and El Paso, Texas, and in Prescott, Arizona, their train being met in each city by Coca-Cola executives, who escorted them on tours of the area. During these drives, Asa felt he was engaged in something productive, because as they rode around he could converse with his employee about business matters.

But, even though the same arrangements had been made for Los Angeles, by the time they arrived on the West Coast, Asa had become fidgety and irritated. "Personally I am very impatient to be at home," he told Howard in a letter filled with business matters. "I am doing no good here and so far as I can see, William will get along well now at home." Although the California weather was ideal and the sightseeing pleasurable, by early March all three Candlers were ready to return to Atlanta. Aboard the *California Limited* headed east, Asa complained: "I continue to be idle," he wrote Howard. "Is this really me?"[82] His frustration turned from boredom to panic, when he and William mounted donkeys and descended to the base of the Grand Canyon, leaving Lucy Elizabeth in the comfort of the hotel at the top. Later he admitted that if he had "conceived of the dangers" beforehand, he never would have embarked on the trek. Everything suddenly seemed alien: the path was too narrow, and the upper trail was dangerously coated with snow and ice. "I simply sat paralyzed as we slowly crept down," he recalled. The water below "appeared to be a slow muddy stream of twenty feet width," but as it grew closer, that stream became "a surprising, roaring, deep river nearly a mile wide." On a "great shelf" about halfway down the trail, the thirty-four "ladies and gentlemen in the party" stopped for lunch. All were "strangers to each other," Asa observed, "and no one introduced any one to any one." For a man used to southern courtliness, this kind of rebuff was painful, especially since none of the riders recognized who he was.

As he thought about the excursion the following day, Asa remembered how frustrated he felt upon realizing he was powerless:

> As I rode across the hot plateau and looked up at the wonderful mountain covered with snow 6000 feet high & realized that the only way I and William could ever get back to Mama was up a narrow steep crooked trail, on a little mule's back and that I could not even be allowed to guide him, just patiently sit on his back, not whip him, not scold him, not coax him, not try to tow him, just fold my hands on the horn of the big saddle and trust him implicitly.

And that inability to control the situation was not only terrifying, it caused profound doubts about religion's place in determining the fate of mankind. He wrote in a letter to Howard:

121

> I thought oh why can't I thus tread life's hills, trust God, go on, be
> patient & after awhile reach the high heights and see Him for myself
> ... He has given me so many unmistakable evidences of His ability
> to carry me safely over dangerous places ... Yet I do not trust him
> and may be lost, one slip, one inch wrong by that mule yesterday
> and I would have gone down 3000 to 5000 feet? Think of it, work
> it out. [83]

Was Asa's fright due merely to the potential physical dangers? Was he
questioning his own faith, or was he merely experiencing another flare-up
of his periodic depression? Most likely it was a little of each, coupled with
an element of his makeup that was so basic it overwhelmed him. Having
always taken charge of his business, his family, his known world, he felt
helpless when trapped in an alien place where he was a virtual stranger,
unrecognized and unimportant. Whatever caused the panic attack, that
ride down the canyon triggered a painful moment of introspection—after a
long period of absence from his high-powered activities—revealing a great
deal about Asa G. Candler's concept of himself. On the train rumbling
eastward, he realized that if he could not manage the circumstances of his
surroundings, his whole world would tumble into an abyss deeper than
the Grand Canyon.

When he returned home, Asa heaved a huge sigh of relief. He was back
on his own turf. Visiting other cities, he told a reporter, made him "more
in love with Atlanta than ever." That appreciation of his home triggered
an increased desire to repay the city for his incredible good fortune, but
before he could activate his plans, a bizarre diversion interrupted him. One
morning shortly after he got back to town, a letter appeared in the stack
of daily mail on his desk. Upon opening it, Asa found a crudely written
demand for $35,000 to be left under the steps of the Inman Park Methodist
Church; if Candler failed to follow instructions or told anyone about the
letter, the correspondent threatened that dire consequences would result.
The note was signed with a black handprint, a scare tactic used by a
variety of early twentieth-century American crooks, some affiliated with
a revolutionary movement in Bosnia and Herzegovina. But the letter in
Asa's hand hardly looked like the work of an international terrorist; rather,
it was scribbled in a rough script and postmarked Atlanta.

The roughness of the extortion letter convinced Asa that the culprit
was a local amateur, and he vowed to catch the troublemaker no matter

what it took. Ignoring the note's threatened "most horrible DEATH" for himself and his family if he failed to comply with the demand to remain silent, he immediately informed his sons and notified the police. Then he devised a trap. In the early morning of the scheduled pickup, the Coca-Cola president went by the church, placed a dummy package under the steps, and turned things over to the armed policemen lurking nearby. But when the blackmailer approached to pick up his money, he saw the not-too-well-hidden cops and hastily retreated. Meanwhile all the Candler households remained poised for a possible attack.

But nothing happened until Asa's office phone rang at two o'clock the following afternoon. The would-be extortionist started by asking about the money, and as he talked the voice on the other end sounded vaguely familiar, although Asa couldn't quite place it. Since he had been advised to keep the caller on the line while he signaled someone nearby to summon the police, he stalled the fellow by haggling over the amount to leave. Finally they settled on $5,000, to be dropped off at a location on Moreland Avenue.

"How do I know I won't be shot in the back?" Candler asked.

"I won't harm a hair on your head if you do what I tell you," the voice replied.

"Well," said Candler, "if there is any shooting I am going to be armed, and I'll shoot as quick as you do." By then the police on the line had traced the phone number.

After he hung up, Asa put together a stack of tissue paper doilies folded to resemble money and tied the bundle into a handkerchief. After that, one of America's wealthiest men—who controlled a huge fortune and could easily have afforded a taxi or asked an employee to drive him to the meeting place—walked out of the Candler Building alone and boarded the next trolley headed for Moreland Avenue. A group of plainclothes officers took the next streetcar and followed him to the designated spot. As Asa descended the steps of the trolley, he spotted a young man in denim overalls riding a mule. To lure him on, he waved the package in the air before placing it under a rock, and, with his task completed, Candler jumped on the next trolley and returned to his office.

Up and down the muddy road the mule circled, its rider's eyes fixed on the rock. Meanwhile, the plainclothes policemen hid in a nearby house and waited. Then as the sun began to set, they crept out and crouched behind rose bushes and apple trees, watching cautiously. Finally, the youth leaned down from the mule and reached under the rock. He started unwrapping the bundle just as the policemen emerged from the shrubbery. After questioning the lad and matching his phone number with the one they had traced, the officers clamped on handcuffs and telephoned Candler from a nearby house. Again, the Coca-Cola president returned to the scene on the streetcar, this time accompanied by two of his sons. Since it was dark when they arrived, Asa needed help from the light of a passing trolley to see the boy clearly enough to identify him. The dreaded "black-hander" turned out to be merely one of his Sunday school pupils named Daniel W. Johnson Jr. He thought that voice had sounded familiar!

Now confronted by his teacher, the seventeen-year-old lost his bravado and nervously confessed to writing the letters. As the police led him away, the youth tried to shift the blame by insisting that he was made to write the letter by three intimidating men. However, when the officers grilled him at headquarters, Johnson's story fell apart. Nevertheless, no one had been hurt, so after spending a night in jail, the police released the boy on a $1,000 bond, and he was consigned to the custody of his father, a respectable sand dealer, quarryman, and contractor. In this unceremonious manner, the "black hand" incident fizzled out, with no further investigation and no trial. Nevertheless, page-one of the *Atlanta Constitution* carried the blazing headline: "BLACKHANDER, WHO DEMANDED $35,000, CAUGHT IN TRAP BY ASA G. CANDLER; YOUNG MAN THREATENED TO DYNAMITE RESIDENCE OF THE COCA-COLA KING." That kind of press coverage turned the episode into a southern style melodrama that rivaled those then on the silver screen. Except in this case, the villain was a teenager wearing overalls and riding a scruffy mule, while the hero was a short, feisty tycoon who faced him down with fearless courage.

Despite his valiant stance, Asa Candler and his children learned a valuable lesson from the incident. Less than a year later, another "black hand" extortion letter arrived at his office in the form of two anonymous letters threatening injury or death for members of his family if he failed to leave $20,000 in a designated location. Not in the least rattled, Asa set about reenacting his previous performance by notifying the authorities, placing a decoy package at the prescribed place, and hiring a detective to work with the police. But this time, the would-be extortionist outsmarted his intended victim. His third letter announced that he had seen the "sleuths" patrolling the drop-off point, so if Asa ignored his demands, he would have to slash the phone lines at his Inman Park residence. The next day the phones at Callan Castle went dead. An infuriated Candler decided to set up another trap with a decoy package left at an agreed location. Fortunately the events that followed worked in his favor. Just as he was leaving the Central Bank with the package tucked into his pocket, detectives following him spotted a disheveled young man creeping along behind the Coca-Cola president. Quickly the police moved to arrest the suspect, who turned out to be an unemployed lumberyard worker. After being held for several days, the man was released on a $1,000 bond.

If nothing else, these attempted blackmail plots taught the Candlers to remain vigilant. So far, Asa had been fortunate with the failed schemes, because the perpetrators were amateurish and bumbling. However, he was fully aware that next time might be different, and his family could be unnecessarily endangered. That realization convinced him that excessive publicity could be counterproductive, a fact that he acknowledged a few weeks later in a speech delivered to the Atlanta Advertising Club. "While the public has its rights of knowledge," he said, "the individual has his rights of privacy, and he must not be unwillingly dragged into the limelight without injustice to himself and also to the public." Never again would Asa Candler be quite so casual when threats occurred, nor would he be quite so bold, allowing the police to do the detection and arresting. And from that time forward, he tried to keep the press out of his personal life, an endeavor that was difficult—if not impossible—to enforce.[84]

A project of a different sort soon diverted the Candlers' attention from extortion schemes. On their return trip from the Western excursion, Asa visited an automobile exhibition in Kansas City. Back in 1902, he had warned his eldest son that motorized vehicles were a mere fad, but within the short space of five years, he not only conceded that cars were here to stay, but he was fast becoming an avid fan. A lighthearted write-up on bank presidents in the *Atlanta Constitution* lampooned Asa for being "an enthusiastic chauffeur" in his expensive car. "He is one of the few who can afford to ride an auto as his hobby," the reporter mused. A cartoon-style illustration accompanied the article, picturing Candler careening downhill in a honking and chugging open car, a chauffeur's cap floating above his head like a halo.[85]

Three years later he decided that the time was right to push forward an auto show in Atlanta similar to the one he had seen in Kansas City. In 1909, thirteen hundred local households owned cars; the city already had thirty-five automobile dealerships, and motorized taxis were beginning to replace horse-drawn cabs. Therefore, shortly after his return from the West,

Asa challenged the Chamber of Commerce to take a leading role in the nation's transportation explosion by sponsoring a large auto show in the new Armory-Auditorium, an idea the Chamber enthusiastically embraced. In conjunction with the exhibition, a group of businessmen agreed to build a two-mile racetrack on land the Candlers owned south of the city near the town of Hapeville.

Georgia authorities soon realized that an onslaught of automobiles coming to town for an auto show and races required paving the existing red-clay roads, which were barely suitable for horses and buggies, much less cars. To boost that project, the *Constitution* offered a $5,000 reward to the county proven to have the best highways. Asa Sr. liked this idea so much that he agreed to join two other men on a press-sponsored inspection tour. Their mission was a full day's drive in a seven-seated, thirty-horsepower White Steamer to rendezvous in Macon with a similar party driving from the southern part of the state. After the tour Asa reported with excitement: "I was charmed and delighted with the condition of the highways between Atlanta and Macon, and with a little work" Georgia should "have a boulevard which will be a credit to any part of the country." The White Steamer, he beamed, "rolled all the way into Macon without a mishap of any sort."

While his father was barreling off to inspect highways, his namesake was all revved up about the proposed raceway, hoping it would be the breakthrough he had been seeking since his return to Atlanta. As treasurer of the Atlanta Automobile and Good Roads Association, Asa Jr. moved rapidly to have the club declare itself principal supervisor of the new raceway. To reward their treasurer for his energies, the organization made him president of the new speedway. During the summer of '09, he and a fellow auto racing enthusiast toured the country to look at other tracks, ending up in Indianapolis, already recognized as the nation's best raceway. A fatal crash during one of the races did little to dampen the two men's enthusiasm, and they returned home more eager than ever to employ top drivers for the Atlanta event.

Helen Candler and the wives of other club officials took on the responsibility of decorating the speedway's new clubhouse in preparation for a barbecue designed to drum up interest in the upcoming races. Five hundred automotive enthusiasts showed up to munch on ribs and spoon down Brunswick stew as they walked around the almost completed raceway. They returned to the track when the celebrity drivers began arriving for trials. Although auto racing had been around since 1895,

126

few Atlantans had ever seen it; thus, as momentum for the big event began to mount, curious people boarded trolleys or drove cars and buggies out to watch the spectacle. They cheered as George Robertson tested his ninety-horsepower Simplex and as Charles Basle circled the track in a sixty-horsepower Renault racing car. Barney Oldfield, the most celebrated driver of all, caused the largest stir when he maneuvered his "monstrous one-hundred-twenty horsepower Benz racer." Not to miss out on the fun, Asa Jr. drove his Pope-Toledo at an unprecedented seventy-eight miles-per-hour clip, later telling reporters that he could have easily reached one hundred, because the track was so smooth that "it was like walking on velvet." Indeed, he boasted, the Atlanta Speedway was "the fastest two-mile motor track in the world."

Similar bombast heralded the opening of the city's first automobile exhibition at the City Auditorium, where workmen had festooned the hall with strings of electric lights alongside yards of bunting and flags. Before the show opened, a beaming Asa Sr. strolled through the cavernous floor reviewing the two hundred new Locomobiles, Pierce-Arrows, Cadillacs, Mitchells, Studebakers, and Packards, as well as smaller cars manufactured by a newcomer named Henry Ford. Although some of the autos had been driven into town, most came straight from the factory in specially fitted railroad freight cars. Asa watched happily as these specimen "machines" were being washed to remove the grease acquired during manufacturing and then waxed and polished, each company hoping to outshine its competitors.

After all the hype and preparation, Automobile Week opened with great fanfare on Saturday, November 6, 1909. "Everything new in motordom is on exhibition," crowed a reporter for the *Atlanta Constitution*, "whether it be new car fixtures, springs, magnetos, carburetors, spark plugs, or new and improved makes of cars, set up resplendent with immaculate upholstering." The night of the opening was a major social event, as the city's upper crust paraded around the auditorium showing off its finery. Lucy Elizabeth— wearing a black gown and hat trimmed in blue plumes—strolled around the showroom with her daughter, Lucy Owens, sporting her new gray satin gown and black hat. The crowd grew quiet when Asa Candler Sr. stepped up to the stage to deliver a welcoming address. The small, graying Chamber president informed the packed auditorium that the first such exhibition in the South would clearly promote "the construction of highways over which the automobile may be successfully run through every community of Georgia and in regions beyond the borders of our state." In his piercing

127

voice, he predicted that although a decade earlier the nation had refused to accept the "horseless-carriage" (not acknowledging that he had been among the skeptics), such obsolete prejudices were rapidly disappearing to make way for "the new automotive era" that "would make the towns more countrified, and the country more citified to the good of all concerned."

At the same time Atlantans were viewing the newest model cars and accessories at the auditorium, others were filling the stands of the speedway. Asa Jr.'s Pope-Toledo and a Chalmers-Detroit had an accident during the November 12 races, but nobody was injured. The big news of that day was breaking "the 50-mile record" and the exciting "12-mile stock chassis race." After a full week of motorcycle races, free-for-alls, and handicap races, many men received trophies, including the Swiss driver Louis Chevrolet—cofounder of the motor company that bore his name—who won the Candler family's prize award.

Accompanied by a military band blaring "Home Sweet Home" and patriotic marches, state officials celebrated the last day of the exhibition and races. Most Atlantans hated to see them end. "Automobile Week is over," lamented a writer for the *Constitution*, "and everybody ... would like to see it all over again. There was a sport about it which gradually took possession of one, and whether your machine won or you won your bet," the experience was exhilarating. In the Capital City Club's box at the speedway, the leaders of Atlanta society confessed that "they would not have been anywhere else but where they were."[86]

Automobile Week marked a moment of triumph for Asa Candler and his children. During the festivities, the Candlers reigned as star attractions at a series of dinners, luncheons, teas, and suppers in private clubs, palatial homes, and downtown hotels, demonstrating to all that they were now firmly grounded in the upper echelons of Atlanta society. And there were several commercial bonuses as well. The Coca-Cola Company bought its first delivery truck, which had been used to transport guests to the speedway, now reconstructed to handle as much as six kegs of syrup. A more significant offshoot of the transportation revolution was the rise of home sales in Druid Hills, as executives and professional men realized that they could live in the suburbs and rapidly reach their offices downtown by car.

When he finished his two-year term as president of the Atlanta Chamber of Commerce, Asa Candler received the praise of his admirers for forcefully backing the bond issue, extending the city limits to create "a Greater Atlanta," hosting educational and industrial conferences, and pushing completion of the auditorium-armory. "He has given not only of his time and judgment," commented a columnist, but he used his funds "for the advancement of the city's general good." Henry W. Grady Jr., son of the well-respected journalist, wrote a letter to the editor praising Candler as "the biggest, brainiest, best man" in Atlanta, suggesting that the city would be wise to elect him its next mayor.[87]

But it was a little too soon for that. Despite all the positive publicity following Automobile Week, opinions remained divided on the character of Asa Griggs Candler Sr. Old Atlantans viewed him as an aggressive upstart, and business rivals judged him as opportunistic. On the opposite end of the spectrum, recipients of his charitable assistance considered him saintly. One of his admirers, Governor Joseph Brown, gave him the honorary title of "Georgia Colonel" and appointed him to serve on his staff, as an aide-de-camp. The two poles of Candler's reputation intrigued Julian Harris, son of author Joel Chandler Harris. In an article based on a conversation with Asa, he concluded that the Chamber of Commerce president was "a very strong and able man ... who will fight hard and spend a great deal to win a small point; and then, if he believes, will in a moment spend or give away a small fortune." But Harris also acknowledged that many Atlantans considered him "close-fisted about everything but the Methodist church" and resented his assumption that he owned "all the town and most of the state." Above all, his detractors were convinced that Candler had fostered prohibition in order to sell more Coca-Colas.[88]

Although that kind of criticism often left Asa feeling vulnerable and depressed, in middle-age he was still charged with the high energy level he had always maintained. He remained heavily involved in the day-to-day operation of the Coca-Cola Company, the Candler Investment Company, the Central Bank and Trust, and the Druid Hills Corporation, in addition to his many duties as president of the Emory College Board of Trustees and Atlanta Chamber of Commerce. Like a puppeteer pulling a tangled jumble of strings, he managed to manipulate a large family, a rapidly mushrooming business, a fast-growing city, and an immense real estate enterprise.

Automobile Week transformed Asa Jr., the once-undisciplined Buddie. His phenomenal success in spearheading and managing the Atlanta Speedway made him a celebrity with an established place in the community, separate from—albeit tangential to—his father's financial empire. Like his progenitor, he was now capturing the headlines every time he made a move of any kind, whether it was admission to the New York Cotton Exchange (shortly before the final sale of Witham Mills in 1910) or becoming a member of the Young Men's Democratic League. He was clearly demonstrating his father's ingenuity and drive, as evidenced by a column in the *Atlanta Constitution* that carried his photograph and summarized his accomplishments. "Young men of the type of Asa G. Candler, Jr. are a credit to any community," the reporter commented. "Wide awake at all times, progressive in everything he undertakes, with intuition to seize upon things, Mr. Candler ranks with the best of the businessmen of Atlanta today." As the son of "one of the city's leading financiers, bankers and capitalists," he "inherits all his good qualities."[89] Never mind that Asa Jr.'s newfound fame was achieved by spending the money the senior Candler had earned, for now at last the unsettled and floundering Buddie was forgotten, and the new achiever was proudly displaying the right to bear his father's name. Only time would tell if he could maintain the momentum.

By the middle of 1910, Asa Jr. once more made automotive news. Spending much of his time arranging new events at the Atlanta Speedway, he was also gaining the reputation of being an "extraordinarily good driver," both on public roads and around the track. As part of a contest sponsored by the New York *Herald-Journal*, he drove from Atlanta to New York in his own forty-five horsepower Lozier, which had cost him the whopping sum of $5,000. Shortly after this marathon, he took his Lozier on a "round-the-state" tour sponsored by the *Atlanta Constitution*. In each town, crowds gathered along the side of the highways to marvel at the "horseless-carriages." Late one night, as they trundled along a red-clay road in rural south Georgia, Asa Jr. and his passengers realized they were miles from any semblance of civilization. Hungry and tired, they plowed on until they spotted "a turpentine still," where they roused a sleepy manager, who confirmed their fears that at that hour no restaurants or hotels anywhere in the vicinity were open. Yet the man wanted to be helpful, obviously impressed that his visitors had the nerve to drive around the state in such a contraption. This admiration moved him to escort the strangers to his general store a half-mile away and give them cans of food, insisting—despite their protests—that he would not accept money for his kindness. They were lucky. When another car ran out of gas in that same wasteland, the crew was forced to walk six miles to the nearest garage to get fuel. Still, most of the drivers completed the 950 mile loop in six days, with Candler's powerful Lozier leading the pack and setting records for speed and endurance.

Asa Jr.'s automobile exploits were curtailed a few months later. He was in the garage behind his Euclid Avenue home fiddling around with the engine of his Renault when a pipe containing gasoline exploded, and flames rushed through the wooden structure. Fleeing the combustion, he dashed to the back door, only to find it locked, so in panic he bashed down the door and fled into the cold night air. Although, fortunately, he escaped with his life, the fire not only consumed the garage, but his Renault, Fiat racer, and Pope-Toledo touring car were totally destroyed. Even before that disaster, Asa Jr. had become bored with auto racing and was slowly turning management of the speedway over to others. It was a typical shift of interests, since throughout his life he had found it difficult to stick with any one hobby after his initial enthusiasm waned. By then, he had discovered a far more exciting modern marvel. Only six years after the Wright brothers' historic flight at Kitty Hawk, Asa Candler Jr. wholeheartedly embraced the "aeroplane."

In the spring of 1910, he arranged for one of the nation's most celebrated early aviators, Charles K. Hamilton—known as "the Man-Bird"—to bring his bamboo, silk, and wood glider for an aerial demonstration at the speedway. Less than two months after his appearance in Atlanta, Hamilton made aviation history by completing the first round-trip flight between New York and Philadelphia. However, his first appearance at the Hapeville track was disappointing, because light winds prevented him from rising more than 375 feet, instead of his usual 500. That failure hardly fazed the cheering crowds in the stands, as they craned their necks and watched in wonder when the weird-looking vehicle lifted off the ground and remained aloft. "The conquering of the air is no longer an idle dream," exclaimed Dick Jemison, writing for the *Atlanta Constitution.* "No language is fitting enough to describe this beautiful maneuver." With a flourish of fanaticizing, he added: "The time is not far off when the automobile will be put in the discard for the flying machine, just like the horse was passed up for the automobile."

A few months after the "Man-Bird" demonstration, Asa Jr. sponsored a flight from Atlanta to Knoxville, Tennessee, by one of the Wright brothers' aviators, and he collaborated with the *Atlanta Journal* to back a three-day series of stunt flights and airborne trials at the speedway. In some events, planes raced automobiles, in others the pilots raced each other; sometimes they dropped make-believe bombs, and in several instances they showed off their prowess by rising high into the clouds. Covering the exhibition, reporters were again fascinated to see human beings soaring above them in giant "man-made birds" that would "have made our forefathers doubt their sanity."[90]

Among those watching these early flights was a twenty-year-old high school dropout named William B. Hartsfield. The wonder that he felt in viewing the "Man-Bird" and subsequent aerial exploits was to change his life and eventually affect the future of the Hapeville track, which a half century later would become the huge international airport that bears his name. Perhaps now forgotten in those infant days of aviation was Asa Candler Jr., who laid the foundations for the new airport, which would be called Candler Field for the next thirty years. From his pioneering efforts to sponsor these air exhibitions, Asa Jr. proved that he was not afraid to venture into uncharted territories, for, like his father, he had the ingenuity and imagination to speculate. However, he had a decided advantage over his parent: ample funds to support his search for prominence and excitement. It was the beginning of an adventure he would pursue with exponentially increasing grandiosity in the years to come.

Despite his accomplishments, members of the Candler family often commented that Asa Jr. drank too much, although at that time of his life alcohol did not seem to seriously affect his public demeanor. Not so his next youngest brother, who was beginning to replace Asa Jr. as the family's bad boy. During his youth, Walter had been a discipline problem in the classroom, yet he always was adept in his studies and able to balance his mischievous streak with a sincere interest in learning. As one of Emory's most enthusiastic alumni, he participated energetically in campus affairs, even though he seemed simultaneously attracted to life's wilder side, a transgression that continued even after he became a husband and father. For several years, his wife Eugenia had been plagued by fragile health, especially after suffering during four pregnancies in rapid succession. When Walter Jr. was fifteen months old, she had another boy, Asa Griggs Candler IV; fourteen months after that, she delivered a girl, Eugenia; and two years later, Mary was born. Each birth had been so difficult that doctors advised the couple against having more children, warning that a future pregnancy could prove catastrophic. Now when she desperately needed Walter's help at home, he rarely stuck around, always finding a number of ways to escape his exhausted wife and house teeming with youngsters.

His recklessness often made its way into the newspapers. For example, one afternoon in 1910, he and a friend were careening down Edgewood

Avenue when he hit a twelve-year-old boy named Buford Ingram, whom he claimed materialized from nowhere to dart in front of the car. To his credit, Walter jammed on the brakes, jumped out of the car, snatched up the boy's limp body, and rushed him to Grady Hospital. Given a diagnosis of severe concussion and multiple injuries, his victim remained in critical condition for several days, until released to the care of his mother, a worker at the Fulton Bag and Cotton Mill. Although the incident was deemed accidental, Walter ended up in police headquarters, charged with exceeding the speed limit and fined $25.75. Not wanting to see a Candler get off so easily, a furious Mrs. Ingram filed suit for $10,000, claiming that her boy had lost the hearing in one ear and was suffering from severe headaches.

At this point the press dropped the story, but it is tempting to speculate that Walter asked his father to send money to Mrs. Ingram and Asa Sr. complied, since young Buford had an almost identical injury (and suffered the same consequences) that he had experienced at about the same age. The potential severity of this accident did nothing to deter Walter from again breaking the law, and within a year he had another brush with police. This time he was pulled over for going over twenty miles an hour in a fifteen-mile zone and fined five dollars. Thus once again he avoided more serious punishment because he was a Candler. Nevertheless, Walter seemed to be courting danger, especially serious at a time when Asa Sr. was planning to elevate his standing at the bank. It was almost as if, unlike his other brothers, he was trying to distance himself from—and indeed contradict—the upstanding reputation his father had worked so hard to achieve.

During the next year, Walter became even more firmly established as the family gadabout. The society pages often noted his appearances at Piedmont Driving Club balls and Chamber of Commerce events, perhaps to demonstrate that his lifestyle had more positive aspects. However these civic and social activities did little to camouflage the more menacing side of his character, displayed when he was behind the wheel. His latest indiscretion was a run-in with a streetcar conductor. Ignoring a trolley stop, Walter barely avoided slamming into exiting passengers. When the motorman reprimanded him for ignoring the pedestrians, he reached into his glove compartment and pulled out a revolver. Pointing the weapon at the driver, he purportedly asked the man to "shut his mouth." Not surprisingly, the conductor summoned the police. Charged with illegally brandishing a weapon, Walter protested that he never really threatened the driver. The gun was on hand, he claimed, because as assistant cashier at the bank, he was transporting a great deal of money. Once again the punishment was lenient, and Walter escaped, quite likely because he was Asa Candler's son.[91]

A decade after Coca-Cola moved into its state-of-the-art "permanent" headquarters on Edgewood Avenue, the business had grown so rapidly that the building no longer served its needs. In late 1909, the company moved for the fifth time in twenty years to larger and more up-to-date facilities at the corner of Marietta and Magnolia Streets. Neel Reid and Hal F. Hentz—two young architects then establishing their reputation for designing some of Atlanta's most gracious estates—drew up plans for a seven-story office building and factory that backed up to the Western & Atlantic Railroad. Space was not the only reason for this relocation; Coca-Cola needed a cleaner and more efficient plant to satisfy the demands of federal authorities. Ever since passage of the Pure Food and Drug Act in 1906, Dr. Harvey Wiley's deputies, Lyman F. Kebler and J. J. Lynch, had been snooping around the factory unannounced, hoping to discover the ingredients in Candler's so assiduously guarded formula.

Howard Candler was one of the privileged few to know the contents of Merchandise Number 5. When he became an executive of the company, his father took him into his office, locked the door, and in hushed tones laid out the "mysteries of the secret flavoring formula." For Howard, this display of paternal confidence was "one of the proudest moments" of his life. But his pride vanished some time later when he walked into the plant one afternoon and found Kebler perched on a ladder, leaning over into one of the large tanks. Standing below, Lynch was scribbling notes. Upon spotting Howard, the agents demanded a sample of Merchandise Number 5, and the easily rattled young man blurted it out. When he realized the severity of his blunder, he summoned his father to come at once. Within minutes, Asa stormed into the factory, shouting at the two men for invading private property without permission. No doubt he then gave his eldest son a severe tongue lashing. But it was too late. The government had gotten what it wanted.

Two days after that incident, federal agents seized a shipment of syrup en route to the Chattanooga bottling plant. The US District Attorney justified the confiscation by saying the shipment failed to meet the standards specified in the Pure Food and Drug Act. As company lawyer, John Candler raced to the scene of the seizure, but he could do nothing to reverse the action. Back in Atlanta he lost no time in informing the press that intervention by Washington would work in favor of his brother's company, for now it could fight the persistent and unwarranted accusations in court. Besides, John charged, since Wiley "was a friend of northern sirup [sic] manufacturers," he was trying to destroy production of "southern soft drinks."[92]

The first act in what was to be a decade-long drama was about to begin.

Part Three:

Spending Money

CHAPTER EIGHT
Prominence and Prosperity

The performance started on a chilly Monday morning in March 1911, as crowds of reporters and interested bystanders pushed and shoved to catch a glimpse of people entering the Customs House in Chattanooga, Tennessee. One of the most celebrated visitors was Dr. Harvey Wiley, the chemist turned government investigator, escorting his new bride. After the seizure of Coca-Cola syrup a year-and-a-half earlier, Wiley and his deputies—acting under authority of the Pure Food and Drug Act—set the wheels in motion for bringing their case to trial. Howard Candler moved silently into the packed courtroom, watching cautiously as his Uncle John's son Asa Warren, along with his father and their law partner Harold Hirsch, took their places alongside two Chattanooga attorneys on the defense side. Across from them, no doubt looking menacing to Howard as they shuffled their papers, were the Tennessee District Attorney and his coprosecutors, one sent from Washington to represent the federal government. After they all settled down, Judge Edward T. Stanford banged his gavel, initiating the opening round of *The United States vs. 40 Barrels and 20 Kegs of Coca-Cola.*

John Candler had insisted that his older brother remain in Atlanta, persuading him to let Howard represent the Coca-Cola administration. Although Asa hated the idea, he reluctantly agreed to stay away. But that didn't prevent him from writing daily letters to his son, making occasional long-distance calls, and trying to manipulate the press. With the large contingent of reporters telegraphing or telephoning bulletins to papers in Atlanta and around the country, he had no trouble following details of the trial. Needless to say, he was chaffing at the bit to get into the fray, certain that the government's brief would accuse Coca-Cola of grossly violating sanitary laws and falsely allege that rodents and insects were swimming in the vats. Though he "anticipated a <u>nasty</u> mean case," Asa assured Howard that even if their defense failed, he knew Coca-Cola was in the right. And he further deflated his thirty-two-year-old son's shaky self-confidence by warning him not to "be <u>gored</u> into <u>indiscretions</u>, words or <u>acts</u>." Nowhere was Asa's frustration more evident than in his interviews with newsmen. In the past few years, he fumed, "spies" from Washington were filing erroneous reports, fabricated by nosy investigators "boldly walking in [to the plant] and refusing to account for their presence until forced to do so."

During the first week of testimony, Howard listened to Lynch, Kebler, and an array of chemists and physicians repeat charges that Coca-Cola had repeatedly failed to meet the standards prescribed by Congress. Their case rested on two counts. The first alleged that among the many "deleterious ingredients" in the beverage, caffeine, which was deemed "poisonous" and "injurious to health," was the worst. The second charge—in the convoluted logic that only federal authorities could have devised—claimed that Coca-Cola was mislabeled, since no coca leaves and only an infinitesimal amount of cola nuts were found in the syrup. As authors Mark Pendergrast and Frederick Allen point out, this last charge was ludicrous, because if cocaine *had* been found in the syrup, the beverage would have been illegal. No wonder the Candlers were worried. It seemed to them that the government was not only determined to condemn Coca-Cola, but it was trying to close down the business. On the first day, Lynch described an inspection of the Edgewood Avenue plant, where he found a "colored man" stirring the kettle in "a dirty undershirt." Not only were his toes sticking out of his shoes, but he was wearing "an old dirty pair of trousers." Worst of all, while he stirred the vat, the man dripped perspiration and spat tobacco onto the floor. The kettle itself, he insisted, "appeared as though it had never been thoroughly washed or scraped for some time." Then he elaborated on the dangerous consequences of feeding Coca-Cola to animals. The press loved it. "DRINK KILLED RABBITS" proclaimed a headline in the *Atlanta Georgian* on March 15, followed by an article describing the poisonous and addictive nature of Coca-Cola.

Lynch "should be prosecuted for perjury," Asa Candler exploded. Heated up and anxious to lash out at his adversaries, he told Howard that he was desperate "to go on the stand." John's call for him to remain in Atlanta was complicated. Quite aware that his older brother would not be a silent observer like his son Howard, and if he was called to testify—which he undoubtedly would be—Asa might lose his temper and say something detrimental to their case. No doubt, there was a more subtle reason for keeping him away. With Asa's propensity to take control over every situation, he was likely to begin instructing the legal team, claiming he knew more about the operations of Coca-Cola than a bunch of young lawyers, especially his youngest brother, who had only recently taken over as the company's lead attorney. Obviously, there were also unrecorded pressures from his family and staff, who must have agreed that Asa should not attend the trial. So the Coca-Cola president remained unhappily in Atlanta, trying to influence the local papers and the bevy of reporters from national news services hanging around his office. Since he had agreed not to go to Chattanooga, he sent Sam Dobbs (his most aggressive relative at Coca-Cola), in hopes that his nephew would "shape the AP notices so they will be just a little less sharp."

As the week dragged on, with witness after witness citing Coca-Cola's "poisonous" effects and the *Georgian* accelerating its inflammatory attacks, Asa Candler's emotions exceeded the boiling point. "I want only our name and character to go unassailed," he fumed. "We must protect these at any cost." Still the parade of prominent toxicologists and physicians mounted the witness stand to rattle off detailed evidence about ominous perils hidden in the syrup. The prosecution's case reached a crescendo at the end of the week when one of the government's lawyers described Edwin Corry, a patient in a Philadelphia insane asylum, who had been driven mad by his addiction to Coca-Cola. All the while, the press kept promising that Dr. Wiley would soon take the stand. But the chemist sat silently in the courtroom, letting his subordinates do the dirty work.

By the beginning of the second week, Asa's spirits lifted. Federal authorities seemed to be floundering around when confronted by cross-examiners. In fact, Asa felt so optimistic that he assured his nephews, Sam and Joe Willard, that not only had the government "almost exhausted its rat, rabbit and frog evidence," but its case was being "torn to shreds in crossing by our attys." He advised the Willards not to "get out of heart" when they read the adverse press coverage, because now he was "confident of winning a verdict" or, at worst, having a mistrial.

Asa really began to relax on March 23, when Coca-Cola's attorneys started presenting their side. As one of their first witnesses, John Candler told the court that he had been drinking Coca-Cola regularly for the past twenty years, and except for two bouts of the grippe during that time, he had never been ill. When asked about Merchandise Number 5, John replied that although it was a "trade secret," he could guarantee it was being manufactured under very sanitary conditions in a Maywood, New Jersey, laboratory. To back that up, the defense lawyers read an affidavit from Dr. Louis Shafer of the Maywood lab that described the manufacturing process. However, the report lacked specificity, because his brother had forbidden him to reveal the specific ingredients.

When called as a witness, Howard elaborated on Coca-Cola's production process, asserting that "negro employees" were always required to put on clean clothes before entering the kettle room. Later that day, the defense called James Gaston, the man seen stirring the vat. He politely refuted Lynch's accusations, insisting that he had never chewed tobacco and couldn't have holes in his shoes, since the "hot licker" would have burned his feet. Lawyers for the prosecution smiled knowingly, as they asked which member of the defense team had coached him to say that. Gaston snapped indignantly that nobody *ever* told him what to say. During the next few days, the defense summoned its own team of prestigious scientists to demonstrate that the percentage of caffeine in Coca-Cola was much less than the amount found in a cup of coffee or tea. Then a chemist from Chicago explained that humans had a far higher tolerance for caffeine than the rabbits and frogs used in the government's tests. In fact, John Candler and his team argued, since caffeine had been part of the formula in the first syrup produced more than two decades earlier, the government's calling it an additive was utter nonsense.

Although Coca-Cola's lawyers seemed to have put the caffeine issue to rest, they were treading on thin ground when it came to the question of mislabeling. Undoubtedly, the company's veil of secrecy did little to allay suspicions that the beverage contained dangerous ingredients. After days of charges and countercharges, Judge Sanford finally threw up his hands and announced that the case could proceed no further without the defense revealing the exact contents of Merchandise Number 5. Following every move from his isolation in Atlanta, Asa realized, with consternation, that they were cornered unless they released Dr. Shafer from his pledge of secrecy. Thus with the company's permission and all eyes focused on the witness stand, the defense lawyers testified that the formula included small amounts of coca leaf, cola nuts, alcohol, and wine. Even though the scientists testified that these last two items were in such infinitesimal quantities that they posed no threat to anyone's health or level of sobriety, the alcohol and wine do seem surprising in light of Asa's vociferous opposition to intoxicating drinks. But he gave little thought to that dichotomy at the time, telling Howard that he was greatly relieved because disclosure of the secret formula demonstrated that there was enough of both coca and cola to save the company from accusations of misbranding, thus seriously weakening the government's argument.

The clincher for the defense came in response to the charge about Edwin Corry's insanity induced by drinking Coca-Cola. Doctors from the mental institution testified that the man was suffering from a congenital neuropathic condition, which had nothing to do with his drinking habits. At the end of the trial's second week, Howard Candler felt so good about the proceedings that he decided to return to Atlanta for the weekend. When he stepped off the train, a group of reporters awaited him. "The able defense," Howard smilingly asserted, has "proven by credible witnesses that the product in its refined shape contained no cocaine or any of its alkaloids." And best of all, they had been able to establish that Coca-Cola "was manufactured under cleanly, hygienic conditions," which meant it was "distinctly a healthful drink." Howard's confidence was strengthened several days later when Dr. Wiley suddenly left Chattanooga, mumbling as he boarded the train that he had been called to a meeting in Washington.

The third week of the trial was a shoo-in for Coca-Cola. Jubilant over the turn of events, Asa was extremely anxious to watch what now promised to be a triumphant conclusion. "I can't avoid wanting to be with you all," he wrote Howard, "but Uncle John advises staying away." He didn't give up, however, insisting that he was "ready to go on a moment's notice." In his stead, he sent Asa Jr., with a "splendid lot of friends," to watch their victorious finish.

The defense lawyers were so confident that they requested a preemptive decision, which amounted to dismissing the case. Judge Sanford and the jury endorsed their decision, because it would shorten the trial, and on April 6, 1911—after almost a month of headline news and a federal expenditure of more than $200,000—the case ended. Most Atlantans were ecstatic. An editorial in the *Constitution* proclaimed: "Seemingly the government, coached by a malevolent outside influence, had made up its mind to blast the reputation of reputable businessmen." Gleefully the writer concluded: "If the government is willing to endlessly play 'sucker' to a personally-conducted confidence game, the tax-payers should not be saddled with the costs." But Wiley was not finished. The preemptive decision left the case open to further legal action, and soon after the Chattanooga trial ended, the government began preparing an appeal. The next act for the Candlers was yet to come.[93]

Candler Family, 1911, (first row) Lucy Magill Candler, Elizabeth Owens, photograph of Asa III, Catherine, John, Howard, Jr., William; (second row), Asa Jr., Helen, twins Helen and Martha atop photo, Howard, Flora; (third row) Bill Owens, Lucy Owens, holding Bill, Jr., Lucy Elizabeth, Asa Sr., Eugenia, Walter, courtesy of Millennium Gate Museum, Atlanta, Georgia

Toward the end of the trial, Asa Sr. wrote Howard that "Sister" was "feeling [the] approach of her expectancy." Two weeks later, on April 1, 1911, Lucy delivered a baby boy, whom they named William D. Owens Jr. Since the Candler offspring seemed to produce children close to the same date, a few months later, Helen and Asa Jr. increased their family with the arrival of twin girls, Martha and Helen and a few months after that Howard and Flora's third child, Louisa, was born. With the arrival of so many babies, the siblings began moving into larger quarters. Howard was already settled in his Elizabeth Street house, and shortly after their son's birth, Lucy and Bill moved out of Callan Castle and into a home of their own, on what was then called "little Ponce de Leon," a narrow road across the park from the wider avenue. To house his five offspring, Asa Jr. also decided to build a residence in Druid Hills on a forty-two acre rolling lot on Williams Mill Road on the outskirts of the city. He called his property "Briarcliff," a name soon adopted for the street leading to it. Their modest five-room house was surrounded by a farm, similar to the one at his childhood home on Seaboard Avenue. Determined to be totally self-sufficient, Asa Jr. not only provided his family's food, but he also dug his own well to supply them with water. Most of all, he now had ample space to accommodate his latest expensive hobby: breeding and exhibiting specimen hens, roosters, and pigeons.

William Candler still remained in the shadows of his older siblings. Plagued by a frail constitution and constant bouts of ill health, he grew into a quiet, introspective young man. Like Howard, he went to work for the Coca-Cola Company, first in the mail room, later as a cashier, and finally as company treasurer. In February 1913, William married Bennie Teabeaut, a pretty, outgoing woman he had met in church. A graduate of Randolph-Macon College, she gave piano and French lessons to private pupils. When she married William in the Methodist church near her family's home in Cuthbert, Georgia, the bridal party marched into the sanctuary through an elaborate arch covered with twinkling electric lights laced among the flowers. As had become a Candler tradition, Uncle Warren presided. After the reception, William and Bennie left for extended travels through the South before returning to live for a while with Asa and Lucy Elizabeth in Callan Castle.[94]

A month before William married, Asa Candler rewrote his will, and in preparation, he made another accounting of his finances, appraising his assets to be $5,263,100, with a debt of about $1,500,000, which, when subtracted, put his net worth at $3,763,000. In slightly more than two decades, his wealth had appreciated a hundredfold. Soon to celebrate his sixty-second birthday, Asa was more ready than ever to retire altogether from the Coca-Cola Company and make Howard president. He confided to Warren that Walter didn't seem "competent" enough yet to be president of the Central Bank. But such musings were pointless, because Asa had no idea of actually relinquishing control over his empire. His will of 1913 divided his estate into two parts: half for his wife and the other half split between his five children, deducting the money they had borrowed but not repaid. Not surprisingly, he had loaned Asa Jr. the most ($100,000), and the numbers declined proportionately to William, who only owed his father $5,000. Asa's calculations omitted the considerable real estate holdings that he had transferred to the Coca-Cola Company after he liquidated the Candler Investment Company a few years earlier. Asa Jr. supervised all the family's land transactions, which were slowly transforming the Candlers into one of Atlanta's largest urban property owners. The star of all those holdings was still the Candler Building, which provided space for more than two thousand people working in four hundred separate offices.[95]

Not satisfied with limiting his grand vision to the Southeast, Asa decided to build a sister edifice in New York. During 1912, he purchased property on Forty-Second Street and began constructing a twenty-four-story office building. He and his two oldest sons frequently traveled to watch their skyscraper rising near Times Square, just west of Seventh Avenue. When they realized that buildings on either side would obstruct views, they bought and demolished the older structures and replaced them with two five-story buildings, one housing a theater for movies and stage shows. Although trimmer than its Atlanta predecessor, the exterior of the soaring "Spanish Renaissance" skyscraper was covered in the same Georgia marble and had similar carved ornamentation above the lower floors. In February 1913, several members of the Candler family traveled to New York for an elaborate dinner at the Astor Hotel honoring Asa Sr. and celebrating the newest gem in the Candler's growing real estate empire.[96]

At the time the New York skyscraper opened, a huge twelve-story regional headquarters and enlarged manufacturing facility was under construction in Baltimore, adjacent to their Coca-Cola factory. The box-like structure—which covered a square block between Pratt, Concord, and Lombard Streets—was designed to bring in a great deal of natural light and to display the latest technological and fireproofing innovations. Negotiations for this giant building had been progressing slowly due to Asa Candler's intransigence. Determined to win both a moral and a commercial victory, he refused to authorize the new building until the owner of a saloon and brewery next door agreed to move to another location. Asa not only wanted to own the entire site, but he objected to having alcoholic beverages sold near any building bearing his name.

Within the next two years, the Candlers acquired a lot on South Wabash Street in Chicago for construction of a Coca-Cola headquarters, and similar buildings would soon rise in Dallas, New Orleans, Los Angeles, Winnipeg, Toronto, and Havana. During that same time, the company purchased property in Kansas City to construct yet another Candler Building, which would also house Coca-Cola's regional headquarters, a proposal Asa Sr. had rejected when Howard suggested it fifteen years earlier. In all of these dealings, the company president conducted the final negotiations, scrutinizing the contracts and evaluating all construction costs.[97]

Shortly after the New York Candler Building opened, Asa and Lucy Elizabeth left New York on the RSS *Olympic* for their first European tour. When they set sail from New York, Asa was enchanted with their flower-bedecked stateroom. The ship was a "floating palace," he wrote, the seas were smooth and the crew was very accommodating. But it didn't take long for him to begin feeling antsy and apprehensive. After they reached their first stop, the Elysée Palace Hotel in Paris, he wrote Florence: "Wife enjoys being here, I do not but will tough it through." That remark sums up his attitude throughout the journey. Just as he had experienced four years earlier as he toured the American West, Asa disliked being in an alien environment where he was unknown and out of control. On this trip, however, he was also confronted by a pervasive awareness of being in a foreign land "amid a people who do not understand my words and whose words I can't interpret." Forced into idleness, without the hyperactivity of his rigorous routine, he was bored and restless, anxious to return to surroundings he could manage. In his correspondence, he sometimes hinted that he actually enjoyed seeing the ancient sights and connecting those places with past historical events, but he always balanced such positive observations with business concerns and wishes that he could return home.

Being anchorless was especially difficult for a man who suffered from frequent bouts of depression. In a letter from Interlaken, he told Warren that he had agreed to travel in Europe as a possible way to induce "nerve steadiness." And periodically he did relax in the new surroundings. The Alpine peaks and cascading waterfalls of melting snow seemed to lighten his sprits, as did a sermon delivered by a Scottish minister in a small chapel near their hotel. Switzerland was, in fact, so energizing that Asa reluctantly admitted that "the trip taken in its entirety" had probably been good for both of them. Sitting in the grand salon of Lucerne's Hotel Schweizerhof with a band playing "Swiss airs," he almost forgot he was in a foreign land with its "curious languages" and "strange" people, especially since that hotel was filled with touring Americans wanting to converse.

By the time they arrived in London five days ahead of schedule, he was exhausted, writing that they both agreed "if the ship were sailing tomorrow" they would "take passage for home." Although he liked seeing interesting manuscripts in the British Museum and visiting the sites associated with John Wesley, the founder of Methodism, London was "so dark and cold" that Lucy Elizabeth had "a return of her la grippe," which caused them to abandon several planned tours. As a whole, England itself displeased him.

Not only was the weather bad, but he detested watching "a noble people" being "harassed by such men as [Prime Minister] Lloyd George and such women as [suffragette] Vera Pankhurst," not to mention "the rumblings from Ulster by the discontent of Ireland," all of which seemed to intensify his allegiance to his own country.

Ruminating about his exhaustion and disillusionment, Asa realized that he was at a great disadvantage, because his "search for wealth" had made him forget many historical facts that he had once known and left him unable to fully appreciate the "wonderful sights" they were seeing. In fact, the overabundance of historical monuments made him feel as "surfeited as a <u>hog</u> who is <u>penned</u> up to <u>eat</u> and be made fat for slaughter." Why, he wondered, did "so many of our <u>ignorant</u> folks come to <u>Europe</u>? They don't know what they are seeing" and don't understand the guides who "speak by rote," while the tourists "march along like tired pigs." Europe, he concluded, was "a world of the past," certainly decadent when compared to the United States, which had been "called by God to do better things than build Abbeys, monuments of brass and stone, Cathedrals and picture galleries." Those objects merely illustrate "materialism," when they should inspire "faith and spiritual growth." Since he still had time and money to direct his material assets into something that would benefit future generations, he vowed that his "days on earth" were "too few to be <u>wasted</u>." It was another moment of introspection made while traveling, one that he would soon act upon. It was at that point, that he began counting the hours until they could set sail for home. Still, they spent several more weeks touring Scotland before he finally got his wish in early August, when they departed from Liverpool on the SS *Corona*. [98]

Asa's negative opinions of Europe and his vows while traveling to make a "contribution to the world's betterment" led him into the most valuable and long-lasting contribution of his lifetime. For many years, he had been donating major portions of his fortune to projects sponsored by the Georgia Methodist College of Bishops, largely dominated by his brother Warren. His gift of $75,000 assured completion of Atlanta's Wesley Memorial Church, and his funds enabled the new Wesley Memorial Hospital to become a reality. But above all, was his favorite Methodist institution: Emory College. As longtime chairman of its board of trustees, he was constantly rescuing the small Oxford, Georgia, institution from recurring financial shortfalls. Since his brother decided over two decades earlier to remove Emory from all intercollegiate athletics, many wealthy alumnae had withdrawn their support, exacerbating the board chairman's fear that the "money entrusted" to him was being plunged into "a crumbling castle."

Shortly before his European sojourn, Asa told a group of Emory journalism students that he was "going to do more for Emory, something that I hope will ever link my name with its glorious work." He only hinted, but never specified, what that contribution might be. He was well aware, however, that the Methodist Episcopal Church, South was losing its grip on higher education. At the time, Vanderbilt University, in Nashville, was the only established Methodist university in the Southeast, and for the past few years, Warren—a former board member—had been embroiled in a feud with the university's chancellor. Their disagreement centered on the composition of Vanderbilt's board and faculty, where other denominations outnumbered Methodists. This highly charged issue sparked a wide rift between the administration, which declared it had the right to choose its own faculty and board, and the College of Bishops, which felt it should dictate all university policies. The quarrel reached a boiling point in 1913, when Andrew Carnegie offered Vanderbilt one million dollars toward a proposed medical school on the condition it would abolish all "denominational control." Warren so strongly disagreed with Carnegie's "impudent proposal" that he lashed out heatedly against the steel magnate, calling his stipulation an "undisguised attempt to disintegrate a Christian university."

Asa received a copy of his brother's speech while he was in Germany, the seedbed of the Protestant Reformation. "I am proud of your courage in the Vanderbilt matter," he wrote Warren. "We need greatly some Martin Luthers," especially when "we are but mocked when we pretend to honor the memory of John Wesley." And now, facing the Southern Methodists' call for strengthening the church's educational ties, he worried that Emory would "yield her principles and be like all other Methodist schools." Under these pressures, he decided that only his brother's "great brain and faithful heart," could "save" the college. Between those lines were strong hints that Asa was devising another of his "rescue" schemes, this one larger and more far reaching than any of the others.

Eight months later, the Supreme Court of Tennessee ruled that Vanderbilt's administration had the right to overrule the bishops and make its own policies. That was the central topic of discussion as Asa and Warren traveled to Oklahoma City in the spring of 1914 for the annual conference of the Methodist Episcopal Church, South. On the long train ride, they figured out a maneuver that they hoped the conference would endorse, and, to their great satisfaction, the assembled body played right into their hands. Most responded positively when Warren delivered a lengthy address to outline their ideas for severing ties with Vanderbilt. The delegates then voted for the proposal and agreed to sponsor two new universities, one west of the Mississippi, another east. It was the exact decision both Candlers had been anticipating. Southern Methodist University in Dallas was selected to be the Western institution, but the conference reached no decision on the Eastern location. Instead, it asked Warren to chair an educational commission to consider bids from various cities and name the final choice at a midsummer meeting in Atlanta.[99]

Immediately, Asa Candler began hatching another scheme. His first challenge was convincing the Methodists' educational commission to locate its Southeastern university in Atlanta, and after that was secured, they would facilitate negotiations toward an affiliation with Emory. But both brothers vowed to say nothing specific until all the preliminary steps had fallen into place. Much to their chagrin, it didn't happen that way. When Asa solicited support from members of the Wesley Memorial Enterprises (an organization formed to consolidate local Methodist charitable donations), one of the recipients leaked his letter to reporters, thus revealing the Candlers' attempt of secrecy. "It is just a case of too much indiscriminate talk by a man with words but short on good sense," an angry Asa wrote Warren. With their cover blown, newspapers pounced on the idea that Candler would be financing the Eastern Methodist university in order to outshine Carnegie. Just as that story hit the press, Emory's trustees gathered for their annual meeting in Oxford. Although Asa tried to keep their deliberations secret, the papers reported that he had agreed to donate $30,000 to remove the college's debt, not mentioning—but implying—that financial solvency was the Methodist Conference's mandatory prerequisite for transforming Emory College into a university.[100]

After the meeting in Oxford, Asa took his wife, daughter, and her family to New York to see the completed Candler Building. Proudly they surveyed the sleek new skyscraper, especially impressed with the elaborate Italian-style atrium and "lower promenade" of the Candler Theater next door. As Asa sat through movies and plays, he felt "conscious smitten" for being idle when the time was right for making a positive step toward fulfilling the church's educational mission. That project, he confessed, had now become "the paramount purpose" of his life. Still begging Warren not to make any public statements until he had decided on another "plan of campaign," he concluded that whenever they made the announcement, he was certain to be annoyed.

Worried that the Atlanta Chamber of Commerce would fail to endorse and financially support his scheme, he sent his family sightseeing and shopping while he stayed in the hotel writing long letters to Chamber members. "If Atlanta does not wake up," he warned one of them, "she is going to lose the biggest and best thing ever possible for her to get." At the same time, he assured Chamber President Mell Wilkerson that rather than ask for a "whirlwind subscription campaign," he wished him to quietly ascertain the "dignified and earnest support of all the best people of our great city." Although Wilkerson was receptive to the idea, he kept pleading for extra time, thus goading an impatient Asa into shooting back that a speedy decision was essential, since the Methodist commission would be making its decision in a week or so. Finally, much to Asa's relief, Wilkerson pledged to raise $500,000 toward building the school in Atlanta, thus assuring the success of his plan.[101]

When Bishop Warren Candler convened the Southern Methodists' educational commission in mid-July, he was able to tell the delegates that Atlanta was promising $1,500,000 toward the new university. Following his brother's dictates, he mentioned the Chamber of Commerce's pledge but deliberately omitted the donor of the additional million. Secrecy, however, was futile. So many leaks had been published that when the commission formally announced Asa Candler's contribution of $1 million, no one was surprised. According to their arrangement, the long-anticipated offer appeared as a formal letter, written from Asa to Warren. It contained no mention of a specific city but no one doubted that he had in mind the *probable* place. In fact, there was really no contest. Despite substantial bids from Birmingham and Durham, Atlanta's offer topped them all, convincing the commission where the southeastern Methodist university would reside. The city was jubilant. "Never in the history of Georgia, or of the south," glowed a columnist for the *Atlanta Constitution*, "has one individual or one corporation given a sum even approximating this to any educational, religious or philanthropic cause. What a splendid inspiration and asset is such a man to a community!" With supreme optimism, the writer proclaimed that Asa G. Candler has "wrought for himself a monument that will stand through the decades," comparable to John Harvard's gift three decades earlier. That praise was just what Asa needed. *He* would show Andrew Carnegie. His million would be directed toward *preserving* religious education, not eliminating it.

Within a few weeks, the commission announced that Bishop Warren Candler would be the new university's chancellor. By that time, a theology department "with a full corps of six chairs" was already scheduled to open that fall at the downtown offices of the Wesley Memorial Association. Given the source of the gift and the prominence of both brothers, the press decided that the new institution should be named "Candler University." Not only did Asa strenuously object to having the school named for him, he was already busily working to tie up the merger with Emory. Once more, he and Warren tried to conceal that information, but long before they released it, the public had been informed.

As soon as Emory was designated to be the school, the trustees voted to keep the Oxford campus in place, operating as an affiliate for feeding students into the larger university, an arrangement which still exists today. Again playing his cat-and-mouse game, Asa told no one where the new Emory campus would be located, even though he had decided that issue several weeks earlier. "If it were not my own property," he wrote Warren a month earlier, "I would unhesitating place it on 50 acres in the Druid Hill [sic] section, where there are several magnificent locations." In deference to fellow Atlantans, he announced that authorities were considering several offers, one from Oglethorpe College in Brookhaven, another from Edwin P. Ansley—who had just built a subdivision five miles north of the city center—and others from downtown property owners.

Never serious about considering any of these proposals, Asa engineered the final decision, when the Candler-dominated Druid Hills Corporation voted to give Emory seventy-five acres at the corner of North Decatur and Clifton Roads. Within the next year, Asa and Warren hired architect Henry Hornbostel to draw up preliminary plans. The Brooklyn-born and Paris-educated Hornbostel was already well-known for designing the campuses of Carnegie Tech, University of Pittsburgh, and major buildings for Northwestern University. His concept for Emory resembled that of St. Peter's in the Vatican, a Catholic influence that was destined to cause later friction. The campus in Hornbostel's original plan centered around a large library with a tall conical dome that, like its Vatican model, would be joined to the adjacent structures by a covered colonnade. In reality, the architect had limited control over execution of the project, since Asa forcefully dictated his preferences, the first being that each building be faced with pale pink, white, and gray Georgia marble, the same material that he had designated for his skyscrapers in Atlanta and New York.

Soon construction was under way, starting with three stone bridges that Hornbostel designed to span the picturesque creeks winding through the wooded location. Before long, Asa watched the law and theology buildings rise across from each other on the quadrangle. Even before the project began, the Candler brothers had planned to create a new Emory medical school and eventually relocate the downtown Wesley Memorial Hospital on the campus. As head of Emory's Building Committee, Warren thus authorized construction of two dormitories, as well as two buildings to house the anatomy and physiology departments that were essential for the professional schools to operate properly. Such frills as Hornbostel's colonnade and large library would have to wait, pending approval of the founding brothers.[102]

The establishment of Emory University in the summer and autumn of 1914 was but a minor newsmaker when set against the crisis unfolding in Europe. At the end of June, when Asa Candler was still in New York with his family, a Serbian anarchist assassinated Archduke Franz Ferdinand of the Austro-Hungarian Empire as he was parading through Sarajevo. The chain of events that followed pitted France, Britain, Russia, Italy, and Serbia on one side against Germany, Austria-Hungary, and Turkey on the other. By the fall of 1914, the "Great War" had become a world event, with fighting ranging from the infamous trenches in France and standoffs on the eastern front between Russia and Germany to battles among colonial powers in Africa. America stayed out of the fray, even though many of its commercial functions were being seriously impaired by the fighting. "The European war has almost scared the life out of business in this part of the world," Asa Sr. wrote Joe Willard. Although the Coca-Cola Company's business was not as good as in 1913, he added, it was surviving "good enough."

Diminution of European trade led Asa to devise another rescue plan. As many Atlantic ports closed, lucrative cotton markets ceased operation, leaving farmers—many having borrowed money in the spring to be repaid with sales of their crops in the fall—with wagonloads of unsold cotton. As that agricultural emergency threatened the nation's economy, the federal government floated several ideas to help farmers. While those plans were stalled in a bureaucratic quagmire, Asa announced that the Central Bank and Trust would loan farmers six cents per pound (the market price) for their unsold cotton, which he would hold temporarily in a corrugated iron warehouse that he was building on Stewart Avenue in south Atlanta. Before the ink dried on the announcement, requests from farmers came pouring in, most being accepted. Although this maneuver may have merely been a cover for making an eventual profit, Georgians—such as the African American minister named H. H. Proctor—were quick to call Asa "a modern Joseph."[103]

By Christmas 1914, however, Asa's mind was not on rescuing farmers but on saving his family. Earlier in the month, his daughter became ill, and physicians diagnosed a serious case of typhoid fever. Outbreaks of the deadly disease, transmitted through contaminated water or food, were frequent scourges during the early twentieth century before the population was routinely immunized. As Lucy's temperature climbed and she teetered on the brink of death, her husband remained by her side night and day. Lack of sleep so weakened his constitution that a few days after he began his vigil, Bill was also stricken with typhoid. By that time, Lucy had passed the crisis point; her fever had subsided somewhat, and—although still in critical condition—she seemed to be stabilizing. Sadly, Bill's illness moved rapidly in the opposite direction, deteriorating into pneumonia. In the days before penicillin and antibiotics, this was an ominous development. Coughing constantly, he grew so weak and listless that doctors, unable to reverse his condition, summoned his mother to come at once from her home in Florida. She arrived just in time to be at his bedside on December 19 when Bill slipped away. Stunned by his unexpected death, the family and their doctors concurred that Lucy should not be told the bad news until she grew stronger

She therefore probably knew nothing about the small private funeral at Callan Castle on the afternoon of December 21 with Bishop Warren Candler performing the brief ceremony, before the family transported the casket to Westview Cemetery for burial. On the day of the funeral, the Central Bank and Trust Corporation, where Bill had been chief cashier, closed at noon so its officers could act as pallbearers, and the city's Board of Aldermen, on which Bill's brother John served, canceled its all-day session. Despite the tragedy, the Central Bank lost little time in realigning its executive branch. Walter Candler became chief cashier to succeed his late brother-in-law; John Owens remained on as vice president, as did Henry C. Heinz, a young man soon to play a significant role in Candler family history. Lucy slowly recovered and decided to stay in her house on "little" Ponce de Leon. The children were comfortable there, and so was she.[104]

Trying to reconstruct her shattered life, Lucy was probably only dimly aware of the ongoing Atlanta drama concerning the fate of Leo Frank, who two years earlier had been convicted of murdering a thirteen-year-old factory worker named Mary Phagan. The entire nation became hypnotized by the trial of a New York Jew in the Deep South, where blacks usually bore the brunt of such accusations. After his conviction, Frank ended up in a Milledgeville prison, awaiting execution, while a wave of bitter anti-Semitism swept the city. Then, during the summer of 1915, discovery of new evidence prompted Governor John Slaton to commute the death sentence to life imprisonment, inflaming an angry mob to storm the prison and hang Frank from a tree in Marietta.

Four months after that lynching, D. W. Griffith's *The Birth of a Nation* began its run at the Atlanta Theater, where it played for a week of packed matinees and evening screenings. Atlantans applauded the brave men in gray, shed tears as Lillian Gish suffered the ravages of war, and even shouted Rebel yells when the Klan rode off to defend Southern honor.[105] Members of the Candler family were no doubt curious to see the Civil War reenacted from a Southern point of view, although they recorded no opinions. Surely, however, they were aware that *The Birth of a Nation* helped revive a dormant Ku Klux Klan, which gathered around a burning cross atop Stone Mountain, vowing to eradicate all religious and racial minorities. Revival of the Klan demonstrates just how vituperative prejudice had become. Although most Georgians of the early twentieth century were determined to keep the "Lost Cause" alive, Atlanta was divided between overt haters and moderates, who frowned upon all forms of mob violence. The Candlers were among the latter, loyal children of the Confederacy, yet unwilling to engage in outward manifestations of religious or racial intolerance. Had any of them spoken out publicly, it might have carried a great deal of weight. But like most Atlantans at the time, they did not want to rile their neighbors, many of whom were members of the Klan, and so they chose not to get involved.

As the Klan marched that hot summer of 1915, Asa was once again preoccupied with family matters. In July, he and his sister Florence traveled to Iuka, Mississippi, to be at the bedside of their dying brother Zeke. Although he had lived eighty-four good years, his passing was hard for Asa, who was close to his elder brother. The following September, his sister-in-law Elizabeth (Lizzie) Slaughter Candler was struck and killed by a speeding train near her home in Villa Rica. Since she had been one of Asa's particular favorites, he rushed to his old hometown to comfort his brother Willie. But the most devastating misfortune of all was occurring in his own household. During the past year, Lucy Elizabeth had suspected that the lump in her breast might be malignant, even mentioning it to Flora, who convinced her to get medical attention. Finally, when she got up the nerve to consult a doctor, her suspicions were confirmed. The dreaded "C word" was barely mentioned by the family in its correspondence or when dealing with the public, so details of her illness remain shrouded in secrecy.[106]

His wife's growing infirmity and difficulty climbing stairs—which she attributed to arthritis—was changing Asa's life in many ways. To make things easier for her and to take his own mind off of her illness, he decided to build a new one-story house in Druid Hills. Their plans were accelerated when an unexpected incident caused them to move sooner than anticipated. One night, their daughter was sitting in the parlor of her house listening to eleven-year-old Elizabeth practicing the piano, when she saw a limousine come up the driveway. Calmly Lucy walked onto her front porch, as three strange men got out of the car, one of them saying he had come to see Mr. Owens. Although Lucy told him that her husband was dead, the stranger asked to speak with her confidentially. Steeped in Southern politeness, she invited him to come inside, but within minutes she realized that his eyes were bloodshot, his appearance was disheveled, and he reeked of alcohol. She really became alarmed when he looked around and whispered that she had better be careful because anarchists had been "killing the rich people for the past several years."

Then the man whimpered that he needed her help, because he had only one quarter in his pocket, and he wanted Lucy to give him a large amount of money. Outwardly calm but inwardly terrified, she commanded the stranger to leave, and to her relief, he obeyed by tumbling out of the door, jumping into the waiting car, and speeding away. Later she learned that her intruder was a Cincinnati native named S. B. Burdett, who had come to Atlanta in hopes of unloading his Coca-Cola stock. When he discovered that Asa Sr. was out of town, he picked up two more men, and together they hired a chauffeur to drive them to Asa Jr.'s home. When Burdett knocked on her door, Helen told him that her husband was visiting a friend on Peachtree Road, so the man from Cincinnati directed his chauffeur to drive him there. Called away from his card game, Asa Jr. listened for only a minute before slamming the door in Burdett's face. Still attempting to contact a Candler, the party took off for Lucy's house. After Burdett's encounter with her ended in his rapid departure, she summoned the police. The following day, they arrested Burdett and held him in the

DeKalb County jail until he scrounged up enough money to pay a $5,000 bond.[107]

This incident—reported by the local papers in minute detail—marked a changing world from the one in which Asa's children had been born. Even though Atlanta was slowly emerging from its small-town beginnings, real crime was rare in 1915. Southerners like Lucy were generally naïve and trusting, considering hospitality to be a sign of good breeding. But life for the city's most prosperous family was different than that of the simple world of her childhood on Seaboard Avenue. Her father and brothers had experienced that reality during the extortion schemes of the past decade. Now the downside of prominence had touched the formerly overprotected Lucy. Asa's only daughter reacted to the unwanted visitor by doing what she always did: she scooped up the children and ran to her parents' home. Shortly afterward, the whole lot of them moved from Callan Castle back to Lucy's house, where her mother had fewer stairs to climb, and Asa could better supervise construction of his new mansion across the park on Ponce de Leon Avenue.

Asa Sr.'s Ponce de Leon house, photograph by John Sumner

In early 1916, the new 8,500-square-foot estate was ready for Asa, Lucy Elizabeth, their daughter, and two grandchildren to occupy. Because of its yellow-brick façade and trim of white Georgia marble, the family labeled it "the lemon pie house." His wife's infirmity prompted Asa to uncharacteristically relinquish command of family matters and leave design of their new home to her. It was Lucy Elizabeth's idea to center all rooms on a huge rectangular interior court, topped by a vaulted leaded-glass ceiling that flooded the hall with pale sea-green light. She readily admitted that she got the idea from the recent film *The Last Days of Pompeii*. Indeed, the estate—which reportedly cost Asa the then-phenomenal sum of $210,000—resembled a silent-movie set, replete with a great deal of stained glass, antique mahogany paneled bedrooms that each adjoined a huge bathroom, and a Louis XV-style music room large enough to house both a grand piano and a pipe organ. Notwithstanding the elegance of the new mansion, a large vegetable patch flourished out in back, while cows, chickens, and horses luxuriated in the spacious barn.[108]

Shortly after he settled into the comforts of his new estate, Asa Candler made a decision that altered the course of his life and reshaped his already illustrious career.

CHAPTER NINE
In Control

Asa Sr., c. 1918, courtesy of Manuscript, Archives, and Rare Book Library,
Emory University

Hoping to secure some relief for Lucy Elizabeth's increasing discomfort, Asa arranged to accompany her to the mineral springs in Mount Clemens, Michigan, for an extended stay during July 1916. Never mentioning the real causes of her physical decline, he said she was suffering from severe arthritis. But the family knew. In the biography of his father, Howard skirted around the truth when describing his mother's illness, hinting that she underwent a radical mastectomy but writing only that "amputation of the affected member and extensive removal of all discoverable involved glands was not enough to stop the spread of virulent malignancy to a vital organ."[109] He did not disclose when the surgery took place or which "vital organ" was affected by the spreading cancer. Clearly, however, Asa was well aware of the seriousness of Lucy Elizabeth's condition and decided to put aside everything so he could focus exclusively on her care and comfort.

However, a troublesome distraction hovered over Asa Candler's good intentions. Prominent Atlantans had been begging him to enter the Atlanta mayoral race, and with the Democratic primary scheduled for late August, they began intensifying their attempts to enlist him. But the more persistent their pleas, the more adamant was his refusal. Still stung from the barbs unleashed by the government's suit against Coca-Cola, Asa was reluctant to provide the press with fresh opportunities to invade his family's privacy, especially in light of Lucy Elizabeth's poor health, which was certainly reason enough for him to avoid taking on new responsibilities. Added to that worry, an unpleasant brush with Atlanta politics continued to gnaw at him, preventing his wholehearted commitment to another civic involvement. Several years earlier, Police Chief James Beavers had initiated a campaign to erase prostitution and bootlegging by conducting surprise raids on suspected locations. This abuse of customary police authority received a public tongue lashing from Mayor James Woodward, who may well have been profiting from and partaking in the illegal trade. For Asa it was an easy call. Not only did he enthusiastically back the chief's anti-vice campaign, but he was thoroughly convinced that Woodward was corrupt, and for that reason he agreed to address rallies calling for the mayor's recall.

Before long, however, what he perceived as a chance to erase evil influences in city hall degenerated into an angry confrontation between Beavers's supporters and much of the business and professional community. Realizing that it was imprudent for him to remain publicly involved in Beavers's defense, Candler (along with a few other prominent Atlantans) quietly stepped back. Since the chief and his backers had been counting on the seemingly incorruptible Candler to help implement the anti-vice crusade, his about-face convinced them to vote overwhelmingly for keeping Woodward in office. Now reinvigorated by his victory, the mayor quickly removed Beavers from his job as police chief and demoted him to a lesser role in the department. For many voters, who had pegged the Coca-Cola president as a man of unflinching moral rectitude, his reversal in this controversial issue indicated an inner weakness. Therefore, in the spring of 1916, Asa tried to redeem his dignity in a major address to the Chamber of Commerce that called for the city to unite in the face of adversity. That speech—along with other voices attempting to restore harmony— gradually helped reestablish Candler's standing with local bigwigs; as his popularity increased, so did calls for him to enter the mayoral race.[110]

But did Asa Candler really want to run Atlanta? The city of two hundred thousand was on the verge of bankruptcy—its streets, schools, and hospitals were dilapidated, city employees remained unpaid, and Woodward was doing nothing to alleviate the problems. With the European war further aggravating the South's economic prospects, businessmen longed to rebuild Atlanta's treasury and recoup its reputation for honesty and stability. Nobody, they believed, would be more apt to avoid graft and corruption than the city's wealthiest citizen. Yet despite ongoing pressure, Candler feigned disinterest, telling his supporters that he could not consider running in the primary race due to his wife's illness. Nevertheless, they persisted. If he would agree to run, they would handle all details of the campaign. By then, the Democratic mayoral primary was less than a month away, and two men—Mayor Pro Tem Jesse W. Armistead and Councilman Claude L. Ashley—had already announced their candidacies. Still, Candler refused to commit.

His seeming intransigence did not deter five businessmen from calling at the Central Bank to inform its chairman that a poll of prominent citizens had selected him to be Atlanta's next mayor. When they arrived, Asa remained in his inner-office and asked his secretary, Walker White, to fend off the visitors by handing each his formal letter stating that his wife's illness prevented him from running. Unmoved, the determined men replied that, whether or not he agreed, they were placing his name on the ballot. At this point, Candler realized that further refusal would be futile, and so he reluctantly capitulated to their request, adding one stipulation: his supporters *must* do all the campaigning. "I have never held public office, nor have I had any desire to do so," he told the *Atlanta Constitution*. "But I have yielded most reluctantly to the expressed desire of a large number of citizens of Atlanta, that I should now give up the duties of my business life to accept the position of mayor with all the heavy burdens that pertain to it."[111]

Regardless of his pretense of sacrificing personal and business interests for civic duty, Asa Sr. had already been making preparations for a possible career change. New tax legislation had recently restricted the Coca-Cola Company to manufacturing and selling *only* syrup and to separate all real estate dealings from the beverage corporation. As part of this mandated restructuring, Asa told the Coca-Cola board at the end of January 1916 that he would resign from the presidency so "men who, as my juniors, have been associated with the Company during my entire incumbency" could take over. As long anticipated, Howard was named president. Sam Dobbs was to remain vice president in charge of sales and advertising, while William Candler would continue as secretary-treasurer. Asa Jr. became vice president to deal with real estate until they could compensate stockholders for profits accrued from property sales. After that happened, the law required them to completely separate their real estate business from the Coca-Cola Company.[112] None of these changes had yet been made public, so the press carried no mention of Asa's planned retirement.

In reality, Asa Candler had grown tired of the business he had established almost three decades earlier. For the last several years, increased governmental surveillance and new federal legislation were transforming the original Coca-Cola Company into an enterprise he found increasingly alien. No longer could he, with the help of a few relatives, maneuver funds and single-handedly manage daily activities the way he had done in the past. Overwhelmed by pressures from what he perceived to be his enemies, he began to realize that there was a downside to developing the business into an ever-expanding, moneymaking enterprise. As banking and real estate increasingly fascinated him, Asa began quietly investigating the possibility of selling Coca-Cola. Several months earlier, he had arranged a secret meeting with an Albany, Georgia, businessman named Ed Brown, brother-in-law of John Candler's law partner Harold Hirsch. Accompanying Brown at their meeting was a New York attorney named Edward Colby, and together the two men offered $25,000,000 to buy the company. The Candler family and the Coca-Cola board began debating the offer, but, reaching no agreement, they temporarily tabled the proposition.[113] In light of Lucy Elizabeth's illness and the pressures for him to enter the mayoral race, Asa was becoming all the more anxious to remove himself from the negative accusations bombarding the company.

Nothing convinced him more to wash his hands clean of it all than a short 1912 film by D. W. Griffith. With cloak-and-dagger intrigue, the melodrama, entitled *For His Son*, tells the woeful tale of a man who invented a drink called "Dopo-Koke," only to discover that his own son had become addicted. Because the potion he concocted contained a large amount of cocaine, his son was unable to break the habit and declined until he reached a melodramatic death. Although the film never specifically mentions Coca-Cola, the implications were clear enough to spark revived misgivings about the beverage's contents. Those new inquiries provided welcome fodder for the government's lawyers, then appealing the *Forty Barrels and Twenty Kegs* decision in a case that was working its way up the federal appellate chain, until it finally reached the Supreme Court. If the nation's high court ruled against Coca-Cola, then nobody would want to buy either the syrup or the company. In Asa's estimation, it was definitely time to be rid of the troublesome business. In May 1916, shortly before a group of Candler's backers petitioned him to run for mayor, the Supreme Court handed down its decision. The long-awaited verdict reversed the earlier ruling by declaring that caffeine was indeed an additive, and the company was guilty of false labeling. Thus five years after the aborted trial that spelled a victory for Coca-Cola, the case was sent back to the Chattanooga courtroom to restart the whole process.[114] That blow to the stability and future of the family's investment ignited the spark for Asa to hand over the presidency to Howard and turn all his energies toward alleviating his wife's suffering and participating in the upcoming election.

Shortly after Asa agreed to run for mayor, five hundred men assembled for a luncheon to launch his campaign. Addressing the cheering crowd at the Piedmont Hotel, the new candidate said: "I have never dreamed that I should stand before so many of my personal friends for the purpose for which I am here. The committee may be making a serious blunder," because if "I stood before this audience today indicted on some criminal act, you would hang me if you so desired," and if you did decide to do that, "I have not kinfolks enough to save my life so great is your enthusiasm for your plans." Obviously, despite his protestations, he was enjoying the spotlight. Soon letters and telegrams filled his desk, all expressing certainty that such a prominent, moral, and wealthy man would clean up a corrupt city hall. True to his word, Asa did no campaigning, allowing his supporters—led by his manager Forrest Adair—to open a headquarters and recruit volunteers for soliciting votes in each city ward. On June 25, Councilman Ashley dropped out of the race, leaving only Candler and Armistead as serious contenders in the primary. The two men drew support from opposite ends of the spectrum. Armistead, a linotype operator and past president of the typesetters union, hoped to win the backing of the labor movement to counter Candler's advantage as darling of the business community. By the time Asa and Lucy Elizabeth boarded the train for their long journey to Michigan, the lines had been drawn for a lively battle.[115]

Hopeful of a therapeutic respite for both himself and his wife, Asa instead found himself as restless and disappointed as he usually was when away from home. He complained to Howard that the water was too "heavily charged with sulphur and magnesia" and so full of "iron that one floats in the tub." The large hotel was also less than he had expected; the guests were "not society folk, mostly plain people from every quarter of the globe." And the "intolerable" heat that kept them from sleeping caused "perspiration day and night," rendering "it impossible for the accruing of benefits" they had come for in the first place. Worst of all, Lucy Elizabeth had not "improved to any noticeable extent," even though she bathed daily in the springs and followed the "doctor's directions with persistent punctuality."

In addition to continuing worries about his wife's health, Asa could not help but fume at the progress of his own Atlanta campaign, which he had been following in local newspapers mailed to him daily. Even though he issued a barrage of statements to the press in hopes of countering negative allegations, his absence was giving Armistead a free hand to bombard him with invectives. Forrest Adair was holding things together as best he could, but his efforts seemed to be in vain as more and more of Armistead's accusations filled the headlines. When the linotype operator attacked Candler's philanthropy as being self-serving and implied that the founder of Coca-Cola was too hoity-toity to campaign for himself, Asa dismissed those charges as "weak public utterances." But when his opponent began questioning his personal integrity and charging that he had paid for his new house through illegal manipulations, he could no longer stand it. Leaving Lucy Elizabeth to continue her regimen at the baths, Asa returned home to defend himself.[116]

As the candidate stepped from the train at noon on August 16, a brass band and raucous crowd of cheering supporters greeted him. After delivering a few brief remarks at the station, Asa accompanied his aides to several precincts to rev up the enthusiasm of campaign workers. Prefacing every speech with repeated assurances that he was only running to serve his city, Candler promised that instead of raising taxes, he would cover the shortfall by reallocating existing funds. Slight variations of these remarks resounded at a concentrated series of rallies during the week preceding the Democratic primary. The *Atlanta Constitution*, which openly endorsed his candidacy, contended that "labor and capital, mechanic and banker marched side by side," convinced that "a business administrative head" would "harmonize fractional differences and set Atlanta again upon the road to constructive and prosperous effort." Asa appeared to be regaining lost ground merely by inserting himself into the campaign.

Nevertheless Armistead continued his attacks. Among other things, his campaign circulated a card containing this verse:

> *Asa Candler is a millionaire.*
> *And does not need the place,*
> *The 'forward and backward' movers*
> *Put him in the race.*
> *So vote for Jesse Armistead—*
> *He is the people's hope,*
> *And don't you be misguided*
> *By Asa Candler's "dope."*

Ignoring such affronts, Candler culminated his campaign on election eve with a confident speech to a cheering crowd at the Grand Opera House. The following day, he cast his ballot early, so that he could visit each precinct to personally inspect the voting. The business community demonstrated solid support for Candler; every real estate and insurance office in the city remained closed all day so employees could vote, and most wholesale merchants, grain dealers, and brokers shut during the afternoon. Jim Crow laws and rigid local restrictions kept nearly all African Americans away from the polls, in essence creating a lily-white, all-male electorate dominated by the middle and upper classes. With the city's black workers disenfranchised and blue-collar whites unable to leave their jobs, Armistead's labor-based following counted for little at the polls, thereby shattering his hopes of garnering a working-class majority.

Candler won the primary with 7,821 of the 11,533 votes cast. In the South at that time, winning the Democratic primary usually assured victory in the December general election, leading the Atlanta newspapers to crown Asa Candler as the city's next mayor. The candidate himself shared that optimism by delivering the traditional acceptance speech, which thanked "every citizen" for choosing him "without reference to his occupation or position." Certain he would be unopposed in the general election, he never bothered to gear up his supporters for the next round of the battle. On the morning after the primary, he sat in his office reading congratulatory telegrams from all over the nation before emerging into the Candler Building lobby to greet a crowd of well-wishers. Still gloating, he told them: "I knew they'd do it. I never had any doubt about it from the first, because I know Atlanta. But I didn't expect such a majority. It's mighty good." The only cloud on his horizon that morning was Lucy Elizabeth's health. So when she wired to say she wasn't feeling well, he hastily made plans to return to Mount Clemens, without the slightest concern for the mayoral race, which, unbeknownst to him, was far from over.[117]

Except for anxiety about Lucy Elizabeth, Asa's mood of nonchalant self-assurance was at its zenith when the two of them returned from Michigan in early September. Words of praise from near and far continued for several weeks, as the primary victory captured national attention. Raymond Everette White, writing for *Leslie's Weekly*, called the election "unique in American history" because "a city's first citizen and richest man, a hardworking, industrious old patriot, worth not a penny under $30,000,000" went to the wards day and night, "asking the people to elect him to an office paying a salary of $4,000 a year!" Relating the details of Candler's life and business history, White assured readers that the Democratic candidate, who was recognized "almost as well on Wall [Street] as on Peachtree Street," had "never turned a crooked deal"[118]

The first jolt to Asa's complacence came after word spread that he was supporting the incumbent Nat Harris in the gubernatorial race against Fulton County Solicitor General Hugh Dorsey, the firebrand prosecutor of the Leo Frank trial. Backed by the vitriolic Tom Watson and the *Atlanta Georgian*, Dorsey was the frontrunner in a three-way contest. To skirt any possible problems in the general election, Asa claimed to have no stakes in the gubernatorial election, and—while never denying his preference for Harris—he promised not to speak out against the popular Dorsey, whose late father had been so highly respected. Clearly he was learning the intricacies of politics.

His shoo-in prospects hit a more serious snag when Atlanta experienced its first major outbreak of labor unrest. On September 30, 1916, trolleys all over town rattled to a halt, leaving abandoned cars clogging the roads. The motormen had walked off the job, they said, because Georgia Railway and Power Company president Preston Arkwright flatly refused to pay them for extra hours and forbade them from organizing a union. The next day, Arkwright attempted to restore order by announcing that the streetcars would operate as usual, manned by nonunion drivers, a move that only made things worse. When scab-driven streetcars rolled down the tracks, raucous demonstrators created such utter pandemonium that Candler was left teetering on a precarious precipice. If he defended the company's stand, as a businessman of his status customarily did, he stood the chance of losing support of the workingmen, who had voted for him in the primary. He was especially vulnerable, since not only was he a member of the transport company's board of directors (and one of its largest stockholders), but Arkwright was his friend, supporter, and neighbor, a fact that union leaders jumped on with glee.

At the height of the turmoil, a group of prominent Atlantans formed an *ad hoc* committee to negotiate a settlement and elected Asa Candler to be their spokesman. Although mediating seemed like a good way for him to establish himself as a moderate attempting to bring peace, he accomplished little, since both union leaders and company officials refused to budge. Because of this stalemate, the walkout dragged on for several more weeks, until Arkwright finally agreed to a compromise that partially satisfied the unions. That settlement did nothing to help Asa's reputation. On the contrary, his involvement as a mediator only increased his vulnerability. A labor rally tagged the Democratic candidate as a privileged business spokesman, and under the guise of an "Anti-Asa Candler Club," his detractors began searching for someone to oppose him in the general election. Thus eleven days before Atlantans went to the polls on December 5, Arthur Corrie—a railroad engineer and union member—agreed to run as an independent. Now Asa found himself embroiled in a contest that pitted capitalism against labor and rich against poor.

With the sudden groundswell of grassroots interest in Candler's new opponent, the Atlanta newspapers decided it was time to incite racial bigotry. In a carefully plotted campaign, the press began insinuating that Corrie had the full support of black union members, a bugaboo that was sure to sway southern voters in 1916. Although Asa refrained from all inflammatory rhetoric, he did not discourage his supporters when they implied that Corrie represented a serious menace to white supremacy. Raising that specter got the expected result. Leading members of the working class—including Candler's former opponent Jesse Armistead—withdrew their support of Corrie and endorsed Candler. With few African Americans registered, and much of the white working class staying away from the polls, Asa won once again. This time, however, he only received 6,168 of the 9,692 votes cast, a slimmer margin than he had in the primary. Despite the down-to-the-wire tension, Asa Candler was at last legitimately Atlanta's mayor-elect.[119]

Whether or not he admitted it to others (or even to himself), the prospect of serving as Atlanta's mayor presented a challenge that Asa Candler could not help but anticipate eagerly. A few weeks after the campaign furor subsided, he formally announced his resignation from the boards of both the NC&StL Railroad and the Georgia Railway and Power Company. At the same time, he informed the press that he was retiring as Coca-Cola president, publicizing the decision that he had made eleven months earlier. Apparently, the papers never connected the legally mandated restructuring of Coca-Cola with Candler's stepping down as company president. Nor was it reported that removal of the volatile Asa Candler from management of the company would send a positive message to potential buyers. For public consumption, his resignation was reported as a necessary move to lessen business responsibilities, so he could devote full time to being Atlanta's mayor.

For the next month, everyone speculated about what kind of administration this multimillionaire would construct. What would be his priorities? His policies? With no pre-announced agenda or program, many sitting municipal servants worried that he would make a clean sweep. But Candler refused to promise anything or outline possible plans, merely answering their queries rhetorically: "How can I tell what I am going to do after I shall become your mayor? I can't because I don't know what's going to come up that needs doing." But he did acknowledge that he was "undertaking a mighty big thing" and "getting into a mighty big hole." He was willing, he added, to "crawl into it," and if he was "too small," he would do his "level best to grow to fit the hole."[120] This colloquial touch, which Candler was able to draw upon when required, must have helped disarm those opponents who had labeled him an enemy of ordinary people.

On a chilly evening in late December 1916, politics were put aside as Asa Candler stood beside his daughter, shaking hands with 150 friends and relatives who had gathered at the new Ponce de Leon Avenue mansion to celebrate his sixty-fifth birthday. Looking around in pleased amazement at the finery surrounding them, guests inched their way along the receiving line in the spectacular central atrium, with its pink-inlaid marble floor, carved marble fountain, and imported European statuary. Lucy Owens, looking radiant in a silver lace and gray velvet gown, welcomed the guests at the door, while each of her sisters-in-law (Flora, Helen, Eugenia, and Bennie) greeted them as they passed along the line. Lucy Elizabeth, who didn't feel well enough to stand for so long, sat among the family, beaming proudly at her two oldest grandchildren—twelve-year-old Elizabeth Owens and fourteen-year-old Lucy Candler—serving punch out of a large silver bowl decorated with holiday greens, fruit, and ferns.

Watching Lucy Owens's every move was Henry Heinz, the tall, muscular assistant vice president of the Central Bank and Trust. A few days earlier, the couple had announced their plans to be married early the following year. Lucy had known Henry since he attended Emory with her two older brothers, and after Bill's death they began seeing each other frequently, an easy association since he worked for her father. A native of New Haven, Connecticut, the outgoing and athletic young man had lived in Atlanta since he was a small boy. After graduating from Emory, he coached football and baseball, also teaching various courses at Southwestern University in Clarksville, Tennessee. Then for a few years he worked for Southern Railroad before returning to Atlanta in 1906 to become assistant cashier at the Central Bank and Trust. A year later, Asa elevated him to the vice presidency and made him manager of their Mitchell Street branch. Often seen at clubs and private parties, Heinz was touted as "one of the most popular of Atlanta's younger citizens." The couple had kept their courtship quiet, so that only the family and close friends knew of their impending marriage. Now the secret was out, making the party in the central court of the Ponce de Leon mansion into a joint birthday, election, and engagement celebration. Those were heady days for the Candler family.[121]

Two days later, in a crowded city council chamber on the first evening of 1917, Asa Candler took the oath of office. In his address to the gathering, the new mayor acknowledged that his first obligation was to deal with the city's $150,000 debt, but that would not keep him from finding "a legal and satisfactory way to provide for some of the many things that a great people want and should have." The financial crisis occupied most of Asa's first few weeks in office, as he sought ways to trim the debt by forcing each department head to curb expenses and by asking the city council to change its methods of allocating funds to individual departments. Although during the campaign he had sworn otherwise, Candler suggested that the city might have to increase water rates and property taxes.

Skirting the issue of raising taxes and preparing the ground for possible salary reductions, the new mayor requested that his own $4,000 annual pay be cut in half. "The city is hard pressed for finances," he explained. "Just leave my salary out of it" and apply it "to some good cause where it will bring results." Everyone knew that the Southeast's wealthiest man did not need the money. Still, the councilmen turned down his offer, probably afraid it would establish a bad precedent for future mayors. As Candler trimmed departmental budgets, disgruntled city employees and other critics found grounds for complaint. At the same time, leading journalists eagerly jumped in to comment about what appeared to be a quagmire of insoluble problems. "Atlanta's financial condition doesn't seem to improve any too rapidly with Your Uncle Asa Candler as the doctor," jibed a columnist from Gainesville, Georgia. "Did the Asa boomers last fall really think that the old gentleman would furnish the money as a free gift gratis for nothing to pay the town's deficits? Were they foolish enough to suppose he would give any part of his million-a-year income to pay for the great honor bestowed upon him?" As it happened, the answer turned out to be yes, although it would not happen right away.[122]

In addition to his overwhelming mayoral responsibilities, Asa had distractions. The first was a happy occasion when on January 15, 1917, Lucy Owens married Henry Heinz at a quiet ceremony in the central atrium of her parents' mansion, attended only by family and "an admiring circle of friends." Afterward, the couple left for an extended honeymoon, first to Palm Beach for the social life, then to Havana for the races, and after a few more stops in Florida, they ended up in New Orleans for Mardi Gras. After their return to Atlanta, the newlyweds decided to live in her parents' expansive residence until they could build a home of their own. Asa must have been pleased to see his daughter married to a man who already belonged to his business "family." On the other hand, she remained his adored child and in a letter written six months after their wedding, he referred to his son-in-law as "Mr. Heints," misspelling his name and being—perhaps intentionally—formal.[123]

Another distraction took Candler away from his duties as mayor during the early months of 1917. Even with a new and all-consuming full-time job, he could not resist reviewing all construction details for Emory University, a compulsion that included calculating costs of everything from dormitory furniture to installation of gas lines. Erection of the new campus had been progressing smoothly up to this point. Supporters had established an Emory Founders Club, which was meeting regularly, students were attending classes at the temporary downtown campus, and alumnae of the college and local Atlantans were regularly submitting donations. But in late January the project hit a snag, after Warren Candler discovered that bills for the theology and law buildings far exceeded the budgeted amount. This so annoyed the bishop that he angrily shot off heated letters to architect Henry Hornbostel and contractor Arthur Tufts, a man he had distrusted since the venture began. Without consulting his brother Asa, Warren complained about a litany of expensive elements that were already in place and expressed his disapproval of the proposed "costly colonnade" and "still more costly central building" that were in the original plans.

Both Hornbostel and Tufts responded with barely disguised irritation. Tufts implied that the bishop had no idea how difficult it had been "to convert a wilderness into the beginning of a great Institution." He then spelled out each step of the project and the problems encountered with building roadways and bridges, laying sewage and water lines, erecting an electrical system, and installing many other necessary services. Inclement weather and the campus's distance from downtown created additional obstacles, the contractor insisted. In a courtlier manner, Hornbostel added: "It is not fair to assume that because the buildings are elegant looking and well built ... they run contrary to your ideas of developing the educational standard of the University." However, the architect did concede they had gone beyond the agreed amount, which meant that "a separate donation" was necessary for building the colonnade.

When Asa found out that his brother had taken it upon himself to criticize the architect and builder without first contacting him, he jumped on Warren at a meeting called to discuss the project. Asa's outburst in front of outsiders hurt the bishop so severely that he offered to remove himself from the building committee and give up the university chancellorship. In a letter to Asa, he explained that he could "not contemplate for a moment the possibility of an estrangement" from his "dearest of brothers," yet he felt the prospect of being an effective chancellor was so seriously harmed by their quarrel that he would not be able to handle the job efficiently. At that time, not only were both brothers extremely busy and thus overly irritable, but their lifestyles had veered off in opposite directions. Asa's new persona as the city's number one citizen, living luxuriously in an elaborate mansion, was the antithesis of the bishop's modest existence as a pillar of piety and guardian of Methodist education. Most significantly, Asa was accustomed to having his way when he donated money, whether to business or charitable ventures; similarly, Warren was accustomed to taking the lead in all matters relating to the church. Although the clash over campus construction did cause a cooling of their warm relationship, the rift didn't last long.

Even though the brothers left no documents to specify when or how they settled their differences, somewhere along the line they must have reached a compromise. Warren remained in the chancellorship for several years after the new campus opened, indicating that Asa ignored his offer to resign. And construction of the grounds continued as planned, with the law and theology buildings completed in time for the beginning of the fall term of 1917. Contrary to the bishop's inclinations, Hornbostel and Tufts both stayed on the job, and crews continued to build dormitories and other buildings specified in the original blueprints. However, Hornbostel's elaborate Vatican-inspired grand colonnade and central library tower were abandoned, a grandiose concept forever consigned to the drawing board.[124]

In spite of Woodrow Wilson's 1917 reelection slogan proclaiming: "He kept us out of war," the president had been edging the country toward joining the European conflict. Initially, many Americans were uncertain which side the United States should support, since much of the large German-American population still sympathized with its homeland. But as German submarines began sinking US passenger ships, sympathies shifted toward the Western Allies, and in early 1917, several incidents brought the United States closer to the conflict. First Germany announced that it was resuming submarine warfare, despite a temporary agreement to stop the bombings. Then, shortly thereafter, the government uncovered a presumed plot, known as the "Zimmerman Telegram," that alleged Mexico was preparing to join Germany in the war. Although the rumor was later proven to be a hoax, American troops were dispatched to the Mexican border after a band of revolutionaries crossed into the United States. Among those assigned by his militia unit to Texas border was John Candler's son, Asa Warren.

All of this was happening as the nation prepared for Wilson's second inaugural on the fourth of March. With great excitement, Mayor Candler joined a group of Atlanta Democrats gathered at Terminal Station en route to attend the ceremony in Washington. Flags waved while a drum and bugle corps ushered the group aboard their special train, its engine painted red, white, and blue, with a banner stretched across the tender reading "Atlanta's Loyal League." The following day, Asa strutted down Pennsylvania Avenue beside a young majorette leading the drum and bugle corps. Marching behind him was a large contingent of enthusiastic Georgians wearing derby hats and business suits, while an oversized American flag floated above their heads.

As the crowd waited for the president to arrive, voices raised to sing a spontaneous rendition of "America," giving a subtle signal that the nation was ready to join in the European fight. Wilson's address picked up on the imminence of that possibility. Although he stressed that his goal was to end hostilities abroad, he added: "We may even be drawn on by circumstances, not by our own purpose or desire, to a more active assertion of our rights as we see them and a more immediate association with the great struggle itself." When the United States entered the conflict a month later, Mayor Candler became one of the nation's most loyal patriots, endorsing universal military training for young men, arranging for a large Stars and Stripes to wave from the pinnacle of the Candler Building, and expressing his hearty approval when the Red Cross named his city its Southeastern headquarters.

Shortly after the War Department designated Atlanta as its Southeastern supply center, two officers called on Asa Candler to request rental space in his huge Stewart Avenue warehouse, a visit that provided another chance for the mayor to demonstrate his skillful balance of altruism and business acumen. Actually, he had plenty of room to store equipment at that time, because America's entry into the conflict opened a lucrative new market for Georgia's cotton farmers. Now with overseas sales removing many of the cotton bales stored in the warehouse, Asa was not only able to accept the government's request, but he could magnanimously donate the space free of charge. Anticipating a food shortage, Candler called on Atlantans to devote portions of their property to raising crops on their own land, and he amplified the call by pledging to plant vegetable gardens in the city's public parks. Asa Jr.—who was already prepared to assist the war effort with produce from his own Briarcliff farm—became chairman of the southeastern quartermaster's reserve enlistment committee and spent many productive hours seeking volunteers to transport supplies. Two months later, the mayor's son and namesake was appointed a director of supplies for the Red Cross, an important position that he embraced with gusto.

On the afternoon of May 19, a jaunty, eager Asa Candler Sr. stood beneath a newly erected flagpole at Five Points to introduce General Leonard Wood, who had just been appointed commander of the Army's

Southeastern Division. For several days, the city arranged festivities, luncheons, and dinners to welcome the general, culminating in a grand parade. At that gala event, long lines of new recruits, the militia, the Governor's Horse Guards, and several marching bands filed past a huge crowd of Atlantans waving American flags. Because General Wood had once been a Georgia Tech football coach, students mingled with soldiers from Fort McPherson, to cheer and wave as they paraded beneath the bunting-draped reviewing stand.

In his introduction of Wood, Candler praised the large turnout by saying: "If there was ever any doubt that the South is patriotic, we have completely dispelled it here." Wood augmented his introduction by complimenting the city for its "great demonstration of patriotism," even though he had to admit that the United States was totally unprepared to send troops abroad. "We are fighting for democracy," he shouted to the milling audience, "and every one of us must make the utmost sacrifice." He ended with the hope that troops from Georgia would "lead the way to France." At his side, beaming with pride for his city and his country, Asa Candler now felt himself to be a key player in the nation's attempt to "save the world for democracy."[125]

Two days after the parade, Candler's mood shifted from euphoria to despair, as Atlanta experienced its worst disaster since Sherman marched through fifty-three years earlier. On Monday, May 21, 1917, flames raced through the old Candler warehouse, and before firemen were able to extinguish the blaze, two new fires erupted in different parts of town. As block after block blazed, stretching firefighters to their limits, a fourth and more serious conflagration started in a Grady Hospital storage annex. Strong winds swept the flames from building to building, so that within hours, the inferno had traveled north to the edges of Piedmont Park and east to Edgewood Avenue, destroying miles of mansions and shacks, office buildings and shops. A call for help brought engines from neighboring Georgia towns, while others rushed to the scene from as far away as Nashville, Knoxville, Chattanooga, and Jacksonville. The same military units that had marched in the parade two days earlier were pulling hoses, loading buckets, and dynamiting a trench in frantic attempts to suppress the blaze. When the fire was finally under control around ten o'clock that night, thousands of homeless—most of them poor blacks—were crowded into makeshift shelters in the city auditorium and Piedmont Park.

From the moment the first fire started at his warehouse, Mayor Candler was manning the front lines. Experienced from many years of fighting urban conflagrations, he used his managerial skills to command operations. It was *he* who called surrounding communities to bring in additional firemen, and it was *he* who found explosives and initiated dynamiting trenches to keep the fire contained. As the blazes lasted through the night, the mayor stayed with the firemen to make sure that even the smallest spark had been extinguished. Not only was Asa Sr. performing his duties as the city's chief executive, but he had much at stake, since the fire was edging dangerously close to his family's valuable Druid Hills properties.

In the final tally, approximately three thousand homes and businesses had been wiped out, and the cost to repair damages was estimated to exceed $3,000,000, at the time a huge amount for a city already in debt. In his first speech the next morning, Mayor Candler commended the firemen and "soldier boys from Fort McPherson" for their assistance. "God has been good to us," he added. "We had a fire yesterday that was not nearly such a calamity as it looked while it was burning." He told the press that investigators had found no evidence of arson; rather, they attributed the racing flames to an unusually high wind velocity. Satisfied with that explanation for the strange coincidence of so many simultaneous fires, the mayor requested no further inquiries. Instead, he and the city council agreed to concentrate on rebuilding the damaged neighborhoods. One of the first moves was to put a new law on the books prohibiting wood-shingled roofs, a ruling Candler had been seeking since he took office. At a specially called meeting, the mayor told leading business executives and selected representatives of the African American community that, although financially strapped, the city would repair and reconstruct the burned-out areas, especially those in the predominantly black Fourth Ward. The community agreed to raise as much money as possible through private donations, with $15,000 coming from anticipated city revenues. Generous contributions to the rebuilding fund, as usual, came from the Candlers and their affiliated businesses.

While most of the council was willing to assist the black community to rebuild, they agreed that the mayor should look into drawing up a "city beautiful" plan, which included parks to divide the races on streets where their neighborhoods met. Although no evidence reveals Candler's views on this issue, he no doubt approved the city council's decision to separate blacks from whites. After all, he was a conservative Southerner, and keeping the races apart (except when they were servants) was an accepted belief.

Jim Crow laws were at their height in 1917, and—although the world war would facilitate some tiny cracks in rigid racial segregation—neighborhood separations remained intact for another fifty years. As Atlanta's burned-out districts were cleared and the rebuilding process got under way, a few small parks cordoned off all-white neighborhoods, and several streets were rerouted or abruptly made into dead-ends to keep African Americans from crossing the line.

Despite unbending segregation, Atlanta (unlike other parts of the South during this era) did raise money to help homeless blacks, albeit without the same sense of urgency it had demonstrated when rebuilding middle- and upper-class white neighborhoods. It is important also to note that from the start, the city's more affluent African American citizens donated private money to their own restoration fund and appointed their own committee to coordinate with the Red Cross in making sure relief funds went to help black neighborhoods. Meanwhile, well-to-do white women spearheaded an effort to send a brigade of "pretty girls"—wearing firemen's helmets and carrying metal buckets—to walk from door to door in unharmed (white) neighborhoods, where they hoped to raise $30,000 for relief of fire victims. Several Candler women participated in this drive, which extended to collecting furniture, clothing, and food for the homeless.

As the estimated costs of rebuilding the fire-ravaged areas inched toward $500,000, the mayor and city council were confronted with yet another financial challenge after the federal government chose Atlanta to join thirty-one other cities in housing a temporary army training base, known as a cantonment center. Even with Washington financing part of the project, Atlanta was faced with the responsibility of donating the land, supervising construction, and extending the existing water system to the base. To obtain the estimated $125,000 needed, Candler set to work, first by convincing the Georgia Legislature to levy a special tariff, and then by arranging for the city to purchase a large tract of land near the suburb of Brookhaven. The Chamber of Commerce agreed to loan money for the water main, and Candler personally underwrote purchase of new pumping equipment. Perhaps not by accident, the chief contractor for the project was Asa's friend Arthur Tufts, who was then in charge of constructing the Emory University campus. Mayor Candler stayed busy all that summer, officiating at parades and rallies, promoting draft registration, implementing the services and supplies needed for the new army facility, and passing ordinances to give the "Home Guard" police status so it could protect incoming troops and their families.[126]

Asa's dedication to the war effort paid off when Treasury Secretary William McAdoo named him Georgia director of the War Savings Drive, a titular honor that added no additional duties to his already demanding schedule. Construction of the large cantonment center proceeded rapidly, and by the first of September the base—named for the Confederate General John Gordon—was ready for occupancy.[127]

When the famous evangelist Billy Sunday arrived at Atlanta's Terminal Station in November 1917, his visit created a far larger stir than all the patriotic events combined. Mayor Asa Candler was among the leading city and state dignitaries gathered to welcome him, and during the six weeks that Sunday preached in Atlanta, Asa and his family joined the crowds flocking to hear him deliver fiery sermons at a temporary tabernacle. Billy Sunday's preaching against sin assisted Asa's own campaign to combat vice and godlessness, which seemed as if it might be boosted when the police department voted to reinstate the reformer James Beavers as its chief. Though Asa claimed he did nothing toward facilitating Beavers's return, critics were quick to accuse him of influencing the police board's decision. Candler adamantly denied all such allegations, but he was no doubt delighted to have a defender of sobriety and virtue again manning the barricades. The mayor's unbending disapproval of vice was so well known that he became the brunt of a good-natured prank. During a police inspection tour of the city's storehouse of confiscated alcoholic beverages, one of the commissioners quietly slipped a bottle of corn liquor into Asa's overcoat pocket. When the party emerged from the darkened passageway, a fake vice squad arrested the mayor, while a sextet sang "How Dry I Am." Candler laughed along with the policemen, but his intolerance of alcohol remained as steadfast as ever.

To no one's surprise, the financial problems that began Asa's mayoral term followed him throughout the year, as he gradually pared down expenses and pushed through tax increases. By December, Atlanta's treasury had a small surplus that allowed salary increases for city workers whose wages had been slashed. Typically, Candler accepted the $4,000 salary due him and then donated the full amount to two charities: relief for the fire victims and a home for nurses at city-run Grady Hospital.[128]

In November 1917, Asa decided to give his Coca-Cola stock to his children, thereby relinquishing control of the company he had dominated for thirty years. A year earlier, prodded by the new federal regulations, Coca-Cola had paid the stockholders a dividend based on their share of the company's real estate holdings. Since each of the five Candler children owned one-one-hundredth of the capital stock, each received a note for $64,000, which they returned for shares in Asa G. Candler Inc. a newly formed family real estate and investment company. Asa appointed Howard to be president of the new business, a duty the conscientious eldest son performed without pay, although Asa Jr. continued to conduct most of the property transactions with his older brother as the watchdog. When the Candler offspring took control, the real estate company was $4,240,848 in debt, a sum their father insisted they liquidate before pocketing any of the proceeds.

Howard described how his father apportioned the Coca-Cola stock "almost equally," keeping only eight shares from Asa Jr.'s portion as repayment for an earlier loan, an amount that was eventually transferred to him in 1925. Asa Sr. also gave sixty-four shares to his wife, a fact omitted from Howard's biography of his father. One member of the extended Candler family, Sam Dobbs, resented the transfer. While four of his first cousins received sixty-nine shares of stock (and Asa Jr. got sixty-one), he was left holding only the twenty-three shares he had all along. As Frederick Allen observes in his book *Secret Formula*, Dobbs "did not inherit any of the wealth he had done so much to create." However, it wouldn't take long for Asa's disgruntled nephew to get his revenge.

Elizabeth Candler Graham, Asa's great-great-granddaughter, describes the dispersion of Coca-Cola stock more dramatically. Repeating a story passed on by her great-aunt, Graham says distribution of the stock was all Lucy Elizabeth's idea. Knowing that she probably would not live long and wanting to make certain that each of her children inherited a fair share of their father's wealth, she summoned all of the family to the central court of her Ponce de Leon mansion on Christmas Day, 1917. When all were gathered under the stained-glass skylight, she handed her children envelopes containing their shares of Coca-Cola Company stock. If this did happen, Asa must have orchestrated the event in deference to his wife's illness, for it is doubtful that a woman who formerly showed little interest in business affairs would suddenly upstage her controlling husband by preempting the momentous distribution. Whatever the actual conditions—whether one accepts Howard's straight-forward account or Elizabeth Graham's more colorful one—the Candler children now controlled the Coca-Cola Company and, along with their father, owned three other corporations:

Asa G. Candler Inc.; the Atlanta Warehouse Company; and the Central Bank and Trust. In April, the four businesses collectively paid $67,232 in municipal property taxes, which amounted to 12 percent of all revenue the city collected that year. The competitive and confrontational siblings must surely have squabbled as they sorted out how to manage and disperse the assets.[129]

With Atlanta still trying to emerge from its own debts, the disparity between the mayor's excessive wealth and the city's relative poverty did not go unnoticed. Despite his success in solving some of the city's most pressing financial problems, Asa Candler found himself under fire for a variety of accusations, many of them blatantly false, others hinging on the truth. One critic, a woman named Bessie Linn Smith, went so far as to publish her own newspaper so she could vent her anger. She accused the mayor of stealing money from a newsboy, of cheating "Doc" Pemberton's widow out of the Coca-Cola patent, and of reevaluating his real estate holding to avoid paying taxes.

This mysterious woman had surely been apprised of affidavits then being presented in the ongoing "Koke case in a California court. In the course of the trial that began in 1914 and dragged on for years, the defense called up Margaret Dozier—an owner of Pemberton's original formula—who testified that Asa Sr. forged her signature on the initial Coca-Cola sales document back in 1888. Corroborated by the claims of J. C. Mayfield, another of Pemberton's partners, her testimony and many others like it revived the question of exclusive rights to the original formula. On several occasions, Coca-Cola's lawyer Harold Hirsch had sued Mayfield and other imitators, winning each time because the opposition failed to present a convincing defense. This time, however, it was different. In hopes of benefiting from a ruling against the Candlers, Mayfield had accumulated enough cash from recent investments to hire a team of well-armed lawyers, and their pummeling of the Atlanta company's lawyers seemed to be succeeding.[130]

Now no longer part of Coca-Cola's management, Asa Sr. had been able to ignore the California trial, and he managed to rise above most public griping about his performance as mayor. But when a troubling episode thrust him into the center of a potential sex scandal, he reacted swiftly and with a vengeance. It all started during the summer of 1917, when a striking brunette named Margaret Hirsch (no relation to the Coca-Cola lawyer) came to his office with a group of women requesting his support for a Red Cross rally. Agreeing to help the women out, Asa arranged several meetings in his office with Margaret to discuss the project. During one of them, she jumped up and pointed to the window, saying excitedly that a man was on the ledge. Candler rose and looked around, but finding no one there turned back to his visitor, only to find that she had removed her hat and coat and opened the door. Across the threshold stood a man, later identified as "Handsome Bill" Cook, who let loose a string of accusations against the mayor for behaving improperly with the woman in his office. Suspecting that it was a setup, Asa rushed downstairs to get Asa Jr. When the two men returned, Cook had vanished, and a tearful Margaret Hirsch was making preparations to leave.

This was Asa's side of the story, released to the press on Valentine's Day 1918. After the incident in his office, he turned all negotiations over to his brother John and their friend Forrest Adair, both deciding that it was best to handle the case swiftly and decisively. Mayoral privileges allowed Asa to convene a specially assembled grand jury, where he related the sequence of events, stressing his suspicions of a conspiracy and insisting that his meetings with the woman had always related to Red Cross work. Cook countered the extortion accusations by claiming that he rushed into the office to restore Hirsch's honor, after finding her and the mayor in a "compromising position." Refusing to buy this explanation, the grand jury indicted the couple for perpetrating a blackmail scheme and hustled them off to the Fulton County Jail to await a trial. During the next few weeks, Adair, John Candler, and Asa Jr. met separately with Cook and Hirsch in their cells, each session producing juicy morsels that filtered into the press. Cook claimed that the Candler team tried to buy them off, while Asa's advocates accused the pair of being involved in a scheme to illegally obtain the mayor's money. In his interview with reporters, Cook said that although he had once been "a man of the world," after hearing one of Billy Sunday's sermons, he realized it was his Christian duty to rescue Margaret from the mayor's wicked advances.

When Cook's trial began in late February, a curious crowd packed the courtroom to enjoy every revelation of "morbid and obscene" evidence. The influence of Candler's office and the power of the men testifying on his behalf assured a verdict in his favor well before the judge banged his gavel. Nevertheless, Asa was forced to reiterate his original statement in even greater detail. His sober accounting proved no match for "Handsome Bill's" salacious testimony that delighted onlookers, who snickered audibly when he accused "old man Candler" of threatening to break up Margaret's marriage. To the crowd's delight, the defense lawyer produced a pair of "silk bloomers" supposedly obtained from Candler's office, but, for unexplained reasons, he decided not to enter them as evidence. Nor did he call up any credible witnesses. If Cook had any chance of avoiding punishment, it disappeared after a witness for the prosecution testified that on numerous occasions he had seen the two defendants together, treating each other affectionately. After less than twenty minutes of deliberation, the jury issued a guilty verdict, and the judge sentenced Cook to a year of hard labor on the chain gang along with a $1,000 fine.

Hirsch didn't fare much better. Because her cohort's trial had produced such pandemonium, spectators and reporters were barred from the courtroom when her case went before a different Fulton County jury. Nevertheless, the *Atlanta Constitution* managed to obtain a blow-by-blow description of her two-hour stint on the witness stand and was thus able to describe how she tearfully accused the mayor of making "every advance that a man could make to show a woman that he wanted to do things that he shouldn't do." She failed to resist his repeated assaults, she claimed, because she needed his cooperation in the Red Cross raffle. Unmoved by her theatrics, the jury found her guilty, and the judge sentenced her to one year on a prison farm and fined her $1,000.

Subsequently, Cook attempted several appeals, but these failed. Nevertheless, the court reduced their sentences after Margaret's husband, Herman Hirsch—a prominent insurance agent—filed for divorce, and upon their release, the two accused blackmailers fled the city together. Asa, however, may not have been as naïve as the courts claimed. As a man of considerable wealth and influence, he was (perhaps not altogether unwillingly) attracted to the entreaties of younger women with ulterior motives, as later incidents would prove.[131]

Compared to the Hirsch-Cook melodrama, the rest of Asa Candler's second year as Atlanta mayor was anticlimactic. War-related activities—from parades to Liberty Loan rallies—took up most of his time. He was called upon constantly to speak at public events, preside over parades, and even dress as a woman in a mock wedding staged for a Red Cross benefit. Even before the Germans surrendered on the eleventh hour of the eleventh day of the eleventh month in 1918, Atlanta had planned its victory celebration. Mayor Candler issued a proclamation, announcing that all businesses and schools would be closed for a grand victory parade, which promised to outshine all others in the nation. Ten thousand servicemen, followed by brigades of veterans, students, Red Cross workers, and an assortment of civilians, wound their way through the downtown streets, while "birdmen" flew overhead in a grand salute. That evening the doors of the city auditorium opened wide for a mass meeting, replete with two brass military bands and a full program of speeches by local dignitaries. Asa presided mechanically over all of these festivities, exerting only as much energy as required to get through them. He was worn out. Two exhausting years as Atlanta's mayor, complicated by his wife's declining health, had taken its toll on a man now approaching his sixty-seventh birthday. A few lines in the newspaper in early December indicate his fatigue. The Mayor Pro Tem "occupied the mayor's chair," the brief notice explained, because Candler "was kept at home with an attack of rheumatism."

His gloomy mood lightened only slightly when, three days before Christmas, his daughter Lucy delivered a baby boy named Henry Charles Heinz Jr. But other than the excitement over the new baby, the Candlers' holiday was quiet, because Lucy Elizabeth was too sick to get out of bed. And under the pall of this impending tragedy, Asa ended his two-year mayoral term without fanfare. Even if he had not been restricted by law from running again, he knew it was time to quit and savor what little pleasure he could from laudatory remarks about his accomplishments in the press or in public addresses. Many applauded the way he reduced Atlanta's debt by trimming down several departments and showing them how to operate more efficiently. Most importantly, they commended his strong and steady leadership during the worst fire in the city's history and the most widespread and devastating war the world had then known. There were many problems yet to be solved, he told reporters, but now those worries were on the shoulders of his successor, James L. Key.[132]

Despite his relief at shedding the responsibilities inherent with running a city, the man of constant action faced a severe letdown when all of that activity suddenly ended. Now with nothing to do, Asa Candler was forced to cope with the awful tragedy unfolding at home.

CHAPTER TEN
Losing Control

T ragedy began to stalk the Candlers three months before Asa stepped down as Atlanta mayor. The first blow coincided with the flu epidemic that started in Spain and spread through the world at a deadly pace, accelerated by the close proximity of soldiers in training camps and trenches. Within a month after the disease reached the United States in September 1918, thousands were infected. Atlanta was especially vulnerable because so many men were crammed into close quarters at Fort McPherson and Camp Gordon. As an emergency measure, schools, theaters, and most public gathering places closed, and people were asked to don gauze masks if they ventured outdoors. Even the long-anticipated and extremely popular Southeastern Fair was canceled due to the quarantine. Yet, despite all the precautions, Atlanta—like the rest of the nation—was devastated by the disease. On October 9, health officials reported eighty cases in the city; ten days later it had risen to 613.

On October 1, as the death toll was reaching its climax, the following small notice appeared in the Atlanta paper:

Mrs. Walter T. Candler, wife of the cashier of the Central Bank and Trust Corporation, died Monday morning at 9:15 o'clock at the residence on Lullwater Road, in Druid Hills. She is a daughter-in-law of Mayor Asa G. Candler.

Against the advice of doctors, Eugenia was once more pregnant. Already weakened by the difficulties of the four previous births, she would have had little resistance to the flu, if she had contracted the deadly virus. However, the cause of her death at the height of the Spanish flu pandemic remains a mystery, partly because the quarantine prohibited gatherings, including funerals—which meant an absence of the usual newspapers coverage—and partly because the family blamed the ill-advised pregnancy for killing her. But whatever the reason, Walter, who had frittered away much of his life, was faced with the sobering reality of raising his four children: Walter Jr. (eleven), Asa IV (ten), Eugenia (nine), and Mary (seven).[133]

The second tragedy had been long anticipated. By the time her daughter-in-law died, Lucy Elizabeth's cancer had ravaged her body, leaving her so weak that she rarely rose from bed. During the preceding two years, Asa had taken her to Johns Hopkins and to a spa in Hot Springs, Virginia, in hopes of curing the disease. But neither of these places was able to slow its progress. A man like Asa, accustomed to managing situations, found it excruciating to stand by helplessly and watch his wife decline. The wearing routine of doctors' visits and changing shifts of nurses were a constant reminder of her imminent demise. While still actively involved as mayor, he had a distraction from the pall that hung over his Ponce de Leon mansion. But after his term ended, a tired and depressed man—thrust suddenly from the spotlight—found himself with a dying wife, no city to manage, and few businesses to supervise. Although he still went daily to his office in the Candler Building and tried to oversee the functioning of the bank, the warehouse, the real estate company, and even Coca-Cola, he had little else to do other than to watch Lucy Elizabeth fade away. During those months, Howard claimed that his mother began to rely on him more than anyone else for advice, even though his father "had always been all a husband could be." Then he added sadly: "I did the best I could, but failed when she needed me most."

The family's vigil ended on Saturday, February 22, 1919, seven months short of her sixtieth birthday. Only Asa Sr., Lucy, and Howard were at her bedside when she died, since Walter was still mired in his own grief, and Asa Jr. and William were both out of town. The newspaper described her last illness as "rheumatism of the heart," never mentioning the cancer that had actually killed her. Lucy Elizabeth's funeral packed the Inman Park Methodist Church, and many mourners trooped out to Westview Cemetery to witness her burial. A eulogy in the *Wesleyan Christian Advocate*, written by Howard's father-in-law, Wilber F. Glenn, described her as "a woman of gentle disposition, strong intellectuality and pronounced benevolent character" whose service to the church "helped to inspire many preachers in their efforts to proclaim the gospel." Other people commenting on her life mentioned her charm, grace, and attachment to her five children and sixteen grandchildren. "She was still young in years," Howard remembered, "and every feature of her radiant beauty was well preserved." Although she was "never ostentatious," he added, she did love to surround herself with tasteful objects and wear beautiful clothes.

Two months after her death, the DeKalb County Court announced the terms of Mrs. Asa Candler Sr.'s will. Each of her five children and her husband inherited a sixth of her $1,270,000 holdings with $12,401 of that sum going to Georgia taxes, then the largest amount ever collected from a single estate. But no inheritance could compensate for the void Lucy Elizabeth's loss created in the family that she had held together for so long. Asa sank into deep depression, took to his bed, and was inconsolable for weeks. Howard wrote that during this period his father walked "a dark and lonely path," feeling his life "to be a purposeless round of empty days filled with the sharp pain of a loss to which he never became reconciled."

Walter was also in bad shape. With the double loss of his wife and mother five months apart, he became so despondent that he totally neglected his children. Consequently, their house on Lullwater Road was in constant turmoil. The two boys rarely attended school, preferring to spend their days hanging around the barn and riding their father's horses, while the two little girls wandered around lost and unsupervised. Never inclined to accept many domestic responsibilities, Walter was said to have buried his sorrows in drink. Needless to say, his father openly disapproved of this addiction (as he did of Asa Jr.'s similar predilection), further exacerbating the tension then fracturing the family. When Lucy Heinz realized how intolerable Walter's household had become, she stepped in with a proposition. If her brother would get the boys back in the classroom, so they wouldn't hang around with "the colored help," she and Eugenia's relatives would take the girls to buy clothes and teach them "the things young ladies needed to learn."[134]

With the family in disarray and Asa Sr. depressed and gloomy, his children made a momentous decision. Recently Coca-Cola had become a financial and managerial burden, intensified when the long-running California "Koke" trial finally ruled in favor of Mayfield and declared that the Atlanta company did not have exclusive rights over either Pemberton's formula or the copyrighted beverage name. The consequences of that verdict threatened to open the floodgates to potential imitators. It was just what Asa had been dreading all these years. As the company's lawyers were frantically putting together an appeal, the five Candler siblings decided it was the perfect time to bail out.

They knew that Sam Dobbs had been quietly working with a group of bankers to construct a funding package for sale of the company. When he approached the five of them with the proposal, it seemed to satisfy all of their requirements, and they gave Sam permission to represent them in upcoming negotiations. In hopes of avoiding a possible disruption of these plans, they agreed to keep the matter from their father until the deal was finalized, not only because he would want to take charge of everything, but also because the man spearheading the transaction was his banking rival, Ernest Woodruff, president of the Trust Company of Georgia. It was a very touchy situation, for even though Asa Sr. had given his five children the controlling stock, the Coca-Cola Company was still the baby he had nurtured since birth. And for him, it couldn't have been a worse time. Distracted and grieving, he might have seemed unconcerned about what happened to the business, but never in his wildest dreams did he expect to lose control of its sale. However, his children wisely realized that if he found out about the matter, he might possibly destroy the pending deal.

Dobbs and the bankers, therefore, came up with a solution. Since many of the financing partners were in New York, he would meet with them there, far away from the scrutiny of Asa Sr. and the Atlanta press. Surreptitiously, Sam collected each of his five cousins' signatures, tucked the papers into his briefcase, and in mid-July headed for a meeting at the Waldorf-Astoria. A few days later he returned to Atlanta with the tentative contract for a $25,000,000 buyout. If the five principal shareholders accepted, the purchasers instructed Dobbs to come back to them by the twenty-eighth of August to conclude the agreement. Still worried that Asa Sr. would obstruct the negotiations, Woodruff's name was absent from the first press release. The notice simply declared that a "syndicate represented by prominent New York banks" had received an option to purchase Coca-Cola. In his statement, the company's president, Howard Candler, said that the reason for the new arrangement "was to extend the sale of the drink manufactured by the company to all parts of the world, making an immense exporting center in Atlanta."

In the weeks that followed, Woodruff received the approval of the bank's board, and six days before the deadline, the *Atlanta Constitution* announced that the Trust Company of Georgia had purchased Coca-Cola with the help of "eastern capital" for "nearly $30,000,000." As part of the agreement, Coca-Cola would reorganize under a Delaware charter and reissue the stock at forty dollars per share. Asa's five children were each promised $15 million in cash and $10 million more in preferred stock. As was typical in many such agreements, the new owners stated that for the time being, the company's management would remain unchanged.

No one seems to know exactly when or how Asa Candler learned that his children had sold the company to Woodruff. He might have read it in the newspaper, or perhaps one of his children told him about it when they released information to the press. But if the public didn't know how Asa Sr. found out, they couldn't help but hear how furious and hurt he was when discovering that the sale had taken place behind his back. None of the Candler siblings wanted to harm their father, especially since their mother had died so recently. On the other hand, some of them, especially Howard, may have been unconsciously—or perhaps consciously—seeing the secret maneuver as a way of getting even for years of parental domination. Since Asa then held only a few shares, he did not even attend the Coca-Cola board meeting that approved dissolution of the Georgia corporation.

Asa Jr.'s daughter Laura remembered that when her grandfather came to their house for dinner after the sale, he could not stop crying about the transaction. Howard—who had favored the arrangement from the start—said he was surprised to learn that his father had been "profoundly shocked" and "particularly chagrined" about negotiations that took place with no one "having even consulted him, taken him into their confidence, or sought his advice in determining the details and terms of the proposal." Perhaps the biggest blow to Asa, Sr. was that his number one son and past confidant had been a key player in what he saw as a form of family sabotage. Many years later, Howard wrote that his father never became reconciled to the sale that so "rankled in his mind." Clearly Asa continued to fume over the transaction and freely admitted it. During an interview with a Kansas City newspaper, he said that he had given his children the business, and they turned around and "sold out" for a "fancy price." "I wouldn't have done that," he told reporters, although he conceded that "from a sale standpoint, they drove a pretty keen bargain."[135]

A good portion of his bitterness was having Ernest Woodruff at the helm of "*his*" business. His children knew he would resent it, possibly because the two men, though similar in temperament and background, were very different in values. Like Asa, Ernest Woodruff was a headstrong bulldog of a man, who had moved to Atlanta from a west Georgia town (in his case Columbus) determined to make a fortune. And, like Candler, he succeeded. When he began negotiations with Sam Dobbs in 1919, Woodruff was president of one of the city's most prominent banks, and he controlled a number of local manufacturing businesses. But where Asa was honest, if canny, Ernest had a reputation for ruthlessness, and where Asa lavished funds on philanthropies and assumed civic responsibilities, Ernest showed little interest in either. Although Woodruff and his associates had promised that the company's management would remain the same, within days they reneged. When directors of the new Coca-Cola board met in mid-September, they removed Howard from the presidency and "promoted" him to chairman of the board, even though for the time being they retained his brother William, as secretary-treasurer. Now the tables turned, and it was Howard who bore the brunt of internal maneuvering behind his back. The *Atlanta Constitution* reported that Asa Sr. had been offered the chance to return as president, but, not surprisingly, he declined. This charade of being fair to the well-respected Candlers was probably cooked up to divert criticism of Woodruff and keep the transition as peaceful as possible.

Behind the entire scheme loomed the victor, Sam Dobbs. The new board named him president in Howard's place, granting Asa's nephew his long-desired chance, not only to head the company, but to serve on a powerful three-man voting trust along with Ernest Woodruff and Trust Company Director Eugene W. Stetson, creating a triumvirate empowered to control all important corporate decisions. To placate Howard, who was crushed by his diminished role, the new board agreed to grant him several minor requests, as long as he limited his demands to functional details of the company's operation. Although not happy with the new arrangements, Howard begrudgingly accepted them. And thus, in September 1919, after much behind-the-scenes manipulating, a few strokes of the pen brought the Candler era at Coca-Cola to a close and ushered in a new era dominated by the Woodruffs.[136]

It didn't take long for Asa's children to tally up their profits from the sale of Coca-Cola or to figure out ways to spend their newfound fortunes. Walter made the first decisive move. Just before the transaction was announced, he married an employee of Central Bank and Trust named Marion Penland. In desperate need of someone to look after his four young children, he chose the baby-faced, twenty-four-year-old daughter of a Roswell, Georgia, businessman. Marion was remarkable for a southern woman of her day. Not only had she graduated from LaGrange College, but she had worked her way up from secretary to the top of the bank's bond department. Her education and drive strongly suggested that she could be counted on to set Walter's chaotic household in order. And besides she was awfully pretty.

Adjusting to her new husband's family did have its challenges, but at first Marion agreed to go along, even complying when his sister—who had been protecting and mothering Walter's brood since Eugenia's death—insisted that the newlyweds take all four children on their honeymoon, so they could become better adjusted to their new mother. Although that was not exactly a good way to start a marriage, for the first year or so Marion really tried to fill the void left by Eugenia's absence. When, for example, in late October the eldest girl turned nine, she invited the neighborhood children to an elaborate celebration at their house on Lullwater Road, where she went out of her way to decorate tables with baskets of chrysanthemums and planned several Halloween games. For the young bride, however, mothering was not her strong suit. She actually preferred accompanying Walter to the whirl of club life, fancy balls, and cocktail parties, which were always written up in the local society columns.

In May 1921, Marion had a daughter they named Marion Elizabeth but called "Bootsie" and—at least for outward appearances—the Walter Candlers displayed the trappings of a normal, happy family. But Walter, who had never been attentive to his four older children, showed only a cursory interest in the new baby. More consuming were schemes to expand his recently acquired wealth. While continuing to remain on the payroll of his father's bank, he began investing in both suburban and downtown real estate, and he seemed to enjoy spending time at one of his buildings on West Peachtree that was devoted exclusively to automobile sales, repair, and services. On the side, Walter started to collect thoroughbred trotters, which he raced at Lakewood Park. That track, however, soon displeased him, and he indulged his obsession by buying a 230-acre plot of land—extending north from Claremont Road to the edge of the Emory University campus—to build a stable and racetrack, naming it the "Lullwater Driving Club" after his home on Lullwater Road. However, Marion, whose aspirations had propelled her to a top bank position, slowly began to realize that the wealthy Coca-Cola heir she married was spending far too much time away from home. From that point on, the couple began their years of constant bickering, which set their marriage on a downhill spiral.[137]

At the same time his younger brother was buying land and horses, Asa Jr. was also finding ways to spend his new fortune. Ever present beneath the surface of the wise and clever real estate executive lurked the rambunctious Buddie, who partied constantly and spent money lavishly.

Shortly after the sale of Coca-Cola, he decided—no doubt impulsively—to buy a hundred-foot, seagoing yacht (used during the war by the US Navy) and had it refitted for private use. Christened the "Helasa," a contraction of his first name and that of his wife, the lavish $100,000 vessel had four double staterooms as well as a large "saloon" and lounge. Upon purchasing it, the new owner and his wife boarded the yacht in New York and began a southward journey, accompanied by two other couples. With plenty of food, plenty of booze, and a staff to serve it, they cruised down the Atlantic coast to Norfolk, where they picked up their daughter Lucy, a student at Randolph-Macon College. She and one of her friends sailed with them until they reached Morehead City, North Carolina. There the girls disembarked to return to school, and the rest of the passengers partied their way to moor the yacht in Jacksonville, until they came back in a few months for a tour of the Caribbean.

In sharp contrast to (and perhaps because of) his two middle sons' profligate lifestyles, Asa Sr. agreed to serve as secretary-treasurer of the Georgia Anti-Saloon League, proudly participating when the organization celebrated implementation of national Prohibition on January 16, 1920. After a prayer service at the Wesley Memorial Church, the revelers followed a torchlight parade through the city, ending at a huge a bonfire to burn John Barleycorn in effigy.[138] Asa's children, especially Asa Jr. and Walter, did not join him in celebrating the onset of national Prohibition, since they no doubt disliked the government's restrictions. However, the eighteenth-amendment to the US Constitution would have little effect on their ability to obtain whiskey; Georgia had been dry for over a decade, and they had always managed to find it.

Helen Candler was also beginning to disengage from her husband's way of life. Although she often went along with him on yachting excursions, she was not always content with the constant partying and often chose to remain at home, while her gregarious husband traveled with his friends around the Atlantic Ocean and Gulf of Mexico. By then, the couple had six children—ranging in age from seventeen-year-old Lucy to five-year-old Sam—and Helen found it necessary to be on hand to supervise the sizable staff of maids, nurses, and gardeners, who tended the rambling grounds and her husband's collections of prize poultry, exotic birds, and rare plants. Also, she had never completely recovered from the bout of cat-scratch fever, which often left her weak and listless. In the early 1920s, the medical profession had not yet diagnosed the condition as a recurring illness, but her family (including her husband) realized that her health was never the same after she received the kitten bite during her first pregnancy. Perhaps to make his wife more comfortable and provide more space for his large brood, Asa Jr. began planning a larger and grander house, one that better suited the country gentleman he had become.

Callanwolde, Howard Candler's house, photograph by John Sumner

But his older brother beat him to it. Cautious Howard may have been the antithesis of Asa Jr., but he, too, had grandiose plans for spending his inherited fortune. His prize was a huge Tudor mansion on a twenty-seven acre wooded lot. The project had begun several years earlier, when he hired Henry Hornbostel to design a house for his William's Mill (soon to be Briarcliff) Road property, at the same time the Pittsburgh architect was working on the Emory campus. Although his father's favorite contractor, Arthur Tufts, began construction in 1917, wartime shortages delayed completion until after the armistice, a fortunate postponement as it turned out. With the millions received from Coca-Cola, Howard was able to build a more elegant estate than he had originally envisioned. He decided to name the mansion "Callanwolde" after the family's presumed Irish ancestral seat, Callan Castle, attaching the suffix "wolde," the Gallic word for forest. Although much of the land was well on its way toward ordered cultivation, dense woods surrounded the house when Howard, Flora, and their three children moved there in 1920. Like his father and all of his siblings, his estate contained a small farm on the grounds, two greenhouses, a gardener's cottage, vegetable gardens, an orchard, and a barn that housed an assortment of horses, working animals, and poultry. At the back of the house, he added a courtyard—patterned after a cloister—surrounded by walkways and formal gardens. Behind that stood a four-car garage with a six-room apartment above it, and six tennis courts, as well as a fifty-foot swimming pool, adjoined by a two-story clubhouse, with dressing rooms below and a full game room above.

Every time he drove up the winding driveway, Howard felt as if he were entering a baronial fiefdom. The 27,000-square-foot Tudor-style mansion, constructed of dark oak half-timbers and stucco, centered around a spacious oak paneled hall leading to a library, music room, dining room, breakfast room, hot and cold kitchens, two pantries, and two porches; on the left-hand side, a wide staircase ascended to eight large bedrooms with attached bathrooms. Howard took special pride in his first-floor study, with its large carved stone fireplace (suitable for a Tudor aristocrat) and a stained-glass window carrying the Candler family crest. Guests—and because of Flora's warm hospitality, there were many—frequently assembled in Callanwolde's cavernous hall to hear performances by celebrated musicians, some of them playing the huge Aeolian organ, its mechanism hidden under stone tracery in arches surrounding the massive front door. When the organ operated at full volume, it boomed throughout the house and vibrated into the back courtyard. The organ gave Howard and Flora such pleasure that they enlarged its capacity by ordering additional pipes and amassing a large collection of rolls, so they could listen to their favorite compositions. Accomplished in both piano and organ, Flora frequently sat at the keyboard, and when she didn't, Howard loaded roll after roll, spending the evening hearing popular tunes, hymns, or classical selections. Basically a homebody, Howard never tired of his vast English barony, brimming with its mixture of decorum, elegance, and every lavish accoutrement then available.[139]

Rest Haven, William Candler's house, photograph by John Sumner

William was the only one of Asa's children to resist pouring his money
into a sumptuous residence, determined instead to use his fortune to fund
his dream of becoming a real estate mogul. When he inherited money
from the sale of Coca-Cola, William was already living in a comfortable
residence on Springdale Road, which he had built during the midteens.
The house, called "Rest Haven," was designed in 1915 by prestigious
Atlanta architects Neel Reid and Norman Hentz. When he, Bennie, and
their daughter, Rena (born in 1914), moved in, it sat on twenty-one acres
of land, with a swan-filled lake, a teahouse, formal gardens, stables, and
a greenhouse. Over the next few decades, the property grew smaller and
smaller, as the couple sold lots to pay off debts. By 1918, when William
Candler Jr. arrived, his family was settled happily in the tasteful two-story
yellow-brick house, where they remained for several decades. Not only
did Rest Haven fit inconspicuously into the Druid Hills neighborhood,
it seemed plain and unpretentious in comparison to the mansions built
by the rest of the family, a perfect reflection of William Candler's more
unassuming personality.

During the 1920s, William organized the Callan Court Company, and
under its auspices he purchased a large swath of land in central Florida and
a four-hundred-square-foot lot on West Peachtree between Fifth and Sixth
Streets. Initially, William planned to build an apartment house on the
midtown property but shelved the idea in favor of hiring Henry Hornbostel

to design a luxury hotel.[140] Before it opened four years later, the project would take several unanticipated twists and turns. By its completion, the United States was well into "the Roaring Twenties," and all five of the wealthy Candler siblings were reaping the benefits accrued from the sale of Coca-Cola. Following in Asa Sr.'s footsteps, they set about reshaping the city's urban landscape through Asa G. Candler Inc., the corporation that their father had organized in 1917.

As they gathered to discuss their holdings, the filial patterns established during their childhoods dominated all transactions. As president of the family firm, Howard served as the conservative watchdog, antagonizing his more adventurous brothers by chastising them for their extravagances, especially Walter and William, who often used their shares of the family business as collateral for their own real estate purchases. Asa Jr. was the risk-taker, frequently making wise—but sometimes foolish—decisions in his job as chief real estate negotiator. Inevitably some of these deals would antagonize Howard as he struggled to keep the company solvent. Given his siblings' volatile natures, meetings of Asa G. Candler Inc. usually dissolved into raucous shouting matches. Only Lucy in the middle kept her brothers from turning the meetings into battlegrounds. Yet, despite their many differences, the Candlers maintained the clan-like public front of mutual protection that their father had so assiduously taught them.

Lucy Candler Owens Heinz—the amicable, loquacious family favorite—was so often touched by tragedy that friends and family wondered how she could maintain her sunny demeanor. Having bounced back after Bill Owens's untimely death, she was able to create a happy life for herself, her new husband, and her children. In the early twenties, they still lived in her father's Ponce de Leon mansion while planning a home of their own on rolling hills a block away. Elizabeth was growing into a teen-ager, her younger brother William was still a rambunctious schoolboy, and young Henry Heinz Jr. was an energetic preschooler. The only dark spot shadowing Lucy's rosy existence was the condition of her younger daughter, born in the spring of 1920. After their initial delight in having this seemingly healthy baby they named Lucy Emilie (but called Mimi), they began to realize that she was sleeping far too much and developing far too slowly. Although Lucy consulted several specialists, none diagnosed the problem and could only advise that Mimi would most likely be mentally impaired. Even though that prognosis proved accurate, she remained a pretty and happy child, with her mother's affectionate personality and head full of golden ringlets.[141]

Living on the premises, Lucy and her family kept her father company as he adjusted to his life as a widower. She had always been his favorite, and he had begun to forget that she had been party to the Coca-Cola sale. He compensated for the sting of that transaction by distancing himself from the business, playing with his grandchildren, chairing Emory's Board of Trustees, and attending the groundbreaking ceremony for the new Wesley Memorial Hospital, when it moved to the edge of the Emory campus. Bill Owens Jr. remembered living in his grandfather's house during this period, often sleeping in Asa's bed and accompanying him on excursions around the city. Best of all were the treats his grandfather would bring home, most notably the pony that arrived when he was still too young to ride it. Although usually affectionate with his grandchildren, Asa could be strict and critical if young Bill strayed from the high standards he expected.[142]

Meanwhile, a sequence of events beginning in 1920 drew Asa Sr. unwillingly back to Coca-Cola. For its first twenty-five years of operation, the company had purchased sugar for four or five cents a pound; then during the war that same pound rose to nine cents, and when wartime controls ended in December 1919, it skyrocketed to more than twenty cents. Because sugar was the beverage's primary ingredient, the escalating price threatened to severely curtail Coca-Cola's profits. The main point of contention was Asa's 1899 agreement with the bottlers from Chattanooga, which froze the price of syrup at one dollar per gallon. By 1920, the parent bottling company was in the hands of two younger men, George Hunter and Veazey Rainwater, who had fostered a chain of independent bottlers around the nation, mushrooming their business into a huge moneymaker, which yielded a twenty-eight-cent profit for every gallon bought by their satellites. Several years earlier, Hunter and Rainwater had come up with the brilliant idea of commissioning an Indiana glassmaker to manufacture a unique and uniform bottle based on the shape of a cacao seed pod. When those new curvaceous green bottles replaced the motley assortment of straight-sided ones, sales soared, and the demand for syrup increased. But as long as sugar prices remained high, enlarged production created a shortfall for the plants manufacturing syrup because they were tied to the 1899 agreement.

Harold Hirsch, who had for years served as attorney for both the parent bottlers and the Coca-Cola Company, tried to broker a deal whereby the two businesses would share the increased expense of sugar. However, the type of informal negotiation that had previously seemed to handle such problems was unacceptable now that the hard-edged Ernest Woodruff headed the company. The only acceptable solution, he insisted, was to abrogate the original contract and raise the syrup price, directing Howard Candler to notify the bottlers that the company was terminating the contract made by his father, thereby increasing the price they would have to pay for a gallon of syrup. Hunter and Rainwater responded immediately by suing the Atlanta headquarters.

The case opened at the Fulton County Superior Court on April 22, 1920, with Asa Candler, Sr. as one of the first witnesses. When the prosecuting attorney, C. T. Hopkins, requested that he explain his original bottling arrangements, Asa snapped he had never granted Whitehead and Thomas "perpetual rights." The contract with them was set to last only for the duration of their "good behavior," he said, and "if at any time these gentlemen had done anything to lower the standard of Coca-Cola," their contracts would have been terminated. Since that was never necessary, Candler continued, the company's relationship with the bottlers remained cooperative and cordial. Indeed, he saw nothing in the contract that forbade the company from raising the price of syrup. When asked if he thought the new bottle was an asset, Asa admitted that it had turned out to be "a very fine source of advertising," although the unique taste of the original syrup was the real reason Coca-Cola had triumphed over the many "spurious drinks."

Next Sam Dobbs described how he had negotiated with Woodruff and the other bankers for sale of the company. During his lengthy discourse, he made a serious gaff by letting slip that the initial meeting with the purchasers had been held in secret, an admission that threw open a Pandora's box of questions. For the next few days, Dobbs squirmed on the witness stand and, in the course of his testimony, he revealed that there were serious gaps in his knowledge of the business's financial transactions. The climax of the trial came when one of the prosecuting lawyers grabbed the Atlanta company's minute book, which lay on the defense's table, and began reading it aloud. Harold Hirsch leapt to his feet, demanding that this private information be stricken from the record. But Judge George Bell refused, overruling Hirsch's objections and allowing the lawyer to continue reading. As he did, the entire courtroom—and ultimately the press—learned every detail of the behind-the-scenes maneuverings.

One of the most shocking revelations was how the company had quietly paid Bainbridge Colby and Edward Brown one million dollars to abrogate their earlier contract, a year before Dobbs turned around and negotiated a similar deal with Woodruff. Part of his reason to end the transaction with Colby and Brown, Dobbs confessed, was to avoid paying $15,000 in "burdensome taxes." Such tax-avoidance schemes captured the headlines for days, especially since Colby had left his law practice to become the US Secretary of State in the waning days of the Wilson administration. As revelation of the company's secrets sidelined the bottling issue, Rainwater and Hunter withdrew their suit in Georgia and filed it anew in a Delaware court. In the meantime, when sugar prices rose to an all-time high of twenty-eight cents a pound, Howard made an unwise move. With Dobbs's approval, he negotiated to buy forty-one thousand tons of Javanese sugar at twenty cents a pound. Very soon afterward, sugar prices plummeted to fifteen cents in September and nine cents a few months later. The Coca-Cola Company was clearly slated to lose millions, and Howard Candler, perpetrator of the deal, was in serious trouble.[143]

Sam Dobbs was in even hotter water. The bungled contract—compounded by his revelation on the witness stand—planted a seed of doubt in Ernest Woodruff's mind. Had he appointed the wrong man to be company president? For the past year or so, Dobbs had been riding a crest of popularity, accrued from his position as Coca-Cola president. Not only had he been asked to serve on several important corporate and charitable boards, but he had been elected president of the Atlanta Chamber of Commerce, his Uncle Asa's old job. Now middle-aged and paunchy, with the characteristic Candler bulldog jaw and deep-set eyes, "Sammy's" picture was often in the paper, as he delivered speeches around town. That celebrity, however, stood to be threatened when Woodruff fully realized the potential repercussions from Dobbs's blundering.

If Sam had left well enough alone, he might have survived. But another misjudgment spelled his doom. Just as sugar prices were making their precipitous fall, he tried to force through an expensive advertising campaign. For Woodruff and most of the trustees, that was the last straw. In no uncertain terms, they strongly opposed the cost of Dobbs's badly timed suggestion, using it as the excuse to criticize his performance as company president and demand his immediate resignation. When reporting his departure, the newspapers spoke vaguely of "irreconcilable differences" between Dobbs and the board. Howard was reinstated as Coca-Cola president, and now it was his cousin's turn to suffer the disgrace of being summarily turned out of the company, where he had worked for the past thirty-two years.[144] As vindicated as Howard must have felt when learning of Sam's dismissal and as gratified as he must have been to be back at the helm of Coca-Cola, he faced a full slate of complications brought about by a bad-news, good-news judicial scenario.

The bad news came from a Delaware judge, who ruled in favor of the bottlers by upholding the original 1899 contract, thereby bringing down the price of Coca-Cola stock and further implicating Howard for negotiating the deal that purchased sugar at such an exorbitant price. The good news was that as lawyers were desperately preparing to appeal that verdict and stave off the company's sliding profits, the US Supreme Court made its pronouncement on the long-running "Koke" case by reversing the California decision and declaring a victory for Coca-Cola. In writing for the majority, Chief Justice Oliver Wendell Holmes stated that use of the name "Koke" was a clear infringement on the Atlanta company's trademark, a ruling that finally ended the troublesome string of court cases that had haunted Asa Candler for so long. But his eldest son, now once again Coca-Cola president, remained in a precarious position under Woodruff's suspicious eye, and for the next two years he stayed suspended on tenterhooks, waiting for another blow to fall.

Asa Jr. had his own dispute with the new Coca-Cola management. In the contract negotiated in 1919, the Candler siblings had each received ten thousand shares of preferred stock, with the stipulation that it be held in a three-man voting trust, then consisting of Woodruff, Eugene Stetson, and board Chairman W. C. Bradley (Dobbs's replacement). Their domination over dispersal of dividends so rankled Asa Jr. that he decided to sue the voting trust for withholding payments to the preferred stockholders. Unknown to anyone in the Coca-Cola hierarchy—probably not even his brother Howard—Asa Jr. filed his suit in Woodruff's home town of Columbus, Georgia, where he hoped to find sympathy among people familiar with their former resident's high-handed maneuvering. When he learned about the suit, Woodruff angrily labeled it "the opening gun of a great legal battle in which the Candler family is seeking to gain control of the Coca-Cola Company once more." To this charge, Asa Jr. snapped that the three men making decisions about *his* stock were the manipulators. When the case arrived on the docket in midsummer 1921, the press called the trial a "great Coca-Cola battle." But the anticipated fight never occurred. After several long, hot court sessions, the judge washed his hands of the entire mess and sent it to the Georgia Supreme Court. However, before that body got around to considering the case, Coca-Cola paid its delayed dividend, prompting a contented Asa, Jr. to withdraw his suit and return to his yacht, birds, and cars.[145]

Asa Sr. left very little evidence that he was particularly upset about his nephew's dismissal as president of the Coca-Cola Company, nor did he express much enthusiasm about Howard's reinstatement. In fact, he seemed to take little more than a cursory interest in the many trial procedures. Not only had he physically and psychologically removed himself from the company, but he had become consumed with a personal affair that was occupying most of his spare time. The involvement began two years earlier, when he served on an advisory committee planning a Confederate reunion. At one of the preliminary meetings, he met an attractive auburn-haired woman from New Orleans with the improbable name of Onezima de Bouchel Roquet. When a few months later the reunion took place in Atlanta's Piedmont Park, Asa Sr. and his new friend were among the crowd of ten thousand visitors from across the South, milling around the grounds, chewing on ribs, and watching mock maneuvers. One day during that time, he invited Onezima to bring a few ladies to lunch with him at the Druid Hills Golf Club, before asking them to visit his nearby home.[146]

When the reunion ended, Onezima wasted no time in initiating a warm and persistent correspondence. Flattered by the younger woman's attention, Asa (who loved to write letters) responded by filling page after page with his current worries as well as his hopes for the future. Although from the start she was outwardly aggressive, Asa seemed to delight in her affectionate advances. In her first note, written to thank him for shepherding her around during the Confederate reunion, she invited him to meet her in New York, and shortly afterward she encouraged him to come with her to Florida, saying she believed it would be "an ideal place for a honeymoon." After Asa responded that a trip at that time would be inconvenient, she replied that "since the 'Mountain won't come to Mahomet,' Mahomet will come to the Mountain." A few weeks later, she said that she would be "stopping off in Atlanta for a day or two with the sole purpose of seeing" him and asked Asa to reserve a room for her at the Ansley Hotel. He probably complied, although no letters survive to prove it. Disturbed about the intensity of his sudden attachment to a stranger so soon after Lucy Elizabeth's death, his children began suspecting he was "showing signs of senility." Even if that were true, one thing was certain: her attention and affection lifted his sagging spirits and revived his energy.[147]

By the summer of 1920, events began to move rapidly. When Onezima sailed to Europe, Asa sent flowers to her stateroom, and when she returned, he met her at the dock in New York and gave her a sapphire ring. Onezima's letters to him now became even warmer and more possessive. "I intend to devote my life to your happiness and comfort," she wrote in November, signing the long letter, "Sweet One." By December, she was addressing him as "My Darling," and by January 1921, she was gushing: "I think of you constantly day and night, in fact, thoughts of you constitute the chief pleasure of my waking or dreaming hours." He, in turn, responded: "I want to sit near you and tell you that I love you as the haven of peace into which I steadfastly believe Providence has directed me." Onezima was then in the process of divorcing Adolphe Roquet in Reno, Nevada. Because the laws of that state required her to remain in the vicinity until the divorce was finalized, she took an apartment there. At her request, Asa counseled her about handling legal details but insisted that she keep his name from any transaction. During early 1922, their plans accelerated. In steamy letters passed back and forth, they agreed to be married as soon as her divorce came through, and he agreed to visit her in the spring to discuss the details. Despite his expressed ardor on paper, Asa cautioned that "influences in Atlanta" were "moving against" them, never revealing the identity of his critics, although all signs pointed to members of his immediate family.

As their romance-on-paper grew warmer, Asa began to assume a paternalistic attitude, scolding her for participating in the suffragette movement. "You are out of that class now," he insisted, "for you told me so when I was last with you." Lightly treating his intolerance for the women's movement, she continued to plead with him to visit her. Just as they were preparing for their rendezvous, he had to cancel because his sister Jessie Willard was in critical condition. When she died, Asa took charge of all the arrangements, in the same fashion he had managed affairs for his widowed sister during much of her life, scheduling the funeral in his Ponce de Leon mansion and shepherding his nieces and nephews to her burial in a Decatur cemetery. [148]

After he settled matters for the Willard family, Asa capitulated to Onezima's entreaties and departed westward. The first stop was Kansas City, where a former Coca-Cola employee "carried" him on an automobile ride to view property that the family owned. Then he went on to California, never telling his children that he was meeting Onezima in San Francisco. In letters to his oldest son, Asa described dinner parties and opera performances, saying only: "I am running [at] a rapid gait for one of my age. My physical machinery appears to be in a healthy state," words that give away little, yet may hint about his relationship with Onezima and his pride at being able to keep up with her.

He did tell Howard that George Reed, who was still running the Los Angeles Coca-Cola office, had driven him up the Pacific coast. It was "the grandest possible scenery," he exclaimed. "Nothing that I saw in Switzerland or Scotland equals these American scenes." He later told Onezima that Reed was "an enigma" and in many ways an "unworthy person," using this description to warn her against associating with people like that. This admonition about the company she kept filtered into several of his letters, suggesting that he had found out something about her companions that displeased him. Still, Asa continued to pursue his courtship through several months of peripatetic traveling. First he was in New York, then Wyoming and Utah, and finally he visited Onezima in Reno, taking her for a jaunt to nearby Lake Tahoe. Again he commented on the "wonderful country" in letters to his son but failed to mention that he was traveling with a companion.

In fact, in his correspondence with Howard, Asa's tone was morose. "No very good reason for me to be here," he said, but "to stay at home or to go only a short distance away I would be restless." He missed his family and his "own Georgia," he wrote, but felt like he was "little benefit to either." And he revealed his frustration about no longer being in the spotlight. "I once was counted with Atlanta's builders, Georgia's active sons, your advisor," he lamented, "now I am companionless, not needed, not called to any service and so I am wandering with those who do not even know me." He expressed similar dissatisfaction in a letter to Howard's daughter Catherine, then fifteen. "Naturally you know I realize that there is now no one to whom I am 'first-love.' I must be ever in the end of the procession of the family, which once I was the progenitor, so when any one of you look down the line to salute me, I rejoice in the recognition." Was this another veiled hint that he had plans to change the "companionless" state of his life? [149]

When he returned home, Onezima began pleading with him to tie up his business obligations, so they could be married immediately after the pending divorce was finalized. In response, he warned that no wedding could take place before the Heinz family moved out of his home. Lucy and Henry had just signed a contract for construction of their new house and hoped to move into it the following March. To ward off anxiety as he waited for news from Reno, Asa stayed busy, seemingly in good health and high spirits. When Emory's fall semester began, he delivered a brief speech at the opening exercises, and the next evening he attended a mock spelling bee given in his honor by the American Institute of Banking.

In the roof lounge of the Ansley Hotel, bankers from around the nation watched in amusement as the former mayor "defeated" all other contenders by consulting a "blueback speller," not so secretly hidden under his arm.

In the fall, he returned to Kansas City to attend an American Legion convention, at which the French war hero Marshal Foch appeared as an honored guest, and when he returned home, he joined a group of dignitaries welcoming the marshal to Atlanta. In the middle of December, Asa presented a loving cup containing four bottles of Coca-Cola to the winner of an Emory track meet, accompanied by students singing "The Coca-Cola Song," whatever that might have been. Shortly after the track meet, Onezima notified him that the divorce was final. And from that point, events spiraled out of control.[150]

Part Four:

Enjoying Money

CHAPTER ELEVEN
Misbehavior

On December 30, 1921, Warren and John Candler went down to their elder brother's office at the Central Bank to congratulate him on his seventieth birthday. But to their surprise, he was nowhere to be found. Inquiring about the vacant office, Asa's secretary remarked nonchalantly that the boss was on his way to California. Although Asa had tried to keep his affair with Onezima de Bouchel secret, his brothers and children had picked up enough hints to realize what was happening. Possibly the family had met Onezima in Atlanta and, even if not, she had friends and other contacts in the city, who were spreading gossip. From what they had heard, Warren and John were convinced that Asa's courtship was a mistake and that Onezima would be an unsuitable wife. So when they discovered their brother was on the way to California, they jumped to the conclusion that he had sneaked away to get married. In a frantic attempt to track him down and prevent the elopement, they contacted the local press, which had teletype connections and access to news services unavailable to private individuals. Needless to say, the local newspapers were delighted to comply with his brothers' request. Asa Candler was a public figure, and the smallest leak about a possible marriage would make a juicy story. After a quick investigation, reporters from the *Atlanta Constitution* found out the name of his Los Angeles hotel and sent him a telegram to ask if the rumors were true.

When Asa received the wire, he was furious. "I have no intention of getting married," he responded angrily, "and I did not come to Los Angeles on the trail of any woman. I celebrated [the birthday] yesterday on the train and nobody is accompanying me. Things have come to such a pass in this country that if a man is supposed to have money he cannot be courteous to any woman without being accused of matrimonial intent. My wife died three years ago," he sighed, "but her death did not eliminate my many friends among women from my life or relieve me of the responsibility incumbent upon every gentleman of being courteous to a woman." He went on to confess: "I met the lady whom gossip is connecting with me in 1918. She was chief sponsor on Colonel Van Zant's staff at the Reunion of Confederate Veterans." Then he added rather sheepishly that he found her both "cultured" and "charming."[151]

Although he never admitted it to his family or the press, Asa and Onezima did spend several days together in Los Angeles, and during that time they made plans for their wedding, tentatively set to take place in San Francisco the following spring or summer. "What I most desire is that you become formally my wife at the earliest possible date," he wrote, explaining that the principal reason he was delaying the nuptials was that the Heinz family was still living in his house but expecting to move out around June 1. After they left, he told Onezima that she could send some of her own possessions to the Ponce de Leon mansion. However, he warned her that they would have to postpone their proposed "foreign journey" to Hawaii until he had fully retired "from active business and public service."

Asa's refusal to set a definite wedding date goaded Onezima into intensifying her pleas for a definite commitment, while her hints to her friends about their engagement leaked back to Atlanta and further irritated his brothers and children. "Rumors of my marriage are abroad," he wrote her in March, "and members of my immediate family are being approached" with all kinds of inquiries. A few weeks later, he elaborated further by saying certain people in town were attempting "to disturb" their relationship, convinced that the fervor of his devotion had "clouded or handicapped" his "reasoning facilities." In light of all the gossip, Asa decided to tell his children that they planned to marry, yet he refused to say when, lest his daughter feel pressured to move. Each of his four sons reacted differently when they heard about Asa's intentions, reflecting their individual personalities. Although Howard feared his father was making a mistake, he promised that once the marriage took place, he and Flora would welcome Onezima into the family; Asa Jr. was more supportive, saying that he and Helen wanted his father to be happy and therefore would love his new wife; Walter opposed the union altogether, and William considered his father's "marriage to anybody" unwise. In his letter telling Onezima about their reactions, Asa never mentioned how his brothers had responded to the news.

By the first of June, Asa was beginning to have second thoughts. Under the prompting of his family, he authorized his nephew, Ezekiel ("Zekie") Candler Jr.—who had just ended ten terms as a US congressman from Mississippi—to conduct an investigation into Onezima's private life. After questioning several of her acquaintances and obtaining testimonies about her character, Zeke provided a report. Asa told Onezima the conclusions were "painful," since many of the people his nephew interviewed suspected that she wanted to marry one of the South's richest men merely for his money. While that may have seemed obvious to everybody else, Asa clung tightly to his romantic fantasies. Certain he could clear up such rumors, he reminded her that there wasn't much money left because he had already "distributed" a "full nine-tenths" of his "material properties" to his church, state, and family. Still confused by the messages he was receiving from Zeke and others, Asa told Onezima that doubts about her Roman Catholic upbringing, her status as a divorcee, and her active support of woman's suffrage were among the disturbing issues being raised. Although he admitted that these things concerned him, he assured her that nothing would diminish his affection.

In the early summer of 1922, Asa promised Onezima that he would soon be coming westward to "claim" her "precious hand and golden heart," but he was unable to travel at that moment. Not only was his sister Lizzie Dobbs critically ill, but the Heinz's home was not yet completed. To prove that he intended to "consummate the engagement," he told her that he had already purchased a wedding ring and arranged for announcements to be printed. Feeling reassured, Onezima arranged to dispatch her furniture to Atlanta, and she organized a trip to New York, where she hoped Asa would meet her. Yet he continued to stall for the next month and even denied having marriage plans when reporters from the *Atlanta Constitution* inquired. Then on August 4—the very day the paper reported his denial—Onezima released news of the wedding to a New Orleans paper. Now he was really cornered, especially after banner headlines blazed across Atlanta's front pages announcing their upcoming marriage.

Based on Onezima's press releases, the papers touted her elevated social status and her heritage from "a very old and distinguished Creole family," as well as her coat of arms and crest, "said to date back to the French Revolution." Added to this stellar background, the reporters wrote that she was considered to be one of the most beautiful and wealthiest women in Louisiana, her "holdings including valuable central business property in New Orleans." In the next few days, stories of her affluence and prominence swelled to include a father, who not only owned "a number of sugar houses," thoroughbred horses, and several steamboats but had been a principal player in the Crescent City's business life. No private citizen's wedding announcement "has ever caused as much talk and produced as many letters of every kind as has mine," Asa wrote Onezima a few days after the news release. Seemingly relieved now that everything was public, he promised to leave Atlanta later in August, so they could be married by the end of the month. [152]

The first and most dramatic interference in Asa's marriage plans was caused by his third son. At that time, much of Walter's life revolved around the racetrack and clubhouse that he had recently built on his new property near Emory University. At the track's inauguration, an event to benefit a Decatur children's home, his sister along with other young "matrons" served as hostesses. Their principal duty was to circulate in the crowd selling programs and refreshments. Hawking a tray of chewing gum in the stands was the beautiful twenty-one-year-old wife of an automobile salesman and racehorse owner named Sarah Byfield. Walter had helped her husband, Clyde, start his business and in the process began paying a great deal of attention to Sarah. That flirtation probably pushed Marion into carrying out the threat she had long been contemplating. Exasperated with all of Walter's excesses, she picked up their daughter Bootsie and fled to her mother's home in California. When his wife left, swearing she would never return, Walter decided to take his other two daughters—eleven-year-old Eugenia and nine-year-old Mary—to Europe. Then, to everyone's surprise, shortly before his departure he asked Clyde and Sarah Byfield to go along, ostensibly to provide female supervision and companionship for his daughters. Possibly already aware of Walter's dalliance with Sarah, Lucy Heinz and Helen Candler expressed strong objections to the arrangement.

But Walter ignored them, and on July 11, 1922, the five Atlantans boarded the SS *Berengaria* bound for France, sharing a large suite with their individual staterooms divided by a small hallway. Enjoying the luxury of their accommodations and the company of several new friends, they crossed the ocean. All was harmonious and peaceful until the Byfields and several others threw a lavish champagne party on the night prior to their landing. As the hour grew late, Sarah and Clyde volunteered to put the children to bed. What happened next depends on who tells the tale. Sarah alleged that when she and her husband reached their stateroom,

Clyde decided to go back to the party, but Sarah said she preferred to stay with the children. After the girls were asleep, she went to her room and prepared to retire for the night. All of a sudden, she claimed, Walter "opened the door, tore the bed clothing off her, grabbed her in his arms and sought to get in bed with her." Sarah said she screamed and raised such a racket that "her husband rushed into the room and immediately engaged in a terrific fight."

As might be expected, Walter Candler's side of the story was quite different. He described how aboard ship the Byfields spent most of their time with "notorious gamblers." Admitting that he had had too much to drink the night of the incident, he said he didn't remember why he ended up in Sarah's stateroom. But "nothing whatsoever of any improper nature" happened, he protested. The next thing he remembered was Clyde bursting into the stateroom, assaulting him and then attacking his wife "in so brutal a manner" that he disfigured her face. Still consumed with fury, Byfield began to search frantically for his pistol, but finding it nowhere, he slammed out of the room. Then as Walter was gathering himself together and staggering across the hall to his own bed, Clyde reappeared with a note demanding $25,000 for the damages inflicted on his wife and his marriage. Given the Candler family's history of attracting extortion plots, the story now takes a remarkably familiar turn. However, unlike his circumspect (and teetotaler) father, Walter made a mess of things. Facing Byfield in what he called "a dazed condition," he said he didn't fully comprehend that he was handing over a $25,000 check. One cannot help but wonder if an innocent man would have so quickly complied to a request for that much money. But more importantly: Had Clyde really become suspicious, or was the whole thing a setup to get Walter's money? These queries would shape the gossip and subsequent legal proceedings.

The next day, when they reached the Carleton Hotel in Paris, Walter began backtracking, confessing that his depleted bank account lacked the funds to cover the check, and so he begged Byfield to end their misunderstanding. Temporarily the delay worked. In the heady atmosphere of a Paris holiday financed with Candler's money, Byfield agreed to take only $2,500 in cash, and they signed an agreement to that effect, supposedly canceling the other $22,500. But Clyde retained the original promissory note as well as the new compromise, later explaining that Walter threatened to destroy his automobile business if he refused the lower amount. During their stay in the French capital, Sarah purportedly remained holed up in her hotel room, claiming that the incident had wrecked her nerves.

After they left Paris, the two parties separated, and within days each man had contacted an Atlanta lawyer. Walter instructed his to file suit for attempted blackmail, while Clyde raised his demand to $100,000. When the Byfields reached New York, they were greeted by a barrage of reporters, tipped off by either Clyde himself or—as he claimed—somebody aboard ship. Not surprisingly, the Atlanta papers wallowed in reporting the peccadilloes of its most prominent family. Splashed across the headlines, the incident aboard ship and its aftermath escalated into a melodrama of Hollywood proportions. Sarah stayed locked in her Atlanta apartment, insisting that Walter's attack had precipitated a "sinking spell" that caused "a nervous breakdown" requiring hospitalization. As she languished in bed, other *Berengaria* passengers began emerging with differing versions of the shipboard brouhaha. One of them, a New York lawyer named August Dreyer, claimed that Walter had promised to pay *him* $5,000 for witnessing the Paris agreement that reduced the payment to Byfield. Anxious to enlist witnesses to their cause, Clyde and his lawyer traveled to New York in hopes of recruiting Dreyer to testify in court on their behalf.

Back on American shores, Walter escaped the Atlanta press by retreating to Maine, where Howard and his family were vacationing. Asa Sr.—whose own romantic folly was simultaneously capturing the headlines—wrote Howard to express his displeasure at learning about Walter's affair. "I have great confidence in your good sense and in your love for and fidelity to your younger brother," he began, and then added:

> I do pray that Walter has not compromised himself. Tell him Papa allows no one to speak evil of him … I am not passing judgment on him till I hear what he has to say. He must face every enemy bravely. Say just as little as possible [as] you advise together affectionately. We must all cling together. We can overcome all if we do. I try to pray every day for all of you. God has been good to us. He will not desert us.[153]

Asa's comments repeat his long-standing credo: With God on their side, their family fortress could defeat any adversary, a conviction that had seen them through past trials.

By the end of August, the ocean liner episode had dissolved into a morass of legal wrangling and malicious slurs. Walter hired the Burns

Detective Agency to investigate the New Yorkers on board the *Berengaria* for possible connections with "blackmail gangs" and, in retaliation, Byfield accused Walter, one of his "horse trainers," and Asa Jr. of storming into his automobile agency in an attempt to make off with the original promissory note and the Paris memo. In their scuffle, Byfield claimed that the Candlers tore off his clothes and ransacked his business.

As it didn't take long for the wire services to pick up the juicy story, Marion Candler heard about the incident while vacationing in Hawaii. At first, she told reporters that she wasn't surprised that her estranged husband had been involved with another woman and was furious to learn that he had gotten himself into such a mess. But after members of the Candler family intervened, she reversed her position: "If I believed for a moment that there was a word of truth in the charges," she said, "I likely would be the first to accuse my husband." A few days later, she departed from Honolulu en route to Atlanta, a journey that entailed several days of traveling by ship to California, where she picked up her daughter and then went a few more days by rail to meet Walter in Chicago. As she stepped from the train with Bootsie in her arms, Marion embraced Walter before turning to speak with the press. Coolly, she announced that she had every intention of supporting her husband and was deeply skeptical about the Byfields' charges. Moved to a burst of purple prose, one reporter described the couple's reunion as if it were a screen scenario, replete with "feminine sobs" and "exclamations of faith," intermingled with "a masculine drawl full of entreaty and an infant's cry of joy."[154] Either the reporter got completely carried away, or Marion and Walter put on quite a performance.

Asa Sr. had instinctively rallied to his son's side when he first heard about the shipboard incident, but he soon began having misgivings, especially after becoming aware of how far Walter's shenanigans had gone. Ever mindful that adverse publicity could be destructive to a business, the senior Candler knew that the Central Bank and Trust was in jeopardy, with its vice president embroiled in such a public legal debacle. For the past three years, Asa had been issuing positive reports about the institution's strong standing, emphasizing that his bank had remodeled the Candler Building facility and opened two new branches. Still actively engaged in management, Asa retained his office at the bank and participated in the daily activities of his employees. Although the bank's prominence— enhanced by recently increased revenues—often prompted inquiries from potential buyers, Asa refused to even discuss a possible merger.

Walter's latest fiasco, however, changed things. After years of grooming his third son to be bank president, Asa realized that Walter was totally inadequate for the job. Not only was he embroiled in an ugly scandal, but he seemed far more interested in horse racing and high living than in the daily activity of higher finance. In addition, Asa feared that his nemesis, Ernest Woodruff—whose Trust Company was fast dominating the Atlanta scene—was maneuvering to take over the Central Bank the same way he had wormed his way into Coca-Cola. It was time for him to be rid of this troublesome worry. Therefore, in September 1922, Asa Jr., acting for his father, signed an agreement with the Citizens & Southern Bank, a fast-expanding Savannah institution with branches all over Georgia and the Southeast. Under terms of their merger, the Central Bank and Trust would cease to exist, and its downtown location and branches would become part of C&S. Asa Candler Sr. and Jr. would join the C&S board, and Henry Heinz would remain a vice president. Although Walter's name was never mentioned in the press release, the omission made it very clear that his relationship with the bank was permanently severed.[155]

With Walter's escapade and the bank merger foremost in his mind, Asa was neglecting Onezima de Bouchel, which only intensified her pursuit. Once again, she used her favorite weapon—the press—to announce that they would marry during September. Shocked by her temerity, Asa vehemently insisted that no date had been set, yet when an inquiring reporter called, he said he had every intention of going through with the wedding. What he failed to tell the press was that Onezima's furniture and personal belongings were already in the Ponce de Leon mansion, and announcements of their marriage were stacked on a table waiting to be mailed. And most significantly, he had already purchased Pullman tickets for his trip to Reno, with return reservations to New York and Atlanta for them both. In fact, he had gone so far as to order flowers and engage a minister to conduct the ceremony.

After Walter's story broke, Asa wired Onezima saying that there was no way he could leave Atlanta until after the "storm" subsided. That message set her temper into such high gear that she turned once more to vent her fury in the press. "Elements" in Atlanta led by Bishop Candler, she exploded, were "mitigating against her proposed marriage" because the Candlers opposed her Catholicism, her divorce, and her suffragette activities. Then she instructed her lawyer to announce that "the acts of two or three envious intermeddlers and slanderers" would not deter his client from carrying out her planned marriage. When a reporter from the *Atlanta*

Constitution called to read Asa the lawyer's statement, he replied: "I don't care to hear it, thank you," and slammed down the phone. Nevertheless, he persevered, making arrangements to depart for Reno on September 16 and marrying Onezima as soon as he arrived. He admitted to his prospective bride, however, that with the exception of support from his sister Florence, "troubles" at home left him "far from being happy" about the situation. Still he continued to beg her to stand by faithfully during his ordeal.

Gnawing indecision, coupled with pressures from all quarters, soon propelled Asa Sr. into the depths of depression. When he was at his lowest, he learned from an unnamed source that during the Confederate reunion of 1919, Onezima had invited two Atlanta men to visit her hotel room. That finally put him over the edge. The twenty-first century's more relaxed sexual mores make such accusations seem not only trivial but downright ludicrous. However, to a generation reared during an era subsumed in Victorian repressions, it was a very serious charge. In Asa's moral code, men did not enter a respectable woman's hotel room, nor did a woman collect men's telephone numbers and make unsolicited calls. No one seems to have considered that she had used similar tactics to lure Candler during the same Confederate reunion, and—although he may not have then visited her hotel room—he had certainly been attracted by her alluring entreaties.

With this latest defamation of Onezima's character weighing heavily upon him, on the day before he was scheduled to leave town, Asa wired his fiancée that "circumstances" made it impossible for him to go through with their plans. He amplified this seemingly final declaration with a long, emotional letter, providing an account of the hotel-room story. "To marry you with these reports in force," he wrote, "could not in any case be right or fair to either of us, even [if] they be untrue." It was a lame (and possibly dictated) excuse from a man struggling to reach a balance between her persistence and pressure from his determined family. All those months of procrastination do suggest, however, that subconsciously he was trying to avoid any kind of firm commitment. Yet at the same time his doubts were increasing, he was continuing to express his undying love and devotion, pathetic appeals that continued right up to the day he called off the wedding! Those paradoxical signals, occurring simultaneously, certainly lend credence to his children's conviction that their father's judgment and decisiveness had undergone significant changes.

As anticipated, Onezima reacted furiously to the break. "Do you expect me to let this hideous slander go unpublished?" she railed, threatening to tell "the whole world" about what he had done and demanding that he reveal the name of the person who had unleashed such an untrue and "clumsy conspiracy." No doubt, she added, the family had fabricated the story of her hotel visitor to destroy her reputation and sever their engagement. But like a poignant parody of then-popular dirty jokes, Asa would reveal no details about the informer other than to say that her accuser was a "traveling salesman."[156]

The story did not end with the broken engagement. Onezima settled into a Chattanooga hotel under an assumed name, encamped like General Sherman ready to advance on Atlanta but waiting until her lawyer went first to scout out the enemy. During this period, Asa wrote two more letters, repeating his continued respect for her and expressing his doubts about her purported impropriety. However, his last communications were clipped and impersonal. The engagement must be broken, he insisted, because the current situation would make a life together "intolerable" for them both. Finally, during early October, Onezima descended on Atlanta, taking a suite at the Winecoff Hotel. It was her last hope, although if anything her visit made matters worse. Asa, accompanied by Asa Jr., called at her suite, and, during a chilly meeting, the formerly ardent suitor broke into sobs. His seemingly pitiful state only underscored Onezima's conviction that he was being duped into breaking the engagement, and that notion provided her with an impetus to retaliate. When the newspapers announced that they weren't getting married, she released an interview in which she depicted herself as a mistreated innocent, who was orphaned at age eight, educated in Catholic convents, abused in her marriage to Roquet, and now slandered by the Candlers. Then she twisted the knife. She could not blame Asa, she said, because he had not come from "generations of the courtly refinement which I inherited from my forebears." His shoddy upbringing and coarse surroundings, she said, prevented him from understanding that making accusations against her character inflicted a "mortal wound."

Back in New Orleans, the former society doyen held court by calling together seventy "richly gowned women of the oldest and wealthiest families" to commiserate with her at the Grunewald Hotel, all the while plying reporters with accusations against Candler's "agents." His children, she said, had attempted to steal their love letters from her lawyer's office and threatened to place Asa in "a sanatorium" if he insisted on marrying her. Eventually, when even the gossip-hungry press became tired of the story, Onezima's lawyers filled the void by announcing that they were gathering data for a "breach of promise" suit. They insisted their action was merely an attempt to restore their client's "good name," with no intentions of collecting "one penny of the Candler fortune"[157]

Just after Asa's seventy-first birthday, at the height of the de Bouchel press frenzy, a civic organization called the President's Club voted to honor the former mayor on the fiftieth anniversary of his arrival in Atlanta. For the occasion, four hundred leading businessmen, professionals, and out-of-town guests gathered in the Piedmont Driving Club ballroom to pay tribute to one of its most prominent citizens. The honoree sat in the center of a head table surrounded by his four sons, his son-in-law, and invited speakers. Following the meal, an array of Atlanta's foremost citizens heaped accolades on Asa for his philanthropic and commercial contributions to the city and presented him with a silver loving cup, inscribed with thanks for "fifty years filled with golden deeds for his fellow-man."

The outpouring of support and affection from community leaders must have buoyed the old warrior, because during 1923 he resumed an active role in civic affairs, appearing frequently at meetings and making speeches around town. He played a leading role in planning Candler Park, which was being built on a large tract of land near Decatur, then part of his large Kirkwood/Druid Hills holdings. In a deal worked out with the city, the family agreed to donate the property for the park that would have playgrounds, a lake, tennis courts, a large swimming pool, and golf links. When work began in July 1923, Asa delivered what the papers called a "splendid talk" and vowed to "make the park into an ideal playground." A month later, when President Warren G. Harding died, Governor Clifford Walker appointed the former mayor to accompany the Georgia delegation attending the funeral in Marion, Ohio. As he threw himself into these activities, Asa seemed to have recovered his old vivacity and much of his energy.[158]

Rainbow Terrace, (exterior and interior) Lucy Candler Heinz's house,
courtesy of Lullwater Estates and Dr. Edna Bay

By that time, he was living alone in his mansion for the first time since
Lucy Elizabeth died, because during the previous summer, his daughter
and her family had moved into their new estate a block away. The Heinzes
called their Mediterranean-style home "Rainbow Terrace," a name chosen
to reflect Lucy's ebullient personality and persistent optimism. Resting at

the crest of a hill—which became a fairyland of pink and white dogwoods in the spring—the two-story mansion sat near the front of the eight-and-a-half-acre lot and opened onto terraced gardens in back. From there, the property swept downward toward a wooded area, where, like her parents and brothers, Lucy and her servants maintained a small farm, replete with cows, chickens, and a vegetable garden.

The local architectural firm of G. Lloyd Preacher & Company carried out the rainbow theme by designing pale-pink stucco exterior walls and pastel plaster interior walls, washed with buttermilk (taken from the Heinzes' cows) to achieve the patina she had seen in an Italian palazzo. Her travels in Europe and frequent trips to Florida supplied many of her decorating ideas, while others came from movie sets, similar to those that had inspired her mother. She admitted that she patterned the staircase and Spanish-style balcony on a film she had seen in Atlantic City. The furniture (painted in pale shades to match the décor) as well as the hand-carved wooden ceilings and woodwork (veined with goose feathers to simulate marble) also suggested the decor of Italian palaces, if not the sets of contemporary movies.

Elizabeth Owens's debut on November 23, 1922, provided her mother with the perfect opportunity to show off Rainbow Terrace. The festivities for Lucy's daughter—who at age eighteen was attending Ward Belmont College in Nashville—began at an afternoon reception, during which girls of her debutante class strolled around the mansion's grand entrance hall sipping punch or nibbling small sandwiches in the adjoining dining room. That evening, Lucy and Henry hosted a ball at the Druid Hills Golf Club (next to their home), where they formally presented Elizabeth to Atlanta society. For still-small-town Atlanta during the 1920s, these debuts were the highlights of the social season. Marriageable young girls met scions of prominent families (or as the newspaper dubbed them, "young men of the dancing set"), who were available to be prospective grooms. The *Atlanta Constitution* covered the Rainbow Terrace reception and formal ball, describing the décor and entertainment in minute detail. According to custom, a photograph of Elizabeth in her ball gown appeared in the Sunday rotogravure section, and the society editor elaborated admiringly on her "golden hair and fair attractions."[159]

Briarcliff, home of Asa Candler Jr., photograph by John Sumner

When her cousin, Lucy Candler, had her debut two months later, the papers were even more effusive, calling her "strikingly handsome" and "one of the most attractive of the young women in fashionable circles," an attribute confirmed by the photograph picturing a pretty, dark-eyed young woman with stylish spit curls in the middle of her forehead. Ever keen not to be outdone by any of his siblings, Asa Jr. presented his daughter to society by starting the celebration with an extravagant reception in his new buff-colored Georgian-revival mansion on the forty-two acre estate he called "Briarcliff." Like Howard, he had built a baronial manor with a number of outbuildings in a park-like setting, but, as always, Asa Jr. sought ways to outdo his elder brother. During construction, the *Atlanta Constitution* reported that he sent his landscape architect on a tour of the East Coast in search of rare plants. To accommodate his collection, he added two additional steel-framed greenhouses, filled with state-of-the-art equipment for nurturing luxuriant flora to surround the swimming pool, water fountain, reflecting pools, maintenance buildings, and a large garage, with room above to house the servants. More than eight hundred species of roses dotted the forty-two acres of land, over which bridges and walkways connected themed gardens, lighted so visitors could roam around the estate at night.

Winter weather discouraged the four hundred guests at Lucy Candler's debutante reception from touring the extensive grounds. Instead, they drove up the semicircular driveway to the columned entrance portico and entered the large wood-paneled entrance hall to greet the elegantly gowned debutante, her mother, and her closest friends, all standing in a receiving line before a screen of palms and ferns, with French flower baskets hanging overhead. Other members of the family acted as hosts to usher the visitors into the dining room for punch and light refreshments. That evening, Asa Jr. spared no excesses at the formal dance for his eldest daughter in the ballroom of the Piedmont Driving Club, which had been transformed into a Japanese garden, replete with wisteria, peach blossoms, and roses. Small pergolas festooned with colorful Japanese lanterns and fresh flowers filled the room, each centered with tables where tuxedoed waiters served a formal dinner slightly before midnight. The society reporter called the assembled finery: "the most brilliant gathering" of the season.[160]

One cannot help but wonder what Asa Sr.—a farm boy from Villa Rica—was thinking when his granddaughters were so extravagantly introduced to Atlanta society. Was he proud or repulsed to know how his family was spending the wealth produced by all his years of hard work? At least, the debutante balls afforded a welcome relief from the continuing press orgy caused by the simultaneous father and son scandals and the legal procedures then in the works. Refusing to speak with reporters about either case, the family closed ranks for mutual self-protection in the established Candler manner. Still, their refusal to talk did nothing to curtail the gossip or prevent the pending litigations from proceeding.

In February, Onezima's lawyers filed a petition claiming $500,000 in damages, and the Atlanta papers once again plastered the front pages with her latest photograph. Alongside it was a lengthy description of her claims, which included a report of her severe "nervous breakdown" caused by the broken engagement, leading to her confinement in a Chicago sanitarium. The ninety-two items of her lawyer's petition reiterated all of her complaints about "members of the defendant's family," who had made a "determined effort" to locate "sources of information derogatory" to her character. When reporters telephoned Asa Sr. for his comments, he told them he had "absolutely nothing to say about the matter," and again he slammed down the phone. However, he did reply the following March, when his own lawyers filed a response to de Bouchel's charges. Admitting that a member of his family *had* investigated "certain suggestions" about Onezima's conduct, Asa denied that they had attempted to "prevent the marriage," adding that the accusations against her and the concurrent publicity (which she had originated) would make it impossible for them to ever "be happily married."[161] And with that, the confrontation quieted down awaiting announcement of a trial date.

Just about the time the Candler family was enjoying debutante balls and enduring yet one more round of undesirable publicity, Howard found himself getting more and more annoyed with Ernest Woodruff. Although now reinstated as Coca-Cola president, the eldest Candler sibling was well aware that he had no real authority, despite his having reduced the company's losses during the few years he had been in charge. Some of his distress stemmed from Woodruff's determination to dominate, and he was well aware that his own conservatism and obsession with detail were seriously exasperating his impetuous boss. But when he discovered that Woodruff was issuing doctored press reports, a scheme contrived to boost stock prices, Howard became so infuriated that he complained openly, a risky maneuver in light of subsequent developments. Through it all, Asa Sr. was neither cheering his son along nor sitting idly in the background. Conversely, while Howard was airing his objections to Woodruff, his father was telling a reporter that had he not given all that Coca-Cola stock to his children, the company "would not have gotten into all the trouble that has attended it during the past twelve months."

As the tension mounted, Howard—who had never been able to withstand pressure and was always suspicious of the schemes to undermine him—must have realized that his tenure as company president was precarious. Yet when Ernest Woodruff announced in early 1923 that he was making his thirty-three-year-old son, Robert, president of Coca-Cola, Howard expressed shock. At that time, Robert Woodruff was an up-and-coming executive at the White Motor Company in Cleveland, Ohio, having risen rapidly from car salesman to vice president. In most ways, he and Howard were quite different. A tall, debonair playboy and dropout from Emory College, Robert was outgoing and personable. In fact, in many ways he bore a greater resemblance to the imaginative and flamboyant Asa Jr. than to the staid, fastidious Howard.

Unlike his hotheaded father, Robert Woodruff was a diplomat. When the Candler siblings united to challenge Howard's dismissal, the younger Woodruff worked hard to placate his predecessors. That wasn't exactly easy, especially when William Candler had earlier become so impatient with the Woodruffs that he resigned as secretary-treasurer; then after his oldest brother was so abruptly fired, he candidly voiced his resentment. But Robert's greatest challenge was dealing with Howard, especially after Flora let it be known that she was very angry at the affront to her husband, no doubt secretly worried that it would send him spiraling into another depression. In hopes of calming things down, Robert took the time to visit Callanwolde and talk quietly with them both in hopes of assuaging the couple's wounded feelings. As a result of that visit, Howard decided to put aside his initial dismay at being ousted by the younger man, and he agreed to negotiate a flimsy truce with the company he had served through much of his life.

When the board of directors created an advisory council and offered him the chairmanship, Howard willingly accepted. Robert Woodruff backed up this gesture of conciliation by telling the press that he was "greatly honored" to have Howard Candler serving as his "associate." In return, Howard remarked that Coca-Cola was "entering into an era of prosperity and expansion," and, therefore, it was "necessary to add to our executive force." He even went so far as to commend Robert Woodruff's "wide experience" that would be of "the greatest aid in shaping the policy of expansion" they hoped to implement. Howard retained his position as chairman of the Coca-Cola Board of Directors for the rest of his life, seemingly reconciled to the reality that he had been permanently removed from the day-to-day operations of his father's former company.[162]

With his older brother nursing his wounds, Asa Jr. became involved in another diversion. In February 1923, he announced plans to establish a "floating school" for four hundred young men from rich families. Probably inspired by exploring the seas in his new yacht, he embraced this project with the same obsessive fervor that he had shown for all his new endeavors, devising a convoluted rationale to justify this latest folly as a form of altruism for the wealthy. In the profligate 1920s, such a notion seemed to make sense, at least it did to Asa Jr., whose older son John personified the overprivileged boy he described to the press. "There are many poor boys who attend schools and buckle down to their work in earnest because they have no other interests," he said to reporters, "but there are many sons of rich men, who have their cars and their clubs and find too much to do other than study." Excitedly, he opened the school's office in the Candler Building, began enrolling potential students (including John and his cousin, Howard Candler Jr.), and purchased the army transport ship *Logan*, with plans to have it remodeled. But only a few months elapsed before the venture began to falter. In early April, Asa Jr. announced that the headmaster he hired had died suddenly, which meant he would have to postpone the opening for another year. Two weeks later, he sold the *Logan* to a Boston company, claiming the renovation costs were "prohibitive." Nevertheless, the indomitable Coca-Cola heir said he had not abandoned the school idea altogether and was seeking another vessel more easily adapted to such purposes. The idea bounced around for several years, but the school never materialized.[163]

It was just one more of the many impetuous ventures that Asa Jr. embraced enthusiastically, only to become bored and move on to something else. After he abandoned the floating school, Asa Jr. decided to take his wife Helen, their two sons, daughter Lucy, and niece Elizabeth Owens on an around-the-world vacation. The three-month journey began with a driving tour through the British Isles and France, and then the Candler party leisurely headed eastward, ending up with an extensive jaunt through Asia. As they were sailing out of the Yokohama harbor on the return voyage, a major earthquake struck Japan, causing severe damage in Tokyo and several other cities. When he got home, Asa Jr. capitalized on this disaster by giving a series of lectures on "the Orient" to various civic and religious groups, and in each talk he described the various cities they had visited, illustrating his remarks with a sampling of the rare treasures they had purchased.[164]

Howard and Flora Candler in Havana, 1923, courtesy of Manuscript, Archives, and Rare Book Library, Emory University

Howard was also channeling his energies toward travel now that he was relieved of all responsibilities at Coca-Cola. For the first few months following his removal from office, he took Flora on several trips to New York, where they indulged themselves with frequent evenings at the opera or theater and spent hours wandering around the city shopping for clothes, home furnishings, and new rolls for the Aeolian organ. Now that he was not "rushed to death with work," Howard and his wife decided to spend a few weeks in Cuba. One sunny day in Havana, they hired a "motor launch" for a tour around the harbor to Moro Castle, and later that day they visited an old Spanish woman who kept monkeys. Snapshots from that excursion survive, one showing the couple standing by the shore, another picturing Flora jauntily posed on a wall carved into a rock cliff. Now approaching middle age, both had put on weight. Howard stands stiffly in a business suit, while Flora is attired in a dress with the fashionable lowered waistline and cloche hat. Ever conscious of the latest styles, she had written to her daughter Catherine during their New York stay: "The girls here are fixing their hair the cutest way, making long hair look like it was bobbed but didn't see a single girl with bobbed hair." The cloche hat hides Flora's hair, so it is difficult to tell whether she had succumbed to the current trend.[165]

In mid-June 1923, Howard and Flora returned to New York for another relaxing get-away, only to find their calm retreat unexpectedly disrupted by shocking news from home. On the morning of June 22, while lounging in his hotel suite leisurely opening the mail, Howard spotted a letter from his father, indicating that a duplicate copy had been sent to Asa Jr. in Europe. It began with Asa Sr.'s usual warm wishes to his "two men sons" and hopes "that their hearts and minds are as one." Howard must have read the next sentences with a growing sense of unease: "We are growing old, our interests are divergent. Profound love for each other will tend to [be] keeping us always very, very dear to each other." At first this might have seemed like is father's usual plea for family unity, but that illusion vanished when he read:

> Tomorrow I am taking to myself a life companion, one I believe who is interested in me and will be a comfort to me. I feel the need of such companionship. She will be only by marriage related to you. I have reason to believe her worthy of your respect, if she by right living proves this to be true, I bespeak for her your confidence and respect. She has been obligated to work hard to support herself and two daughters, 10 years old … We will be in New York from about June 24th till July 2nd at Hotel Biltmore.

223

In other words, the old rascal had sneaked off to be married! Fearful that his sons and brothers might again try to stop him, he concealed his intentions until the day before the ceremony.

The bride was thirty-six-year-old Mae Little Ragin, a widow who ran a stenographic service in the Candler Building. In the picture on the front page of both major Atlanta papers, she appeared to be a stately brunette with smiling eyes and a round face. Ironically, when she and Asa met six months earlier, she was employed as a typist at his brother John's law firm while they were preparing their response to Onezima de Bouchel's suit. Although Bishop Warren Candler attended his brother's hastily organized wedding, he did not perform the ceremony, as he had for every other family member. Instead, Mae's minister, Ben Lacy of the Central Presbyterian Church, presided. Asa's two other living brothers, John and Willie, also attended, as did Lucy and Henry Heinz, several Candler grandchildren, and a few members of Mae's family, including her ten-year-old twin daughters, Mary and Julia. Noticeably absent were Asa's four sons, leading one to speculate that he deliberately planned the secret wedding knowing they would be away. Even if they had been in town, it is highly unlikely that William and Walter would have attended, given their strong opposition to their father marrying anyone.

The couple had planned to be wed at Mae's home on North Avenue, but because her mother was ill, they transferred to Emory's Theology Building chapel, financed several years earlier by the groom. It was an extremely simple ceremony with no attendants and no music. Asa, in a black mohair suit, and Mae—wearing a navy crepe "traveling suit" and tan, satin hat—walked arm-in-arm down the chapel aisle. The wedding was so inconspicuous that students studying nearby knew nothing about it. As soon as the service ended, guests followed the newlyweds to the small Emory depot and watched them board the Seaboard Airline train bound for Washington, where the couple spent three nights at the Willard Hotel before traveling on to New York.

Due to Asa Candler's prominence as the founder of Coca-Cola and former mayor of Atlanta, the surprise wedding made headlines all over the nation. The response of his stunned family was less than laudatory, to say the least, since most of them looked upon the new bride with scorn. Asa's granddaughter, Laura Candler Chambers, later complained about the tycoon's choice of the woman to replace her sainted grandmother. "There were plenty of widows out there that would have loved to have gone out with Asa Candler," Laura commented bitterly. But "no, he had to pick this thing that nobody had ever heard of." Furthermore, Asa Jr.'s daughter complained that the papers referred to Mae's twin daughters as the "Candler twins," while her own twin sisters, Martha and Helen, were ignored.

Howard and Flora, however, offered their congratulations and sent flowers to the honeymoon suite at the Biltmore. The new groom responded with gratitude: "Your renewed devotion" will "ultimately justify my policy in withholding name, date, and place from you all previous. Experience caused fear of harsh criticism undeserved and undesired."

The newlyweds returned to Atlanta a few days earlier than expected and settled into Candler's Ponce de Leon mansion, with Mae's twin daughters in tow. During the summer, family and friends entertained them at teas and dinner parties, and for the time being, Asa appeared to be happy. When told about the marriage, Onezima de Bouchel shrugged that she was "entirely unconcerned." With perhaps a degree of sadness, the Candlers would soon realize that they would have been far better off if they had allowed Asa to marry his first choice for a compatible "life companion." [166]

CHAPTER TWELVE
Trials and Tributes

For the Candler family, 1924 got off to a bad start and didn't get much better. First came the long-anticipated courtroom drama, prompted by Onezima de Bouchel's attempt to get $500,000 in damages from Asa Sr. The case—dubbed the "heart balm suit" by the press—began in the US District Court on January 30 with Judge Samuel H. Sibley on the bench. Because Georgia law prohibited Asa and Onezima from testifying, the action boiled down to a squabble over legalities. But no legislation prevented the two of them from attending the trial. On the first day, Onezima, "attractively clad in a dark dress trimmed in moleskin" appeared promptly at 10:00 a.m. with an entourage of friends from New Orleans, while Asa Sr., with his new wife at his side, did not arrive until nearly one thirty that afternoon, sitting down quietly beside his sons, Asa Jr. and Walter, who were already in the courtroom. Although he glanced furtively at his former fiancée when he entered the room, neither of them looked directly at each other for the remainder of the session.

The first question to arise was the validity of Onezima's divorce from Roquet, which Candler's attorneys argued was invalid, thus rendering any marriage illegal. However, her lawyers interrupted the proceedings to read a dispatch from Reno, ascertaining that she had received the divorce decree in September 1921. Although that should have quelled the matter, it didn't. The real theatrics came when one of her lawyers began methodically reading each of the twenty-one letters that Asa had written to "Dear Sweetums," a salutation that Candler's attorneys corrected as actually being "Dear Sweet One," claiming a misreading of the handwriting. But the title "Sweetums" stuck and entered all subsequent retellings of their romantic entanglement.

The next day the melodrama reversed courses, as Harold Hirsch read thirty-two of what he termed Onezima's "pursuit letters." The defense team announced it would make no effort to attack the plaintiff's character, rather the attorneys would demonstrate that Candler had conducted himself "in a considerate and gentlemanly manner" and had made no public announcements of either the engagement or its dissolution. Onezima had been the one, he explained, to initially contact the press and then travel to Atlanta in "a desperate attempt to retrieve what apparently had been lost after months of careful planning." In short, the lawyers pegged her as "the aggressor," who manipulated the engagement with "consummate skill" long before she had obtained her divorce. When the defense began closing arguments, de Bouchel's attorney jumped to his feet to express his "amazement" that they never mentioned the alleged visit of the mysterious man to their client's hotel room. But, too smart to take the bait, Candler's team continued doggedly to demonstrate that the Nevada divorce would be considered illegal in Georgia. At this impasse, the judge dismissed the jury and called a private Saturday session for the two attorneys to quibble over legal technicalities.

Then national news intervened. On Sunday, February 3—the day after the lawyers convened privately—Woodrow Wilson died. In memory of the former president, city officials announced they were shutting all government facilities on February 6, the day of the funeral. Consequently, Judge Sibley said he wanted the Candler-de Bouchel case finished before the court closed down. When the trial reconvened on February 4, the day was cold and gray with intermittent snow. Still the legal disputes droned on, as dreary as the weather outside, the same quarrels over the divorce's legality and Onezima's aggression, repeated and rehashed in mind-numbing detail. Finally around midday, the two sides adhered to the judge's demand for closure and turned the case over to the jury. Both Asa and Onezima were in the courtroom that morning, as their lawyers presented final arguments, but both departed when the jury left for deliberations. In the decision that came back rather quickly, Asa was cleared of all charges with no obligation to pay anything to Onezima. It was a predictable verdict, for no panel of twelve Atlanta men would dare convict their city's former mayor and favorite philanthropist of any wrongdoing.

Asa was in the lobby of the Candler Building surrounded by friends when he learned of the outcome. To the milling reporters, he said simply: "I have no statement to make except that I am very happy." Onezima was far more vocal when she received the news while lunching at the Piedmont

Hotel with her entourage. Once again she issued a lengthy diatribe claiming that "technical legal reasons" subverted the true meaning of her suit. Howard, who was in New York, sent his father a congratulatory wire after learning of the verdict, and Asa responded that the trial proceedings left him so upset he could "scarcely write." The *Atlanta Constitution* called the decision "the closing chapter in one of the most sensational breach of promise suits ever tried in the South."[167] But just as that chapter closed, another equally difficult one was about to open.

Three days after the jury issued its verdict, the *New York Times* reported that Mrs. Asa Candler Sr. had been arrested by none other than Asa's friend, Atlanta Police Chief James L. Beavers. Mae's indiscretion—revealed in bits and pieces over the next few months—constituted yet another sad assault on Asa's dignity. While extreme loneliness and boredom had no doubt propelled him into the whirlwind courtship of Onezima and hasty marriage to Mae, his vulnerability to female aggression seems also to have resulted from a considerable decline in his judgment and reasoning. For several years his children had been suspecting he was becoming "senile," and they soon began noticing physical impairments as well. In December 1923, when Howard escorted his father to a "Coca-Cola family" dinner in Baltimore, he was saddened to see that Asa's "muscular deterioration" caused "a slinging and dragging motion of the right foot." Aboard the train, Howard also noticed that his father was having difficulty boarding the car and climbing into and out of the berth. These symptoms could mean that Asa was then in the early stages of any number of debilitating illnesses, arthritis, or perhaps small strokes, or maybe Parkinson's disease. Aware of that growing disability, he may well have been seeking a wife to serve as his nurse.

But if Asa had hoped to marry a caretaker, he chose the wrong person. Mae was rude to his friends, he later confessed, and he suspected that she was meeting a man somewhere, since she left the house early many mornings and didn't return until late in the evening. When Asa instigated an investigation, he discovered that she had been visiting a building on Juniper Street. Alerted to the situation, Chief Beavers and Captain A. J. Holcombe began knocking on doors until they found her in an apartment with two men: W. J. Stoddard, president of a dry cleaning business, and G. W. Keeling, a brick manufacturer. In searching the premises, the policemen discovered a half-empty quart of liquor, giving them grounds to arrest the three for violating the city's prohibition laws. "We were just having a little party," Mae purportedly said. "I don't see any harm in that." Then she asked the chief if the Candlers had sent him, to which Beavers reprimanded her for "doing a thing like that to Mr. Candler." In self-defense, Mae told the officers that she had spent the previous night with a girlfriend, who was away at work, and the men merely dropped by for a visit. Dismissing all of their excuses—especially Stoddard's claim that their get-together was "a business conference"—Beavers booked them for running a "disorderly house" or "dive." After a cursory interrogation at police headquarters, the trio was released on three one-hundred-dollar bonds and ordered to appear at a scheduled hearing a few days later.

In consideration of Asa Sr.'s recent courtroom ordeal, the Atlanta papers chose to ignore the incident, but after the *New York Times* picked up the story, the local press was trapped. Still they waited until the day of the scheduled hearing to report Mae Candler's arrest. At the police recorder's hearing, the three defendants appeared promptly, but to their surprise Beavers was nowhere to be found. After learning that Beavers was ill, the judge postponed the hearing until his return. Almost a month elapsed before the chief recovered, and then the hearing was further postponed because Stoddard and Keeling's lawyer was busy preparing to represent Clyde Byfield in his suit against Walter Candler. By this time, Mae had moved out of the Ponce de Leon mansion and was living with her mother.

On the morning of the hearing, Mae and her sister filed into the small but packed facility, and she was told to sit on a small piano stool in the corner. Stoddard, the first witness, accepted full responsibility for possessing the liquor, saying that the question of guilt or innocence was moot since none of them had broken any law. Then to everyone's surprise, Beavers confessed that Asa Candler's friend, Forrest Adair, had put him up to the arrest. Seeming to enjoy his own performance, the chief admitted that his real purpose in raiding the apartment had been to help the former mayor, yet when questioned, he admitted reluctantly that he could find no serious reasons to charge the three defendants of a crime. Upon hearing that, the judge concluded that the apartment could not be categorized as a disreputable "dive," and there was insufficient evidence to indict either Mae Candler or G. W. Keeling. However, W. D. Stoddard was fined $300 for possession of alcohol. Left unsaid was the overhanging reason for the entire matter: disclosure of circumstantial evidence that suggested Asa Candler's young wife was committing adultery. That revelation broke no law except the Ten Commandments.

A few weeks later, Beavers found himself struggling on the docket, accused by the city council of violating his duties as police chief, of demonstrating "conduct not becoming of an officer," and of disobeying a municipal ordinance that prohibited policemen from "arresting anyone involved in possible divorce proceedings." When the case came before a police committee, once again the arrest of Mae Candler and her companions provided the principal evidence. This time, however, the prosecutors revealed that Asa Sr. had originally asked the police chief to conduct the raid. This discovery caused the judge to accuse Beavers of perjury, since in the first hearing he said the call came from Forrest Adair. Even though lawyers for the defense insisted that the Candlers were not getting a divorce, Beavers's use of city employees to intervene in a private matter provided grounds for the council to demand his permanent dismissal, not only as chief but from ever being part of the police force, an action many had been seeking since Mayor Candler reappointed him to the job seven years earlier.[168]

If Mae's tawdry behavior was not enough to satisfy the gossip-hungry public, Walter Candler's trial a few days after the hearing satisfied the press orgy even more. By then, Walter was once again sponsoring the annual trotters race to benefit the Children's Home, not at his own smaller track but at Lakewood Park, where he drove his prize horse "Bogalusa" in the opening race. In the interim between the fateful voyage on the *Berengaria* and the trial almost two years later, Walter and Marion had reconciled, but the Byfields had separated. All outward signs, therefore, indicated that the Candlers were happily reunited. To demonstrate her readmission into the family circle, Marion gave a bridge-tea at their "Lullwater Driving Club" for participants in the Lakewood trotting race and horse show, with a guest list that included several of Walter's teen-aged nieces.

Marion even made a few cameo appearances at the Byfield trial, held in DeKalb County the following spring, its witness box dialogue seeming to parody popular conceptions of the flamboyant 1920s. On the first day, the star was Sarah Byfield, who—having recently won a beauty contest judged by Rudolph Valentino—was now working in New York as a "beauty clay" salesperson. Her seductive glamour and spirited remarks enlivened the proceedings, as she turned the witness stand into a platform for lambasting both her husband and Walter Candler. During one cross-examination, Candler's attorneys, Reuben and Lowry Arnold, succeeded in making her admit that Clyde had beaten her unmercifully aboard ship and that her marriage since the European voyage had been "two years of torture." Such testimony really stymied her own lawyer, ex-governor John Slaton, who was struggling to portray Clyde Byfield as a noble savior protecting his wife from her assailant's lust.

Despite her swipes at Clyde, Sarah stuck fast to her version of the evening in question. Walter had often visited her stateroom unannounced, she said, and that night he stumbled in drunk, partially dressed, and "panting as if he was out of breath." Then she teasingly told the court that when she "saw and felt what he was trying to do," she shouted: "Don't treat me like this; if my husband comes in he'll kill you." During cross-examination, her physician—who had been called to testify about how Walter's actions had destroyed her physical and mental health—ended up confessing that he had performed surgery on Sarah shortly after she returned from Europe because of "a premature childbirth" brought about by "nervous or physical shock." The word "abortion" or even "miscarriage" remained unspoken in newspaper coverage, and it is doubtful if paternity of the lost baby ever came up during the trial.

The Arnolds had lined up a stellar slate of local business executives, state legislators, professors, even the president of Emory University, to present evidence on Walter's behalf. Parading these distinguished witnesses to the stand the next day, the attorneys attempted to establish Candler's unblemished reputation in the community, and by so doing they accused Clyde Byfield of maneuvering a carefully planned extortion scheme. Walter confirmed this by testifying that when Clyde broke into the room that night, he pulled a Central Bank & Trust check out of his pocket and thrust it in his face for a signature, as if he had prepared ahead for the frame-up. The most damning evidence against Byfield came from employees of the *Berengaria,* brought over from England with Candler money. The ship's chief inspector stated that when he investigated "the disturbance" the morning after it occurred, Byfield was boasting about Walter's $25,000 check, and the ship's stewardess said she had been alarmed to see how drastically Sarah's face had been injured. Then the night watchman reported that after hearing the ruckus he knocked on the stateroom door and found Byfield "in his shirt-sleeves" asking for a gun. At the same time, he noticed that Candler was fully clothed and not at all disheveled.

On the following day, as the opposing attorneys were preparing to deliver their closing arguments, spectators were startled to see a surprise visitor enter the courtroom. Amidst a chorus of excited whispers, Asa Candler Sr. slipped in quietly and sat beside his son. He wasn't there long before his presence worked its way into the trial. When Asa Sr. arrived, Byfield's attorney was just beginning to accuse the Candler family of abusing the power of its wealth, prompting a red-faced Reuben Arnold to leap up and shake his finger at the prosecutors. "That aged gentleman sitting over there," he fumed, has donated a great deal of time and money to build "schools and hospitals and other institutions," and it is high time for the public to "take steps to stop these plots to extort money out of such a family." Shortly after this outburst the closing arguments began, and at their conclusion the jury left to deliberate. At 1:00 a.m. the foreman reported a deadlock, and the judge ordered the men sequestered for the weekend. When the court reconvened the following Monday, it took only an hour for the jury to declare Walter Candler "not guilty."

One month later, Walter was again in court, this time in Fulton County, testifying in his suit against Byfield. Again the same attorneys reiterated the same details of that critical night, only now Walter found himself floundering, when he was forced to admit that he—along with one of his employees and his brother, Asa Jr.—had indeed stormed into Byfield's automobile dealership, purportedly searching for the paper that Byfield had signed to cancel the original promissory note. In this instance, Walter's unwise incursion overrode whatever benefit the Candlers' prominence might have given him, and *this* jury concluded that he still owed Clyde the promised money. On and off for the next two years the two cases traveled through the appellate process, going all the way to the state Supreme Court. But all legal bills amassed by this courtroom wrangling accomplished little for either of the litigants. Byfield was unable to collect the $100,000 he sought, and Walter had to honor his pledge to pay $22,500, plus the 7 percent interest it had accrued in the ensuing years. In the end Sarah and Clyde divorced, and Marion remained in Atlanta, at least for the time being.[169]

In the midst of Walter's courtroom ordeals, his brother William opened his hotel. Several years earlier, he had to abandon Hornbostel's blueprint because of exorbitant costs and begin seeking additional funding sources. Eventually he decided to team up with the Biltmore Hotel chain, which insisted on using its own architectural firm to complete the project. The expanded facility did retain a few features of the Hornbostel design, most notably a large landscaped courtyard filled with "ancient trees" and luxuriant foliage that led up to the main rear entrance. On the night of April 20, 1924, colored spotlights illuminated that courtyard, as "beautiful women" accompanied by "chivalrous and handsome men" drove their

Studebakers and Packards up to a columned portico and stepped into what one reporter crowned "the most handsomely constructed hotel in the world." Guests on opening night walked through the two-tiered lobby and entered a "palatial" Georgian ballroom, where they dined and danced to the music of Enrico Leide's orchestra. At a center table, members of William Candler's immediate family—including his father and Aunt Florence—sat with visiting hotel executives. While the invited dignitaries were enjoying the opening festivities, Atlanta residents were listening to a blow-by-blow description on one of the first live broadcasts of WSB (Welcome South Brother) radio, located on the hotel's top floor.[170]

Elizabeth Owens, c. 1925, courtesy of Vesta Owens Jones

Shortly after the Biltmore opened, two members of the Candler family married. The first was twenty-year-old Elizabeth Owens. When she told her mother several months earlier that she planned to wed Dr. Bryant ("Bry") King Vann, those close to Lucy knew that at first she was uncertain about her prospective son-in-law, despite his excellent credentials. Vann, who had graduated from Harvard and served in the field artillery in France during the recent war, came to Atlanta to attend the Southern Dental College, where he received a degree in 1923. Nearly a decade older than his bride, Bry was beginning his dentistry practice and living in a boarding house. As family gossip would have it: when the "struggling dentist" read newspaper coverage of the 1922 debutante class, he told friends that he planned to marry one of them. When he succeeded in winning the hand of a Candler heiress, it was enough to persuade some of the family that Bryant Vann was surely a "gold digger."

Despite her initial misgivings, Lucy Heinz swallowed her feelings and arranged an extravagant wedding at Rainbow Terrace. A reporter for the *Atlanta Constitution* embellished every "cascade" of lace and every flower petal, heaping praise on the nuptials for "exceptional brilliance and splendor" and for drawing "prominent social interest throughout the south." Lucy did put on quite a show. The bridal party, waiting on either side of the balcony overlooking the great hall, met at the staircase and descended in pairs to an aisle lined with lighted white candles, as a small orchestra—under the direction of family friend Enrico Leide—played the bridal march. Elizabeth, on the arm of her stepfather Henry Heinz followed her bridesmaids to the altar, where Bishop Warren Candler stood before the palm-covered fireplace waiting to perform his familiar role for the next generation. To match the mansion's decor, the bridesmaids and other attendants wore pastel, rainbow-colored gowns, while throughout the house a profusion of roses and lilies carried out the rainbow theme.

An assortment of Candlers participated in the ceremony: Lucy Heinz was her daughter's matron of honor, William Owens the junior groomsman, Henry Jr. the ring bearer, and four-year-old Mimi was a flower girl. Candler cousins from each branch were also included in the wedding party. Asa Jr.'s daughter Lucy became the maid of honor; Howard's daughter Catherine was a bridesmaid; William's daughter Rena a junior bridesmaid; Walter's daughter "Bootsie" a flower girl; and the rest of Elizabeth's cousins served punch and kept the bride's book. This rare concordance of the usually quarrelling brothers was a tribute to Lucy, who had always been able to unite her fractious family.

The *Atlanta Constitution* described Elizabeth Owens Vann as a "stately beauty," attributing her "gracious manner and charming personality" to inheritance from her late grandmother "whose name she bears." That same reporter gushed: "She is a beauty of a lovely blonde type, with exquisite fair coloring, and is one of the most attractive young girls in society." Portentously, however, the marriage started off with a mishap. As

Elizabeth and Bry were being chauffeured to the railroad station for their honeymoon, an oncoming car crashed into them. Although no one was seriously hurt, the newlyweds were so shaken that they postponed their trip for a week. When they returned to Atlanta at the end of the month, Elizabeth adhered to family tradition by moving into Rainbow Terrace with her new husband.[171]

Just after the Vanns left for their delayed honeymoon, Asa Jr.'s daughter Lucy married Homer Thompson at Briarcliff. Homer had been a baseball star at the University of Georgia and was now employed at a Coca-Cola bottling company. The judgmental Candlers disapproved of Thompson as much as they did of Vann. In fact, hoping to persuade his daughter and niece to change their minds, Asa Jr. had taken them both on the extended foreign journey the previous summer. But when his daughter refused to relinquish her fiancé, Asa Jr. outdid his sister by staging a major spectacle. To accommodate the guests, he had a pavilion built across the driveway on the southern side of the mansion, and on the opposite end, he added a large music room that could double as a formal dining-room seating up to seventy-five guests.

The actual wedding capped several weeks of entertaining, including an *al fresco* rehearsal dinner in Briarcliff's sunken gardens. The main event resembled an outdoor pageant, with bridesmaids—several of Lucy's friends and her sister, Laura—wearing simple short dresses and proceeding through the garden into the new pavilion. Bishop Warren Candler, by now a regular at family nuptials, performed the ceremony, while all the rest of Asa Jr.'s children and his nephew Henry Heinz Jr. participated in the ceremony. This marriage, however, lacked the full family participation of its predecessor at Rainbow Terrace. Conspicuously absent were Howard, Flora, and their children, who had left shortly after Elizabeth's wedding for a tour of Europe. However, representatives of the press were plentiful. The rotogravure section of the *Atlanta Constitution* carried a full page of photographs, picturing the bridal procession crossing a garden bridge, a full view of the decorated sunken gardens, and Lucy in an ankle-length gown and lace veil carrying a flowing bouquet of orchids and lilies-of-the-valley, all cultivated in her father's greenhouse. In his letter to Howard, Asa Sr. described the wedding as a "brilliant affair" on a "beautiful night" with the moon shining "on the scene as if prepared for the occasion," adding that his namesake had "provided everything, lights, flowers, music, to make a great picture never to be forgotten."

Lucy and Homer's honeymoon getaway was even more dramatic than her cousin Elizabeth's had been. After sneaking out of the ongoing party, they silently wove their way around the gardens, carrying Lucy's luggage to their car, sequestered at the end of the property. They drove to the Thompson home nearby to pick up his bags, parking in an alley behind the house to avoid being seen. But just as the couple was stealing up to the back door, they heard a shot. Seconds later, a bullet whizzed so close to Lucy's head that it singed off a piece of her hair. Fearful that they were being assaulted by robbers, Homer pushed his bride back into the car and off they sped. Later they found out that a neighbor—knowing that Mrs. Thompson was attending a family wedding—had been watching the house, and upon spotting a car in the alley hauled out her rifle and blasted away at what she presumed to be burglars. Since fortunately no one was hurt in the farcical incident, Homer and Lucy's less than auspicious start to their honeymoon provided the family with jokes for many years to come.[172]

Around the time his granddaughters were entering into marriage, Asa Candler Sr. had come to a decision to terminate his own, charging in a divorce suit that his wife had humiliated him with her "unbearable" conduct. Not only had she been rude and insulting to his friends, but she paid "not the slightest attention to the making or keeping of a home" and spent too much time with her suspected paramour. Such behavior, he said, was "a deliberate attempt to wound and harass" him. After living apart for the past four months, Asa concluded pathetically that her attraction to him must have been prompted by acquisitive motives rather than "the result of love." A few days after news of the divorce commanded a full column in the Atlanta papers and a notice in the *New York Times*, Mae told reporters that she would not contest it, especially since her husband had already agreed to give her $60,000 as settlement.

Then, before those proceedings were completed, the well-publicized relationship took some unanticipated twists and turns, again inviting police scrutiny and unwanted reporters. As Asa's estranged wife was driving her car through Buckhead late one afternoon, a five-year-old girl named Mary Elizabeth Lunsford suddenly broke away from a group of children playing on the sidewalk, darted in front of Mae's car, bounced onto her fender, and landed in the gutter with a fractured skull. Police summoned an ambulance that rushed the child downtown to the Piedmont "Sanitarium," where surgeons attempted to save her. During the police interrogation that afternoon, Mae tearfully insisted that her "machine" had been "traveling at a moderate rate of speed," about twenty miles an hour, and she had "slammed on the brakes" as soon as she spotted the girl. But it was too late. "I deeply deplore this terrible thing," she sobbed, "and have suffered untold agony since it happened." After hearing her defense, the officers let her go without an arrest.

When the child died the following day, however, Mae was indicted for involuntary manslaughter and charged with exceeding the speed limit and engaging in "careless and reckless driving in utter disregard for human life." Although a grand jury judged the accident "unavoidable" and dismissed the case, it didn't end there because Mr. and Mrs. Lunsford sued Mae for $25,000 in damages, holding Asa Candler as a codefendant. The couple appeared a month later before the grand jury, but again the Candler family's prestige won out, and the girl's death was declared an accident. However, before that final verdict, Mae crept back to her former husband, fearing that the Lunsford family would require a financial settlement, and she would be unable to pay it without his help. The upshot was that Asa dropped the divorce proceedings, and she ended up moving back into the Ponce de Leon mansion, a startling development that none of Asa's children would discuss with reporters. However, no one doubted that all of his offspring were dismayed and disgusted by his change of heart.

Probably to avoid facing his family at Christmas, Asa decided to take his wife to spend the holiday at New York's Biltmore Hotel. On a cold, cloudy December 25, 1924, he wrote his children, ostensibly to wish them a Merry Christmas. Depressed by the dismal weather, he chose to remain in his "warm room," since he disliked "going out at all." Maybe he would take Mae "sight showing in day time," he wrote, but would not go "to shows at night." In the short letter, the patriarch apologetically referred to the sudden reconciliation and abandonment of his divorce suit: "Well, I'll try to make the best of it all," he lamely remarked, "try to so live that you can all continue to feel kindly of me." Then he added:

> I rejoice that you are all comfortably situated. Want you to be kept in perfect health. Try to think of me as I <u>was</u>. God has blessed me as the world sees it more than most of those with whom I have associated during all my past life … Know I love you and love me much.

This pitiable comment from a despondent and lonely man sounded like his last will and testimony. And in many ways it was.

As Asa Sr.'s lonely vigil in the New York hotel indicated, he had become aware of his declining health. Recognizing his precarious state, he began donating the bulk of his assets to Emory, including his portion of the family's real estate company. Earlier in the decade, he had been a major donor for the Wesley Memorial Hospital when it moved to the Emory campus, and the five Candler siblings joined in donating a wing in memory of their mother. Asa Sr.'s last major contribution to the university was a library. In June 1925, he had been strong enough to attend the groundbreaking ceremonies, and wielding a symbolic axe, he posed for photographers. Initially, he had opposed having the building bear his name, but the trustees voted unanimously to override his wishes, and today the three-story, classical-style Asa G. Candler Library occupies one end of Emory's main quadrangle, adjoining its much larger replacement, donated during the 1960s by the then-Coca-Cola president, Robert W. Woodruff.

In the summer of 1925, Asa Sr. took his wife to Europe, in hopes that the vacation would improve his health. Although no correspondence from this trip survives, his earlier distaste for the continent must have been intensified by his growing frailty. The journey did take its toll, however, since a few weeks after they returned to Atlanta, he was felled by a fairly severe stroke. After staying at Wesley Memorial Hospital for over a month, he remained partially bedridden at home for many weeks more. While recovering, Candler still insisted on going down to his office occasionally and seemed to enjoy presiding over meetings of Emory's trustees. In February 1926, his favorite sister, Florence Harris, died. For several years, she had been living in his Ponce de Leon mansion, and when she passed away, Asa not only arranged the funeral service at the Inman Park Methodist Church but drove with his family to bury her next to Colonel Harris in Cartersville. However, when the new Candler library at Emory formally opened a few weeks later, he was too ill to attend the inaugural ceremony.[173]

With their father ailing and spending most of his time at home, his children were conscientious about frequent visits, when they weren't too wrapped up in their own diverse lives. As always, Howard preferred to remain out of the limelight. Happily married and devoted to his children, he spent much of his time improving Callanwolde or serving on cultural and corporate boards and as an advisor to Coca-Cola. Like his father, he devoted many volunteer hours and spent a great deal of money supporting

Emory. After Asa Sr. became too ill to preside over the board of trustees, Howard replaced him as chairman. During the uproarious twenties, he and Flora lived quietly, often attending concerts or operas, followed by musical evenings at Callanwolde, where selected virtuosi performed chamber music recitals or vocal performances in the great hall. Except for being seen pursuing his business, cultural, and charitable interests, Howard carefully guarded his privacy and that of his family.

Not so his next youngest brother. With a determination to be noticed, Asa Jr. loved to have everyone read about his various pursuits, ranging from fast cars, to farming, to yachts, to exotic flora and fauna, to real estate. In March 1925, he announced that R. H. Macy & Company, which had recently embarked on an expansion program, would erect a department store on a Candler-owned lot fronting Peachtree Street. Davison-Paxon-Stokes, one of Atlanta's most respected emporiums, agreed to lend its name and prestige to the new downtown store, with the understanding that Macy's would merchandise, staff, and manage it. A few days after the plans were published, Macy's President Jesse I. Straus arrived in Atlanta to be honored at an elaborate banquet at the Biltmore Hotel. During the long evening of speeches, the *Atlanta Constitution* editor, Clark Howell, praised the "patriotic spirit" of Asa G. Candler Jr. and his brothers, who deserve all the credit for convincing Macy's to make Atlanta its first southern location. In his brief response, Asa Jr. told the audience: "I have always dreamed of a great department store for that location and my dream has at last come true."

Huge crowds jostled to get in when the new Davison-Paxon (Stokes had retired) store opened two years later. Shoppers from Atlanta and the surrounding towns rushed down the aisles and up the elevators, purchasing twenty-five-percent more merchandise than had been anticipated. On opening night, the city threw another lavish banquet at the Biltmore, attended by "the flower of Atlanta social and civic activities and business life," along with Jesse Straus, his brother Herbert, and numerous other Macy's executives. One local establishment—that may not have been so happy to see the new Macy's affiliate come to town—was Atlanta-owned Rich's, which had just finished constructing a larger and more modern facility a few miles away. However, the two department stores managed to coexist for over six decades, competing energetically for the city's ready-to-wear and home furnishings trade.

At the same time that Asa Jr. was buying, selling, and developing property for the family corporation, he frequently struck out on his own, and—as in everything he did—his interests were eclectic. To promote his prize cattle and encourage Georgia's livestock industry, he combined forces with William H. White Jr., a fellow aviation enthusiast, who happened to own a large meatpacking plant on Howell Mill Road, at the edge of the stockyard district and adjacent to several railroad lines. As was his style, Asa Jr. talked White into enlarging his business and announced that he hoped to turn Atlanta into the premier meatpacking center of the Southeast. Toward that goal, they hired one of Chicago's top stockyard executives to manage the facility, and at first their only problem was complaints from passersby who had to hold their noses when in the vicinity.

But the stench went far beyond the slaughterhouse. Two years after its founding, the state-of-the-art White Provision Company was experiencing a cash shortfall, which forced Asa Jr. to reorganize the company and take over as president, telling the *Atlanta Constitution* that he hoped to quadruple the factory's output to reach an annual income of $10,000,000. However his task was rendered impossible after investigators discovered that White had been borrowing company funds to purchase shares of a Kansas City cattle business and dipping into the corporate till to speculate in cotton futures. When his manipulations were discovered, stockholders initiated a suit against White. On the witness stand, Asa Jr. explained that he had loaned his former partner $150,000, believing that it would be used to enhance the sinking revenues. However, he was shocked to learn that White was speculating with the struggling company's fund. The jury must have believed him and ended the trial by fining White for his actions. As a means of paying it off and settling up his many debts, White declared bankruptcy. A few weeks later, Asa Jr. announced that he was buying the entire thirty-five acre public stockyard and planned to oust the tenants, so he could use the property for other purposes. The deal, however, was stalled for years, mired in litigations brought by the evicted tenants. Eventually Swift and Company took over the White Provision Company, and Asa Jr. moved on to new business pursuits

Later in the decade, Asa Jr. purchased property at the intersection of Highland and Ponce de Leon Avenues, and like much of his family, he became involved in Atlanta's growing hotel industry. On the site, he constructed a nine-story apartment hotel, known as 750 (later 1050) Ponce de Leon, or the Briarcliff. The U-shaped building—faced with red brick above a white stone base and roofline decorated with a brightly colored terracotta frieze—was composed mainly of private living quarters. At the time it was considered one of the most fashionable and modern residential addresses in the city. As was characteristic of apartment hotels built in the first third of the twentieth century, the Briarcliff had a dining room and shops on its ground floor.[174]

Some of Asa Jr.'s erratic decisions and undisciplined dash from one business or hobby to another was accelerated by his addiction to alcohol. His wife bore the real brunt of his drinking, which often led to public misconduct and overt womanizing. Augmenting Helen's problems was her fragile health, attributed to the blood poisoning suffered during her first pregnancy, which was aggravated by the difficulties during each of her four subsequent deliveries. Doctors eventually diagnosed her illness as Bright's disease, since in those days the destructive effects of recurring cat-scratch fever were unknown. Added to her physical infirmities, Helen was often depressed, a condition no doubt exacerbated by her husband's misbehavior. As her health declined during 1926, Helen's son John and daughter Laura took her for treatment at Johns Hopkins Hospital in Baltimore. But despite five months of extensive tests and experimental medications, the doctors expressed little hope for her recovery. She returned home, lingered a few months, and died on January 29, 1927, at age forty-six. Her husband of twenty-six years held the funeral at their home, followed by burial at Westview, the cemetery southwest of the city that he had recently purchased.[175]

Less than nine months later, Asa Jr. married his personal secretary, Florence Stephenson, who was fifteen years his junior. During Helen's long illness, she often attended business and even family functions with her boss and frequently visited Asa Sr. at his home. The *Atlanta Constitution* noted that she was "a young woman of unusual brilliance and charm" with an "engaging personality." But the *New York Times* and newspapers around the country reported that by marrying his stenographer, Asa Jr. was "following the example set by his father." Some papers even mentioned Walter's marriage to Marion as another example of a Candler millionaire marrying a younger employee. Understandably, such comments offended Florence, since she considered herself to be a longtime friend, confidant, and companion to her boss, not just his secretary. Most of all, she knew him well enough to tolerate and participate in his many idiosyncratic pursuits. The couple married quietly at Briarcliff, with only four people in attendance: Bishop Warren Candler—who not surprisingly officiated— and his wife Nettie, along with the bride's father and sister. After the ceremony, the newlyweds took the *Crescent Limited* to New Orleans and then boarded a liner to cruise through the Panama Canal to Honolulu, where they remained for several weeks.[176]

The absence of Asa Jr.'s four siblings and all of his children suggests that there had been objections to his remarriage. The best indication of this is that only four days after the ceremony, his son John wed Elizabeth (Lib) Brandon in a long-planned church wedding in Richmond, attended by most of the Candler family. Perhaps Asa Jr. decided to marry when he knew his children would be in Virginia, and thus avoid their disapproval, following his father's example of a few years earlier. But the big question is why he had not attended his oldest son's wedding. In later years, John and his father were business partners and apparently close. In 1927, however, John may have been upset because his father remarried so soon after Helen's death. As it turned out, Asa's marriage to Florence lasted the rest of his life, and his children not only accepted her but took her into the family fold.

Many Atlantans traveled to Richmond for John Candler's wedding, since the bride's uncle, Morris Brandon, was a prominent local leader. Candler family members were also there to see Howard Jr. as his first cousin's best man. As quarrelsome as Howard Sr. and Asa Jr. remained, their sons were best friends. Both had been pals throughout high school and both went to Emory together, even though Howard Jr., like his father, was a more serious student than his fun-loving, bright, and irrepressible cousin. A year later, the two young men reversed roles, and John was Howard Jr.'s best man when he married Ruth Ozburn. These and several other Candler weddings during the twenties were lavish affairs with elegant decorations and, naturally, their Uncle Warren performing the ceremony.[177]

Despite all the adverse publicity that Walter Candler suffered in the early '20s, like his brother Asa Jr., he still courted publicity. Fortunately, by the end of the decade, that coverage was more positive. After his career at the Central Bank ended, Walter embarked on several business ventures of his own, one of special note being an automotive center on West Peachtree Street, not far from the car dealership owned by Clyde Byfield. But following the shipboard scandal and its aftermath, Walter transferred his garage to a larger downtown facility, where he could provide more up-to-date service and have a larger showroom. Around this time, he also opened the Lullwater Shirt Factory to produce blue work shirts that turned out to be a moderate success. Probably his most lucrative enterprise was the Candler Hotel in the Atlanta suburb of Decatur, begun by a group of businessmen concerned that the area had inadequate facilities to accommodate visitors. Having put up most of the money to build the four-story brick building, Walter had considerable input in drawing the architectural plans. With its sixty guest rooms, shops, a restaurant, and comfortable, home-style lobby, the Candler became a Decatur landmark for many years. At last, Walter was able to demonstrate that he was capable of thriving on his own in the business world.[178]

When the hotel opened, Walter and Marion were still married, although their relationship was rocky, and she was frequently taking their young daughter for extended stays with her mother in California. While his wife and Bootsie were away, Walter threw himself into his favorite pastime: racing prize trotters. Often entering national competitions, he began accumulating trophies, especially for the horse Bogalusa, sired by the famous stallion Peter the Great. In 1924, he hired Lewis Crook, the architect of Emory's new Candler Library, to design a manor house for the racetrack property he called Lullwater Farms. Equally as imposing as the Druid Hills mansions of his brothers, sister, and father, Walter's large Tudor-style house was constructed of granite quarried from the grounds and half-timbers taken from his own trees.

Lullwater Farms estate, Walter Candler's house, photograph by John Sumner

Like Callanwolde and Briarcliff, the Lullwater Farms estate sought to emulate the domain of an English aristocrat, albeit with a distinctive southern flavor. The center of the L-shaped residence featured a three-story round tower topped with a castellated observation platform, while the surrounding land held several outbuildings, recreational facilities—including an Olympic size pool and tennis court—and a large lake created by a dammed creek that generated power for the estate. Adjacent to the new racetrack stood a unique log clubhouse. More rustic than the main house, it too had a central tower, pitched roof, and tall stone chimney. Shortly after he and Marion moved in, Walter gave a party celebrating the twentieth anniversary of his graduation from Emory. Forty members of his class came to swim, boat, play tennis, and gather around the large stone fireplace in the clubhouse for a fried chicken dinner and an exchange of memories. During the reunion, Walter's classmates elected him to be the alumni chairman of Emory's class of 1907, a job he maintained enthusiastically for the next twenty years.[179]

Asa Candler Sr.'s last recorded public appearance was at the opening of the first six holes of the Candler Park golf course in April 1926. Six months later, he was rushed to Wesley Memorial Hospital (now called Emory Hospital) with a far more debilitating stroke that left him paralyzed and unable to speak. Recovery, the doctors pronounced grimly, was doubtful, and they proved to be correct. Now the once-dynamic entrepreneur remained trapped in a semi-mute state for the next three years, never leaving the hospital, and for the most part, only partially aware of what was happening in the world that he had formerly controlled. Mae, his children, and grandchildren visited almost daily, all plying him with food he probably never ate and family gossip that he rarely comprehended. His granddaughter Bootsie remembered visiting the hospital with her father and seeing PawPaw "laying in that bed, just staring at the ceiling." Another caller was Dr. Joseph Jacobs, whose soda fountain had dispensed the first Coca-Colas. After one such visit, Jacobs told Howard that as he sat at the bedside of his "dear friend of nearly half a century," his "heart overflowed with sorrow." Asa "seemed to recognize" him, Jacobs wrote, "and smiled at times," during a conversation that the pharmacist "tried to make as cheerful as possible."

On December 30, 1926, numerous messages wishing Asa Candler a happy seventy-fifth birthday arrived at Wesley Memorial, accompanied by floral arrangements from city, state, religious, and educational organizations.

Close family and friends filled his hospital room, while others left notes at the front desk. For the next two years on December 30, similar tributes marked his seventy-sixth and seventy-seventh birthdays. But the Coca-Cola founder was only dimly aware of these good wishes. At the end of 1928, it was clear that Asa Sr. would not last long. Frequently the family had been called to his bedside assuming death was imminent, but each time the indomitable old patriarch managed to continue breathing. No one really knew whether he realized that several of his grandchildren had married. Nor did he seem to know in April 1928 that his eighty-two-year-old brother Willie had passed away at his home in Villa Rica. And similarly he was unaware that in January 1929 his brother John's son, Asa Warren Candler, had died quite unexpectedly in a room near him at Emory Hospital.

By the time Asa Warren was buried, seventy-seven-year-old Asa Griggs Candler Sr. was approaching his own end. It came quietly on Tuesday afternoon, March 12, 1929. After all the false alarms, only Lucy was at his bedside. That was perhaps fitting, for he had always doted on his daughter. Asa Jr. was in Europe at the time, but his son John went immediately to the hospital upon hearing the news, followed shortly by Howard Sr., Walter, William, and Henry Heinz. John wrote his father that when his Uncle Howard arrived at the hospital, he produced a "most remarkable document." Four years earlier, realizing that his health was failing, Asa Sr. had placed two items in sealed envelopes and delivered them to his friend Fred Patterson, Atlanta's leading mortician. One was the biography he wished to appear in the newspapers, the other held instructions for his funeral. John commented that the handwritten letter was "couched in beautiful English, without the waste of a single unnecessary word," and the message itself was "in no sense ambiguous." Indeed, ambiguity was never a component of Asa Candler's makeup.

It turned out to be impossible for the family to restrict the newspaper coverage to the modest autobiography that Asa had requested. "It would have been unjust" to the press, John wrote, "and would have undoubtedly brought forth considerable criticism." Clearly nobody could have stopped the torrent of adulation that poured forth. Banner front-page headlines ran in all local newspapers, announcing the death of the "multimillionaire financier, civic leader, philanthropist and founder of the Coca-Cola Company, a man whose multitudinous affairs did more to build up the city than any other resident." The *Constitution* described him as "perhaps the most widely known citizen Atlanta ever had." Similar reverential assessments of Asa Candler's life and contributions filled newspaper columns across the nation.

On the day of the funeral, flags in Atlanta flew at half staff; Emory University canceled classes; and around the world, all Coca-Cola bottlers and manufacturing plants closed for the day. At eleven in the morning, an invited crowd of prominent Atlantans assembled in the flower-filled court of the Ponce de Leon mansion to attend services that had been carefully orchestrated by the man they were eulogizing. Not wanting to burden his friends, Asa had requested that employees of Patterson's Funeral Home carry the casket, and he specified which men among his family, friends, and acquaintances should be honorary pallbearers. He tried to show a similar impartiality with his many contacts in the Methodist Church, asking that the dean of Emory's Theological School preside at the service. Therefore, the current occupant of that position, Franklin N. Parker, delivered a brief and simple eulogy. According to the instructions, a small family burial at Westview Cemetery was to follow that afternoon, but a pouring rain forced the cemetery to postpone the interment until the next day. John told his father that the family adhered to Asa's wishes as closely as possible "with only little interference from Mrs. Candler."

Even though Asa Candler's five children were already enjoying the bulk of his fortune, the young widow did receive compensation. Half of the $500,000 that remained in the estate was divided between his church, Emory University, and the household servants; the other half went to his wife. Four years after her husband's death, Mae sued the five Candler siblings, claiming that her late husband had granted her an additional $250,000 in a codicil, which also gave her the Ponce de Leon mansion and shares of Asa G. Candler Inc. Ultimately, she settled for part of the requested money but received no stock in the real estate company, nor could she retain the house, which was ultimately sold. Shunned by the family from the moment Asa married her, Mae was henceforth ignored and ultimately ostracized by all the Candlers.

In his will, Asa Candler wrote the epitaph he deemed appropriate: "To my household, my children and to their children, and the generations that follow, I bequeath my good name as it has come to me from an honorable and honest ancestry. My chief aim in life has been to help and not hurt my fellowman." A writer for the *Atlanta Constitution* followed this theme by commenting: "Thus the closing chapter to a great career was written and the book was quietly closed, even as he would have wished." Although "he was being proclaimed as a business genius and his fame spread through the business world," the writer continued, "he went from business triumph to greater triumph and became known, not only as a man of power but a man of heart as well." Although Asa Candler had asked not to have any flowery eulogies, he no doubt would have been pleased to know that he was being remembered as "a man of heart."[180]

CHAPTER THIRTEEN
Wild and Unfathomable Things

On a rainy Christmas afternoon in 1929, eight months after the family patriarch died, several of his descendants attended the opening of Atlanta's Fox Theater. One of the prime movers in building the fantasy movie-house was Lucy's husband Henry Heinz, a former Potentate and active member of the Shriner's Yaarab Temple, which owned the new theater. During the mid-1920s, when the Shriners purchased the property on Peachtree Street for its new headquarters, Heinz had insisted that the meeting house also include a public auditorium. But as treasurer for the project, he soon became alarmed when costs for the elaborate Arabian-Nights-style structure spiraled. As a precaution, he convinced the Shriners to offset the enormous construction costs by leasing the auditorium to the Fox Theaters Corporation.

Like the entire audience attending the opening ceremony, members of the Candler clan gawked in amazement at the huge theater with its minarets, onion dome, and Egyptian Ballroom, redolent of a Hollywood-inspired exotic romance. Sitting in the courtyard auditorium, surrounded by false castelled ramparts under a ceiling of flickering stars and wafting clouds, they were thrilled when the huge Möeller organ rose from a pit below the stage, booming its melodies throughout the theater. They watched excitedly as the spectacle opened with Enrico Leide conducting the Fox Grand Orchestra in Elgar's "This Shrine of Beauty," followed by the "Sunkist Beauties" dancing to the strains of "By the Beautiful Sea." As lanterns on the faux palace dimmed, the Candlers settled back to view the very first Mickey Mouse cartoon, *Steamboat Willie,* followed by the Fox Movietone News, and finally the feature film, *Salute,* starring George O'Brien and Helen Chandler and featuring Stepin Fetchit.[181]

Casting his eyes over the enthralled crowd, Henry Heinz must have felt a glow of pride for helping create the "Fabulous Fox," a magical place to escape from the panicked gloom that followed the stock market plunge two months earlier. However, unlike most Atlantans, the Candler siblings seemed largely unaffected by the crash, since their lifestyle was continuing as usual. In fact, during 1931, the *New York Times* published a list of millionaires based on the value of their insurance policies. Two Candler names appeared toward the bottom: Asa Jr. (insured at $1,450,000) and William (insured at $1,385,000). At a time when a four-course steak dinner cost fifty-cents, a million dollars was considered to be a megafortune. To put the Candler wealth into perspective, number one on the list was Pierre S. DuPont, who valued his life at $7,000,000.[182]

During the free-spending 1920s, it had been Asa Candler's second son and namesake who found the most lavish and adventurous ways to spend his inheritance. In many ways, Asa Jr. personified the decade's popular stereotype, living recklessly and drinking heavily, often taking extended cruises in his newest yacht, *Amphirtrite*. When the craft docked in Miami in 1928 after an extensive West Indian jaunt, federal officials boarded the craft and confiscated eighty-eight bottles of liquor. A reporter for the *Washington Post* commented that "the party included a number of young women said by officers to be Atlanta high school girls." Although no names appeared in the paper, the girls aboard were probably Asa's sixteen-year-old twins, Helen and Martha, with some of their schoolmates. Perhaps, as friends of the family contended, the seized liquor consisted merely of "small souvenir bottles which the girls were bringing back." The police made no arrests, nor did they seize the boat, suggesting that the press report bordered on sensationalism, which was as common then as it is today. But the incident clearly signifies that Asa Jr.'s lavish spending and an erratic lifestyle was setting less than a stellar example for his offspring.[183]

Insight into Asa Jr.'s penchant for flamboyance during the 1920s—both in the way he lived and the way he handled money—is exemplified by the intensity with which he once more embraced aviation, combining his propensity for wheeling and dealing with his father's canniness. Until 1925, the family had retained ownership of Candler Field in Hapeville, the racetrack that doubled as a landing strip, but by the mid '20s, the property was in such dire need of repair that few planes could land there. To avoid undertaking the project himself, Asa Jr. appealed to the city in hopes it would buy the site. However, the city council was hesitant to spend public funds on such a "modern" undertaking, even though other southeastern municipalities were already building airports. When the councilmen finally decided that Atlanta needed a decent landing strip, the debate shifted to whether the city should purchase and rehabilitate Candler Field or construct a new airport someplace else. As a lure to persuade the council to buy his property, Asa Jr. said he would give the city free use of the site if it would pay the taxes. One councilman in particular—the young and newly elected William B. Hartsfield—was pushing to have Atlanta take over the Hapeville property, and after much debate, he was able to persuade the council to accept Candler's offer.

Two-and-a-half years later, Charles Lindberg landed his famous *Spirit of St. Louis* at Candler Field. Crowds lining the sidewalks cheered as he paraded through the city on what the mayor declared to be the official "Lindbergh Day." That evening, several Candlers went to the Ansley Hotel for a banquet honoring the hero, and afterward William and his family welcomed the young aviator to the Biltmore Hotel, where he spent the night.[184] Shortly after Lindbergh's visit, three well-known pilots—Doug Davis, Beeler Blevins, and A. B. McMullen—received permission to construct hangars around the edges of Candler Field. However, these and other pilots complained that the piecemeal expansion of the old racetrack was much too dangerous for large planes to take off and land. In 1928, Pitcairn Aviation designated Atlanta as a possible base for mail and passenger service, but only on the condition that the unlighted and uneven runways be properly reconstructed. If the airport remained unsatisfactory, the company announced it would locate its southeastern center elsewhere. Worried that Atlanta would be overshadowed by another city, municipal authorities agreed to purchase Candler Field in the spring of 1929 for $94,500, slightly less than the $100,000 Asa Jr. had requested. With repaved runways and a new lighting system, Pitcairn (now rechristened Eastern Air Transport) began operating airmail service and regular passenger flights from Atlanta to New York, Washington, Richmond, Jacksonville, and Miami.

After the city improved the airport, Asa Jr. was one of the first Atlantans to throw himself into flying, exhibiting the same zest, excessive spending, and eye for publicity that characterized all of his enthusiasms. In 1929, he hired Beeler Blevins to help him buy a maroon Waco open-cockpit biplane with a Wright 165 horsepower engine. A photograph of Asa and Florence—wrapped in winter coats, wearing helmets and goggles—appeared in the *Atlanta Constitution*. Posing for the camera beside their plane with its "Briarcliff" insignia on the fuselage, the couple told reporters that they had just returned from an excursion over Atlanta that included an aerial view of their Briarcliff estate. Asa commented that, although this was his wife's first flight, he had already used Blevins as his pilot for several business and pleasure trips.

By the fall of 1929, Asa Jr. had purchased another craft, this one a seven-passenger Lockheed Vega monoplane costing more than $20,000. The new toy—an aviation original, recently flown by the ace Wiley Ford—combined "great speed" (142 miles an hour) with "limousine-like luxury in the ship's appointments." Because the Lockheed Vega flew at an increased speed of 160 miles an hour, it was able to complete an eight-hundred-mile, nonstop jaunt facilitated only by an auxiliary gas tank. On one of their first trips in the Vega, Florence and Asa encountered such a heavy fog returning from Dallas, that Blevins had to navigate the last leg by hovering 250 feet above the ground and following the West Point Railroad tracks to Candler Field. Another time, they flew eight hundred miles to New York in a record five hours, so they could attend a welcoming party for Atlanta golfing champion Bobby Jones, who had just docked after winning the British Amateur Open. The Candlers had hoped to transport Jones back home to see his children and then fly him to Minneapolis, where he was scheduled to play in the US Open. But the golfer declined their invitation, feeling it would be safer to take the train to Minnesota and see his children later.

In a long article about Asa Jr. and his planes, Atlanta society writer Medora Field Perkerson remarked: "Mr. and Mrs. Candler fly about the country as casually as the average person goes motoring" and have even "established a record for foreign travel" by flying to Havana. "No one else in the city," Perkerson wrote, "has adopted the airship as quite such an everyday means of transport for the entire family." Florence Candler even had a "special outfit for flying, fashioned for her along severely tailored lines by Abercrombie and Fitch in New York." While he was employed by the Candlers, Blevins taught Asa Jr.'s children Martha and John to be pilots, and when the lessons were completed, their father bought each a plane in hopes they would continue flying.

In July 1931, Asa and Florence traveled to Los Angeles to trade the Vega for a $23,000 low-wing Lockheed Orion that could speed through the skies at 220 miles an hour. Blevins agreed to pilot the couple in the new craft for what was hyped as a record-breaking twenty-two-hundred-mile cross-country flight from Burbank, California, to Savannah, Georgia, with only one stop in Dallas. However, the trip—which both pilot and passengers had so eagerly anticipated—seemed jinxed from the outset.

A heavy fog covered the California coast as they prepared to take off before dawn, delaying their departure for two hours. Then, crossing the Rockies, they encountered an even thicker fog, which forced Blevins to veer southward in search of clearer skies. That detour, coupled with the inclement weather, slowed them down and depleted their gas supply so drastically that they had to make an unexpected stop in El Paso. After refueling, Blevins flew the three-hundred-mile hop to Dallas, but when he landed, mechanics discovered that the plane had been damaged slightly, although luckily Asa, Florence, and the pilot escaped without injury. By the time the Orion was repaired, it was too late to fly any further, thus shattering any chance of breaking a transcontinental record. Bad weather and bad luck having prevented Candler and Blevins from making aviation history, the unpredictable Asa Jr. turned toward Europe to seek his next all-absorbing adventure.[185]

Meanwhile, Walter Candler was not sitting by idly allowing his older brother to outshine him in adventure, so he took up flying, too. Having no plane of his own, Walter was among the first Americans to take a long journey on commercial flights, one of his earliest being an odyssey from Buenos Aires to Miami. He had completed a cruise that began in Havana and traveled down the west coast of South America via the Panama Canal. Leaving the ship in Valparaiso, Chile, Walter crossed the Andes by train to Buenos Aires, but after several more days touring Argentina, he was eager to return home, and the quickest way to get there was via a number of connecting flights. From Buenos Aires, he flew to Rio, Trinidad, Martinique, Santiago, St. Thomas, and finally Miami, a nine-day, eight-thousand-mile journey on six different airplanes, written up in March 1930, as the longest flight ever taken by an Atlantan.

As this long, solitary trip implies, for all practical purposes Walter and Marion were living separate lives. When Walter returned from his South American jaunt, they were together at the debut of his oldest daughter, Eugenia, in March 1930, but a few weeks later, when his younger daughter, Mary, married, Marion's name was not mentioned among the family members attending the wedding. Their life together had been tumultuous from the start, one serious bone of contention being religion. Walter had stayed contentedly in the Methodism of his parents, while Marion was a Christian Scientist, who fought tooth-and nail to keep their sick daughter away from doctors. Bootsie remembered a serious fight between her parents when Marion stood outside in the driveway screaming hysterically as

Walter drove her to the hospital to have a tonsillectomy. Around 1931, the couple separated permanently, and Marion moved to California to be near her mother. Three years, later, Walter agreed to give her temporary custody of Bootsie, along with a monthly alimony of $400; their divorce was finalized in August 1934.[186]

In contrast to the flamboyant lifestyle of Walter and Asa Jr., their oldest brother, Howard—careful to avoid unwanted press scrutiny—continued to pursue his unassuming course of public and charitable service. One of his largest contributions in the early 1930s was Emory's Glenn Memorial Church, nominally a gift from his wife and her brother, Thomas K. Glenn, board chairman of Atlanta's First National Bank. Although the university had been planning to build a permanent Methodist church on campus for several years, the ripple effect created by the stock market crash greatly weakened Emory's potential for finding donors. It was then that board Chairman Howard Candler came to the rescue by pledging $250,000 toward construction of the facility, with the stipulation that it be named after Flora and Tom's late father, Wilber Fisk Glenn.

Around the time he was arranging to fund Glenn Memorial Church, Howard departed from his negative view of his younger brothers' personal real estate ventures. During the late '20s, he and a group of men bought an old hunting resort at the northern end of Cumberland Island, off the Georgia coast. The principal residents of the large, semitropical island were descendants of Andrew Carnegie's brother Thomas, whose family owned a huge swath of land. The prestige of the Carnegie name, coupled with the potential for growth, bode well for the men's investment to become a moneymaking venture. But when the stock market crashed, the hunting resort crashed with it, leaving Howard and his son to bail out the others by buying the property. In the next few years, they remodeled the hotel to be a family beach retreat, which they christened "High Point." There two, and soon three, generations of Candlers spent their summer holidays in a secluded spot away from the public eye.

On the sunlit beaches of Cumberland Island and in the oak-paneled dignity of Callanwolde, Howard and Flora—known lovingly by their grandchildren as "Popee" and "Danny"—presided gently and quietly over their growing clan. During the thirties, their daughter Catherine and her husband Bill Warren lived at Callanwolde with their three children, while Howard Jr., his wife Ruth, and their three children lived nearby on Lullwater Parkway. Every Sunday, the family would converge at Callanwolde for an afternoon of swimming, followed by dinner in the large, formal dining room. Within the family and the community, Howard Sr. was often teased for criticizing the extravagances of his children and grandchildren, and in return, they ribbed him for being so parsimonious in his personal life that he never bought new clothes unless absolutely necessary and drove an old Packard until it became a collector's item. That fiscal conservatism made Howard Candler a stable presence on many corporate and charitable boards. His father would certainly have been pleased to learn that all those lectures on thrift and economy had taken root on at least one of his offspring.[187]

The staid and conservative Howard—who did little to conceal his disdain for Asa Jr.'s freewheeling ways—must have been more furious than ever when he learned that his next youngest brother had embraced another and even more eccentric venture. According to one account, while Asa and Florence were traveling somewhere in Eastern Europe during the late summer of 1931, they attended the final performance of a down-and-out circus. Upon learning that all the stock was for sale, Asa made one of his snap decisions. Why not buy the circus and reassemble it on the grounds of his Briarcliff estate? Another version relates that he was drinking in a bar somewhere in Germany when somehow he agreed to pump enough money into a bankrupt circus to keep the performances going, and when the season ended, he arranged to ship the animals and most of the equipment across the Atlantic, purportedly wiring his architects: "Bought circus, build zoo."

Purchase of the circus was only the first step toward an even larger and more bizarre undertaking. On his return to the United States, Asa Jr. asked a wildlife importer in Nashua, New Hampshire, to acquire additional animals through negotiations with a scouting company in Hamburg, Germany. In tough economic times, the Germans must have been shocked and delighted to receive an order from Atlanta, Georgia, that included requests for pairs of pumas, panthers, lions, bears leopards, chimpanzees, baboons, grivets, monkeys, buffalos, elephants, and a variety of birds from Africa, Asia, and South America. Winifred Griffin, half owner of the New Hampshire farms, explained: "fine animals like these don't grow on bushes," and furthermore, finding the "proper mates" is more difficult, because the company had to ascertain "just the right size, markings, and dispositions for each pair of wild animals." With a budget of over $50,000, Asa apparently saw himself as a modern Noah, perpetuating the species, in what was described as "the finest private collection of animals in the South."

Gathered from many native habitats in Asia and Africa, the animals were packed into crates and loaded aboard ships for voyages that often lasted as long as twenty days. To keep them placid and free from injury, the importers sedated their cargoes, but even with medication many of them suffered from extreme seasickness. One trainer admitted that he fed them Jamaican rum for five days, joking that neither the animals nor their future owner cared that they were defying the Prohibition laws. Initially unconcerned about the details of transporting such a huge menagerie, Asa subsequently had to figure out ways to bring the beasts from New York to his Atlanta estate, and in typical Buddie fashion, he came up with an ingenious solution. Realizing that circuses transported animals all the time, he arranged for Ringling Brothers, Barnum & Bailey in Sarasota, Florida, to lend him specially fitted boxcars. All went well until a shipload of animals docked in New York and had to wait several days before a circus train was available. Unfazed, Asa asked Mayor Jimmy Walker to house the animals in Madison Square Garden, where circuses usually performed. But his brilliant idea turned into a major headache. Some of the creatures broke loose and went on rampages through the surrounding neighborhood, breaking storefronts and stopping traffic, until angry policemen and frantic trainers could round them up and return them to Madison Square Garden. Not surprisingly, the merchants with the shattered windows and damaged stock sued Candler to recoup their expenses. This escapade was only the first in a string of legal battles caused by Asa Jr.'s newest folly.

By April 1932, trainloads of animals began arriving at the Emory depot. Shepherding the precious cargo were teams of experienced trainers, who nursed and coddled the smaller animals and kept the larger ones from breaking down their stalls; after their arrival at the station, these same men had the difficult task of persuading the beasts to exit from the boxcars. A pair of baby elephants—which Candler named "Coca" and "Cola"—proved especially difficult to unload. Groggy from rum and sedatives, they had to be dragged with ropes down the gangplank. Waiting there to greet them was Asa Jr., accompanied by his brother Walter, along with a crowd of neighbors, curious to see the menagerie as it slowly emerged. The best part was to follow. After assembling all of the new arrivals on the platform, the trainers led them in a parade through residential Druid Hills, for a two mile walk to the Candler estate on Briarcliff Road. As the fantastic procession coursed by, amused adults snapped their Brownie cameras, while children ran along the sidewalks, cheering to see such a spectacle in their usually tranquil neighborhood.

255

A few weeks after he settled the animals and birds into their new surroundings, Asa invited a group of sixty-five children to celebrate the birthdays of his grandchildren, three-year-old Nancy and year-old Asa V. By that time, three full-grown elephants—"Delicious," "Refreshing," and "Rosa" (named for the family cook)—had joined "Coca" and "Cola," and the entire group performed tricks, before being hitched to wagons that rode the excited children around the grounds. Also transporting the children was a team of Shetland ponies pulling an old stagecoach acquired from the European circus. During the following summer Asa opened his zoo to the public two days each week, and on other days he orchestrated special events for charities. One was a special "circus day" for the Shriner's Scottish Rite Hospital. Children in wheelchairs, braces, and casts watched gleefully as elephants, bears, ponies, and monkeys performed their routines in a circus ring. After visiting a concession stand for lemonade, the children were taken around the zoo to see the animals. Favorites were the Royal Bengal tiger (named "Jimmy Walker," after the helpful New York mayor), a Nubian lion, and the varieties of flamingos, ostriches, and parrots.

Later that year, another elephant and an antelope joined the collection, making their way southward by truck and stopping overnight at Washington's National Zoo. With its six elephants and an assortment of exotic animals, Asa's zoo was a paradise for the Candler grandchildren and cousins. His daughter Lucy and her family visited often, and her husband Homer trained the horses to pull the stagecoach and taught them new tricks. Asa V grew up thinking that a zoo in his grandfather's yard was "just the way things were." Other kids, he said, might be thrilled to ride ponies, but he thought nothing of sitting atop an elephant. His grandfather was creative when it came to facilitating his growing collection. To service all the animals, Asa Jr. drilled another well on the property, and the large amount of water it supplied filled a huge, new swimming pool with a fountain in its center. The pool soon turned the front lawn of Briarcliff into an elaborate amusement park, especially after Asa fitted it with neon lights, locker rooms, and a concession stand. For twenty-five cents (to help override escalating costs), visitors could go for a swim and then wander over to see the zoo before stopping by the circus ring to watch the animals perform tricks.

At its peak in 1933, Asa's zoo housed one hundred animals, including six elephants, a Bengal tiger, four lions, four leopards, two lynxes, two polar bears, four Himalayan bears, a brown bear, sixty-three monkeys, a puma, a camel, two zebras, two ostriches, two nilghau (rare oxen), four American buffaloes, four deer, two elks, nine ponies, seven sea lions, six alligators, and three hundred exotic birds. In the depths of the Depression, a display of wealth could easily be construed as frivolous, even cruel, thus provoking some of the most desperate to try tapping into the Candler millions. A young Southern Railway employee named John Lee Butler wrote a letter threatening to kill all the animals unless Asa paid him $1,000 toward his wife's medical expenses. Butler was just one of the more inventive. What he didn't realize was that he was facing an experienced pro. Asa Jr. made one phone call to the police and then promised to meet Butler at a movie house in West End, where a waiting policeman nabbed him when he attempted to pick up the money.

Other threats to Asa Jr.'s financial resources were coming from his Druid Hills neighbors. Because the zoo's cages sat at the front edge of the estate next to Briarcliff Road, the architects designed a high stone wall around the entire enclosure, ostensibly to avoid escapes. But the wall was not enough. Animals frequently slipped out to create pandemonium in the quiet neighborhood, prompting a group of concerned residents to demand that Candler employ more stringent measures for keeping his collection confined. When they met with the zoo's curator, Fletcher Reynolds, neighbors were assured that the existing facilities were "100 percent effective" in stopping the animals from running away. But the creatures didn't know that. All year long, neighbors phoned about sightings of birds and beasts tramping down their gardens, destroying their roses, and frightening their children. Attendants spent day after day and night after night conducting rescue missions. That meant scouring the surrounding yards in search of a stray lion or tiger, using food to coax the creature to climb into a station wagon, so they could transport the frightened animal back to its cage.

As might be expected, these roaming creatures prompted a slew of lawsuits. One neighbor, Mary L. Smith, filed for $25,000 worth of damages to her property, claiming that the "roaring of lions, trumpeting of elephants, screeching of baboons, chattering of monkeys, calling of birds, and similar noises," not only kept her awake all night but depreciated the value of her home. Several months earlier, Mrs. Smith had complained to police that a loose baboon in her yard had allegedly climbed into the front seat of her car and grabbed her purse; then she fell and broke her leg in several places as she tried to wrest her bag away. Another resident of Briarcliff Road, Walter B. McClellan, sued Candler for $20,000, on grounds that the deed to his property guaranteed the neighborhood would remain residential.

In his petition, McClellan told the court that before Candler's "nuisance" existed, their home "was peaceful and quiet, and conducive to repose and relaxation." But now the air was "filled with hideous sounds" from animals "that growl, roar, bellow, bleat and cry out" at odd times. Worst of all, in dry weather, dust "laden with disease germs" floated in the air. In fact, "the proximity of so many dangerous, ferocious wild beasts, even though they are supposed to be safely caged and confined," brought fear, even terror to the neighborhood. At the same time neighbors were filing these animal-related charges, attorney Will D. Thomson sued Asa Jr. for the $7,600 he owed his firm for handling nine separate litigations. It was proving to be the costliest craziness of his unorthodox career, mounting up tabs that even Asa Candler Jr. had trouble paying.

At first he managed to avoid responding publicly to the many charges, leaving the negotiations and payments to his lawyers. But pressures were increasing so rapidly that in September 1933, rumors that he was being forced to sell the zoo began circulating. Although Candler vehemently denied that his "zoological garden" was closing, he did announce the dismissal of his curator, Fletcher Reynolds, who told the papers he was returning to the animal park in New Hampshire, because Candler was "overburdened with debt" and couldn't afford to keep him. A month later, Asa gave his baby elephant "Coca" to the Atlanta zoo at Grant Park, to replace an elephant that had recently died.

Aware that he could neither fend off the neighbors nor keep up the enormous project, Candler began conversations with New York's Central Park Zoo. However, municipal authorities there rejected his asking price, and the deal fell through. Meanwhile, Atlanta Mayor James Key began pressuring him to donate the menagerie to his own hometown. Finally, after much negotiating, Candler agreed to give the entire collection to the city's Grant Park Zoo. Complicating his largesse was the size of the existing park space, which was far too small to accommodate so many animals, birds, and reptiles. But when the zoo's managers requested twice the acreage and more than double the existing facilities to house the new collection, the city told them there was no surplus money to pay for such a large expansion. Even though the newspapers were collecting dimes from schoolchildren to cover the cost of the cages, those coins could not begin to pay for the extra construction. City officials were able to offset labor costs through a $20,796.50 grant from the Federal Emergency Relief Administration (FERA), part of the Depression era's WPA program. Still lacking $15,000, the Atlanta government launched a larger fund-raising drive, stressing the business and educational advantages of having a large public zoo. However, in the ongoing economic slowdown, that too failed to meet its goal.

Despite the meager funds and inadequate space, the transfer process began in March 1935, with several weeks of intermittent deliveries that left the administrators frantically searching for places to put the menagerie. Ultimately, the Grant Park Zoo was forced to sell those animals it could not house, and since elephants required the largest quarters and greatest upkeep, they were the first to go. Coca remained but the other five Candler elephants went to circuses around the country, while newborn lion cubs were sent to a preserve in Florida. Asa Jr. gave the Atlanta zoo its first tiger, the popular "Jimmie Walker," but zoo authorities were far from happy when, several days after his arrival, the beast reached a giant paw into the adjoining cage and fatally mauled a leopard. To even out the holdings at Grant Park, Candler agreed to buy twelve new monkeys, which occupied less space than the larger animals. His gift to the city also included the transfer of his zookeeper, Johnny Dilbeck, who spent the next two decades as an Atlanta employee.

After the animals departed from Briarcliff, the large pool with its spouting fountain remained opened to the public for another decade. Even though the zoo and all its activities seriously depleted Asa Jr.'s fortune and damaged his relations with neighbors, the project revealed the big-hearted generosity of its owner and thrilled many a visitor. Asa, himself, experienced enormous pleasure opening his spacious grounds to admirers, witnessing the amusement of children, and inviting the press to gloat over his acquisitions. Most of all, the project revealed that down deep, he was still Buddie. Middle-aged and paunchy he might be, yet the warm, creative, impractical, and irrepressible boy in him exulted in living out his childhood fantasy of running off to join a circus. If realizing that dream threatened to diminish his wealth, the pleasure of his ride must have made it seem worthwhile.[188]

Another member of the Candler family, Henry Heinz, was then serving his community by following a much less quixotic or fiscally precarious path than that taken by his brother-in-law. By participating in business, civic, and social organizations, Henry had become such a valuable contributor to city projects that a member of the Civitan Club proposed his name for Atlanta mayor. He declined the offer, however, because he could not take time away from his already overloaded schedule. In June 1927, he was elected chairman of the International Kiwanis Club (then only including the United States and Canada) and to celebrate that prestigious position, a group of business leaders—accompanied by Enrico Leide and members of his orchestra—welcomed him as he stepped from the train at Terminal Station. Added to the numerous duties associated with that office, Heinz had equally taxing responsibilities in his job as vice president of the Citizens and Southern Bank and secretary-treasurer the Dinkler Corporation, which had charged him with helping plan a new $10 million hotel.

Barely scathed by the Depression, Henry and Lucy seemed to be living a charmed, secure, and extravagant life. But that was before unanticipated tragedies struck—not once but twice—with blows that no amount of inherited wealth or local prestige could fend off. In September 1934, at age fourteen, their daughter Mimi developed such a high fever that she could not be roused. Although her frequent seizures often left her listless and drowsy, this time her prolonged sleep seemed different. When the usual treatment failed to bring down her fever, Lucy rushed her to Emory Hospital, where physicians concluded that she suffered from encephalitis, the probable cause of her long-term illness. As they were preparing her for a spinal tap to relieve some of the pressure, the girl suddenly stopped breathing, and despite the doctors' frantic efforts, Mimi's life ended abruptly. The death of their youngest child so devastated Lucy and Henry that they could not bear to spend Christmas at home, and so they decided to take sixteen-year-old Henry Jr. with them for a Florida vacation. Lucy's son Bill Owens and his wife Louise planned to meet them there, as did her daughter Elizabeth and her husband, Bryant Vann.

Elizabeth Vann had been in poor health ever since her marriage, due to recurring bouts of tuberculosis, an illness said to have prevented the couple from having children. When she first became ill, her mother took her to an Asheville clinic, where the climate was reputed to be favorable for tubercular patients. But Lucy became dissatisfied with the slow progress of her daughter's healing, and attending physicians advised her that Elizabeth would receive equally beneficial treatment in Atlanta. For almost two years thereafter, the young woman remained bedridden in her mother's home until she began to show signs of improvement. When she seemed fully recovered, Elizabeth and Bryant moved to a house they built on an extension of the Heinz property facing Lullwater Road. After Mimi died and Lucy continued to grieve, Elizabeth decided it might comfort her mother if she joined the family in Florida for Christmas. Besides, the sunshine of Miami might improve her health.

The Heinz family, accompanied by Bill and Louise Owens—who were then living in Washington while he worked as a government contractor—started their Florida vacation by fishing in Inverness, before they proceeded on to Miami, where Elizabeth and her husband were meeting them. Since the Owens' had already planned to spend Christmas in Atlanta, Lucy and Henry put them on the train going north, then headed south to Miami, knowing Elizabeth and Bryant were en route there by car. The Vanns left Atlanta as scheduled and were making good time as they approached Waycross, near the Florida border. But just before they reached the south Georgia town, the rear wheels of their car locked and skidded into a tailspin that threw the vehicle over an embankment. When the tumbling automobile came to a stop, Bryant was able to escape without a scratch, but Elizabeth was flung into the backseat and was pinioned under her husband's heavy bag of golf clubs. Not only were her nerves severely shaken, but she suffered from numerous lacerations and bruises. Nevertheless she refused to go to a hospital near the scene of the accident, insisting that she and her husband would take the train back to Atlanta and seek treatment there.

The next morning, when Bill and Louise Owens reached Atlanta, the family chauffeur greeted them at the station with news of the accident. Immediately, they tried to contact Lucy and Henry, but they too were traveling by train, and—given the slow communication systems of the early 1930s—hours passed before the Heinzes could be reached. Despite reports from their son that his sister's injuries were not serious, Lucy and Henry canceled the rest of their vacation and headed for home. At first, Elizabeth seemed to be doing well, and her doctor felt certain that she was recovering satisfactorily. That is until, like her late father, she developed pneumonia. Therefore, by the time her mother arrived after a slow two days on the railroad, her daughter's condition had worsened, and the prognosis was grave.

Meanwhile much of the family and many of Atlanta's leading citizens had gathered on December 29 for a joyous occasion: the wedding of William Candler's daughter, Rena, at St. Mark's Methodist Church. Although most of the wedding guests had heard about Elizabeth Vann's accident, they were under the impression that it had not been too serious. No doubt they began to be suspicious when they noticed the absence of Lucy and Henry Heinz on the bride's side of the sanctuary. Then, during the elegant Biltmore Hotel reception following the ceremony, they found out that Rena's first cousin was fighting for her life. Sadly, the day after the wedding, thirty-one-year-old Elizabeth Owens Vann died in her Lullwater Road home, with her mother and husband by her side. For Lucy, it was a cruel ending to what had already been a tragic year. A shocked Candler family attended the private funeral at the Vann's home on New Year's Day 1935, with an array of Candler cousins serving as pallbearers.

The presence of the extended family at Elizabeth's funeral provided only temporary relief and solace for Lucy, who had lost both of her daughters within three months. Even though Mimi's lifelong illness left her mentally and physically debilitated, her sudden death—at the moment doctors were proposing to improve her condition—had been devastating enough. Then the tragedy of having Elizabeth recovering from the accident only to be felled by pneumonia, struck an almost unendurable blow. Holidays are meant to be happy family occasions, and hoping to make the best of things, she and Henry had finally gotten away to relax in Florida, anticipating Christmas with Elizabeth and her husband, before they all returned home for Rena's wedding. Then suddenly and traumatically, they were plunged into yet another cycle of optimism, followed by the seemingly incomprehensible passing of a loved one, far too young to die. But somehow, Lucy possessed the disposition and *joie de vivre* that had helped her slowly recover from the unexpected death of her first husband and would get her through this next battle with grief—saddened no doubt—but still resilient.

Henry, too, was having a hard time getting over their year of loss. His professional and volunteer work kept him busy during the day, and he was gradually able to overcome the sorrow of the recent deaths by eventually settling with Lucy into another round of travel and socializing at the many receptions, teas, and dinner parties they had once so enjoyed. Their two sons were a comfort, too. Although Bill Owens was then living in Washington, the government job lasted only a few years more before he returned to Atlanta. In their youth, Bill and his half-brother Henry Jr. were bitten by the flying bug, instigated by their "Uncle Bud" and his son John, who took them for frequent jaunts in their private planes. As a result of these exalting flights, both young men trained to be pilots. In 1939, Bill began working for Delta, and, around the same time, Henry got a similar job with Eastern Airlines. Eventually both of Lucy's sons and their families would live nearby, as did her son-in-law Bryant Vann, all on hand to attend family dinners and other celebrations at Rainbow Terrace.[189]

In the mid '30s, the Candler family faced another shocking tragedy, this one involving Lucy's youngest brother, William, in many ways one of the family's highest achievers. Through his participation in civic affairs and the prominence of the Biltmore Hotel, he had become a well respected businessman. Although less flamboyant than Asa Jr. or Walter and more adventurous than Howard, he retained a public persona of dignity and accomplishment, even though he was often an unwise administrator of his own investments. After the Biltmore Hotel opened, he followed his father's footsteps by rising to the top of the Atlanta Chamber of Commerce, and between 1926 and 1930 he served as its vice president. During those years he chaired the fund-raising arm of the "Forward Atlanta Movement," a public relations campaign, headed by Ivan Allen Sr., designed to promote the city's commercial and tourist advantages. Under William's direction, a battery of volunteers called on local businesses and easily raised the $1 million needed for promoting Atlanta as a mecca for financial investment and manufacturing. Thanks to the efforts of William Candler and others, when the Depression ended the "Forward Atlanta" drive, the city found itself recognized nationally as a prospective location for business and industry.

While managing the Biltmore Hotel and serving on various boards, William devoted his spare time to devising new avenues for investing his inherited fortune. One was the Candler Lumber Company, which later changed its name to Edgewater Estates, its essential purpose being acquisition of central Florida property during the 1920s land speculation boom. His dream was to develop a planned community for mixed commercial and residential use near Kissimmee, adjacent to the ranch that he built as a family retreat. During the late '20s and early '30s, he spent hours planning the community, which he dubbed "Intercession City," traveling often to Florida to check on the status of his investment. The flip side of William's complex character was that of risk-taker. His youthful escapades—such as speeding away on his pony when he was seven or his inability to stay long in any one school—may have been a warning that a wilder persona lurked beneath his seemingly stable facade. In his multiple business ventures, he often veered close to the edge by borrowing on his share of the family real estate company to lever his losses.

Despite clear signs that fewer people would be able to afford visits to his luxury hotel during the Depression, William failed to take steps to adequately protect his $6 million investment, in case it suffered from a serious slump in reservations. Thus when the Biltmore began losing money, he found it necessary to take funds from the hotel's surplus to pay his bills. This move depleted the capital so drastically that the hotel could no longer disburse the promised dividends to investors, leading disgruntled bondholders to file three separate suits. Ultimately, the hotel management was forced to declare bankruptcy and enter into a "friendly receivership." In August 1932, Judge E. E. Pomeroy of the Fulton County Court ordered the Biltmore's board to furnish a list of all bondholders, place the bonds in the hands of a special committee, and inform the public about the company's mandatory reorganization plans. The bankruptcy weighed heavily on the hotel's principal owner, who was spending a great deal of time trying to reorganize the corporation so it could emerge from its debt.

The financial downturn led William—who like his brothers had always been fascinated with automobiles—to channel his attention on his hobbies, one of which was driving. During the late '20s, he agreed to chair the motor vehicle maintenance committee of the National Conference on Street and Highway Safety, and in that capacity he issued a report in 1930 advising people to inspect their automobiles for mechanical defects. In addition to the many worn-out cars on the road, he warned, "a large number of vehicles" were "being operated in an unsafe condition because of neglect on the part of the owners," enumerating headlights and tires along with other features that needed constant maintenance. William may have kept his cars in good condition, but he was reckless when it came to speed. Consequently, shortly after filing the automobile safety report with the National Conference, he had a serious accident.

On his way home after visiting his Florida property, and probably driving well over the speed limit, he hit a pig on a back road near Perry, Georgia. William was trapped in his car for a couple of days, until an unnamed African American farmer driving through the countryside in a mule-drawn wagon found him and transported the almost lifeless victim to the nearest hospital. The diagnosis was a fractured skull, but the identity of the unconscious patient remained a mystery because—mistrusting the hospital staff—the man who had saved his life kept the wallet and other personal belongings. A day or so later, the farmer took the contents of the wallet to his minister, and they telephoned William's family in Atlanta. Immediately, his wife Bennie procured a doctor and nurse to accompany her to Perry in a specially equipped Pullman car, in which she planned to transport her husband back to Atlanta. But after examining the patient, the Atlanta doctors felt he was too ill to travel, and he remained hospitalized in Perry for several weeks. Before William was released, he was able to meet his rescuer, who came to his bedside and returned all of his personal belongings.

Six years later, William was not so fortunate. Now burdened by the Biltmore's financial woes, he was once more returning from his Florida property, this time hurrying to meet attorneys and businessmen to discuss emergence from bankruptcy. With him was his friend and lawyer, George Spence. They had originally set out for Forsyth, Georgia, to meet an attorney named Sam Hewlett. But when they arrived there, they discovered that Hewlett had gone to McRae with Governor Eugene Talmadge, so they turned around and drove to McRae, only to find out that Hewlett was now in Valdosta. By then it was late at night, and William found himself once again driving on back country roads. As the men approached the small town of Naylor, eleven miles from Valdosta, they encountered a cow crossing the road. William swerved to miss the animal and again flipped into a ditch. But this time the crash ignited a fire in the engine, and plumes of smoke filled the car before Spence could break a window to get air. When rescuers arrived, they found the attorney had suffered only minor injuries, but William was in critical condition. The frantic rush to a hospital in Valdosta proved fruitless. He was pronounced dead on arrival.

The untimely death of her forty-six-year-old husband was devastating to Bennie. Weighted down by debt and facing bankruptcy, she proved herself to be a strong survivor, as positive and resourceful as her sister-in-law Lucy, who was perhaps her closest family ally. At the time of their father's death, her daughter Rena and her husband were living in Augusta, and eighteen-year-old William Jr. was in college. When she got herself together, Bennie sold their house on Springdale Road and moved into the Biltmore, personally taking over management of the hotel and reorganizing the business to salvage the venture and keep it running. Business picked up in the late thirties, allowing her to book passage to Europe. Aboard ship Bennie met Howell Ross Hanson, a financier from a wealthy Pennsylvania family, and in June 1938 they married in the Candler Theological Seminary at Emory, with all of her Candler in-laws in attendance. Although the Reverend Dr. William Rumble officiated, he was assisted by Bishop Warren Candler, now almost eighty. Bennie and her new husband lived in the hotel that her first husband had built, and she continued her duties as the establishment's very capable manager.[190]

After his separation and divorce from Marion, Walter Candler concentrated on his several businesses and his horses. The garage in downtown Atlanta was so successful that President Roosevelt, who came frequently through the city on his way to Warm Springs, appointed him to serve on the six-man National Motor Vehicle Storage and Parking Code Authority. No great admirer of Roosevelt's New Deal policies, Walter and his brothers no longer followed their father's unbending loyalty to the Democratic Party. Perhaps for that reason, men serving on the Motor Authority chose Walter as their spokesman when the entire committee voted to resign because of a price-fixing clause in the NRA motor vehicle code. When interviewed about his decision, Walter told the press that he strongly objected to the "cut-throat competition" encouraged by the new legislation.

When his short stint on the federal committee ended, Walter devoted more time to his business enterprises and to racing trotters on the Lullwater track, and he still continued to travel. Speaking to a San Francisco audience in 1935, he warned that a recent trip to Asia taught him "that American businessmen must get back to fundamentals immediately or our markets will be glutted with cheaply made Japanese goods." Now free to rant against the current administration, he added: "It's high time to break away from the idealistic, fantastic dreams of President Roosevelt and run our businesses as they should be run. The Japanese are about to offer a serious threat to our economic well-being." It was a prescient remark that was soon echoed around the United States.

Walter Candler, c. 1940, courtesy of Manuscript, Archives, and Rare Book
Library, Emory University

In October 1939, Walter married for the third time. His new wife was Rebekah Skeen of Atlanta, an attractive socialite, three decades his junior. Despite his children's objections to the age disparity, it seemed to be a good match. Her parents were friends of the family, and Rebekah fitted easily into his lifestyle, seeming to enjoy traveling and horseracing as much as Walter did. They both took pride in the victories of their trotter Duke of Lullwater and the colts he sired, pictured several different times on their Christmas cards. Rebekah also shared Walter's love of Shakespeare, a passion developed during his days at Emory, and they often invited friends to gather at their home for readings of plays and poems. Gone was the disorderly behavior and excessive drinking that had overshadowed his early life, as Walter Candler settled down to become a responsible and contented individual.[191]

Asa Jr. had a little bit harder time curbing his erratic lifestyle. After the creation and ultimate termination of his zoo, he grew restless, searching for new hobbies and projects to absorb his excess energy. Still he appeared fated to invite mishaps. A year before William's shocking death, he had a serious automobile accident, a recurring curse for the Candler family. As he, Florence, two of her nephews, and her maid were returning home from Panama City, Florida, the car developed mechanical difficulties south of Atlanta near Griffin and flipped over. Although—in the days before seatbelts—all of the passengers were thrown out onto the road, miraculously no one was killed. Several, however, were injured, some seriously. Because of the Candlers' prestige, Asa Jr. was able to summon several ambulances from Emory Hospital to transport the wounded back to Atlanta, where all were treated. One of Florence's nephews had broken his back and remained hospitalized for an extended period. As a result of this near catastrophe, a chauffeur drove Asa Jr. for the rest of his life.

In August 1940, Asa Candler Jr. celebrated his sixtieth birthday with family and close friends surrounding him. Florence had ordered his portrait to be painted by a local artist named Emma Jennings, and for its unveiling they threw an outdoor barbecue. It was just one of many large gatherings at Briarcliff during the '30s. In the era when "theme" parties were in fashion, they held a costume ball with guests dressed as their favorite comic-strip characters. Perhaps best remembered by Asa Jr.'s descendants were the holiday festivities. On Christmas Eve, Asa and Florence always invited the adult children and grandchildren to attend a formal dinner at Briarcliff, attired in tuxedos and evening gowns. Then the next day, the younger family members participated in a raucous celebration in the banquet-size dining room, where a huge tree laden with gifts filled the corner. The children anxiously awaited Asa's son-in-law Homer Thompson—dressed as Santa Claus—to enter the room and distribute gifts to each of them. As these reminiscences indicate, Asa Jr.'s branch of the Candler family still managed to continue living in luxury, even during the Depression. Nevertheless, Asa was never fully able to recoup the losses he incurred from the skyrocketing expenses of his extravagant zoo and the litigations resulting from it. Not only did he have to watch his pocketbook more carefully by the end of the decade, but his excessive consumption of alcohol (unfortunately affecting some of his children) was catching up with him.

At some point in the late '30s, Asa Jr. stopped drinking, a courageous move he attributed to an epiphany. One day, riding home "half drunk" in the back of his chauffeur-driven car, he said a voice told him: "You must get rid of your self; you must renounce your self; you must reject your self." For the past three years, he had begun attending church services regularly, always praying that he could be rid of his addiction. But to no avail. Then he remembered that he had once tamed an angry Bengal tiger through long, patient sessions, which ultimately quelled the beast's fear caused by living in captivity. Upon thinking of this, Asa decided "that God was trying to get past" his own fears so he could be similarly tamed.

Whether the Lord actually intervened is a matter only Asa and his Maker knew. But the binge that induced heavenly intervention proved to be his last. In a published confession, he declared that "false pride had erected a barrier" between his "soul and God." With this revelation, he suddenly became religious, immersed himself in church activities, developed close clerical friendships, and made a public confession of his alcoholism and subsequent redemption. To make sure he would never retreat, he tied a red ribbon around a whiskey bottle and placed it on the mantelpiece, where it remained for many years.

When the zoo and its consequences stretched his finances beyond their limits, Asa Jr. was forced to liquidate some of his holdings during the '30s, and as part of the process, he sold his shares of Asa G. Candler Inc. to his three remaining siblings. With profits from that sale, he formed his own real estate company, known as Briarcliff Inc., bringing his sons John and Sam into the business. At first, the new corporation dealt primarily with owning and operating Atlanta apartment houses, but over the next decade it gradually branched out to encompass other ventures. Still resourceful and now sober, Asa Candler Jr. was able to maintain his important position in the city and reclaim the dignified reputation he had once so assiduously sought. Respectability did not, however, signal the end of his wild and often erratic plunges into new passions and obsessions, as future events would prove.[192]

CHAPTER FOURTEEN
Murder in Druid Hills

Lucy Candler Heinz and Henry Heinz, c. 1940, courtesy of Vesta Owens Jones

On the night of September 28, 1943, Henry and Lucy Heinz were sitting in the library of Rainbow Terrace listening to the radio. Like many other Atlantans tuned in that night to WSB, the Heinzes had probably been chuckling at the antics of "Fibber McGee and Molly," as the season's first broadcast got under way. Afterward, the couple no doubt stayed tuned in to hear Bob Hope and then Red Skelton, Lucy stitching an award patch on her Red Cross cap, Henry glancing at the newspaper from time to time. At ten, Lucy put down her sewing and told Henry she was going to bed. He replied that he wanted to stay up to hear the latest war news at ten.

Over time, sixty-year-old Lucy had accumulated some extra pounds, yet her soft complexion and even features were still appealingly pretty. Henry Heinz Sr., now in his early sixties, had retained his erect, muscular physique, although now he too was growing paunchier around the middle. His name was constantly in the newspaper, often in tandem with Lucy's, since their parties at Rainbow Terrace seemed scarcely to have been affected by either the recent economic downturn or wartime rationing. Because of his prominence in the community and his many years of experience in the financial world, Henry had been chosen Atlanta chairman of the Third War Loan's banking division. He took his duties with the loan drive very seriously, and it was to hear results of the latest local war bond campaign that he was sitting alone in his library listening to the radio that early autumn night. On the broadcast, he would have learned that Allied troops were working their way up the Italian peninsula and heard of the latest developments in the US bombing of Germany and Austria. The latter would have been of particular interest, since his son Henry Jr. and stepson Bill Owens were US pilots, Bill a captain in the Army Air Force, Henry transporting packages to wartime Britain as part of the Ferry Command.

Undoubtedly, Lucy must have also had the war on her mind as she prepared for bed, for like Henry she was concerned for her sons, and, to aid the war effort, she had been volunteering at the local Red Cross. As she stepped from the shower that night, Lucy said she heard dogs barking, which made her uneasy, since in the past those barks had signaled prowlers on the grounds. Only recently intruders had entered their home, on one occasion stealing $210 out of Henry's wallet, on another taking $80 from her purse. In reporting the last break-in, Henry told police that he had seen a large Negro man running down the driveway, an incident which prompted him to purchase a gun that he kept in the drawer of his bedside table.

So when he heard dogs barking that September night, Henry, too, feared it was another burglar and called, "Mama, Mama," summoning Lucy to come at once. Grabbing a bathrobe, she rushed down the stairs and dashed across the lengthy entrance hall toward the library at the opposite corner of the house. When she drew closer, she saw her husband wrestling with a tall man in a skullcap with a bandanna covering his face. "I'm not sure whether he was a real dark white man or a light-skinned

Negro," she said later, although she could not recall whether she had seen the assailant's masked face or only his back. However, she did notice that he was about the same height as her husband (five feet eleven inches). A clothes-conscious woman, Lucy was able to remember that he was dressed "very neatly" in "light brown trousers with a pink or red stripe in them and either a blue shirt or sweater." He also had on "a vest with one color cloth in the back and another in front, ... a handkerchief or some kind of cloth tied across his face and knotted behind his neck, ... a cap that fitted tightly and it was pulled down behind, so near the handkerchief knot that I couldn't see his hair. I do distinctly recall that he appeared to be a very neat man."

These were amazing details coming from a woman who would have been severely shaken by what was transpiring. Even though the incident was no doubt permanently frozen in her head, she was unable to tell reporters whether her husband or his assailant had said anything. Perhaps that was because, as soon as she saw the intruder, she hurried back to their bedroom to follow her earlier promise to Henry: if they ever spotted another burglar, she would get his pistol. After she retrieved the gun and was racing toward the library, Lucy heard the unmistakable sound of gunshots, and when she reached the library door, she was horrified to see Henry sprawled across the sofa, bleeding profusely. No prowler was in sight. A hysterical Lucy grabbed the phone and began a series of frantic calls to the police, Grady Hospital, her daughter-in-law (Louise Owens), and her son-in-law (Dr. Bryant Vann), both of the latter living only minutes away.

In the midst of catastrophe there is often humor—albeit dark—and the farcical chain of events that ensued played out like a scene from *The Keystone Kops*. The first policemen to respond, Marion Blackwell and Bill Miller of the Atlanta force, had not only investigated the previous robberies at Rainbow Terrace but had spoken several times with the Heinzes. Answering Lucy's call, they sped down Ponce de Leon Avenue, arriving with sirens blaring and searchlights beaming. Without wasting a moment, the two policemen rushed in opposite directions: Blackwell to the back door and Miller to the front. Breathlessly, Lucy gave Blackwell a brief description of the man she had seen in the room with her husband, exclaiming excitedly that she feared he might still be in the house or on the premises. So Blackwell scuttled back to the squad car to radio headquarters for help, and as he was making the call, a shot whizzed past his head. Assuming it was the robber, he fired back into the thick bushes.

Meanwhile, hearing the commotion, Miller jumped off the porch, spraining his ankle in the process. Just then, another bullet whizzed out of the shrubbery, and Miller also fired into the dark underbrush. At that moment, two more Atlanta policemen—replying to Blackwell's call for help—drove up and stepped into the crossfire, just as a man emerged from the bushes shooting. From four corners, the officers converged to tackle the suspect and pinion him to the ground. "Let me up," cried their victim, displaying wounds inflicted by police gunfire. "I'm not the burglar. I was called by Mrs. Heinz." It turned out to be Dr. Bryant Vann, Lucy's son-in-law. He told police that when Lucy called, he had tried to come across the path linking their two houses, but finding it too overgrown, he ran around to the front, hiding in the surrounding shrubbery, with his .45 caliber automatic cocked and aimed at what he assumed to be the prowler.

Within the next few minutes, the house was teeming with action, a scene that the senior police officer and evening watch captain, Herbert Jenkins, described as "a carnival." A streetcar that had been clanging its way down Ponce de Leon Avenue seemingly saw the police and Vann firing at each other and stopped to let driver and passengers hop off to watch what looked like a clip from a shoot-'em-up Western. A swarm of vehicles had pulled into the circular driveway: the ambulance, doctors, a brigade of city and county policemen, reporters, family members, and neighbors. It was bedlam: Lucy was understandably hysterical, Vann was lying seriously wounded on the front lawn, and Henry Heinz's lifeless body was still sprawled across the sofa.[193]

When her phone rang, Louise Owens was in her kitchen on Lullwater Parkway, making formula for her five-month-old son. Her husband Bill was then in India flying over "the hump" to China. As she picked up the receiver, she heard her mother-in-law screaming: "Quick, quick, see if you can get a doctor, a burglar shot Daddy." Louise tried telephoning a neighborhood physician but was unable to reach him, and feeling that she was needed urgently at Rainbow Terrace, she summoned the live-in nurse to watch the baby, grabbed her visiting stepfather, and drove the half-mile up to the Ponce de Leon mansion. When she attempted to enter the driveway, a policeman asked her to park on the street, and he escorted her and her stepfather toward the front door. As they made their way through the darkness, Louise spotted the form of a man lying on the grass and assumed it was the wounded burglar, not having any idea that it was her brother-in-law Bryant Vann. Inside Rainbow Terrace, she found Henry

Heinz's body still on the sofa, and Lucy pacing up and down, wringing her hands, and moaning: "Where's the ambulance? Where's the doctor?"

Louise tried to remove Lucy from the scene, but the hysterical woman refused to budge until a doctor could be found. Finally, her daughter-in-law reached a physician, who agreed to come at once. As he approached the house, the doctor also saw Bryant Vann lying on the lawn and stopped to tend his wounds. When he came into Rainbow Terrace, Lucy insisted that he look at Henry, but after a perfunctory examination, he gently told her: "My dear, he's gone." At having her worst fears confirmed, Lucy fell apart, ranting that there was nothing left to do but "go out and jump off of a cliff." In hopes of calming her down, the physician administered a sedative injection, and much to everyone's dismay, Lucy had such a severe reaction to the drug that the pandemonium increased, and the family hastily summoned a nurse. Finally Lucy relaxed enough for Louise and the nurse to put her in bed. By that time, Florence and Flora had arrived, all of Lucy's brothers being out of town, and the women looked on in stunned silence as Patterson's Spring Hill Mortuary took Henry's body away. The ambulance, which had originally been intended for Heinz, rushed Bryant Vann to Emory Hospital, where he was treated for bullet wounds in his shoulder and arm.

Before dawn the next day, all of Atlanta knew Henry Heinz had been murdered at Rainbow Terrace, and panic spread over Druid Hills. In the wee hours of the morning, police responded rapidly to the report of an intruder at Preston Arkwright's residence, across the park from Rainbow Terrace. Upon checking the premises, they found evidence that someone may well have entered through a window and exited from the back door. Later that night, officers picked up an African American man and took him in for questioning, but when he produced a valid alibi for his whereabouts at the time of the murder, they let him go. It was the first of the countless false alarms that would deluge police headquarters for months to come.

When the city awoke on the morning of September 29, banner headlines atop *The Atlanta Constitution*'s front page provided a detailed account of the murder scene, prompting curious onlookers to block traffic in front of Rainbow Terrace, now cordoned off by barricades. Inside, policemen and detectives were roaming through the house in search of clues, but they found little more than three damaged bullets lodged in the wall, a shirt button, and the workings of a Bulova watch. Family members insisted that such a cheap watch could not have belonged to Henry, so the Bulova became an important piece of evidence. As they scoured the house, investigators also discovered a partially opened window in the dining room, and they dusted its sills and Venetian blinds for fingerprints. Later at headquarters, the inspectors sent the dusted fingerprints, photographs of the items they had found, and the Heinz and Vann guns to the FBI lab in Washington.

Two days after the murder, a large crowd of family and friends attended the funeral of Henry Heinz in the chapel of Patterson's Spring Hill mortuary, sorrowfully watching as a procession of business leaders carried the coffin bearing Henry Heinz's remains down the center aisle. After the service, they followed the hearse and procession of cars to Westview Cemetery to witness the banker's interment. Among the mourners was Henry Heinz Jr., who was based in Miami and therefore able to return to Atlanta for his father's funeral. But Lucy's other son, Bill Owens—half a world away in India—would have to wait until the war ended to say his final good-byes. So would Bryant Vann. From his hospital bed on the day of the funeral, Vann revealed his side of the story to policemen and reporters. After returning home from a "State Guard drill," he explained, he was taking a bath when the phone rang, and Lucy shrieked: "Oh, 'Bry' come quick. Somebody's killing Mr. Heinz." As he rushed over to Rainbow Terrace, he began "formulating a plan to catch the burglar" by crouching along the side wall and moving to the rear of the house. But as he was carrying out this strategy, the shooting began. Unsure whether the bullets were being aimed at him or at his mother-in-law, he fired back. Then when he emerged from the bushes he had no chance to identify himself before the police began "unmercifully" beating him. "I don't hold anything against the officers," he added wistfully. "I guess they did think I was the burglar. I certainly didn't know they were policemen."

A much shaken Lucy—sequestered from the public at an undisclosed location—had recovered enough to speak with investigators a few days after Vann's interview. In her lengthy, often rambling, account she said that at first she thought he had "seen a rat or something. We once had a large rat in the solarium," she digressed, "and I thought maybe he had found one in the library and wanted me to bring a broom or something." Getting back to the incidents leading up to Henry's murder, she told the interrogator about her first view of the intruder and her discovery of the body. In another digression, Lucy speculated that she thought her husband had probably refused to give the man his wallet, even though she had "begged him not to put up a fight if he was robbed." Henry, however, always replied: "Nobody's going to take my money from me." And then she explained that he had "once coached athletics, so had an idea that he could whip any man his size." Due to the shock of seeing her husband's body, she told her interviewer that she did not recall hearing the gun battle going on outside and was later distressed to learn that the wounded person had been Bry, whom she considered to be "just like a son."

Despite attempts to quell it, gossip about the possible murderer proliferated. A vivid assortment of imaginative speculations and bizarre conspiracy theories grew out of Bryant Vann's shoot-out with police. The most persistent alleged that Lucy and her son-in-law were having an affair and had together plotted the murder. Other tales implied that Lucy had hired the killer, and the police were protecting her because she was from such a prominent, wealthy family. Still another insinuated that Vann and Heinz had an argument, during which the dentist shot his step-father-in-law, and in order to protect her late daughter's husband, Lucy invented the story of the prowler as a cover-up. Although the rumors persisted, none jibed with the findings of the FBI report. The bullets on the library floor, the experts concluded, were from a .38 caliber Smith & Wesson revolver, which matched neither Vann's .45 caliber automatic nor Heinz's pistol. This information, combined with Lucy's observations and the small amount of money remaining in Henry's wallet, led the police to conclude that the motive had definitely been robbery. The wallet—which should have been a prime source for fingerprints—had been handled by so many people that it had no value as evidence. Since the murder occurred before the days of DNA and other more sophisticated detection techniques, the bullets, the fingerprints, and the inner workings of the watch were the only items the investigators had.

Based on Lucy's description, the Georgia State Patrol, along with a combined team from the Atlanta and DeKalb County police departments, continued to search the area for the "large Negro man." However, Chief M. A. Hornsby of the Atlanta squad admitted that they were a long way from finding the killer. In response to this, the Candler family, along with several businesses and local governmental organizations, posted a $2,500 reward for information. They thought they had their man, when an escaped African American convict broke into four homes in a rural area northeast of Druid Hills and set fire to a chicken coop. A police posse tracked him down, hauled him back to prison, and extended his sentence, an action that prompted newspapers to write that the Heinz assassin was safely behind bars. But those hopes fizzled after the FBI's forensic experts reported that his fingerprints failed to match those found at the now-vacant Rainbow Terrace. And so the search for Henry Heinz's murderer continued, interrupted only by arrests that raised hopes and created headlines until the police released the suspect of the moment.

Further fueling the rumors that Lucy was somehow implicated in her husband's death, the Candlers requested that there be no coroner's inquest. The police agreed that it would serve no useful purpose, but to many the idea of preventing further inquiries seemed suspicious. After all the tragedies Lucy had borne, she was hit hardest by Henry's murder, partly because she was suffering from severe shock and partly because prying reporters and curiosity seekers rendered her private life so public that she had little time to sufficiently grieve. Finally, when the hubbub died down, she moved as quietly as she could to the Biltmore Apartments to live near her sister-in-law, Bennie. The beautiful Mediterranean mansion on Ponce de Leon, with its array of pink and white dogwoods, was cordoned off, boarded up, and abandoned.[194]

Sixteen months after the murder of Henry Heinz in January 1945, police arrested a plausible suspect, an African American named Horace Blalock, who was picked up shortly after he broke into the Peachtree Road home of Atlanta attorney Hughes Spalding. When the police searched Blalock's residence, they found a "bandana handkerchief" similar to the one Lucy had described covering the face of Henry's assassin. Frank French of the Fulton County FBI quickly identified Blalock's fingerprints as being identical to those taken from the Venetian blinds at Rainbow Terrace. With this seemingly indisputable proof, the police locked Horace Blalock in the Fulton County Tower, where a crew of investigators subjected him to an intensive grilling. The thirty-five-year-old railroad worker denied having killed Henry Heinz but admitted that he had broken into the estate several weeks before the murder and had taken eighty dollars from Lucy's purse.

After this admission, policemen took him to Rainbow Terrace to have him demonstrate how he had robbed the house. During that excursion, Blalock told authorities that he had undergone surgery a few days before the murder and was in too much pain to have wrestled with Heinz. Although Grady Hospital confirmed his operation and subsequent hospitalization, Frank French would not relent. Fingerprints taken from such a well-kept and meticulously dusted house, he insisted, would not have remained on the slats two weeks after having been placed there. Hurriedly the Atlanta headquarters assembled an eight-man lineup and asked Lucy Heinz—along with two other people whose homes the suspect had allegedly robbed—to view it. Without hesitation, all three pointed to Blalock, who was tall, husky, and "not very dark." To make certain of her identification, Lucy asked all the men to turn around so she could view them from the back, since that was how she had originally seen the intruder. When they turned around, she asked them to take off their coats. Again she pointed to Blalock.

Her identification gave the police grounds to continue grilling the prisoner in his Fulton Tower cell. After fifteen hours of interrogation, Blalock broke down and asked for a pencil and paper, in order to explain why he had committed the crime; all witnesses to the questioning assured reporters that the police had not used pressure to coerce the confession. His rambling declaration—scribbled on three sheets of a yellow legal pad and subsequently published *verbatim* in the Atlanta papers—told the story of his surgery, adding that the insurance policy issued by the railroad only paid seven dollars per week, which was not enough to support his family. For that reason, he drove to the Heinz home, where he saw the couple "sitting in the side room." He waited until "Mrs. Heinz went to the bedroom," and thinking they had both retired for the night, he broke open the dining room window and walked down to the library. Spotting Lucy's sewing bag but thinking it was a pocketbook, he crept in to steal it. Then he saw Heinz reading in the corner of the room. "I turn to run," Blalock wrote, "and fell over the table and he grabbed me. We tussle for a few mins. He was so strong I could hardly hold him. So he got my gun before I did and point it at me and shoot my thum [sic] half in two." Eventually, Blalock said, he "got the best" of Heinz, but in an attempt to retrieve his gun, he twisted the banker's hand so that the weapon he was holding pointed directly at him. "It was fire every once in awhile," the confession stated. "I didn't know how many times it is fire." When he was able to wrest his gun away, Blalock said he ran out of the house and rushed home to tend his wounded finger. Unable to sleep, he rose early the next morning, drove out to a bridge in Marietta, and threw the gun into the Chattahoochee River. The rest of the letter was an entreaty for mercy, ending with a plea for Lucy Heinz to spare him so he could see his "children grow up and not make the same mistake" he had.

Now that Blalock had confessed to the murder, the Fulton County judge ordered him transferred to the DeKalb County jail to await a grand jury hearing. This overlapping jurisdiction of city and county further muddied the complicated case, since Rainbow Terrace was in the city limits of Atlanta but also in DeKalb County. Because most of the metropolitan area was in Fulton County, residents of DeKalb were skeptical about anything the Atlanta or Fulton authorities legislated, and this mistrust triggered a new round of speculation about Blalock's innocence. The intense police interrogation, they said, forced a poor and desperate black man to admit to the crime as part of a plea bargain for getting off more easily. For this reason, the DeKalb police chief warned that with so many loose ends, they should proceed cautiously before making a judgment. But nobody listened. Anxious for closure, the press and public were overwhelmingly in favor of a rapid conviction. In an attempt to expedite the proceedings, policemen took Blalock to the Chattahoochee bridge the next day and asked that he show them exactly where he had thrown the gun. As they peered into the fast-moving river, all agreed that too much time had elapsed for them to ever retrieve what might have proven their most significant piece of evidence. Under these circumstances, the authorities concluded that the existing data (Blalock's confession, the fingerprints, and Lucy's identification) provided sufficient grounds for a prosecution. Meanwhile, a reporter discovered that the suspect had been playing an illegal local lottery called "the bug," and he conjectured that gambling was the *real* reason he resorted to robbery. After all, the papers insisted, at $200 a month his salary from the railroad was certainly sufficient for supporting a family of five.

On the morning after Blalock made his confession, the DeKalb County solicitor asked both the suspected killer and Lucy Heinz to return to Rainbow Terrace. A few reporters accompanied the solicitor as he followed Lucy into the deserted mansion that she had abandoned over a year earlier. Now on the market, the once-grand house was laced with cobwebs, and only a few scattered furnishings remained. Walking cautiously into the library, Lucy pointed out where chandeliers, chairs, and tables had been situated, and again she gave her account of her husband's murder. While she was escorting the police through her former home, Blalock waited with guards outside, his lawyer having advised him against taking part in any reenactment of the crime. When Lucy and her entourage emerged from the house, she and her husband's suspected killer stood several feet apart on the wide front terrace. Lucy glanced over at Blalock a few times but never spoke directly to him. Instead, she complained to the police that proximity to the unshackled suspect was making her very nervous.

From this point on, things progressed rapidly. The very next day, the DeKalb County grand jury convened to deliberate the case, whereupon Lucy once again identified Blalock and repeated her story, expressing relief that her ordeal was over and praising the police for solving the crime.

Due to all the hype and advance publicity, the grand jury convened only a short while before handing down an indictment of Blalock. On January 21, headlines in the Atlanta papers—"HEINZ MURDER MYSTERY SOLVED"—rendered judgment before the trial even began, instantly flinging the once-gripping murder into the old news bin. Ironically, the speed with which Blalock's arrest and arraignment transpired caused an even more intense whispering campaign in DeKalb County, where many were convinced beyond question that the two jurisdictions had struck an underhanded deal. "The widow of a rich capitalist," they said, had easily triumphed over an innocent Negro, and Blalock had been accused of a crime he didn't commit. Critics even accused Lucy of appearing too nonchalant at the hearing and being improperly attired for a widow.

A month later, Judge James C. Davis of the Stone Mountain Circuit presided over the three-day trial of Horace Blalock. Atlanta police investigators set up a projector and screen in the courtroom to demonstrate how the detectives had matched the fingerprints on the sill and blinds at Rainbow Terrace with those of the accused man. Then the judge asked Lucy, this time wearing a black suit and veiled hat, to testify before the jammed courtroom. Looking tired and haggard as she mounted the witness stand, the victim's widow said that continuing rumors about her involvement in the murder of her husband had made her ill. Nevertheless, she followed the judge's requests to retell her account of that fateful night two years earlier. Her testimony deviated little from the one she had given previously, except that when the defense lawyers grilled her about why she had picked Blalock out of the lineup, she seemed a little hesitant, saying that the accused man "looked a lot like" the person she had seen wrestling with her husband.

The prosecution called up several other witnesses, one of the leading ones being a jeweler named Harold Jacobson, who explained how he had sold the suspect a watch with workings similar to those found in the Heinz library. Even though cheap watches did not have serial numbers, Jacobson continued, he felt sure of his identification because Blalock had come into his shop a few days after the murder, seeking new workings to fill the empty case. In their closing arguments, the defense lawyers tried one last appeal to leniency by asking the twelve white jurors to consider whether the police had used unscrupulous means to coerce Blalock into confessing. Planting that seed of doubt had no effect on the jury's pronouncing a guilty verdict, but it did influence their two-day debate about the severity of the sentence. Although nine of the jurors wanted to send Blalock to the electric chair, the three in opposition were able to convince the others that "reasonable doubts" heard during the trial provided sufficient grounds for recommending life imprisonment.

Officer Herbert Jenkins of the Atlanta police force, one of the chief investigators of the murder, was a close friend of Judge James C. Davis and a key witness at the trial. In later years, he told his son that he and Davis were thoroughly convinced Blalock was guilty because of his jailhouse confession and the fingerprints that matched those found at Rainbow Terrace. Jenkins later revealed that he and the judge were concerned that the continuing rumors would cast doubt not only on the court procedures but on the honesty of the Atlanta police investigation. For this reason, they wanted to settle the case as rapidly as possible. That fear of adverse publicity probably explains why, after printing Blalock's confession, the Atlanta papers failed to cover the actual trial. Complicating matters even further, Scott Candler—Milton Candler's grandson and Lucy Heinz's second cousin—was the very powerful DeKalb County commissioner at the time of the trial and quite likely had influence over both the judge and the jury.

Less than two years after the trial and sentencing of Horace Blalock, Judge James C. Davis was elected to represent Georgia's Fifth District in the US Congress, a position he held for sixteen years, and Herbert Jenkins became Atlanta Police Chief, serving in that post for a quarter-century. As of this writing, the Archives Department of the DeKalb County Court has been unable to find the transcript of the trial, although it is listed in their ledger that contains all court cases taking place during January 1945. However, when an archivist searched their storehouse, the document was nowhere to be found, and no one had any idea where it might be.[195]

After the trial, Lucy Candler Heinz began slowly and quietly creating a new life for herself, spending more and more time in New York, where she started going out with her old friend Enrico Leide, the same man who had provided music for so many family occasions when he was conductor of the Atlanta Symphony. After that organization hired someone to take his place, the Italian widower taught for a while at Brenau College in Gainesville, Georgia, before accepting a job as director and export manager for a machinery manufacturer in New York. Having known each other for many years and sharing a love of music, Enrico and Lucy found they were becoming more and more compatible, although their backgrounds were different, she being a Southern Methodist, and he being an Italian

Jew. They married in a quiet ceremony in Lucy's apartment at the Atlanta Biltmore on February 5, 1946, telling family and friends that they would divide their time between her hometown and New York.

Now able to afford a more leisurely life, Leide gave up commerce and returned to his first love, music. With his new financial security, he and Lucy moved into a Fifth Avenue apartment overlooking Central Park, and he accepted a position as guest conductor for the New York Philharmonic. Atlanta society writer Edith Hills Coogler visited Lucy and her husband in New York and later described their life together in glowing terms. Most days the couple lunched at leading restaurants, she wrote, and then spent their evenings at home, Leide playing the cello and his wife accompanying him on the piano. On other evenings, he might work on a score as she sat beside him sewing. One of her cousins, Annie Beall, commented that Lucy was "having the time of her life" and seemed "so extremely happy with her Italian" that she was taking Italian lessons. Beall also remarked that Bill Owens Jr. had never become reconciled to his mother's remarriage because he was "so devoted to Mr. Heinz." Nevertheless, her cousin admitted that Lucy knew how "to live and be happy," a pleasure she certainly deserved. Eventually, her children and grandchildren grew to accept "Uncle Leide" into the family, spending a great deal of time with the couple during their prolonged stays in Atlanta. Her granddaughter remembers Lucy's vivacity and generosity during those years, indulging all of her offspring with gifts and affection, and she has fond recollections of family gatherings, many of them including Bryant Vann, Lucy's son-in-law.[196]

During the next decade, the highly publicized murder receded from memory, and when Horace Blalock's case came up for parole on May 18, 1955—only ten years after he had received a life sentence in the state penitentiary—a brief hearing before a police panel granted his release. Neither the state of Georgia nor DeKalb County kept records of parole hearings, and no known newspaper covered the event. The docket of the State Board of Pardons and Paroles simply states that the sentences of Blalock and three other men were suspended "in the best interest of the prisoner and society." A year after Blalock was promised release, his wife charged him with abandonment, leading prison authorities to place him on probation for twelve months. When those restrictions ended, he moved away from Atlanta and was last seen in Vidalia, Georgia, working for an automobile company.

The release of an accused African American in the segregated South—after he had served only ten years for murdering a prominent white banker—ignited a new wave of speculation. Did he promise the Atlanta police that he would confess to the murder on the condition that they grant him a milder sentence, essentially the same punishment he would have received for burglary? When the Candler family united, as it always did, their refusal to discuss the case renewed suspicion that Lucy knew more than she wanted to reveal. One of Asa Jr.'s granddaughters later commented that after Blalock went to prison, Lucy "sent the chauffeur up" to get the address of his family. Then she "went to the grocery store and got forty or fifty dollars worth of groceries," and drove with the chauffeur to deliver the food to his wife. Lucy apparently told Mrs. Blalock: "You can't help what your husband did. I don't want you to go hungry." If this really happened, it poses additional questions: Did Lucy, somehow, feel guilty because her testimony had sent a man to prison? Or was she touched by his plea for mercy? After all, she had once expressed such definite negative racial opinions. Depending on your point of view, the anecdote could be interpreted as an indication of her sympathetic nature, a display of her class' *noblesse oblige* largesse, or evidence of the doubts gnawing at her conscience.[197]

These questions will probably never be answered. Yet, like all overpublicized crimes, the Heinz murder has inspired continuing conjectures about possible intrigues and conspiracies. But despite the temptation to play amateur detective, such imaginative forays amount to little more than an exercise in futility. Not only has all of the original evidence vanished, but records of the DeKalb County Court have virtually disappeared. Albeit the absence of those records fuels continuing speculation, but such guesswork is little more than a game. Blalock's explicit confession—especially his explanation that he shot Heinz accidentally when the banker tried to take away his gun—must, therefore, stand as the solution to a case that is now far too "cold" to be otherwise solved.

CHAPTER FIFTEEN
And So It Goes

The family real estate business (Asa G. Candler Inc.) lasted until the late 1940s. Asa Jr. bailed out in the late thirties, and Lucy sold part of her share to the realtor Jack Adair in 1947, donating the remainder to Emory. A year before that, Emory purchased Walter's portion for $2,500,000. But Howard, who had not squandered his inheritance, donated his full share of the family business to his alma mater. His gift to the university's endowment was said to total more than $5 million in holdings, including much valuable Atlanta property as well as Coca-Cola stock. A year later, when the New York Candler Building on Forty-Second Street sold for more than $2 million, Emory profited from Howard's generosity.[198] No longer tied together by the business, the four remaining children of Asa Griggs Candler Sr. became increasingly involved with their travels and multiplying offspring.

For the most part, the Candlers avoided the public eye; that is, all but Asa Jr. Instead of inviting the press into his life as in the past, much of the publicity he received during the 1940s was unsolicited and definitely unwanted. Ever the innovator and entrepreneur, he had opened a laundry, dry-cleaning, and storage facility on the premises of his estate, putting to productive use the artesian well he had tapped to feed the zoo animals and supply the swimming pool. Since he was devoting most of his time to buying and selling real estate and developing Westview Cemetery—a purchase of the 1930s—he turned over management of the laundry to his sons John and Sam. At first the business prospered, with people from all over Atlanta bringing items to Briarcliff to be washed, dry cleaned, or stored for the winter. But before long, the far-too-casual operation began losing money. Then in June 1943, a fire totally destroyed the entire facility, leaving hundreds of infuriated customers demanding compensation for lost clothing.

The following year, a police investigation into causes of the fire discovered that the Candlers had been charging one cent per bundle for insurance, from which they had amassed more than $5,000 per year, purportedly to cover all of the garments on the premises. However, further exploration disclosed that the business was coinsured to cover only 80 percent of the damage caused by the fire. Added to this, the Candlers were charged with not having used the collected fees to pay the insurance premiums. In short, the family could not begin to collect the estimated $300,000 needed to include all the stored items. Worse yet, only the laundry was covered for fire damage and—as it turned out—the dry-cleaning and storage facilities incurred the greatest losses. When presented with this information, a federal grand jury indicted the three Candlers on two counts: first for misrepresentation, since customers were not told the truth about their insurance coverage, and second for redirecting their losses, because they had attempted to limit liabilities by separating the failing laundry from the more lucrative real estate division.

Asa Jr. and his sons were each asked to post $5,000 bonds. At the time of the trial in April 1944, John was under a great deal of stress due to the death from cancer of his wife Lib. Although for several years he had been helplessly watching her slow and painful decline, the shock of her actual passing—coupled with the reality of being left with their four children and the catastrophe at the laundry—drove John more deeply into the kind of binge drinking that had recently sent him for treatment at various out-of-town clinics. The courtroom scene made matters worse, as John, his brother, and his father watched former customers (many of whom were friends) parade to the witness stand waving receipts that promised insurance coverage. Servicemen from Fort McPherson and the Naval Air Base told how they had lost hundreds of dollars worth of military uniforms, and several women complained that they had left their fur coats at Briarcliff, because Sam Candler assured them that for a two-dollar charge their clothes would be stored and insured.

Under questioning, John and Sam admitted that they had not been keeping a very close watch on business operations, yet they vehemently denied ever having conspired to defraud customers, further asserting that the accusers were claiming far greater compensation than the stored items were worth. Addressing the charge of redirecting their losses, the Candlers' lawyers explained that separation of the real estate company could not have been an attempt to doctor the books, since John had purchased the business in 1942, well before the fire. As character witnesses, several clergymen and well-known Atlantans endorsed these statements by emphasizing that they had long known the Candler family and were convinced that all three men were honest in their business dealings. After three hours of deliberation, the jury concluded that there was insufficient evidence to charge Asa Jr. or his sons of a crime, but it did require them to reimburse customers for their losses. That penalty wielded the final blow to the laundry, which had never recovered from the devastating fire.[199]

In the next few years, John Candler began investing in real estate; his key project was development of one of the city's first shopping centers on Ponce de Leon at the corner of Highland Avenue, known as "The Plaza." In this and other endeavors, he displayed the wise business abilities of his father and grandfather. But John's accomplishments and attempts to embark on a new life were not to last long. Despite his continuing efforts to end a dependence on alcohol, grief and heavy responsibility drove him into spells of binge drinking. Even a second marriage to a young and devoted woman named Thesis Fowler could not end his addiction. A year after he married, John once again entered a clinic, where the doctors were treating patients with an experimental therapy that involved injecting insulin into their systems. Shortly after he returned home from this treatment, he suffered a fatal heart attack, which the family blamed on the clinic's unorthodox methods. He was only forty-one.

At the time of his son's death on Valentine's Day in 1947, Asa Jr. was traveling with a group of friends, all of whom returned home for John's funeral. The immediate issue after John's death was custody of his children. Asa Jr. and Florence asked that all four live with them at Briarcliff, since John's young wife worked and could not handle the responsibility. But Lib's widowed mother, Mrs. George Brandon, also wanted custody of her grandchildren, and the case ended up in court. The family confrontation was settled with a compromise: the two younger children, Helen (nicknamed Nena) and John Jr., went to live with their maternal grandmother, while the two older ones, Nancy and Asa V, moved into Briarcliff with Asa Jr. and Florence.[200]

While the two teenagers lived with him, Asa Jr. owned a 1,200 horsepower Lockheed Lodestar that accommodated fourteen passengers. Now and then, he used the plane to take his grandchildren on vacations, and at other times, he paid for them to travel, once sending Nancy and Helen on an extensive tour of the West. Mostly, however, Asa Jr. filled the airplane with groups of men accompanying him on big-game-hunting expeditions. By the late '40s, those journeys to stalk and shoot animals had developed into yet another of his expensive obsessions. His first trips took him to Canada, Alaska, and various areas of the American Northwest, where he boasted of hanging from a cliff to shoot a longhorn sheep and of being charged by a Kodiak bear. To display these prizes, Candler built an eighty-foot by sixty-foot trophy room adjoining his principal office at Westview. On exceptionally high walls, he displayed heads of polar and brown bears, longhorn sheep, moose, and elk; beside them he hung splayed skins from these and other animals, along with a full-sized stuffed Rocky Mountain goat. Thus with a curious reversal of hobbies, the eccentric millionaire—who once housed and cared for live animals—now began exhibiting dead ones.

Recent financial setbacks and lifelong extravagances forced Asa Jr. to consider selling Briarcliff, and after several dead-end negotiations, he accepted an offer from the federal government, which planned to locate a new Veteran's Administration hospital on the property. After the sale, Asa Jr. and his family moved out of their mansion and took over the top floor of his Briarcliff Hotel. Once settled, he decided to take his grandson, Asa V, on a safari in Kenya, announcing that he hoped to return with enough game to decorate the empty wall of his trophy room. They set out in July 1949, flying to New York on his private plane and then boarding a Pan American "clipper ship" for a stop in London to buy hunting outfits before continuing by air to Nairobi. Equipped with big-game rifles and a multitude of cameras, the Candler party followed an East Indian guide through the jungles west of Mombasa, camping in a luxurious site, replete with electricity, plumbing facilities, and a crew of Africans to cook, wait on them, and assist with the hunting.

Each day, Asa Jr. drove with the guide into the jungle, remaining seated in the "shooting car" until the others had cornered the prey, and then he would alight from the vehicle to participate in the kill. For Candler's sixty-ninth birthday on August 27, the guide sent out three hundred engraved invitations for a party in Mombasa, which described the guest of honor as "a well-known North American big game hunter and real estate man." During the six-week trek, Asa Jr. and his namesake shot thirty-four animals—including his prize, a huge bull elephant—as well as two lions, several deer and antelopes, a rhino, a giraffe, and a zebra, very nearly replicating the assortment of beasts that had populated his zoo sixteen years earlier.[201]

The hunting expedition ended with an unexpected bang. Upon arriving in Atlanta, Asa Jr. discovered that another business problem had again catapulted his name into the headlines. This time the difficulty centered around his management of Westview Cemetery, the resting place of his parents, his first wife, his youngest brother, his baby son, his oldest son, as well as his brother-in-law and mother-in-law. By the late 1940s, he and Florence (comanagers of the cemetery) were undertaking a large "beautification project," beginning with construction of a community mausoleum, a café, and the large trophy room. Their modifications also called for extensive reconfiguring of the grounds, a project that had already begun. But many relatives of those buried there felt that the supposed improvement was destroying—not enhancing—the city's second oldest and largest burial ground. They were particularly distressed that the owners were destroying much of the foliage, eliminating the picturesque lake, and knocking down all of the Victorian-era monuments. Upset by these changes, 250 unhappy families filed a class-action suit against Westview, accusing Asa Jr. and his wife of mismanaging the "perpetual care" trust fund. The disgruntled clients complained that not only were the grounds and plots of their loved ones in extreme disrepair, but their own expensive plantings had been removed without prior notification. These protests caused such a stir that the Fulton County Superior Court slapped an injunction on the cemetery, ordering cessation of all further work until the Candlers and their employees answered the charges.

Since the judge's ruling only prohibited the cemetery from disturbing older graves, bulldozers continued to uproot avenues of magnolias, using the displaced dirt to fill in the lake. As this was happening, headlines about the "desecration" of fifteen hundred graves hit the Atlanta papers, intensifying the pressures. Former Congresswoman Helen Douglas Mankin led a bevy of concerned politicians on a tour of the cemetery, afterwards telling reporters that she had been reduced to tears to see the destruction of monuments dedicated to famous Georgians. Candler shot back that he was merely lowering all markers and simplifying the landscape, to bring the facility out of the "horse and buggy days" and into the modern era. His model, he said, was the Lincoln Memorial Cemetery in Washington, DC, which permitted no monuments and only metal gravestones. "I have taken money from my own pocket for the beautification of the cemetery," he told the press. "If the Lord lets me live long enough and the people of Atlanta will cooperate, Westview will be the most beautiful place in the world."

While the "renovation" continued, irate descendants requested an audit of the books, but Asa refused to comply unless the court demanded it. That happened in late November, when Asa, Florence, and two Westview employees were summoned to explain their actions at a preliminary hearing. Candler defended the changes, arguing that not only were revenues from the perpetual-care trust inadequate for maintaining the graves, but families were expected to tend their own plots, due to dramatically rising labor costs. That defense fell flat, however, when irate relatives testified that they *were* taking care of the graves, only to have the Westview crews mow down their plantings. And, worst of all, they accused the Candlers of using their maintenance trust funds to build the cemetery's new café and elaborate trophy room. Several weeks after the hearing ended, a bevy of angry families defied cemetery rules and swarmed through the gates, armed with lawnmowers and other yard tools, determined to carry out their own repairs. Realizing that any attempts to halt the takeover would only exacerbate his problems, Asa Jr. had no recourse but to allow it. If this wasn't humiliating enough, he then had to face expulsion by the Georgia Funeral Directors for violations of their ethics code. It was the first time the organization had ever ousted a member.

A few months later, Mamie and Henry Oattis brought a well-publicized $55,500 damage suit to trial. The elderly couple described how the crew at Westview had desecrated the grave of their grandson, an eighteen-year-old Georgia Tech student who had died as a result of a football injury. Asa once again explained that he was following the "national trend" toward "level lot cemeteries" to avoid unnecessary expenses. That excuse from a Coca-Cola heir did not sit well with the jury, which fined him $40,300 in actual and punitive damages. In order to pay the fine, he began transferring his real estate holdings to the Westview Corporation, a maneuver Mrs. Oattis and the other litigants contested on grounds he was employing unscrupulous maneuvers to "render himself insolvent." This time, the Georgia Supreme Court ruled in Candler's favor, declaring the transfer to be a legal way of handling his debts.

With this ruling and eleven other suits pending, Asa and Florence tried to smooth things over by opening the cemetery's chapel to the public, hiring a new publicity director, and bringing three professionals into the administration. They limped along this way for a while before finally deciding to sell the property to a Washington, DC, company for more than $2 million, the new owners agreeing to pay the remainder of $350,000 owed to the litigants. Now sufficiently chastised and financially burdened,

Asa Candler Jr. refrained from investing in any more businesses. The Westview debacle proved to be the final drama in his indefatigable search for new commercial ventures. However, this was not his last appearance in the headlines.[202]

In hopes of achieving some positive press and perhaps restoring his reputation, Asa Jr. made a highly visible altruistic gesture. The elephant named Coca—his gift to Atlanta's Grant Park Zoo almost two decades earlier—had recently died, presenting the perfect opportunity for a heroic deed. In early 1950, Asa sponsored a letter-writing contest in the *Atlanta Constitution* entitled: "Why I Would Like to Help Select Coca-II." From seven hundred thousand letters written by children in Georgia and surrounding states, he and his advisers chose six boys and girls—ranging in age from eight to fifteen—to travel to the animal preserve in Nashua, New Hampshire, where he had purchased animals for his zoo. At the end of March, Asa Jr. departed on his private plane, accompanied by the selected youngsters and the director of the Atlanta Parks Department.

Their first stop was Washington, DC, where Asa took his charges on a tour of historic sites, ending with a visit to his Emory classmate, Vice President Alben Barkley. Then they flew to Boston for another sightseeing expedition and stay at the Parker House Hotel. At the animal preserve the next day, Candler stood back as the contest winners reviewed the selection, eventually choosing a seven-year-old Siamese elephant. After a visit to Lexington, Concord, and the Massachusetts Legislature, they spent another night in Boston before returning home. Again Asa employed his skill in eliciting publicity by hiring a crew from Paramount Pictures to record the visit, presenting the reels to an Atlanta television station, which aired the story a few days later. Redeemed somewhat in the public eye by the elephant-choosing expedition, Asa finished his public life dramatically, proving to the end that he was one of Atlanta's most exotic residents.[203]

Two years after he chaperoned the children to New Hampshire, Asa Jr. was diagnosed with cancer. Surgery at Emory Hospital came too late, and he only lasted a few months more before passing away in January 1953, at age seventy-two. His obituary was front-page news in Atlanta and ran in papers all over the nation. His funeral at Westview drew a panoply of dignitaries, including Governor (and soon-to-be US Senator) Herman Talmadge, who was one of the pallbearers. There—in the chapel named after his wife, at the cemetery that seriously depleted his fortune—he was laid to rest on a grassy knoll filled with family tombs. The shortcomings of Asa's unconventional reputation were forgotten when three of his closest clerical friends, along with distinguished Atlanta business executives, delivered eulogies. Harrison Jones, former chairman of the Coca-Cola board, captured him perfectly as "a dreamer and a doer," continuing:

> His mind was never at rest, but always full of plans. Many of those plans for the benefit of the community were more matured than one would think from a man with so many plans. He never thought in small things, but all things which appealed to him were large in scope.[204]

The Janus-like quality of Asa G. Candler Jr.'s unique personality instigated accolades on the one hand and lawsuits on the other. Innately kind and creative, he maintained his childlike and open personality throughout his life, attracting young and old. His grandchildren reminisce nostalgically about his generosity as well as his eccentricity. In the course of his peripatetic life, Asa Jr. proved to be a bighearted friend to people around the world, but the impetuousness—which haunted his life from start to finish—seemed to court calamity. Some quirk in his makeup prevented the "Buddie" component from considering the consequences of his reckless pursuits. And with a fortune to spend (and waste), he could always command a loyal following to comply with his unpredictable whims. For those who knew him, both casually and intimately, he was one of life's most unforgettable characters.[205]

Howard, who died of a heart attack in 1957, was the next of the siblings to go. Because of his prominence as an Emory benefactor and community dignitary, his obituaries were even more effusive than Asa Jr.'s had been four years earlier. Unlike any of his brothers, Howard had carefully guarded and retained his fortune, and, as chairman of Emory's board of trustees, he donated such a large amount to the university that it honored him with several special tributes. He delivered the commencement address in 1946, received Emory's prestigious Alumni Award in 1953, and his large oil portrait hung for many years alongside his father's in the Candler Library.

During the 1940s, Howard began accumulating data to write the biography of his father, contacting old friends and relatives, scouring documents, and consulting with local historians. The result was *Asa Griggs Candler*, published by Emory University in 1950. With no pretense of impartiality, Howard wrote an adoring peon to the parent he had striven so hard to please. A small, limited edition was distributed among friends and family, although the author refused to accept money for the hefty volume and would not allow the book to be sold commercially. His reward was a profusion of congratulatory letters that recalled past events and praised the book's accuracy. With Howard's cooperation, Emory University staged a special centennial celebration of its founder's birth in 1951, featuring a display of memorabilia from Asa Sr.'s life and the beginnings of Coca-Cola.[206]

Because the eldest of the five siblings had been long haunted by the personal doubts and filial obligations that his father implanted, the biography provides an excellent study of how those contradictions shaped Howard's character. For all of his seventy-nine years, he remained the family's responsible watchdog, frugal guardian of the Coca-Cola profits, conscientious scholar, and unselfish benefactor, a role that Asa Sr. had entrenched in him with every conversation, every letter, and every phone call. The book *Asa Griggs Candler* not only sums up the reverence and the conflicts of those responsibilities, but it conveys a loving portrayal of the man who enabled his son's privileged existence. Beyond supplying a glimpse into the Candler family's past, as viewed through the eyes of a principal participant, the biography is spiced with a wealth of anecdotes found nowhere else. Thus the adulatory volume stands as a fitting tribute to his illustrious father from the least colorful—but perhaps the wisest—of his children.

Lucy lived for another five years, the later decades of her life turning out to be less traumatic than the 1930s and 1940s. Her marriage to Enrico Leide seemed fulfilling, as she happily commuted between New York and Atlanta. On her extended visits home, she seemed to enjoy the company of her children and grandchildren, inviting the little ones to spend the night in her new Howell House apartment, lavishing the girls with gifts from J. P. Allen, and entertaining them all with stories of her youth and early adult life. Other times she would host family dinners or go shopping with old friends. Often she spent time with her sons and their wives, Louise and Henry Jr.'s wife, Martha, who began to replace the daughters she had lost. Her grandchildren, nieces, and nephews fondly remember her many kindnesses and her incessant (and often loud) chattering. In New York, she reveled in Leide's musical world and the associations he made as guest conductor of the American Symphony. Her first heart attack was a mild one, hardly causing more than a temporary interruption in the pleasures of travel, family visits, and attending plays and concerts in New York.

Having lived her life with a romantic flair, Lucy even managed to die in circumstances that parodied the movies she so enjoyed. The setting was the steamship *Caronia*, headed across the Atlantic in September 1962, as the Leides were happily anticipating a leisurely cruise around the Mediterranean coast. But those plans were never to materialize. When they were sailing just beyond the Canary Islands, Lucy suffered a second heart attack, and unlike the previous one, this coronary proved to be fatal. Dying at sea presented special problems for her children, for while shocked and grieved, they were faced with the complicated task of bringing the body back to Atlanta. A sad group of mourners gathered at Westview Cemetery, where she was laid to rest alongside her first two husbands and two daughters, not far from three of her brothers and her parents. Like her siblings, Lucy lived her life to the fullest, enjoying the fruits of her father's labors. Of all Asa's five children, in the long run she was probably the toughest. Despite repeated losses, she displayed the capacity to handle her sorrow appropriately and then rebound cheerfully to resume the role of matriarch to her offspring, loyal peacemaker among her brothers, and close friend and confidant to her wide circle of friends. Her children, nieces, and nephews remember her ebullience, her generosity, and her piercing and affectionate voice that made family gatherings so unforgettable.[207]

Walter, who outlived all of his siblings, died when he was eighty-one years old. Remembered for his many contributions to Emory—including a lecture series established in his name—he would no doubt have been pleased that the obituary notices cited his various late-life commercial successes, as well as his championship trotters and their victories. Having sold his estate by the time he died, Walter and Rebekah were residing at the Candler Hotel in Decatur. On his eightieth birthday, his wife arranged a surprise party following the races in Lexington, Kentucky, with his one remaining son and three daughters in attendance. His oldest son and namesake had been tragically burned to death in 1951 at age forty-five, when a butane lantern overturned at his ranch near Kissimmee, Florida. Walter Jr.'s death ended a life spent mainly in aimless wandering, although toward its end, he did settle down as part owner of the Bar-L-Ranch, which he operated with his cousin William Candler Jr. on the Edgewater Estates that William Sr. had purchased during the '20s. Fourteen years later, William Jr. took his own life at his home near Orlando.[208]

These and several other tragedies plagued the succeeding generations. Like much of the modern world, the Candler family has experienced the ups and downs of joys and sadness. Yet at this writing, many of Asa and Lucy

Elizabeth's descendants still live comfortably in Atlanta and surrounding areas, blending so easily into local social, cultural, and business life that few of the city's many newcomers (or even longtime residents) are aware of the lofty position their family once occupied. Many Candler descendants attended Emory University, several achieving advanced degrees, some maintaining the family's involvement in real estate; some are in the clergy, some in medicine. The majority experience normal, productive lives and perpetuate the names Asa, Sam, Martha, Lucy, Elizabeth, Howard, William, and Walter, thus confusing anyone trying to untangle Candler family relationships.[209]

When the railroad finally reached Villa Rica in the 1890s, the old village adjacent to the mines was abandoned, and a new town center developed nearer the tracks. The old Candler homestead was subsequently demolished, as were most of the places Asa Sr. remembered from his childhood. However, the graves of Sam and Martha, where the siblings gathered each year on the Fourth of July, rest undisturbed near those of some of their descendants in the old cemetery at the end of Candler Road. In the late 1920s, Willie Candler sold the general store (which had moved to the new commercial district) and concentrated his efforts on the Villa Rica bank that he had established at the end of the nineteenth century. Today his offspring—several of whom still live in or around this rural community—have prospered from the bank's success.

The house on Seaboard Avenue in Atlanta was razed in 1961, but all of the other Candler residences outlasted their occupants. In a city that tears down old buildings at a rapid clip, it is unusual that those houses managed to survive.[210] Callan Castle, in Inman Park, where Asa and his family lived from 1903 until 1916, is now a private residence for a young family, who are working hard to restore it to its original state. Asa's estate on Ponce de Leon Avenue, dubbed "the Lemon Pie House," has gone through several transformations. When his children took over the property after their father's death, the mansion stood vacant for several years until sold to a family. Then in the 1940s it became a boardinghouse, and in the early '50s it served as an American Legion headquarters. Finally, the Chrysostom Melkite Greek Catholics purchased the house and converted it into a church. Today Lucy Elizabeth's elaborate central court—patterned after the set of the silent movie *The Last Days of Pompeii*—is a sanctuary filled with pews, still topped by the green and white stained-glass canopy that she chose. Asa Candler would have been pleased, though perhaps perplexed, by the Byzantine origins of the denomination that occupies the house where he spent his last years, but he would have been delighted to know that a Christian congregation now worships there.

A few years following Henry Heinz's murder, Lucy sold Rainbow Terrace to a Georgia Tech dean, who lived there for a few years. Then for the next two decades the large home changed hands periodically, perhaps because residents often reported hearing strange, spooky creaks and groans, some ascribed to supernatural beings. After the body of a suicide victim was found on the premises in 1976, people were convinced that the house was "hexed." And so once more Rainbow Terrace sat deserted and vacant for over a decade, windows broken and balconies hanging, a squatting place for homeless people and critters. Even the April panoply of pink and white dogwoods on the rolling grounds did little to dispel the gloom. Finally, in the early 1980s, a developer rescued the property, turned the mansion into luxury condos, built a string of townhouses cascading down the hill where the gardens once stood, and converted the barn into a residence on the adjacent road. Today the development, known as Lullwater Estates, is a thriving segment of the popular Druid Hills scene, where homeowners in the main house live luxuriously in the bedrooms once filled with noisy Owens and Heinz children, or in the dining room and large solarium where Lucy entertained so lavishly, and even in the library where Henry Heinz was murdered.

The most famous of all Candler mansions is Howard's Tudor-style Callanwolde. Flora, who died in 1968, perpetuated Howard's generosity to Emory by contributing to various school projects, endowing an annual concert series, and capping off her munificence by moving out and donating her home to the university. During the late '50s and early '60s, Emory occupied the twenty-eight-acre estate, where professors and administrators held conferences in the dining room, botany students researched plants in the greenhouses, and music students learned to play the Aeolian organ. But Callanwolde proved too expensive to maintain, so Emory sold it to the First Christian Church, which reduced the property to twelve acres. When the church decided to move, an artist bought the mansion and leased out rooms to painters, sculptors, potters and the like, thus further altering the house and grounds.

Aware that the showplace was in jeopardy, an ad hoc committee of the Druid Hills Civic Association intervened in 1972. With the help of the Federal Housing Authority and the DeKalb County Recreation Department, the association purchased the estate for $360,000 and arranged for its placement on the National Historical Registry. Formation of the Callanwolde Foundation in 1983 facilitated renovations, and today the house is an art center offering classes and sponsoring exhibitions. The stately front hall is often leased for private parties, weddings, or fundraisers, and on these occasions the newly restored Aeolian organ booms through the premises, melodically re-creating the many musical evenings that Howard and Flora so enjoyed.

Briarcliff was not as fortunate as Callanwolde. After Asa Jr. and Florence moved in 1949, the US government bought the estate to use as a veteran's hospital. When that plan fizzled, the state of Georgia took over the property and converted the large house into a hospital for recovering alcoholics. Considering the family's struggles with that addiction, that purpose was perhaps appropriate, although the new owners had to dramatically reconfigure the interior to suit their purposes. Then, after a few years, the state turned the facility into the Georgia Mental Health Institute, making further alterations. For several decades, the elegant home was used as a mental hospital, with most of its interior gutted to create patient rooms, conference areas, and doctors' offices. About five hundred feet downhill from Asa Jr.'s former residence—where Japanese gardens and stables once stood—Georgia authorities constructed an amalgam of brick buildings for more hospital facilities and offices.

After the Mental Health Institute closed in the 1990s, the state sold the property to Emory University, which now uses the office buildings for its adult education program. However, the deteriorating Georgian mansion still stands ghost-like and shuttered, windows boarded, graffiti-covering its crumbling walls, a sad reminder of its glamorous past. At the time of this writing, Emory has not yet decided what to do with Asa Jr.'s home or the site of the former zoo and pool. But the original owner would probably be pleased to know that the animals he shot and mounted in the Westview trophy room have been preserved and now reside in Atlanta's Fernbank Science Center.

Walter's Lullwater Farms endured a better fate than Briarcliff. In the late fifties, he sold the entire estate and all 185 acres to Emory, receiving close to one million dollars, a hefty price in those years. The federal government bought the eastern segment for the long-awaited veteran's hospital, and Emory used the remainder as an auxiliary campus. Although the clubhouse burned and the racetrack was plowed over and cultivated, the large Tudor mansion remained, first to house Emory staff and graduate students, then, after extensive renovations, to serve as the university president's home. Since Walter lacked space in his apartment at the Candler Hotel for many of the antiques and other furnishings, they were left *in situ*. As a loyal Emory alumni, he was no doubt pleased to visit the first presidential resident, Dr. Sanford Atwood, and see that his former home remained intact, with its surrounding grounds preserved as a nature sanctuary. Today runners sprint around the lake, and conscientious undergraduates study under the leafy umbrella, while faculty members and doctors take their daily constitutionals around the luscious grounds.

When William's wife Bennie moved to the Biltmore in the late '30s, she sold their home, Rest Haven, to a family named Baker. Although it has changed hands several times, the yellow brick house—on the shady street surrounded by other comfortable Druid Hills dwellings—has remained a private residence. Before Bennie's death, Sheraton bought the Biltmore Hotel and operated the facility for several years. After that chain abandoned the building, it avoided the wrecking ball because farsighted individuals placed it on the historical registry. Recently the Biltmore's new owners turned the massive facility into a mixed-use office building and condominium. On the Biltmore's roof, the pyramidal WSB radio towers still stand as sturdy remnants of the important role the hotel played in its heyday.[211]

The Candler Building in Atlanta, Howard Candler wrote, was his father's "first love," and he gloated over "its elegance, its distinctiveness, its monumental atmosphere" all of his life. Howard commented that the structure incorporated his father's "ideals in its architecture, his conception of completeness in its facilities for usefulness and comfort." Indicating his own veneration for his illustrious parent, he added:

> He was a man of demonstrative sentimental impulses. This building rests upon a foundation of solid granite, its extra heavy skeleton of huge steel columns, beams and girders clothed with white Georgia marble and terra cotta will continue staunch and stable for many years.[212]

This is a very prophetic statement, although not quite in the sense Howard intended it. If the memory of Asa Candler Sr. has faded in the American memory, his egocentric skyscraper still stands, now overshadowed by much taller giants. Yet, after recent renovations by its new owners, the graceful Candler Building remains an important landmark, as does its Times Square equivalent. The annual commemoration of Sam and Martha

Candler's birthdays on the staircase of the Atlanta edifice ended years ago. But the marble busts of Asa's ancestors still keep watch over lawyers, doctors, and CEOs, who ride up the brass-fronted elevators to their offices that look out over a city that scarcely resembles the one once dominated by the Candlers. Most of all, the ever-expanding Emory University and Coca-Cola—one of the world's most recognized American products—stand out as testimonies to Asa Candler's impressive and long-lasting legacy.

Acknowledgments

I wish to thank Virginia Cain Smith and all the staff at Emory University's Manuscript and Rare Books Library (MARBL); Philip F. Mooney, director of the Coca-Cola Archives; and Mike Brubaker and the staff of the Atlanta History Center Archives. I also received suggestions and information from Jennifer M. Jones at Callanwolde, Rev. Fr. John Azar of St. John Chrysostom Melkite Catholic Church, Rodney Cook of the Millennium Gate Museum, and Paul Graham of the DeKalb Historical Archives. Special thanks to Ernest Blevins, Doug Mabry, Spencer Crawford, and all the other helpful citizens of Villa Rica. The interesting conversations with members of the Candler family—especially Asa Candler V, Asa Candler VI, Bill Candler, Helen (Nena) Candler Griffith, Elizabeth Candler Graham, Nancy Candler Nutter, Jim Candler, and Vesta Owens Jones—added so much to my understanding of their ancestors. Also James S. Jenkins provided information about his father's role in the Heinz murder case, and Amy Lathi graciously escorted me through the Candler's Inman Park home. And most of all, I am indebted to Mary Lu Mitchell and Anne Palumbo for their careful reading of the manuscript.

Selected Bibliography

Archives

Coca-Cola Archives, Coca-Cola International Headquarters, Atlanta, Georgia.
Georgia State Archives, Morrow, Georgia.
Manuscripts, Archives, and Rare Books Library, Emory University.

Newspapers

Atlanta Constitution
Atlanta Georgian
Atlanta Journal
Atlanta Journal-Constitution
New York Times
Villa Rica News
Washington Post

Books

Allen, Frederick. *Secret Formula: How Brilliant Marketing and Relentless Salesmanship Made Coca-Cola the Best-Known Product in the World*. New York: HarperCollins, 1994.

Ambrose, Andy. *Atlanta, An Illustrated History*. Athens, GA: Hillstreet Press, 2003.

Anderson, Mary T. *The History of Villa Rica: City of Gold*. Villa Rica, GA: Bicentennial Committee, 1976.

Bauerlein, Mark. *Negrophobia: A Race Riot in Atlanta, 1906*. San Francisco: Encounter Books, 2001.

Braden, Betsy and Paul Hagan. *A Dream Takes Flight: Hartsfield Atlanta International Airport and Aviation in Atlanta*. Athens: University of Georgia Press, 1960.

Bullard, Mary R. *Cumberland Island: A History*. Athens: University of Georgia Press, 2003.

Candler, Charles Howard. *Asa Griggs Candler*. Atlanta: Emory University, 1950.

Candler, Warren A. *Bishop's Address: An Address Delivered by the College of Bishops to the General Conference of the Methodist Episcopal Church, South*. Oklahoma City, May 6–23, 1914.

Coleman, Kenneth. *A History of Georgia*. Athens: University of Georgia Press, rev. 1991.

Collins, Orvis F. and David G. Moore. *The Enterprising Man*. Lansing: Michigan State University, 1964.

Garrett, Franklin. *Atlanta and Environs: A Chronicle of Its People and Events*. Athens, GA, Lewis Historical Publishing Company Inc., 1954. Three volumes. Reprint, University of Georgia Press, 1969.

Graham, Elizabeth Candler and Ralph Roberts. *The Real Ones: Four Generations of the First Family of Coca-Cola*. Melbourne, Australia: Bookman, 1992.

Hammond, Edmund Jordan. *The Methodist Episcopal Church in Georgia*. Atlanta, 1935.

Hauk, Gary S. *A Legacy of Heart and Mind: Emory since 1836*. Atlanta: Emory University, 1999.

Hammond, Edmund J. *The Methodist Episcopal Church in Georgia*. Atlanta: Methodist Episcopal Church, 1935.

Hartle, Robert Jr. *Atlanta's Druid Hills: A Brief History*. Charleston, SC: History Press, 2008.

Hays, Constance L. *The Real Thing: Truth and Power at the Coca-Cola Company*. New York: Random House, 2004.

Jenkins, James S. *Murder in Atlanta! Sensational Crimes that Rocked the Nation*. Atlanta: Cherokee Publishing, 1981.

Jordan, Bruce L. *Murder in the Peach State: Infamous Murders from Georgia's Past*. Atlanta: Midtown Publishing, 2000.

Kemp, Kathryn W. *God's Capitalist: Asa Candler of Coca-Cola* . Macon, GA: Mercer University Press, 2002.

Kidney, Walter C. *Henry Hornbostel: An Architect's Master Touch*. Pittsburgh History & Landmarks Foundation, 2002.

Koehn, Nancy F. *Brand New: How Entrepreneurs Earned Consumers' Trust from Wedgwood to Dell*. Boston: Harvard Business School Press, 2001.

Kuhn, Cliff, Harlon E. Joye, and E. Bernard West. *Living Atlanta: An Oral History of the City, 1914–1948*. Atlanta History Center and University of Georgia, 1990.

Lovett, Charles Candler. *Love Ruth: A Son's Memoir*. Atlanta: Callanwolde Fine Arts Center, 1999.

Martin, Harold H. *William Berry Hartsfield: Mayor of Atlanta*. Athens: University of Georgia Press, 1978.

May, James W. *The Glenn Memorial Story: A Heritage in Trust*. Atlanta: privately printed, 1985.

Oliver, Thomas. *The Real Coke, the Real Story*. New York: Random House, 1986.

Oney, Steve. *And the Dead Shall Rise: The Murder of Mary Phagan and the Lynching of Leo Frank*. New York: Pantheon Books, 2003.

Pendergrast, Mark. *For God, Country & Coca-Cola: The Definitive History of the Great American Soft Drink and the Company That Makes It*. New York: Basic Books, 2000.

Poling, Clark. *Michael Graves, Henry Hornbostel.* Atlanta: Emory University Museum of Art and Archaeology [now The Michael Carlos Museum], 1985.

Seabrook, Charles. *Cumberland Island: Strong Women, Wild Horses.* Winston-Salem: John H. Blair, 2002.

Sulloway, Frank J. *Born to Rebel: Birth Order, Family Dynamics and Creative Lives.* New York: Pantheon Books, 1996.

Watters, Pat. *Coca-Cola:An Illustrated History.* Garden City, NJ: Doubleday, 1978.

Young, James Harvey. *Pure Food: Securing the Federal Food and Drugs Act of 1906* Princeton: Princeton University Press, 1989.

Articles:

Auchmutey, Jim. The Nightmare of Rainbow Terrace." *Atlanta Journal-Constitution Magazine*, October 30, 1945.

George M. Battey. "The Mystery of Ninian Beall's Burial Place Remains Unsolved." www.geocities.com/Athens/5568/ninian2.html?200829.

Booth, Michael. "The Classic Style of the Coca-Cola Homes, Callan Castle and the Homes that Coke Built." *Southern Living* (Spring, 1986): 94-99.

Jenkins, Herbert. "My Most Bizarre Murder Case." *Atlanta Journal-Constitution Magazine*, Aug. 22, 1971: 12–16, 22.

Kennedy, Robert J., and Parks Rusk. "The New Biltmore in Atlanta." *National Hotel Review* (June 14, 1924), entire issue.

Newton, Louie D. "Atlanta's Untold Story: The Atlanta Biltmore a Veritable City Within Its Walls." *The City Builder* (March 1925): 28–32.

Abbreviations in Notes

Names:
> AGC: Asa Griggs Candler
> AGC Jr. Asa Griggs Candler Jr.
> CF: Candler family
> FCH: Florence Candler Harris
> FG: Flora Glenn
> FGC: Flora Glenn Candler
> HH: Henry Heinz
> JSC: John Slaughter Candler
> LBC: Lucy Beale Candler
> LCO: Lucy Candler Owens
> LCH: Lucy Candler Heinz
> LCL: Lucy Candler Leide
> LEC: Lucy Elizabeth Candler
> LEH: Lucy Elizabeth Howard
> MBC: Martha Beale Candler
> OdB: Onezima de Bouchel
> WAC: Warren Akin Candler
> WC: William Candler
> WO: William Owens
> WTC: Walter Turner Candler

Archives:
> AHC: Atlanta History Center
> C-C: Coca-Cola
> GA: Georgia Archives
> MARBL: Manuscripts and Rare Books Library, Emory University

Unpublished memos and articles:
CHC, "True Origins:" CH Candler, "The True Origin of Coca-Cola: Additional Facts Relating to its Early History," typescript, C-C Archives.

D. S. Candler, "A Brief History:" D. S. Candler, "A Brief History of Coca-Cola," typescripts, C-C Archives.

JSC Memo: John Slaughter Candler's memo, box 7 CH Candler Papers, Manuscripts and Rare Books Library, Emory University.

Newspapers:
 AC: Atlanta Constitution
 AJ: Atlanta Journal
 CCT: Carroll County Times
 AJC: Journal and Constitution
 NYT: New York Times
 VR News: *Villa Rica News*
 WP: *Washington Post*

Books:

Allen: Frederick Allen, *Secret Formula*

Anderson: Mary T. Anderson, *The History of Villa Rica*

CHC, *AGC*: Candler, Charles Howard, *Asa Griggs Candler*

Graham and Roberts: Elizabeth Candler Graham and Ralph Roberts, *The Real Ones*

Hauk: Gary S. Hauk, *A Legacy of Heart and Mind*

Kemp: Kathryn W. Kemp, *God's Capitalist*

Pendergrast: Mark Pendergrast, *For God, Country & Coca-Cola*

Endnotes

Chapter 1: Farming and Praying

1. Description of ceremony is in *AC*, Dec. 7, 1910, CHC, *AGC*, 26, 245; for comment about mayoralty, see *AC*, Jan 23, 1910.
2. See the list of Beall children, CHC, *AGC*, 493.
3. Information about the gold rush and early Carroll County comes from Anderson, 10; Betty B. Cobb, "Gold Rush in Carroll County," unmarked clipping from 1926, CFP, MARBL, and *VR News*, Jan.-Mar., 1878.
4. Information about Sam and Martha Candler comes from his obituary, *CCT*, Dec. 1872; Anderson, 2–5; CHC, *AGC*, 1–33. I want to thank Doug Mabry, Spencer Crawford, and Ernest Blevins for additional information about Sam Candler.
5. Descriptions of the Candler children and their accomplishments is in CHC, *AGC*, 34–37 J. M. Hamrick, Fayette County bios, www.usgwarchives.net; JSC memo.
6. MBC to FCH, Dec. 11, 1862, GA Archives
7. Descriptions of the family are in CHC, *AGC*, 44; Graham and Roberts, 23–25; JSC memo, and Cobb, "Gold Rush."
8. Information on the Civil War is in MBC to FCH, n.d. [probably 1863 or 1864], GA Archives; .MCB's letters are reproduced Graham and Roberts, 30–32; also see JSC memo.
9. These stories are found in CHC, *AGC*, 45–46, 51; and Cobb, "Gold Rush."
10. The entire letter is in CHC, *AGC*, 55. For a man who saved few mementoes from his early years, it is significant that Asa kept a copy of his letter to Dr. Griggs among his personal possessions where it was found after his death. AGC's statement about being a physician is in Britt Craig, "What They Wanted and What They Got," *AC*, Dec. 17, 1911.
11. AGC's job with Howard discussed in JSC memo and Alan Rogers, "Rise of Asa G. Candler from Poverty to Wealth," *AC*, Jun. 17, 1907.

Chapter 2: Mixing Concoctions

12. Information about AGC's first years in Atlanta are in *AC*, Jan. 10, 1923; Rogers, "Rise of Asa G. Candler"; CHC, *AGC*, 65; Kemp, 16–17; and AGC to Messrs. Leek and Williams, Cartersville, Jan. 10, 1873 in Josephine Smith to the Coca-Cola Company, Jun. 29, 1971, C-C Archives.

13. Comments about Sam Candler are in *CCT*, Nov. 21, 28, 1873.

14. Information about the immediate aftermath of Sam's death and sale of the farm are in AGC to CHC and AGC. Jr., Nov. 13, 1897. AGC Papers, box 1, folder 1, MARBL; *CCT*, Nov. 21, 1873; Letters quoted are MBC to FCH and Jessie Willard, Thus. [no month] 27, 1873, and MBC to FCH, Jan. 27, 1874, GA Archives. Also see, CHC, *AGC*, 66; JSC memo; Kemp, 33; CHC, *AGC*, 66–69.

15. LEH's family called her "Lizzie" but AGC already had a sister and a sister-in-law with that nickname, so he preferred to call her Lucy. Because there were so many Lucys in the next few generations, in this narrative, she will be called, Lucy Elizabeth, as she was generally known to adult members of the Candler family. Other information about their courtship and AGC's job is in JSC memo; AGC to LEH, May 28, 1877, C-C Archives; CHC, *AGC*, 74. The ad mentioning AGC is quoted in Kemp, 22–23.

16. Info about MBC's homes and the early years of AGC's marriage are in CHC, AGC, 776–77; and Carroll County Archives News, Newspaper Abstracts, Jan., Feb. Mar., 1878.

17. The birth of CHC and LEC's trip to Carrollton are in AGC to FCH, July 15, 1878, George Howard to AGC, Nov. 24, 1878, AGC to CHC, Dec. 2, 1897, AGC Papers, box 1, folder 1, MARBL. Graham and Roberts, 47; and Kemp, 25–26.

18. CHC, *AGC*, 188–189, 229.

19. The move to Edgewood, remarks about MBC and purchase of the pharmacy are in Kemp, 33; CHC, *AGC*, 189–90; Garrett, II, 11–12; MBC to FCH, Aug. 9 [probably 1882], GA Archives; and LEC to LBC, Oct. 25, 1897, AGC papers, box 1a, folder 2, MARBL.

20. CHC to LBC, April 11, 1900, AGC Papers, box 1a, folder 5, MARBL.

21. LEC's trip to Mississippi are in AGC to LEC, May 25, 27, 28, 1885, AGC Papers, box 1, folder 1, MARBL; parts quoted in CHC, *AGC*, 205–07.

Chapter 3: Serendipity

22. Origins of C-C come from "Testimony of John S. Candler," *The United States vs. 40 Barrels and 20 Kegs of Coca-Cola*, US District Court … at Chattanooga, Mar. 13, 1911; CHC, "True Origin," and D. S. Candler, "A Brief History of Coca-Cola," C-C Archives; conversation with Doug Mabry, Pendergrast, 26–34.

23. The Horse Guards was officially known as Company B, First Battalion of the Georgia Cavalry; Julian Harris, "Asa G. Candler, Georgia Cracker," *Uncle Remus Magazine*, reprinted *AC*, Nov. 7, 1909.

24. AGC's purchase of C-C is mentioned in an article from the *AC*, Aug. 18, 1888, quoted in CHC; "True Origin" "Dr. Jacobs, Dean of Druggists, Tells of Early Days of Trade," *AC*, Aug. 5, 1917; AGC to WAC, Apr. 10 , Jun. 2, 1888, AGC Papers, box 1, MARBL.

25. For Candler family activities and AJC Jr.'s schooling, see CHC, *AGC*, 211–212. Today AGC Jr. would probably be diagnosed with AHDD, but at the end of the nineteenth century, such ideas were nonexistent, an idea contributed by Elizabeth Candler Graham.

26. CHC's memories and early days of Coca-Cola are in CHC, *AGC*, 106, 110–12, 211–12; "Asa G. Candler & Co," *AJ*, May 1, 1889, in AGC papers, box 3, MARBL.

27. Correspondence with Dr. Alexander in *AC*, Jun. 21, 1891; mixing the formula, AGC's 1890s budget, and other issues are in CHC, *AGC*, 84–94; "WE Stood,"AGC papers, box 1a, folder 1; AGC to J. G. Green, Apr. 1, 1890, Sam Willard to CHC, Feb. 10, 1929; CHC, "True Origins"; D. B. Candler "Brief History," C-C Archives.

28. The first five-man board of directors included AGC as chairman, Robinson as secretary-treasurer, and his brother John along with two brokers as members. This information is in C-C Trustees Minute Book, I; Sam Willard, untitled memo (1929);

D. B. Candler "Brief History;" CHC, "The True Origin;" and Alberta Orr Cofer to Miss Harb, Aug. 22, 1971,C-C Archives; CHC to Robt. Woodruff, Nov. 12, 1948, CHC Papers, MARBL.

29. WAC, AGC, and Methodism are in CHC, *AGC*, 197, 213–15, 354–55; AGC to WAC, Apr. 10, Jun. 2, 1888, AGC Papers, box 1, folder 1, MARBL; Hauk, 45.

30. CHC's activities are in CHC, *AGC*, 219, 352.Clipping in CHC papers, box 1, folder 6, MARBL.

31. Subsequently GMA moved to suburban College Park and in the latter twentieth century dropped its military association, turned coed, and became the Woodward Academy.

Chapter 4: Leaving Home

32. Letters from: AGC to CHC (and sometime AGC Jr.) while they are at Emory are those of Sep. 22, 24, Oct 11, and Nov. 5, 1894; Jan. 29, Sep. 26, 1895, Sep. 1894, n.d. (autumn, 1894), Jan. 5 and Feb. 28, Nov. 27, 1895, Jan. 20, 27; Feb. 21, 1896, Sep. 24 , 29, Oct. 16, Oct. 18, 1897; AGC to WAC, Jul. 19, 1886, AGC Papers, box 1, folders 1–3, MARBL.

33. FCH Scrapbook, CF Papers, box BV1, MARBL.

34. Information about MBC, her birthday and death are in MBC to FCH, undated (early 1890s), GA Archives, and FCH Scrapbook, CF Papers, box BV1, MARBL.

35. Letters to and from LEC to LBC are May 23, Oct. 11, undated late Oct.– early Nov., and Nov. 23, Dec. 10, 17, 1897, some from 1897 undated. Those of AGC to LBC are from May 29, Sep. 3, 7, 1897, AGC Papers, box 1a, folder 2; LEC to LBC, Sep. 3, 1897, AGC to LBC, May 22, Sep. 2, and Oct. 19, 1897, report card for LBC, Dec. 22, 1897. Those of WTC to LBC, Sep. 11, 19, Oct. 8, 10, 23, 25, Nov. 4, 1897. All of these letters are found in either AGC Papers, box 1a, folder 2, MARBL or C-C Archives. One LEC to LBC is printed in Graham & Roberts, 262–63. In 1891, Florence formally incorporated her school as the West End Institute, calling together Asa and several other family members to write the charter, CF Papers, box 5, folder 6.

36. In the spring term, CHC's cumulative average was a low B. Although he received As in English composition, he got Cs in the sciences, thus lowering his average from the previous year. There is no record of AGC Jr.'s actual grades. For CHC and AGC Jr.'s housing problems, see AGC to CHC and AGC Jr., Jan. 27, AGC to CHC, Feb. 21, 1896, AGC Papers, box 1, folder 1; and LEC to LBC, Oct. 25, 1897, AGC Papers, box 1a, folder 2, MARBL.; Graham & Roberts, 81.

37. LBC's final months in Cartersville, in LEC to LBC, Oct. 21 undated (Late Nov., early Dec.), Dec. 17, 1897; AGC to LBC, Dec. 14, 1897; WTC to LBC, Dec. 9, 1897, AGC Papers, box 1a, folder 2, MARBL; LEC to LBC, Oct. 21, 1897; CHC to LBC, Oct. 21, 27, 1897, C-C Archives.

38. The Inman Park church and death of George Howard are in *AC*, Apr. 16, 1898; *AJ*, Apr.16, 17, 18,1898; Florella Glenn to Flora Glenn, Apr. 18, 1898, CHC Papers, box 17, folder 3, MARBL.

39. The new Coca-Cola plant is in CHC, *AGC*, 119–22; and AC, Dec. 11, 1898.

40. CHC to LBC, Oct. 21, 1897, AGC Papers, box 1a, folder 2, and notes entitled "Sister," Apr. 30, Jul. 12, 1899, CHC Papers, box 7, MARBL.

41. Letters to CHC about his career and travels in the Midwest are AGC to CHC, Mar. 30-Jun. 19, 1899; Aug. 10, 1899, CHC to LBC, Jul. 13, 1899, AGC Papers, box 1, folder 2; and notes entitled "Sister," CHC Papers, box 7, MARBL. The minutes of the C-C board of directors, 1896; CHC order book, 1899; and F. Robinson to CHC, Apr. 24, May 5, 1899, are in the C-C Archives.

42. The C-C bottling negotiations are in CHC to Franklin Garrett, Sep. 10, 1948, C-C Archives; AGC to CHC, Feb. 28, 1895, AGC Papers, box 1, folder 1, MARBL, Hays, 15–22; Pendergrast, 70-73; Allen, 105–07.

43. Information on the Emory graduation of 1899 comes from *AC*, Mar. 22, 1899; Notes entitled "Sister" July 12, 1899; invitations to LBC, box 1a, folder 10, CHC to LBC, Jul. 13, 1899, box 1a, folder 4, AGC to CHC, Jun. 3, 8, 1899, AGC Papers, box 1, folder 3, MARBL; AGC Jr. to CHC,

Jun. 19, 1899, and George Reed to CHC, Jun. 19, 1899, C-C Archives.

44. AGC Jr.'s period in California comes from AGC Jr. to AGC (and sometime) LEC, Jul. 10, 1899; Jun. 19, to CHC, Aug. 9, 12, 1899, C-C Archives, one reprinted in Graham and Roberts, 176; and AGC to CHC, Apr. 7, 17, Sep. 9, 11, 29, 1899, AGC Papers, box 1, folder 3, MARBL; Apr. 11, 14, 16, 18, 1900; G. Patterson, to CHC, Mar. 30, Apr. 2, 5, 10, 1900, C-C Archives.

45. CHC's return home from the Midwest and subsequent trip to California are in AGC Jr. to CHC, Aug. 12, 1899 Apr. 11,14, 16, 18, 23, 1900, George Patterson to CHC, Mar. 30, Apr.2, 5, 10, 1900, C-C Archives; AGC to CHC, Sep. 9, 11, 29, 1899, Apr. 7, 17, 1900, AGC Papers, box 1, folder 3, MARBL.

Chapter 5: Changing World

46. For the remainder of the book, the name Asa Candler Jr. is used instead of Buddie, except where his nickname seems more appropriate. His beginnings at Witham are in AGC Papers, box 1a, folder 4, MARBL; and CHC, *AGC*, 298–299.AGC to CHC, Aug. 30, Sep. 20, 1900; AGC Jr. to LBC, Sep. 17, Sep. 25, 1900, AGC Papers, box 1a, folder 5, AGC to CHC, Jul. 12, 1899, box 1, folder 4, MARBL; AGC Jr. to CHC, n.d. (Aug. 1899), Aug. 11, 12, 1899, C-C Archives; CHC, *AGC*, 298–99.

47. Letters relating to CHC's European trip, his return NY, and the C-C connection are found in AGC to CHC, Jul. 6, July 12, Oct. 3, 1900, LEC to CHC, Jul. 22, 1900, AGC Papers, mss. 1, box 1, folder 4; CHC to LBC, Nov. 16, 20, 1900, AGC Papers, box 1a, folder 5, MARBL; F. Robinson to CHC, Aug. 24, 27, 1900, C-C Archives; CHC, *AGC*, 158–59.

48. Letters about the Willards are AGC to CHC, Apr. 23, 25, 1901, box 1, folder 5, MARBL

49. AGC Jr.'s courtship and marriage are in *AC*, Jul. 18, 19, 1901; AGC to CHC, Feb. 27, 1901, box 1, folder 5; AGC Jr. to LBC, Apr.17, May 3, 9, 14, 1901, AGC papers, box 1a, folder 3, MARBL; Graham and Roberts, 181–84.

50. FGC was the eighth of the Reverend Wilber Fisk Glenn's ten children. He had been a former chaplain in the Confederate army, his ministerial career later taking him to Vernon, Mississippi, and Cave Springs, Georgia, before moving his growing family to Marietta, where Flora was born. Finally he settled in Atlanta to be pastor of the First Methodist Church and left the pulpit to become editor of the *Christian Advocate* (Warren Candler's old job), a position he retained for the next decade.

51. Letters discussing CHC's NY breakdown are in CHC to FG, Sep. 5, 21, 23, 26, 29, Oct. 23, 1901, Oct. 26, 1901, CHC Papers, box 17, folder 5 and AGC to CHC, Sep. 1901, AGC Papers, box 1, folder 5, MARBL.

52. Letters relating to CHC's trip through the South are in CHC to FG, Dec. 15, 1901, Jan. 17, 19, 1902; CHC Papers, box 17, folder 5 and AGC to CHC, Feb. 1, 1902, AGC Papers, folder 6, MARBL.

53. CHC's return to NY and Coca-Cola business are in AGC to CHC, March 22, Apr. 28, May 2, 17, Jun. 2, 1902, AGC Papers, box 1, folder 6, CHC to R .W. Woodruff, Nov. 18, 1948, AGC Papers, box 1, folder 11, MARBL.

54. Letters relating to Helen's baby are AGC to CHC, Mar. 22, May 7, 10, Aug. 9 and 18, 1902, AGC Papers, box 1, folder 6, MARBL and WTC to CHC, Aug. 19, 1902, C-C Archives; also see Graham and Roberts, 185–86.

55. Letters relating to the beginnings of the new house are AGC to CHC, Apr. 15, 1902, AGC Papers, box 1, folder 6, WTC to LBC, May 27, 1902, AGC Papers, box 1a, folder 8, MARBL.

56. Letters relating to LBC's first year at Wesleyan are CHC to LBC, Sep. 15, 1900, Mar. 8, 1901, WTC to LBC, Sep. 17, 1900, and AGC to LBC, Mar. 14, 1901C-C Archives; AGC Jr. to LBC, Sep. 25, 1900, AGC Papers, box 1a, folder 5; and AGC to CHC, Sep. 20, 29, 1900, AGC Papers, box 1, folder 4; LEC to LBC, Feb. 22, Mar. 14, (Feb., Mar.), 1901, AGC papers, box 1a, folder 9; Essie to LBC, Feb. 3, 1901, AGC Papers, box 1a, folder 3; Notes entitled "Sister," Feb. 3, Mar. 24, 1901, CHC Papers, box 7, MARBL.

57. LBC's letters to WO and about LBC's and WTC's travels are LBC to WO, May 11, and undated 1902, AGC Papers, box 18, folder 10, AGC to CHC, Apr. 28, May 2, 17, Jun. 11, Jul. 26, Sep. 24, 1902 box 1, folder 6; notes entitled "Sister," Jun. 3, 1902, CHC Papers, box 7, MARBL; CHC to LBC, Jul. 8, 1902, C-C Archives. The race riot is in *NYT*, May 26, 1902

58. CHC's experiences at C-C in NY are in AGC to H.T. Applewhite, Jun. 2, 1902 ; AGC to CHC, Jun. 11, Aug. 23, 25, 27, Sep. 24, 25, Oct. 1, 1902, AGC Papers, box 1, folder 6, MARBL.

59. Letters relating to LEC's trip to NY are CHC to LBC, Oct. 2, 1902, AGC Papers, box 18, folder 10; AGC to CHC, Sep. 24, Oct. 1, Nov. 29,1902; CHC to AGC, Feb. 24, 1903, AGC Papers, box 1, folder 6; and Notes entitled "Sister," Oct. 26, 1902, CHC Papers, Box 7, MARBL.

60. Letters about AGC Jr.'s experiences at Witham are in AGC to CHC, May 10, July 26, Aug. 2,1902, Feb. 21 and 24 1903; CHC to AGC, Feb. 24, 1903, AGC Papers, box 1, folder 6, MARBL; and CHC, *AGC*, 300–02.

Chapter 6: Creating Families

61. For descriptions of Callan Castle and LBC's wedding, see *AC*, Jun. 12, 1903, .Michael Booth, "The Classic Style of the Coca-Cola Home: Callan Castle and the Homes that Coke Built," *Southern Homes* (Spring 1986), 86–92; Actor Cordell, Callan Castle's Grandeur Restored," *AJC*, Nov. 10, 1985; Yolande Gwin, "Home in Inman Park was Asa Candler's Favorite,", *AJC*, " Mar. 12, 1972; "Asa Candler Home in Inman Park is Newcomer on Tour," *AJC*, Apr. 28, 1978. Letters about the fountain are AGC to CHC, Feb. 21, 26, 1903; CHC to AGC, Feb. 24, 1903, AGC Papers, box 1, folder 6; AGC to FCH, Jun. 12, 1903, FCH Scrapbook, CF Papers, box 5, MARBL.

62. Information about CHC's last years in NY comes from CHC to AGC, Mar. 12, 1903, AGC to CHC, Mar. 10, 24, 1903,AGC Papers, box 1, folder 6, MARBL.

63. AGC to CHC and FGC, Dec. 5, 1903, AGC Papers, box 1, folder 6, MARBL.

64. *AC*, June 4, 1904; also see CHC, *AGC*, 233.

65. The death of AGC III is in the *AJ*, Jan. 10, 1905; Graham and Roberts, 192; and CHC, *AGC*, 301.

66. For descriptions of the Candler Building, see *AJ*, Jan. 21, 27, Mar. 18, 19, 1904; *AC*, Feb. 28, 1904; Kemp, 69; *AJ*, Jan. 21, 1904; Jan. 28, Oct. 4, Dec. 15, 1905, and Jan. 10, 1906. Also see "The Candler Building," promotional brochure (Atlanta, 1906); and CHC, *AGC*, 255–57.

67. AGC Jr.'s attempt to enter the city council is in *AC*, Jun. 23, 30, 1906. During the early twentieth century the city council was officially named "The Board of Aldermen." However the term "City Council" was often used instead.

68. For changes at C-C, see CHC, *AGC*, 138–39; Pendergrast, 105, 107–10; Allen, 75–77. For discussion of Howard's house, see Inman Park Spring Festival brochure, 2009.

69. For details of the riot and AGC's speeches, see Bauerlein, 206–09, 253 and *AJ, AC, NYT*, Sep. 23, 24, 25, 26,1906; and *NYT*, Sep. 23, 24, 1906 Feb. 6, 1907.

70. *AC*, Nov. 22, 1906.

71. AGC to WAC, Aug. 5, 1907, AGC Papers, box 1;JSC to WAC, Aug. 6, 1907, WAC Papers, box 14, MARBL; for the outcome of the case see AC, Jun. 23, 1907; Pendergrast, 110–12.

72. Lucy's travels in LCO to WO, Jul. 20, 1905, Jul. 7, 1907, AGC Papers, box 18, MARB; for LEC's activities, *AC*, Mar. 9, 14, Apr. 24, 1907.

73. Mark Bauman, "Candler, Walter Turner," C-C Archives; also see, Graham and Roberts, 274–75; *AC*, Dec. 11, 1907.

74. *AC*, June 19, 23, July 7, 1907 and unidentified clipping of 1910, box 21, AGC Papers, MARBL.

75. For details of these negotiations, see Kemp, 84–107 CHC, *AGC*, 269–70; *AC*, Dec. 25, 27, 1907, Aug. 14, 1908; Garrett, II, 511–12.

76. For Asa Sr.'s activities see *AC*, Nov. 13, 27, 1907; Feb. 24, Mar. 3, 8, 10, 20, 21, Sept. 22, 1908; Dec. 8, 29, 1908; Jan. 16–18, 1909; Julian Harris, "Asa G. Candler, Georgia Cracker," *Uncle Remus Magazine*, reprinted *AC*, Nov. 7, 1909; and Garrett, II, 545–47. The photograph with Taft is reproduced in *The C-C Bottler*, I, (April 1909), 7.

Chapter 7 Visions of Grandeur

77. Druid Hills, AGC Papers, boxes 8–12, MARBL; *AC*, May 20, Sep. 22, 1908; Elizabeth A. Lyon, "Frederick Law Olmsted and Joel Hurt: Planning for Atlanta," Dana F. White and Victor A. Kramer, eds. *Olmsted South: Old South Critic/ New South Planner* (Westport, CT: Greenwood Press, 1979), 165–93.

78. AGC to Joel Hurt, May 20, 1908, and Druid Hills Inc. papers, AGC Papers, box 9, MARBL. AGC owned 2,250 shares of the Druid Hills Company, which was nine-tenths of the corporation; Preston S. Arkwright (the Georgia Power Company president) held 125 shares; JSC obtained 50 shares; 25 went to the Adair brothers; 25 to C-C's lawyer, Harold Hirsch; and 25 to his law partner, William D. Thompson.

79. JSC's law partner, Harold Hirsch, was a major C-C attorney, and Joseph Jacobs, owner of the pharmacy that first served C-C, was his lifelong friend. When in 1916, Jewish organizations held a drive to relieve Eastern European Jews displaced during World War I, AGC made a generous donation, unlike most other leading Atlanta Christians, whose names were absent from the published list. *AC*, Jan 30, 1916; Druid Hills Inc. papers, AGC Papers, box 9, MARBL; Kemp, 73.

80. Matters concerning AGC's siblings are in *AC*, July 5, Dec. 8, 1905, Aug. 2, 1906, Aug. 27, Sep. 22, 1908; Apr. 4, 1909; Yolande Gwin, "Judge John Candler Built Home in 1909,"*AJC*, Feb. 27, 1972; and AGC to FCH, Apr. 12, 1905; AGC to WC, Feb. 4, 1909, AGC Papers, box 1, folder 6, MARBL.

81. William went from Donald Frazier to the Zetler School, to the Peacock School for Boys, to Boys High, and finally to Culver.

82. AGC to WAC, Feb. 4, 1909; AGC to CHC, Feb. 25, 26, 1909, AGC Papers, box 1, folder 7, MARBL.

83. This comment was in AGC to CHC, Mar. 7, 1909, AGC Papers, box 1, folder 7, MARBL. Other reports of the western trip are in AGC to WC, Feb. 4, 1909, AGC Papers, box 1, folder 6, MARBL; and *AC*, Feb. 12, Mar. 13, 1909.

84. The story of the first extortion attempt is in *AC* Apr. 7, 8, 1909; the second is in *AC*, Dec. 19, 20, 2, 24, 1909; also see CHC, *AGC*, 223–34. AGC's remark on returning home is *AC*, Mar.

11, 1909; and his speech to the Advertising Club is *AC,* May 2, 1909.

85. Alan Rogers, "Unknown Hobbies Daily Ridden by Well Known Atlanta Bankers," *AC,* Aug. 26, 1906.

86. References to Automobile Week and its preliminary events are in *AC,* May 26, Sep. 12, Oct. 14, 23, 31, Nov. 4, 6, 7, 13, 14, 1909; and CHC, *AGC,* 247.

87. *AC,* Dec. 1, 17, 1909, Jan. 23, 1910.

88. Julian Harris, "Asa G. Candler, Georgia Cracker," *Uncle Remus Magazine,* reprinted *AC,* Nov. 7, 1909.

89. *AC,* Nov. 27, 1910.

90. For AGC Jr.'s activities with automobiles and aviation, see *AC,* Dec. 8, 1909; Jan. 1, May 3, Sep. 14, 15, 25, Dec. 4, 1910; Sep. 10, 1911.

91. WTC's activities are in *AC,* Oct. 27, Nov. 18, 1910; May 24, 1912; Sept. 14, 1913; and Graham and Roberts, 276, 280–81.

92. For information on Coca-Cola's troubles, see CHC, *AGC,* 136–37, 122–23; *AC,* Apr. 23, Oct. 24, 1909; Pendergrast, 116; and Allen, 56–57.

Chapter 8: Prominence and Prosperity

93. For more information on the trial, see *The United States vs. 40 Barrels and 20 Kegs of Coca-Cola,* US District Court … at Chattanooga, Mar. 13, 1911; Pendergrast, 116–19; Allen, 58–65; *AC,* Mar. 14-Apr. 7, 1911, and *The Atlanta Georgian,* Mar. 15, 1911. The letters quoted are: AGC to CHC, Mar. 14, 15, 16, and 23, 1911, and AGC to S. & J Willard, Mar. 21, 1911, AGC papers, box 1, folder 7, MARBL.

94. Information on the family comes from AGC to CHC, Mar. 20, 1911, AGC Papers, box 1, folder 7, MARBL *AC,* Jun. 17, 1911; Oct. 10, 28, Dec. 18, 19, 20, 27, 1912; Jan. 2, 1913; *Atlanta City Directory,* 1911–1912; *AC,* Feb. 7, 1913; and Graham and Roberts, 285–86.

95. CHC owed his father $35,000; AGC Jr. $100,000; LO, $20,000; WTC, $12,000; and WC, $5,000. Information on the new will and Atlanta business transactions comes from AGC to WAC, Jan 11, 1913, AGC Papers, box 1, folder 8, MARBL;

CHC, AGC, 259–60; and AC, Apr. 6, 15, 1909; May 27, 1910; Jan. 3, 1913, Oct. 5, 1913.

96. The NY Candler Building was designed by the architectural firm of Willauer, Shape & Bready; see *AC*, Feb. 13, Mar. 31, 1912; Feb. 13, Mar. 31, 1912; CHC, *AGC*, 262–63; Candler Building brochure, AGC Papers, box 5, MARBL.

97. Other Candler buildings are discussed in CHC, *AGC*, 276–86; *AC*, Jan. 18, 1914; Jul. 8, 1913; and Charles F. Wilkinson, "Asa G. Candler Pioneer Capitalist," *Building Management* (Jul. 1915), 56–57, 69.

98. Information on the Candlers' European trip comes from AGC to CHC, Jun. 19, Jul. 7, 23, 29, 1913; AGC to FCH, Jun. 22, 1913, AGC to WAC, Jul. 7, 12, 1913 AGC Papers, box 1, folder 8, MARBL.

99. For a thorough discussion of the Vanderbilt controversy, see Kemp, 119–25 and CHC, *AGC*, 388–94; other information comes from *AC*, May 13, 1913. Asa's letters to Warren are AGC to WAC, June 29, Jul. 7, 1913, May 27, 1914, AGC papers, box 1, folders 8 and 9, MARBL; for Warren's ideas, see W. A. Candler, "The Place of Our Universities in the Educational System of Our Church" (reprint of article) WAC Papers, MARBL.

100. The meeting is discussed in *AC*, May 8, Jun. 10, 1914; J. S. Jenkins to WAC, May 1, 1914, WAC to J.S. Jenkins, May 7, 1914, WAC Papers, box 24, folder 1; HY McCord to AGC, May 21, 23, 1914, AGC Papers, box 1, folder 9, Various letters in WAC Papers, box 24, folder 3, MARBL; Kemp, 123, 126; CHC, *AGC,* 391–92.

101. The NY Candler Bldg. discussed in *NY Times*, May 8, 1914. Asa's NY correspondences are AGC to A. J. Lamar, Jun. 2, 1914; AGC to Mell R. Wilkinson, Jul. 16, 1914; AGC to WAC, Jun. 30, Jul. 6, 8, 1914, AGC Papers, box 1, folders 8 and 9, MARBL. WAC's letters to clergymen, May, Jun. 1914; and minutes of meeting of the Education Commission of Methodist Episcopal Church, South, Jun. 17, 1914, WAC Papers, box 24, MARBL.

102. Final plans for establishing Emory University are in *AC*, Jul. 14, 16, 17, 19, 24, Aug. 9, Sep. 24, Nov. 21, 1914, Aug. 22, 1915. The formal letter from AGC to WAC, Jul. 14, 1914 is in

AGC Papers, box 1, folder 9, MARBL and reprinted in CHC, *AGC*, 397–99. Minutes of Druid Hills Directors, Aug. 13, 1914, are in AGC Papers, box BV 3, MARBL.

103. AGC's business views are in AGC to Joe Willard, Oct. 14, 1914, AGC Papers, box 1, folder 11, MARBL. His WWI rescue plan is discussed in *AC,* Oct. 20, 21, 25, 1914, Sep. 15. 1915; and Kemp, 99–102.

104. Bill's death, funeral, and Lucy's illness are mentioned in *AC* Dec. 18, 21, 23, 1914, Jan. 13, 1915 and clippings in CF Papers, FCH scrapbook BV2, MARBL.

105. Review of *Birth of a Nation* is in *AC*, Dec. 5, 14, 1915; and reproduced in Garrett, II, 666–68.

106. At the time of Zeke's death, his son and namesake, Ezekiel S. Candler Jr. was serving in the US House of Representatives in a seat he occupied for twenty years. See *AC*, Sept 14, 1915. Other family illnesses and deaths are in CHC, 207–08, 243–44.

107. LCO's caller is in *AC*, Sep. 17, 18, 1915.

108. The Candler's Ponce de Leon Ave. house is discussed in *AC*, Apr. 17, 1915; Graham and Roberts, 88. Yolande Gwin, "Asa Candler Mansion Now Owned by Melkite Church," *AJC*, Feb. 13, 1972; Margaret Shannon, "A Dream Cut Short, Asa G. Candler Mansion Never Fulfilled Mission, " *AJ*, July 28, 1946, and Medora Field Perkerson, "Handsome Residence of Asa G. Candler, Sr.," *AJ*, July 15, 1923.

Chapter 9: In Control

109. CHC, *AGC*, 207–08.

110. For details of the Beavers case, see Kemp, 176–86; *AC*, Jul. 27, Aug. 1, 2, 20, Dec. 9, 1915, Jan 4, 6, Apr. 11, May 19, 1916.

111. *AC*, July 20, 1916; Kemp, 192–93.

112. *AC*, Feb. 5, 1916; AGC to CHC, Sam Dobbs, AGC Jr., WC, Feb. 1, 1916, AGC Papers, box 1, folder 11, MARBL.

113. In 1908, AGC had been in conversations about selling C-C with Samuel Brown, Ed's father, but Brown withdrew when the federal government began investigating the beverage's content, Allen, 55–56.

114. For C-C's problems, see F. Allen, 55–56, Pendergrast, 120–21; and D. W. Griffith, *For His Son* (Biograph, 1912).

115. *AC*, July 21, 23, 26, 27, 31, 1916; Kemp, 192, 195.

116. AGC's trip to Michigan is in *AC*, Aug. 4, 10, 1916, and AGC to CHC, Jul. 29, Aug. 2, 8, 9, 1916, AGC Papers, box 1, folder 11, MARBL.

117. Primary campaign and election is in *AC*, Aug. 17, 20, 23, 25, 26, 1916; Kemp, 199; the poem "Jesse W. Armistead for Mayor," is in AGC papers, box 21, MARBL.

118. Raymond Everette White, "A Remarkable Municipal Fight in Georgia," *Leslie's Weekly*, September 21, 1916.

119. For a thorough description of the strike and campaign, see Kemp, 201–15; Garrett, II, 687–88; and *AC,* Oct 2–4, 7, 8, 5, 24, 30; Dec. 5, 7, 1916.

120. Quotes about the general election come from *AC,* Aug. 27, 1916; Dec. 19, 23, 1916.

121. Information about HH comes from *AC,* Dec. 31, 1916; *AJ,* Sep. 29, 1943; *AC,* Sept. 30, 1943.

122. Quotes and information about AGC's beginnings as mayor comes from *Gainesville Eagle,* Jan. 11, 1917; clipping in box 21, AGC Papers, MARBL; CHC, *AGC,* 328; *AC,* Jan. 2, 3, 5, 7, 9, 12, 14, Dec. 23, 1917; Kemp, 222–23.

123. Quotes relating to LCH's wedding are from AGC to CHC, Sep. 22, 1917, AGC Papers, box 1, folder 11; unidentified clipping in FCH scrapbooks, CF Papers, box 5, MARBL; and the collection of Vesta Owens Jones.

124. AGC's dealings with Emory and disagreement with WTC are in *AC*, May 14, Aug. 22, 1915, Jan. 8, 13, 20, 23, Mar. 3, 26, 28, 1916; and marginal calculations jotted down on a letter to him from the Atlanta Gas Co. to AGC, June 20, 1916; WAC to AGC, Feb. 17, 1917, AGC Papers, box 1, folder 11, MARBL. Drawings of the original plans are in Andrew W. M. Beirele, "Unbuilt Emory," *Emory Magazine,* v. 63-64 (March, 1987), 54–57; Kemp, 130–32.

125. Information on the beginnings of WW I in Atlanta is from: *AC*, Jan. 19, 1916, Mar 5, 6, 22, 28, 29, Apr. 4, 15, 22, 25, 29, May 6, May 19, 20, 1917; *AJ,* May 20, 1917; Kemp, 233, 237; CHC, *AGC,* 313; Garrett, II, 715.

126. Reporting of the fire is in *AC* & *AJ*,, May 22, 23, 1917; Garrett, II, 700–05. In the rebuilding drive, AGC, personally gave $1,000, as did the Central Bank and Trust, the Atlanta Warehouse Co., and the C-C Co. In addition, several members of the extended Candler family each gave smaller personal donations.

127. The temporary Camp Gordon should not be confused with the 1950s base with the same name in Augusta, Georgia. Information on it and other war-related activities is in *AC*, May 26, 29, Jun. 8, 12, 15, 17, 19, 21, 27, Jul. 4, 12, 28, 29, Aug 7, 31, Sep. 2, 5, 1917; Kemp, 238–40; CHC, *AGC*, 329.

128. Information on Billy Sunday's visit and the remainder of AGC's first year as mayor is in *AC*, Oct. 10, 17, 24, Nov. 3, 4, 9, 10, 11, Dec. 23, 1917; Garrett, II, 710–11; Kemp, 224–25; 230–32; *AGC*, 327–28.

129. For dispersal of the C-C stock, see CHC, *AGC*, 266–68; Graham & Roberts, 88; *AC*, Apr. 20, 1917; Allen, 91.

130. The accusations against AGC and court cases are in unidentified clipping, Oct. 1917, CHC Papers, box 11, MARBL; Kemp, 227; Pendergrast, 126; Allen, 84.

131. For a full account of the Hirsch-Cook case, see Kemp, 240–44., *AC*, Feb. 15, 16, 17, 20, 22, 23, 24, 26, 27, 28, Mar. 12, 13, 14, 15, 16, 17, 30, 31, Apr. 3, 1918.

132. Information about the remainder of AGC's mayoral term, came from Garrett, II, 745–47; .*AC*, Feb. 13, 17, Apr. 7, Nov. 12, 13, Dec. 8, 1918; Jan. 7, 1919.

Chapter 10: Losing Control

133. For the death of Eugenia and the flu epidemic in Atlanta, see *AC*, Oct. 1, 9, 19, 1918; Graham and Roberts, 275; Garrett, II, 735–36.

134. For LEC's death and its aftermath, and Walter's problems, see Graham and Roberts, 87, 275–76 Kemp, 252. *AC*, Feb. 23, 24, 26, 1919; CHC, *AGC*, 207–09, 422; and CHC to C. B. Galloway, Apr. 9, 1919, AGC Papers, box 1, folder 11, MARBL.

135. Information on the sale of C-C and AGC's reaction comes from Pendergrast, 129–31; Allen, 91–94, 95–97; CHC, *AGC*, 184–85; *AC*, Aug. 1, 22, 1919; Garrett, II, 767–68; Graham

and Roberts, 91. AGC's statement in Kansas City is in an unidentified clipping, CF Papers, box 5, MARBL.

136. Ernest Woodruff's takeover of C-C is discussed in Allen, 98–100; *AC*, Sep. 17, 1919; Garrett, II, 769.

137. Information about Walter's remarriage and its immediate aftermath comes from *AC*, Aug. 14, 17, Oct. 31, 1919, Jun. 19, Aug. 14, Oct. 23, 1921, Feb. 8, 1922; Graham & Roberts, 276.

138. AGC Jr.'s activities and AGC's temperance comes from *AC*, Oct. 26, 1919, *AC* and *AJ*, Jan. 11, 1920.

139. Information on Callanwolde comes from "History of Callanwolde," Callanwolde Fine Arts Center, 1986; Yolande Gwin, "Callanwolde Has a Past," *AJC*, Jan. 30, 1972; Katherine Barnwell, "Emory Gets a Gift with a Colorful Past," *AJC*, Oct. 25, 1959; "The Candlers—Their History and Their House. Callanwolde," unidentified clipping, box 22, and correspondence with the Aeolian Pipe Organ Company, box 15, CHC Papers, MARBL.

140. For WC's house and commercial ventures, see Hentz & Reid, plans of WC house, Jun. 22, 1915, AHC; Yolande Gwin, "Rest Haven ... Still Stands, *AJC*, Jan. 16, 1972; *AC*, Jan. 25, 1920; "William Candler," Garrett, III, (1954), 509–10.

141. LCH's family and AGC Inc. are discussed in Graham and Roberts, 260–61, 266–67.

142. Interview with William Owens Jr. by David Jones, 1994.

143. The case is discussed in Pendergrast, 135–40; Allen, 108–20; *AC*, Apr. 24, 25, 28, 1920; *AJ*, Apr. 27 28, 1920.

144. Sam Dodd's activities and his dismissal from C-C are *AJ*, Jan. 6, 10; Oct. 25, 1920; *AC*, Oct. 26, 1920; Pendergrast, 140–41; Allen, 120–21.

145. The Koke case and AJC Jr.'s dispute with C-C are discussed in *AC*, Jun. 20, 1921; Jul. 7, 8, Aug. 4, 18, 19, 25, 1921, Feb. 4, 1922, Feb. 2, 1924; Pendergrast, 141–42; Allen, 123–24.

146. The Confederate reunion is discussed in *AC*, Jul. 22, 31, Oct. 6, 1919; Jan. 1, 1922; Kemp, 253–54.

147. Details of their romance and correspondence are in Kemp, 254–62, 282,.295–99; also see Graham and Roberts, 120. The correspondence (OdeB to AGC and AGC to OdB, Oct. Nov. 1919, Jan 1920, Nov 26, Dec. 21, 1920, Jan 22, 24, Feb

7, 18, 1921, Feb. 6, 1922,) are reproduced, *AC*, Jan. 31, Feb. 1, 2, 1924.

148. Lizzie Dobbs's death, funeral, and aftermath are in *AC*, Feb. 18, Mar. 23, Apr. 23, 1921.

149. Letters to and from CHC and his family are AGC to CHC, Apr. 6, 11, Jul. 22, 23, and no date 1921;telegram CHC to AGC, Apr. 17, 1921, AGC to Catherine Candler, Jun 2, 1921, AGC Papers, box 1, folder 11, MARBL.

150. AGC's activities are in Sep. 29, 30, Oct. 22, 29, Dec. 18,1921; *AC*, Feb. 2, 1924.

Chapter 11: Misbehavior

151. WTC and JSC's visit and AGC's response are in *AC*, Jan. 1, 1922.

152. The report of the courtship is in *AC*, Aug. 4, 5, 6, 1922; *AJ*, Aug. 4, 6, 1922; their correspondence AGC to OdB, Feb. 6, 1922, Mar. 24, 1922, Apr. 5, 1922, May 8, 11, 18, Jun. 1, 9, 15, 25, 1922, Aug. 10, 11, 12, 1922, is reproduced *AC*, Jan 31- Feb, 2, 1924; also see Kemp, 265.

153. AGC to CHC, Aug. 1922, AGC Papers, box 1, folder 11, MARBL. For details of WTC's encounters with Sarah Byfield see *AC* & *AJ*, Apr. 27, Aug. 15, 16, 17, 18, 19, 20, 21, Sept. 7, 1922; Graham and Roberts, 277–78.

154. Marion's return is in *AC*, Aug 22, 24, 31, Sep. 3, 6, 8, 12, 1922.

155. Sale of the bank and events leading up to it are in *AJ*, Oct. 10, 1920; *AC*, Oct. 24, 1920, Feb. 8, 1921, May 21, Jun. 13, Sept. 17, 1922.

156. During the early and midtwentieth century, jokes were ubiquitous about women making love to traveling salesmen. For details of the breakup, see AGC to OdB, Aug. 15, 1922, reproduced *AC*, Feb.1, 1924; *AC*, Aug. 17, 25, Sept. 8, 11, 12, 15, 28, 1922; Feb. 18, 1923; *New Orleans Times-Picayune*, Aug. 25, 1922; for a full discussion, see Kemp, 265–68; *AC*, Aug. 1922.

157. AGC to OdB, Sept. 30, Oct 3, 5, 1922, reproduced *AC*, Feb.1, 1924; See Kemp, 270; *AC*, Oct. 14, 1922.

158. AGC's activities are found in *AC*, Jan. 7, 10, Apr. 3, May 17, 25, Aug. 10, 1923; assorted clippings and letters in box 11, folder 1, CHC Papers and clipping from *NY Tribune* in CF Papers, OB4, MARBL.

159. Descriptions of Rainbow Terrace come from *AC*, Feb. 26, 1922, Jan. 14, 1923; and Yolande Gwin, "Old, Forgotten Showplace," *AJC*, Aug. 1, 1996; Elizabeth's debut is reported in *AC*, Nov. 23, 26, 1922.

160. At some later date AGC Jr. converted the third floor of his Briarcliff mansion into a seventy-by-fifty-foot ballroom, topped by a vaulted ceiling and lined with gold-leafed walls, where he held the debutante balls for his other daughters. His daughter Lucy's debut and description of Briarcliff are in *AC*, Jan. 2, 10, 1923, Aug. 14, 1921, Jan. 11, Apr. 15, 1923. Also see Kenneth H. Thomas, "Summary of Proposed National Register Nomination," 1988, Candler Homes file, AHC; Celestine Sibley, "Conversion of Candler Home," *AC*, Sept. 22, 1952.

161. *AJ*, Mar. 12, 1923; *AC*, Feb. 18, 1923; *AC* and *NYT*, Mar. 13, 1923.

162. Information on Robert Woodruff's becoming C-C president and CHC's reaction are in *AC*, Jul. 8, Aug. 4, 18, 19, 25, 1921, Feb. 4, 1922 Apr. 27, 29,1923; CHC to C. Culpepper, Apr. 24, 1923, CC Archives; Allen, 131–56; Pendergrast, 151–57.

163. For information on the "floating school,' see *NYT*, Feb. 21, 1923; *AC*, Feb. 21, Apr. 3, 13, 1923; Hugh Park, "Floating College That Vanished," *AJ*, Jul. 18, 1968.

164. For AGC Jr.'s trip, see *AC*, Sep. 4, 15, Nov. 11, 16, 1923; unidentified clipping in the CF Papers, box OB4, MARBL.

165. CHC's travels are in CHC to C-C, Feb. 21, Mar. 19, 1923; FGC to CC, Jan. 23, 1923, CHC Papers, box 1, folder 11, MARBL.

166. Information about AGC's marriage comes from AGC to CHC, Jun. 19, 25, 1923, and various clippings in CHC Papers, box 11, folder 1, MARBL; *AJ*, Jun. 20, 1923; *AC* Jun. 21 Jul. 2, 30, Aug. 1, 1923, and *NYT*, Jun. 21, 1923; Graham and Roberts, 124.

Chapter 12: Trials and Tribulations

167. The AGC-OdB trial is discussed in *AC* Jan. 31, 1924; *AC* and *AJ*, Feb. 1, 2, 3, 6, 1924; AGC to CHC, June 25, 1923, AGC Papers, box 1, MARBL; Kemp, 274–76.

168. Mae Candler's difficulties are discussed in *NYT*, Feb. 4, 8, 11, 13, 1924; AC, Mar. 4, Feb. 13, 24, 1924; *AC* and *NYT*, Mar. 4, 1924. One of the most adamant of Beaver's accusers was Alderman Jesse Armistead, AGCs opponent in the Democratic mayoral primary seven years earlier. For the case, see *AC*, May 23, June 1, 6, 1923.

169. WTC's trials are in *AC*, Mar. 7, 8, 9, 10, 11, Apr. 9, 10, 11, 12, 15, May 23, Jul. 25, 26, Dec. 17, 1924, Sep. 10, 27, 1925; *NYT*, Mar. 11, 26, Sep. 27, Dec. 16, 1924, Mar. 26, Jul. 19, 26, Sep. 11, 27, 1925.

170. The Biltmore opening is in *AC*, Feb. 22, 1923, Apr. 20, 1924; Robt. J. Kennedy and Parks Rusk, "The New Biltmore in Atlanta," *National Hotel Review* (June 14, 1924), 18; *AC*, Apr. 20, 1924; www.cr.nps.gov/nr/travel/atlanta.

171. Details of Elizabeth Owens Vann's marriage are in *AC*, Mar. 30, Jun. 12, 1924; Graham & Roberts, 306–07.

172. Details of Lucy Candler's marriage are in Graham & Roberts, 306; *AC*, June 17, 29, 1924; *NYT*, June 20, 1924; AGC to CHC, June 21, 1924, CHC papers, box 1, folder 11, MARBL. The description of Briarcliff is in Kenneth H. Thomas, "Summary of Proposed National Register Nomination," 1988, Candler Homes file, AHC.

173. AGC's marital difficulties and declining health are in *AC* Oct. 9, Jul. 21, 25, 10, 16, Dec. 6, 11, 1924, Sep. 18, Nov. 6, 7, 9, 10, 11, 1925; *NYT*, Jul. 21, 25, Dec. 11, 1924, Sep. 23, 1925; and *Macon Daily Telegraph*, Dec. 12, 1924; AGC to CHC, AGC Jr., WC, and family, Dec. 25, 1924, CHC to C. Candler, Dec. 6, 1924, CHC Papers, box 11, folder 1, MARBL.

174. For AGC Jr.'s business dealings, see *AC*, Oct. 18, 19, 1924, Mar. 8, 13, 1925, Dec. 12, 1925, Aug. 3, 1926, Mar. 13, 22, 1927; *AC*, Nov. 11, 14, 18, Dec. 20, 23, 1923; Dec. 12, 1925; *NYT*, Mar. 9, 1925. Also see, www.artery.org/WhiteProvision; Garrett, II, 813; Carole Ashkinaze, "New Life for a Great Old Hotel," *AC*, Aug. 30, 1979; application for nomination for historical preservation, Sep. 28, 1982.

175. For Helen Candler's illness and death, see Graham and Roberts, 203–06; *AC*, Jan. 30, Feb. 1, 1927; *NYT*, Jan. 30, 1927.

176. AGC Jr.'s marriage to Florence is in clippings CF Papers, box 2, MARBL; *AC*, Oct. 9, 10, 1927; *NYT*, Oct. 10, 1927; Graham and Roberts, 207–13.

177. For these and other Candler weddings of the 1920s, see *AC* and *AJ*, Oct. 12, 30, Nov. 23, 1927, Dec. 2, 1928, Nov. 18, 1928, Jan. 4, 1929; *AJ*, Dec. 2, 4, 1928, Sep. 3, 1929; Graham & Roberts, 317–19, 328–29.

178. When the Candler hotel opened in the fall of '27, a single room rented for $40 to $75 per month, while the monthly rate on a two-room suite was $75 to $125, actually a competitive, yet luxury, price for the time. *AC*, July 12, 1925; Jan. 8, Oct. 17, Dec. 5, 19, 26, 1926; Feb. 7, 1927; *AC* and *AJ*, Oct. 11, 1927.

179. For information on Lullwater Farms, see *AC* and *AJ*, May 25, 1924, Jan. 7, Aug. 5, 1925; Jul. 8, 1929; *NYT*, Mar. 21, Aug. 30, 1924; Jan. 7, Aug. 5, 1925, Jul. 8, 1929. "Room to Breathe," *The Emory Alumnus*, November, 1958, 5–9; Yolande Gwin, "Candler Estate Retains Elegance," *AJC*, Jan. 9, 1972; and Paige Parvin, "Estate of the Mind," *Emory Magazine* (Winter 2005), 16–21; and Scrapbook, Class of 1907, box OBV1, WTC Papers, MARBL; *AC*, Apr. 24, May 29, 1927.

180. AGC's last illness, death, and subsequent events are in CHC, *AGC*, 335–36, 432–33; Graham and Roberts, 124–27; AC Feb. 26, Mar. 30, Apr. 5, Jun. 21, Dec. 31, 1926, Dec. 30, 1927; Mar. 13, 14, 15, 16, 17, 1929; *AC* and *Washington Post*, Aug. 16, 1933; J. Jacobs to CHC, Jan. 6, 1927, AGC Papers, box 11, MARBL; for reproduction of the eulogies, see CHC, *AGC*, 448–82; John Candler's letter is reproduced in Graham and Roberts, 125–26.

Chapter 13: Wild and Unfathomable Things

181. James C. Bryant, "Yaarab Temple and the Fox Theatre: Survival of a Dream," *Atlanta History* (xxxix, summer 1995), 20–21. By the mid-'30s, the banks foreclosed and the Yaarab Temple was forced to sell its interest to the Atlanta City Council, which in

turn sold the theatre to Mosque Inc, a private corporation that operated it for the next twenty years. Bryant, "Yaarab, 6–17; and www.foxtheatre.org/history.

182. *NYT,* Sep. 12, 1931; Graham and Roberts, 214.

183. *WP,* Apr. 1, 1928.

184. AGC Jr.'s business exploits come from *AC,* Oct. 12, 1927; *AJ,* Oct. 10, 1927; Garrett, II, 831–33.

185. For Candler Field and AGC's planes and voyages, see *AC,* Feb 14, 15, Mar 10, 11, 13, 17, 1925, Apr. 4, Oct. 23, Nov. 26, Dec 13, 1929, Jul. 10, 12, 1931; *AJ,* Feb. 16, 1930, Jan 2, 4, 1931; *NYT* Jun. 28, Jul. 1, Nov. 25, Dec. 11, 1930; Jul. 8, 12, 1931;. Ambrose 147–48; Braden and Hagan, *A Dream Takes Flight,* 13–14, 27–58; Martin, *William B. Hartsfield,* 12–16;Garrett, II, 850–51; Unidentified clippings, Oct. 28, 1929, Feb. 19, Jun. 30, 1930, CF papers, MARBL; sale of the Vega, on www.dmairfield.com/NC49M. The airport retained the name Candler Field for several more decades until (during Hartsfield's mayoralty) it became the Atlanta Airport and today is Hartsfield-Jackson Airport.

186. Information about WTC's life during this period comes from *AJ,* March 23, 1930, March 11, 1930, Oct. 29, 30, 31, Nov. 1, 1930; Graham and Roberts, 279–80; clippings in box 1, WTC Papers, MARBL.

187. Although designated from the outset to be a church, the initial charter of Glenn Memorial allowed Emory to use the auditorium for university assemblies. A few years after it opened, FGC donated funds for a separate Sunday school and a parsonage on Clifton Road near the campus and personally supervised all details of construction and decoration. For this and other information about CHC's activities during this period, see May, *Glenn Memorial,* 71–72, 74–78; Graham & Roberts, 156–57,166, 217–18; Seabrook, *Cumberland Island,* 180; Bullard, *Cumberland Island,* 342; Lovett, *Love Ruth,* 47–49, and http://www.glennumc.org/history.htm.

188. Information on AGC Jr.'s zoo came from interview with Asa Candler V, 2006, and other Atlantans; Graham and Roberts, 214–17; Gail King, "History of Druid Hills, part 2," for the Druid Hills Civic Assn., www.dekalb.k12.ga.us/Druid Hills/nieghborhood/history-dh-com2.rtf; Francis Desiderio,

"Raising the Bars: The Transformation of Atlanta's Zoo, 1889–2000," *Atlanta History*, 18–20;*WP*, Nov. 7, 1932; *NYT*, Aug 7, 14, 1932; and clippings from Atlanta papers dated Apr. 20, 21, May 1, Aug 7, 1932; Feb. 7, Mar. 1, 2, 3, Aug. 24, Sep. 21, Oct. 25, 1933; Dec. 23, 1934; Feb. 7, 1935 in CF papers, box 2, folders 2 and 3, MARBL.

189. Information about the Heinz family's activities and tragedies comes from Graham & Roberts, 267–68;.*AC*, Mar. 6, 1926, May 18, Jun. 9, 11, 1927; *AJ*, Dec. 30, 31, 1934, Jan. 1, 1935; interview with Vesta Owens Jones, 2008; video interview of Louise Owens, 1994, by Dr. David Jones; and clippings C-C Archives.

190. Details about WC's later life and death come from *NYT*, May 19, Nov. 12, 1930, Aug. 28, 1932, Oct. 3, 1936, Jun. 17, 1938; *AJ*, Aug. 25, 1932; James Robert Thompson,"The Forward Atlanta Movement," (master's thesis, Emory University, 1948), 77–75; Garrett, III, 509–10 ;Graham and Roberts, 287–89; Clippings in the C-C archives from the Thomasville *Times Enterprise*, Oct. 3, 1936, Waycross *Journal-Herald*, Oct. 4, 1936, and other newspapers.

191. Information about WTC's later life is from *AJ*, Dec. 27, 1933; *NYT*, June 20, 1934; Graham and Roberts, 280–82; and unidentified clippings, dated Sep. 9, 10, 1935, Oct. 24, 25, 1939, WTC Papers, MARBL.

192. Discussion of AGC Jr's life during this period is in Graham & Roberts, 221–27; "Soft Drinks," *Time Magazine* (April 8, 1935); "God Came In," *Time Magazine* (Apr. 9, 1951), 34.

Chapter 14: Murder in Druid Hills

193. Details of HH's murder and events immediately following it are in AC and AJ, Sep. 29, 30, Oct. 3, 1943 Herbert Jenkins, "My Most Bizarre Murder Case," *AJC Magazine*, Aug. 22, 1971.

194. Details of the events immediately following HH's murder come from a video interview of Louise Owens by Dr. David Jones, 1994; *AC* and *AJ*, Sep. 29–30, Oct. 1–19, 1943; Yolande Gwin, "Old, Forgotten Showplace," *AJC*, Aug. 1,

1976; Graham and Roberts, 271; James. S. Jenkins, *Murder in Atlanta,* 36–40.

195. Information about the arrest and trial of Horace Blalock is in *AC* and *AJ,* Jan. 18, 19, 21, 1945; *NYT,* Jan. 19, 1945; clippings in the Coca-Cola Archives, conversation with James S. Jenkins, Dec. 2009; and Jenkins, *Murder in Atlanta,* 47–50.

196. LCL's marriage and subsequent events come from interview with Vesta Owens Jones, 2007; *AC,* Feb. 5, 1946; Edith Hills Coogler, "Enrico Leides' Home Life in New York," *AJ Magazine,* and Annie Beall to Frances Candler, Aug. 1, 1947, CF Papers, box 2, MARBL.

197. Information about Blalock's parole and later life comes from State of Georgia, Board of Pardons and Paroles Records, May 18, 1955, Georgia State Archives, Morrow; Conversation with James S. Jenkins, Dec. 2009; Jenkins, *Murder in Atlanta,* 51; Graham & Roberts, 270.

Chapter 15: And So It Goes

198. Davenport Steward, "Last Candler Stock Transfer Likely Soon," *AJ,* Aug. 12, 17, 1947; *NYT,* Aug. 11, 1947, Mar. 7, 1950.

199. Details of the laundry case and trial come from Graham and Roberts, 230; *NYT,* Apr. 22, 1944; clippings from *AJ* and *AC,* Feb. 2, 3; Apr. 10, 12, 14, 17, 18, 19, 21, 22, 1944, CF Papers, box 2, MARBL.

200. Information about John Candler's death and subsequent events comes from *AJ,* Feb.15, 16, 1947; *NYT,* Feb. 16, 1947; Graham and Roberts, 230–23; and conversations with Nancy Candler Nutter; Helen (Nena) Candler Griffin and Asa Candler V, 2006–11.

201. Information on the trophy room and the African safari comes from interview with Asa Candler V, 2006;.*AC,* June 24, 1949; Andrew Sparks, "Wings for his Friends," Charles Elliott, "Asa Candler Will Hunt Big Game In Africa," and "Candlers Leave to Hunt Africa's Biggest Game;" AGC Jr. (with Andrew Sparks), "How I Killed an Eight-Ton Elephant," all in *AJ Magazine,* Sep. 15, 1946; May 29, Jul. 17, Oct. 16, 1949.

202. The Westview Cemetery case is in *AC* and *AJ*, Jul. 7, 14, 15, Nov. 23, 24, Nov. 25, 27, 28, 30, 1949, Feb. 8, 9, 10, 14, 15, 1950, and undated *AJC*, clippings, box 2, CF Papers, MARBL; and clippings in C-C Archives.

203. The trip to find Coco II is in *AC*, Mar. 27, 29, Apr. 2, 1950.

204. *AJ*, Jan. 13, 1953; *AC* Jan. 12, 1953; *AC* and *AJ*, Jan. 17, 1953; *NYT*, Jan. 12, 1953; clippings in box 2, CF Papers, MARBL, and in C-C Archives.

205. AGC Jr.'s death and funeral are from *NYT*, Aug.12, 17, 1947; Clippings, box 1, folders 13, 14, CHC Papers, box 1, MARBL.

206. Information about CHC's later life and death comes from clippings and letters, box 11, CF Papers and box 1, CHC Papers, MARBL: *NYT*, Oct. 2, 1957; *Washington Post*, Oct. 2, 1957; *Emory Alumnus*, Sep. 1947, Nov. 1957; "Asa Griggs Candler: A Centennial Exhibit at Emory University;" (1951); Mark K. Bauman, "Charles Howard Candler," CC Archives.

207. Information about LCL's last days and death comes from *AJ*, Sept. 6, 1962; *NYT*, Sept. 7, 1962; and interview with Vesta Owens Jones, 2007. Less than a year after LCL's death, Enrico Leide married, Ann Fiorentino Beichler, a widowed lawyer and fellow Italian American resident of the Howell House, *AC*, Oct. 25, 1963; Aug. 26, 1968.

208. For information about WTC's later life and death, see *AJ*, Feb. 12, 1951; *NYT*, Feb. 12, 1951; *AJC*, Feb. 7, 1965; *AC*, Apr. 26, 1967, and clippings, box 1, WTC Papers, MARBL and C-C Archives.

209. For more details of later generations, see Graham and Roberts, 305–34.

210. Frank Daniel, "Old Candler Seaboard Home to Fall Under Razer's Maul,' *AJC*, May 14, 1961; Michelle Green, "The Homes That Coca-Cola Built," *AC*, Oct. 18, 1979; Margaret Hylton Jones, "The Candler Homes Revisited: A Short History," *Emory Mag.*, 48 (Apr. 1972), 2–3; *Southern Homes*, Spring 1986, 94–99; AJC, Jan. 11, 1981.

211. Information on the Candler houses may be found in *AJ*, Aug. 23, 1951, Jul. 7, 1952; Aug. 26, Nov. 22, 1976, *AC*, Sep. 22, 1952; Aug. 17, 1961; *AJC*, Jan. 16, Jan 9, Feb. 6, 1972; *AJC*, Aug. 1, 1996, " Mansion to Church," http://www.

stjohnmelkite.org/candler.html; clippings DeKalb Historical Society and C-C Archives; conversation with Jim Candler of Villa Rica, and visits with Prof. Edna Bay and the residents of Lullwater Estates. Frank Daniel, "Old Candler Seaboard Home to Fall Under Razer's Maul,' *AJC*, May 14, 1961; Michelle Green, "The Homes That Coca-Cola Built," *AC*, Oct. 18, 1979; Margaret Hylton Jones, "The Candler Homes Revisited: A Short History," *Emory Mag.*, 48 (Apr. 1972), 2–3; *Southern Homes*, Spring 1986, 94–99; AJC, Jan. 11, 1981.

212. CHC memo, Oct. 18, 1946, CHC Papers, MARBL.

Index

A

Adair, Forrest 163, 164, 180, 229, 230
Allen, Frederick 140, 178, 306
Applewhite, H.T. 84, 95, 96
Arkwright, Preston 166, 167, 274, 316
Armistead, Jesse W. 161, 163, 164, 165, 167, 325
Asa G. Candler Inc 178, 194, 246, 268, 284
Atlanta
  Auto Week, 1910 125–128
  city auditorium 116, 117, 126, 127, 174
  Cotton States Exposition of 1895 57–58
  Edgewood suburb 31, 32
  fire of 1917 174–176
  flu epidemic of 1918 183
  in 1873 21–22
  in World War I 172–174
  Kimball House fire 33
  Piedmont Exposition of 1887 40
  race riot of 1906 109–111
  Reynoldstown 42
Atlanta Chamber of Commerce 2, 110, 116, 126, 128, 129, 133, 151, 161, 176, 197, 263
Atlanta Medical College 88
Atlanta Speedway 126, 128, 129, 130, 131

B

Beall, Justiana 5, 8
Beall, Noble 5, 6, 8
Beavers, James 160, 177, 228, 229, 230, 319
Berengaria 208, 210, 211, 230, 231
Biedenharn, Joseph 52, 73
Biltmore Hotel, Atlanta xiii, 194, 232, 239, 250, 261, 263, 264, 297

opening 232–233
Blackwell, Marion 272, 273
Blalock, Horace 277, 278, 279, 280, 281, 282, 283, 329
  arrest and conviction 277–280
  trial of 280–281
Blevins, Beeler 250, 251, 252
Briarcliff 119, 144, 173, 218, 235, 241, 244, 250, 254, 255, 256, 257, 267, 284, 285, 286, 287, 296, 324, 325
Briarcliff Hotel 287
Briarcliff Hotel (1050 Ponce de Leon) 240
Brown, Ed 162, 196
Byfield, Clyde 208, 209, 210, 229, 230, 231, 232, 242
Byfield, Sarah 8, 10, 208, 209, 210, 230, 231, 232, 323

C

Callan Castle 99, 100, 104, 112, 124, 144, 154, 157, 294, 304, 314
  building of 91–92
Callanwolde xiii, 191, 192, 221, 238, 244, 253, 295, 299, 303, 322
Callaway, Martha Candler 144, 225, 249, 251
Candler, Antoinette (Nettie) 29, 30, 92, 241
Candler, Asa III 104
Candler, Asa IV 132, 184
Candler, Asa Jr (Buddie) xiii, 2, 31, 42, 43, 44, 47, 50, 51, 53, 55, 56, 63, 64, 65, 68, 69, 71, 74, 75, 76, 77, 81, 82, 85, 91, 92, 93, 94, 97, 98, 100, 101, 103, 104, 105, 107, 110, 112, 113, 114, 115, 126, 127, 128, 129, 130, 131, 132, 143, 144, 145, 156, 162, 173, 178, 180, 184, 185,

187, 189, 190, 191, 194, 198,
206, 211, 212, 214, 218, 219,
220, 221, 222, 223, 225, 226,
232, 234, 235, 239, 240, 241,
242, 245, 249, 250, 251, 252,
253, 254, 255, 256, 257, 258,
259, 263, 267, 268, 283, 284,
285, 286, 287, 288, 289, 290,
291, 296
and African hunting expedition
    286–287
and aviation 132, 249–252
and Briarcliff laundry 284–286
and stopping his alcohol addiction
    268
and the Briarcliff zoo 254–259
and the floating school 222
and Westview Cemetery 288–290
at Emory College 56–57, 63–65, 74
death of 290–291
in California 75–77
in Hartwell 81–82
marriage to Florence Stephenson
    241–242
marriage to Helen Magill 84–85
Candler, Asa Sr. xi, xii, xiii, xiv, xv, 1, 2,
    3, 5, 10, 11, 12, 16, 17, 18, 19,
    20, 21, 22, 23, 24, 25, 26, 27,
    28, 29, 30, 31, 32, 33, 34, 35,
    36, 37, 38, 39, 40, 41, 42, 43,
    44, 45, 46, 47, 48, 49, 50, 51,
    52, 53, 54, 55, 56, 57, 58, 59,
    60, 61, 62, 63, 64, 65, 66, 67,
    68, 69, 70, 71, 72, 73, 74, 75,
    76, 81, 82, 83, 84, 85, 87, 89,
    90, 91, 92, 93, 94, 95, 96, 97,
    98, 99, 100, 101, 102, 103, 104,
    105, 106, 107, 108, 109, 110,
    111, 114, 115, 116, 118, 119,
    120, 121, 122, 123, 124, 125,
    126, 127, 128, 129, 130, 133,
    134, 139, 140, 141, 142, 143,
    144, 145, 146, 147, 148, 149,
    150, 151, 152, 153, 154, 155,
    156, 157, 158, 159, 160, 161,

162, 163, 164, 165, 166, 167,
168, 169, 170, 171, 172, 173,
174, 175, 176, 177, 178, 179,
180, 181, 182, 183, 184, 185,
186, 187, 188, 190, 193, 194,
195, 196, 197, 198, 199, 200,
201, 202, 205, 206, 207, 208,
210, 211, 212, 213, 214, 215,
219, 220, 222, 223, 224, 225,
226, 227, 228, 229, 230, 231,
232, 235, 236, 237, 238, 239,
241, 242, 244, 245, 246, 247,
251, 286, 292, 293, 294, 296,
297, 298, 303, 305, 306, 307,
308, 309, 310, 314, 315, 317,
318, 319, 330
ancestry 7–8
and charity 114–115, 153–154
and patent medicine 34
and religion 49–50
as Atlanta mayor 169–170, 172–177,
    178–182
"black hand" schemes against
    122–125
boyhood of 11–18
campaign for Atlanta mayor 160–
    161, 164–168
courtship and marriage 1876 26–28
death of 245–246
European trip, 1913 146–148
giving Coca-Cola stock to his children
    178–179
house on Seaboard Avenue 34, 35,
    42, 43, 44, 45, 48, 52, 56, 58,
    71, 85, 91, 92, 100, 145, 157,
    294
in Cartersville 18–20
Ponce de Leon home 157–158, 294
Western trip, 1909 120–122
Candler, Asa V 256, 286, 287, 299,
    327
Candler, Asa Warren 42, 139, 172
death of 245
Candler, Bennie Teabeaut 145, 169,
    193, 264, 265, 277, 297

marriage to Howell Hanson 265

Candler, Bishop Warren Aiken xi, 3, 5, 11, 12, 17, 24, 25, 28, 29, 30, 41, 48, 49, 50, 54, 55, 56, 58, 60, 64, 67, 76, 85, 93, 100, 101, 102, 119, 120, 145, 147, 148, 149, 150, 151, 152, 153, 154, 171, 172, 205, 224, 234, 235, 241, 242, 265, 302, 318

and the founding of Emory University 149–152

as Emory University Chancellor 170–172

as president of Emory College 50, 54, 63–64

Candler Building xiii, 2, 4, 106, 108, 114, 123, 146, 147, 166, 173, 184, 211, 221, 224, 227, 297, 315

Candler family ceremony on the stairs 2–5

opening 106–107

Candler, Charles Howard Jr. 104, 221, 242, 253

Candler, Charles Howard Sr. xii, xiii, xv, 2, 3, 22, 26, 28, 30, 31, 32, 34, 42, 43, 44, 45, 46, 47, 50, 51, 53, 54, 55, 56, 57, 63, 64, 65, 68, 69, 70, 71, 72, 73, 74, 75, 76, 77, 81, 82, 83, 84, 86, 87, 88, 89, 90, 91, 92, 93, 94, 95, 96, 97, 99, 100, 101, 102, 103, 104, 105, 108, 120, 121, 134, 139, 140, 142, 143, 144, 145, 146, 160, 162, 163, 164, 178, 184, 185, 186, 187, 188, 191, 192, 194, 196, 197, 198, 199, 201, 206, 210, 218, 220, 221, 222, 223, 225, 228, 234, 235, 238, 239, 242, 244, 245, 253, 254, 263, 284, 291, 292, 295, 296, 297, 302, 305, 306, 307, 315, 330

and Cumberland Island 253

and Emory College 54–56, 63–65

and Moreland Academy 43, 44, 123

biography of his father 291

death of 291

in California 76–77

in Europe 82–83

in New York 83–84, 85–87, 95–97

marriage to Flora Glenn 101–103

on the road for Coca-Cola 71–73, 87–89

replacement by Robert Woodruff 219–221

Candler, Charles Samuel III 92

Candler, Charles Samuel, Jr.(Charlie) 11, 12, 17, 24, 25, 26, 27, 58, 59

Candler College in Cuba 67

Candler, Daniel (Asa Candler Sr.'s grandfather) 8

Candler, Dan (Zeke's son) 35, 44, 52

Candler, Elizabeth Brandon (Lib) 242, 285, 286

Candler, Eugenia Bingham 3, 112, 132, 169, 183, 185, 189, 321

death of 183–184

Candler, Ezekiel (brother of Samuel Sr.) 7, 9, 13

Candler, Ezekiel Candler Jr. 207

Candler, Ezekiel Sr. (Zeke) xi, 10, 11, 13, 14, 15, 23, 34, 35, 36, 58, 155

Candler Field xiii, 132, 249, 250, 251, 327

Candler, Flora Glenn 3, 86, 87, 88, 89, 95, 101, 102, 103, 104, 108, 144, 156, 169, 191, 192, 206, 221, 222, 223, 225, 235, 239, 253, 274, 295, 296, 305, 313

Candler, Florence Stephenson 241, 242, 250, 251, 252, 254, 267, 274, 286, 288, 289, 296

Candler, Helen Magill 3, 85, 91, 92, 93, 103, 104, 113, 126, 144, 156, 169, 190, 206, 208, 222, 241, 242, 326

death of 240–241

Candler Hotel in Decatur 242, 293, 297

Candler Investment Company 105, 107, 115, 129, 145

Candler, John (Asa Jr.'s son) 104, 221, 241, 242, 245, 251, 262, 268, 284, 285, 286

Candler, Judge John xi, 2, 3, 4, 11, 12, 15, 17, 19, 24, 25, 26, 28, 29, 31, 39, 42, 48, 58, 59, 60, 66, 67, 101, 111, 119, 134, 135, 139, 140, 141, 142, 143, 162, 172, 180, 190, 205, 224, 245, 246, 305, 306, 309, 316, 326

Candler, Lucy Beall xiii, 32, 34, 35, 36, 42, 44, 47, 50, 53, 58, 59, 61, 62, 63, 65, 66, 68, 69, 70, 71, 72, 74, 82, 84, 85, 93, 94, 99, 100, 109, 282

and schooling 63, 65–66

at Wesleyan College 92–93

marriage to Bill Owens 100–101

Candler, Lucy Elizabeth Howard xii, xiii, 2, 26, 27, 28, 29, 30, 31, 32, 34, 35, 36, 42, 43, 44, 45, 47, 49, 50, 51, 52, 56, 58, 59, 60, 61, 62, 63, 65, 66, 68, 69, 72, 82, 85, 86, 87, 91, 92, 96, 100, 103, 111, 120, 121, 127, 145, 147, 156, 157, 158, 159, 160, 162, 164, 166, 169, 178, 182, 184, 185, 199, 216, 294, 305, 308

daily routine in the 1890s 62–63

death of 184–185

illness 155–156, 164

Candler, Mae Little Ragin 224, 225, 228, 229, 230, 236, 237, 244, 246, 325

Candler, Marion Penland 188, 189, 208, 211, 230, 232, 241, 243, 244, 252, 253, 266

Candler, Martha Beall 3, 4, 5, 6, 7, 8, 9, 10, 11, 12, 13, 14, 15, 17, 23, 24, 25, 26, 28, 29, 30, 32, 42,

58, 59, 60, 106, 294, 297, 305, 307

death of 59–60

Candler, Milton Sr. xi, 3, 10, 11, 13, 14, 18, 23, 24, 25, 58

Candler, Noble 3, 9, 10, 24, 28, 31, 35, 42

Candler Park 215, 244

Candler, Rebekah Skeen 267, 293

Candler, Sam (Asa Jr.'s son) 190, 268, 284, 285

Candler, Sam (Milton's son) 52, 75

Candler, Samuel Sr. xi, 3, 4, 5, 7, 8, 9, 10, 11, 12, 13, 14, 18, 23, 106, 294, 297, 307, 308

death of 24

Candler, Sarah (Asa Candler Sr.'s grand-mother) 8, 14

Candler, Walter Jr. 113, 132, 184, 293

Candler, Walter Sr. xiii, 3, 36, 42, 44, 47, 53, 61, 62, 63, 65, 68, 69, 92, 94, 96, 103, 104, 105, 112, 113, 132, 133, 134, 145, 154, 184, 185, 188, 189, 190, 194, 206, 208, 209, 210, 211, 212, 224, 226, 229, 230, 231, 232, 241, 242, 243, 244, 245, 252, 253, 255, 263, 266, 267, 284, 293, 296, 297, 305, 315, 321, 322

and horse racing 188–189, 230, 243, 267

at Emory College 112

marriage of 112–113

marriage to Marion Penland 188–189

marriage to Rebehak Skeen 267

Candler, William Jr. 193, 265, 293

Candler, William Jr. (of Villa Rica) 65

Candler, William of Callan Castle 7

Candler, William of Villa Rica (Willie) 3, 10, 17, 23, 24, 25, 26, 27, 47, 58, 155, 224, 245, 294

Candler, William Sr. xiii, 3, 47, 53, 61, 62, 68, 69, 92, 103, 104, 120, 121, 145, 162, 184, 188, 193,

194, 206, 220, 224, 233, 245,
249, 250, 261, 263, 264, 265,
297, 305, 316, 322
death of 265
marriage to Bennie Teaubeaut 145
Carnegie, Andrew xi, 149, 150, 151,
152, 253
Carroll County, Georgia 7, 9, 12, 15,
16, 17, 18, 23, 29, 39, 306, 307,
308
Cartersville, Georgia 18, 19, 22, 23,
26, 28, 29, 35, 43, 47, 51, 60,
61, 62, 63, 65, 66, 238, 308
Central Bank and Trust 105, 106, 115,
129, 153, 154, 169, 179, 183,
188, 205, 211, 212
Chambers, Laura Candler 100, 113,
187, 224, 235, 241
Chambers, Rena Candler 193, 234,
261, 262, 265
Cherokee County, Georgia 5, 7
Cherokee Nation 6
Citizens & Southern Bank 212
Civil War 12, 155, 307
Cleveland, President Grover 40, 57,
117
Coca-Cola xi, xii, xiii, xiv, xv, 2, 3, 38,
39, 40, 41, 42, 44, 46, 47, 48,
49, 51, 52, 56, 60, 61, 63, 67,
68, 69, 71, 72, 73, 75, 81, 83,
87, 89, 90, 91, 92, 93, 94, 95,
96, 100, 103, 105, 107, 108,
111, 112, 114, 115, 120, 123,
124, 128, 129, 134, 139, 140,
141, 142, 143, 145, 146, 153,
156, 160, 161, 162, 163, 164,
168, 177, 178, 179, 184, 185,
186, 187, 188, 189, 190, 191,
193, 194, 195, 196, 197, 198,
199, 200, 201, 202, 212, 220,
221, 222, 224, 228, 235, 238,
245, 246, 284, 291, 292, 298,
299, 301, 302, 303, 304, 305,
306, 308, 309, 311, 317, 329,
331
and cocaine xii, 37, 48, 60, 61, 90,
108, 111, 140, 143, 163
beginnings of 37–41
bottler case 195–197
bottling 51–52, 72–73
early days of 46–49
Edgewood Avenue headquarters 68
expansion of 68
fifth headquarters 134
Merchandise Number 5 44, 48, 61,
134, 141, 142
sale of 160–163, 185–188
*The Coca-Cola Company vs. Henry A.
Rucker* 90–91
The U.S. vs 40 Barrels trial 139–143
U.S. headquarters in 1913 146
Colby, Edward 162, 196, 197
Cook, "Handsome" Bill 180, 181
Corrie, Arthur 167
Curtwright, Bill 45, 47, 52
Curtwright, George 47

D

Davidson, Helen Candler 144, 225,
249
Dobbs, Elizabeth Candler (Lizzie) 3,
10, 12, 24, 44, 58, 207
Dobbs, Samuel Candler 24, 44, 89,
108, 115, 141, 162, 178, 186,
187, 188, 196, 197, 319, 323
Donald Fraser School 53, 61, 104
Dorsey, Governor Hugh 166
Dozier, Margaret 41, 179
Druid Hills xi, xii, xiii, 118, 119, 128,
129, 144, 152, 156, 175, 183,
193, 199, 215, 217, 243, 255,
257, 274, 276, 295, 297, 302,
316, 327
Candler's purchase of 116–118
D. W. Griffith's *For His Son* 162
D. W. Griffith's *The Birth of a Nation*
155

E

Edgewood 31
Edmondson, Mary Candler 132, 184, 208, 252
Eldredge, Louisa Candler 144
Emory College xi, 8, 18, 24, 29, 49, 54, 60, 104, 112, 114, 120, 129, 148, 150, 152, 220
Emory University xi, xii, xiii, xv, 10, 21, 46, 70, 74, 152, 153, 170, 176, 189, 195, 201, 208, 222, 224, 231, 238, 244, 246, 253, 266, 291, 294, 296, 298, 299, 301, 302, 304, 305, 306, 328, 330
  building of 153, 171–172
  Candler Library 237–238
  founding of 146–152

F

Few, Ignatius 8, 13, 18
Fox Theater, Atlanta 248

G

Georgia Military Academy 53
Glenn Memorial Church 253
Glenn, Wilber Fiske 184, 253, 313
Goldsmith, Dr. William T. 30, 31
Governor's Horse Guard 40, 58, 116
Graham, Elizabeth Candler xv, 178, 299, 306, 309
Grant Park, Atlanta 258, 259, 290
Griffith, Helen (Nena) Candler 286, 299
Griggs, Dr. Asa 11, 18, 19

H

Hallman, Marcellus B. 27, 28, 31
Harding, President Warren 215
Harris, Col. James W. 23, 44, 238
Harris, Florence Candler 3, 10, 12, 13, 14, 16, 18, 23, 25, 26, 29, 32, 35, 43, 44, 51, 53, 55, 58, 59,
60, 61, 63, 65, 66, 92, 93, 101, 119, 147, 155, 213, 233, 305, 310
  death of 238
Harris, Joel Chandler 4, 51, 129, 248
Hartsfield, Mayor William B. xiii, 132, 250, 302, 303, 327
Hartwell, Georgia 81, 85, 91, 93, 97, 98, 104
Heinz, Emilie (Mimi) 194, 234, 260, 262
  death of 260
Heinz, Henry 154, 169, 170, 201, 212, 216, 224, 234, 245, 248, 249, 259, 260, 261, 270, 271, 272, 273, 274, 275, 276, 277, 278, 279, 280, 283, 295, 299, 305
  murder of 270–273
  solution 276–277, 282–283
Heinz, Henry Jr. 182, 194, 234, 235, 262, 271, 275
Heinz, Lucy Candler 182, 184, 185, 194, 201, 208, 216, 217, 224, 234, 245, 260, 261, 262, 270, 271, 272, 273, 274, 275, 276, 277, 278, 279, 280, 281, 283, 295
  marriage to Enrico Leide 282
Hirsch, Harold 139, 162, 179, 195, 196, 227, 316
Hirsch, Margaret 179, 180, 181
Holland, Ed 9, 37, 39
Hornbostel, Henry 152, 153, 171, 172, 191, 193, 232, 303, 304
Howard & Candler 31
Howard, George 19, 22, 23, 26, 27, 28, 30, 31, 33, 66, 308
Howard, Maria Luisa 26, 30
Hunter, George 195, 196, 197
Hurt, Dr. John W. 84, 91
Hurt, Joel 52, 316

I

Inman Park 52, 66, 67, 86, 92, 93, 99,

103, 104, 111, 113, 118, 119,
122, 124, 238, 294, 299, 311,
314, 315
Inman Park Methodist Church 112

J

Jacobs, Joseph 37, 38, 39, 40, 244,
309, 316
Jacobs Pharmacy 38, 39, 41
Jenkins, Police Chief Herbert 273, 281,
299, 303, 304, 318, 328, 329
Jones, Bobby 251
Jones, Vesta Owens 233, 270, 299,
320, 328, 329, 330

K

Kappa Alpha 55, 57, 74, 112
Kebler, Lyman 134, 140
Kemp, Kathryn xv, 303, 306, 308, 315,
316, 318, 319, 320, 321, 322,
323, 325
Key, Mayor James 182, 258
Kimball House Hotel 22, 33, 40

L

LaGrange College 27, 28, 86, 188
Leide, Enrico 233, 234, 248, 260, 281,
292, 329, 330
Leide, Lucy Candler 282, 284, 292,
293
death of 292–293
Leo Frank case 154, 166, 303
Locomobile 89, 95
Lowndes, George 39
Lullwater Farms 243, 244, 296
Lynch, J.J. 134, 140, 142

M

Macy's xiii, 239
Mayfield, J. C. 179, 185
Methodist Episcopal Church, South
12, 49, 50, 67, 114, 149, 302,
318

Miller, Bill 272, 273
Murphy, George E. 67, 92, 105

N

Neal Bank 114, 115, 116
New York Candler Building 146, 150,
284
Nutting, Nancy Candler 256, 286, 299

O

Olmsted, Frederick Law 118, 316
Owens, Elizabeth 2, 103, 104, 156,
169, 194, 217, 222, 233, 234,
260, 261, 262, 325
death of 260–262
debut of 217
marriage of 233–235
Owens, Louise 260, 261, 272, 273,
274, 292, 328
Owens, Lucy Candler 2, 101, 103,
112, 127, 144, 154, 156, 157,
168
marriage to Henry Heinz 170
Owens, William Jr. 144, 194, 195,
234, 260, 261, 262, 271, 273,
275, 282
Owens, William Sr. 2, 93, 94, 99, 103,
105
death of 153–154

P

Pemberton, Charley 37, 41
Pemberton, John S. (Doc) xii, 27, 33,
37, 38, 39, 40, 41, 68, 179, 185
Pendergrast, Mark 140, 306
Piedmont Driving Club 133, 215, 219
Preacher, G. Lloyd 217

R

Rainbow Terrace 216, 217, 234, 235,
262, 270, 271, 272, 273, 274,
275, 277, 278, 279, 280, 281,
295, 304, 324

Rainwater, Veazey 195, 196, 197
Reed, George 63, 71, 81, 87, 201, 312
Reid, Neel 134, 193
Rest Haven 193, 297, 322
Robinson, Frank 38, 39, 40, 41, 44,
    47, 48, 49, 60, 61, 68, 72, 89,
    108, 309, 311, 312
Roosevelt, President Franklin D. 266
Roosevelt, President Theodore 67, 86
Roquet, de Bouchel Onezima 199,
    200, 201, 202, 205, 206, 207,
    208, 212, 213, 214, 219, 224,
    225, 226, 227, 228, 305
Ruffner, Marion Candler (Bootsie)
    189, 208, 211, 234, 244, 252,
    253

S

Spanish American War 67
Sunday, Billy 177, 180

T

Taft, President William Howard 116,
    120
Talmadge, Governor Eugene 265
Talmadge, Senator Herman 290
Thompson, Homer 235, 236, 256, 268
Thompson, Lucy Magill Candler 91,
    92, 93, 103, 104, 169, 190, 218,
    219, 222, 234, 235, 236, 256
  marriage of 234–236
Trust Company of Georgia 186, 188,
    212
Tufts, Arthur 171, 172, 176, 191

V

Vanderbilt University 149
Vann, Bryant 233, 234, 235, 260, 261,
    262, 272, 273, 274, 275, 276,
    282
Venable, Willis 38, 39, 40
Villa Rica xi, 3, 9, 14, 15, 18, 22, 23,
    24, 25, 27, 28, 37, 43, 58, 59,
    60, 61, 92, 117, 155, 219, 245,

294, 299, 301, 306

W

Walker, Woolfolk 41
Warren, Catherine Candler 108, 201,
    223, 234, 253, 323
Watson, Tom 109, 166
Wesley Memorial Church 148, 190
Wesley Memorial Hospital 114, 148,
    153, 238, 244, 245
West End Institute 43, 61, 63, 66, 310
Westview Cemetery 154, 184, 241,
    246, 275, 284, 287, 288, 289,
    290, 293, 296, 330
White Provision Company 40, 57, 86,
    126, 161, 166, 220, 240, 320
Wiley, Dr. Harvey 108, 109, 134, 135,
    139, 141, 143, 251
Willard, Jessie
  daughter of Jessie Candler Willard
    29, 84, 93
Willard, Joe 29, 38, 40, 44, 47, 52,
    141, 153
Willard, Sam 25, 29, 44, 47, 52, 141
Willard, Sarah Justina (Jessie) 10, 12,
    24, 25, 29, 44, 58, 84, 85, 200,
    308
Wilson, Eugenia Candler 132, 184,
    208, 252
Wilson, President Woodrow 172, 173,
    197, 227
Wine Cola 37, 41, 56
Witham, Billy 81, 82, 92, 97, 104, 130
Witham Mill 82, 92
Wood, General Leonard 173, 174
Woodruff, Ernest 186, 187, 188, 195,
    197, 212, 220, 322
Woodruff, Robert xv, 220, 221, 324
Woodward, Mayor James 160
World War I xi, xiv, 316
  armistice 181–182
  start of 152–153
World War II xiv, 270–271

Made in the USA
Las Vegas, NV
31 May 2021

23977483R00203